ESSAYS

ON THE

SUPERNATURAL

ORIGIN OF CHRISTIANITY,

WITH SPECIAL REFERENCE TO THE

THEORIES OF RENAN, STRAUSS, AND
THE TÜBINGEN SCHOOL.

BY

REV. GEORGE P. FISHER, D. D.

PROFESSOR OF CHURCH HISTORY IN YALE COLLEGE.

NEW YORK:
CHARLES SCRIBNER & CO., No. 654 BROADWAY.
1867.

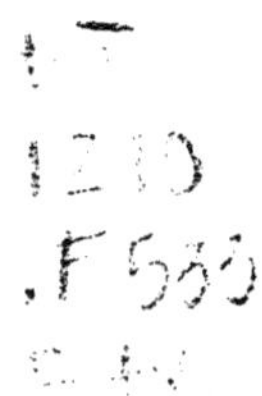

JOHN F. TROW & CO.,
PRINTERS, STEREOTYPERS, & ELECTROTYPERS,
50 GREENE STREET, N. Y.

PREFACE.

Although this volume does not claim the character of a complete treatise, yet the Essays which compose it form a connected whole and deal with the most important aspects of the general theme under which they are placed. That theme is the origin of the religion of Christ—whether it be "from heaven or of men." The validity of the distinction between the Natural and the Supernatural is assumed, and something is done in various parts of the work—for example, in the Essay on Miracles—to elucidate this distinction. The fact of the constant presence and agency of God in Nature is held to be perfectly consistent with the proposition that the world is a reality distinct from Him.

This being his theme, the author has deliberately abstained, as far as was practicable, from discussing the special questions involved in the subject of Inspiration, such as the alleged discrepancies between the various Gospel narratives. The question here considered is not that of Inspiration, but of Revelation. A great advantage is secured by keeping these two topics apart, and I have given heed to the canon of Paley that "*substantial* truth is that which, in every historical inquiry, ought to be the first thing sought after and ascertained."

The portion of this work which has lately appeared in the form of Articles in Theological Reviews, has been much revised and, it is hoped, rendered more worthy to be submitted to the public. Especially is this true of the Essay on the *Genuineness of the Fourth Gospel*, which has undergone not only a careful revision, but also a material amplification, since its first publication in the *Bibliotheca Sacra*. And in this place I gladly express my acknowledgments to an accurate scholar, Mr. Ezra Abbot, of Harvard College Library, for a number of important suggestions, as well as corrections, which he has kindly communicated to me, and of which I have availed myself in the present edition of that Essay.

In the preparation of these dissertations, the author has chiefly made use of German writers, because in Germany these subjects have been canvassed of late with more earnestness and a greater outlay of learning than elsewhere. Germany has been the theatre not only of the most formidable assault upon the claims of Revelation, but also of the most effectual vindication of those claims. But I have diligently resorted to the original authorities, and have withheld my sanction from statements which did not appear to be sustained by their testimony. Although many of the special topics which are handled in the following pages, have only recently been brought forward, I have still found frequent occasion to consult Professor Norton's *Genuineness of the Gospels*, a work which combines thorough learning with signal impartiality. I may be permitted to add that no attempt has been made to provide the reader with a bibliography upon the topics embraced in the present work. It would have been easy to multiply references to books, but it has been thought best to mention only such as are most important to the student.

The leading feature of the present volume is the consideration given to the system of the Tübingen school of historical critics, and especially to the tenets of the late Dr. Baur, incomparably the ablest, as he is the most conspicuous, representative of this school. Although the Tübingen criticism is to be considered the ripe form of the one type of Unbelief peculiar to our age, as Deism was characteristic of the last century, and although this movement, from the learning and ingenuity of its promoters, is more entitled to notice than any other leading form of skepticism which has ever appeared in the Church, I am not aware that any full examination of it has been attempted before in English, unless the work of Mr. Mackay, a zealous partisan of the school, is to be counted an exception.[1] It will be observed that comparatively little space is devoted to the book of M. Renan. This is due partly to the fact that much that might properly be said respecting his work, is anticipated in the previous Essays, and partly to the conviction that its claim to scientific attention is small, compared with that presented in the productions of Baur and Strauss. The same remark is applicable to the Essay on the opinions of Theodore Parker.

These Essays are mainly devoted to the vindication of the genuineness and credibility of the New Testament Narratives. But in the final Essay, I have examined the Pantheistic groundwork on which most of the fabrics of skeptical criticism are reared. If Pantheism is here met by other arguments than those furnished in the Hamiltonian "philosophy of nescience," it is because this philosophy did not appear to be requisite, and for the still better reason that I am not persuaded of its truth. It would seem that the

[1] The *Tübingen School and its Antecedents*, by R. W. Mackay. London, 1863.

human mind can *know* in a proper sense of the term—though it be inadequately—the Being above it, whom it yet resembles in spiritual constitution; that it can exclude its own limitations without thereby turning its knowledge of the object into a mere negation. But whatever may be the reader's opinion upon this question, the considerations which are here advanced in refutation of Pantheism remain valid, and are sufficient, it is believed, for their end.

On one point it may be well to guard against misconstruction. From the prominence given to the subject of miracles, it might be supposed by a cursory reader, that these are considered the leading proof of Revelation. That the fact is quite otherwise, a more attentive perusal of this volume would immediately show. On the contrary, it is claimed that faith in the primal verities of religion has an independent root of its own. Such is the ancient and accepted teaching of Christian theology; the view not only of the Reformers, but also of all the mediaeval writers, including even the free-thinking Abélard. In keeping with this doctrine respecting the origin of faith in general, it is further held that the principal, most convincing source of faith in the divine origin of Christianity is the impression directly made on the spirit by the teaching, the life, and the death of its founder, and by the adaptedness of the Christian system to the practical necessities of the soul. But while all this is true, the investigation of the historical origin of Christianity is by no means superfluous. It must be remembered that the number of minds whose immediate discernment of the excellence of the Gospel delivers them from all doubt, and enables them to dispense with other proof of its divine origin, is comparatively small. The greater number of the cultivated class need to be fortified by evidence of a different nature; they need at least that obstacles should be removed out of the way, and that the historical conscience, if the phrase may be allowed, should be freed from uncomfortable misgivings. And it surely behooves the preacher of Christianity to address himself to the consideration of living questions, and not be content with answering objections which are no longer rife in the minds of thinking men. The older Apologies, like the ordnance of a former day, contain most valuable materials, but they are no longer serviceable until they are refitted in accordance with an altered state of things.

Yet the disappearance of one after another of the previous types of unbelief, while the Christian faith still remains a living power, may teach a lesson of modesty. It is too much the habit of a class of writers to speak of Christianity as an antiquated system, and of faith in Revelation as something left behind by "the spirit of the age," "modern thought," "the consciousness of the nineteenth century." There is a cant on the side of unbelief, as well as among some of its opponents. It is well to bear in mind that these boastful phrases, or others analogous, were in vogue in the last century among those whom the later infidelity of the present day is forward to charge with shallowness.

While these sheets are passing through the press, the information reaches me of the sudden death of my revered friend and former instructor, President Wayland. It affords me gratification, which I shall, perhaps, be pardoned for expressing, that he lived to read most of these Essays, and volunteered to convey to me in warm terms the too generous appreciation with which he regarded them. If any of these grave topics are found to be superficially handled, or if, in any respect, there is a want of fairness in the treatment of adversaries, these faults must be set down to a departure from his example and from the enlightened spirit of his teachings.

NEW HAVEN, *October* 7, 1865.

CONTENTS.

VIII.

IX.

X.

XI.

XII.

XIII.

ESSAY I.

THE NATURE OF THE CONFLICT OF CHRISTIAN FAITH WITH SKEPTICISM AND UNBELIEF.

We purpose, in several Essays, to examine the foundations of the Christian faith, with particular reference to some of the leading theories of unbelief which are in vogue at the present day. It will aid us in performing the work we have taken in hand, if, at the outset, we present a statement of what we conceive to be the real question or questions, with which the controversy of Revealed Religion with Skepticism, in our day, is chiefly concerned. This discrimination seems important on account of the multiplicity of controverted points relating to the subject, which are brought into popular discussion. Physical science, historical study, metaphysical speculation, has each its own inquiries to raise and doubts to suggest, and the effect of the simultaneous agitation of so many different topics, none of them unimportant to a Christian believer, is, doubtless, to breed confusion. We shall do a service, therefore, as we hope, to some of our readers, if we stop amid the "confused noise" of the battle, survey the field where so many are running to and fro, and direct attention to the really essential points which are threatened, though not, as we trust, imperiled by the assault.

We shall not delay long for the purpose of characterizing the prevailing *tone* of the existing skepticism and unbelief, as contrasted with similar phenomena at other periods in the past. Yet not to leave this interesting topic altogether untouched, we extract a passage from a late volume of Bampton Lectures, in which the peculiarity of the present development of skepticism is correctly described. "The unbelief of the present day," writes the author, "differs from that of the last century in tone and character; and in many respects shares the traits already noticed in the modern intellectualism of Germany, and the eclecticism of France. It is not disgraced by ribaldry; hardly at all by political agitation against the religion which it disbelieves: it is marked by a show of fairness, and professes a wish not to ignore facts nor to leave them unexplained. Conceding the existence of spiritual and religious elements in human nature, it admits that their subjective existence as facts of consciousness, no less than their objective expression in the history of religion, demands explanation, and cannot be hastily set aside, as was thought in the last century in France, by the vulgar theory that the one is factitious, and the other the result of priestly contrivance. The writers are men whose characters and lives forbid the idea that their unbelief is intended as an excuse for licentiousness. Denying revealed religion, they cling the more tenaciously to the moral instincts: their tone is one of earnestness: their inquiries are marked by a profound conviction of the possibility of finding truth: not content with destroying, their aim is to reconstruct. Their opinions are variously manifested. Some of them appear in treatises of philosophy: others insinuate themselves indirectly in literature: some of them relate to Christian doctrines; others to the criticism of Scripture documents: but in all cases their authors either leave a residuum which they profess will satisfy the longings of human nature, or confess with deep pain that their conclusions are in direct conflict with human aspirations; and, instead of reveling in the ruin which they have made, deplore with a tone of sadness the impossibility of solving the great enigma. It is clear that writers like these offer a wholly different appearance from those of the last century. The deeper appreciation manifested by them of the systems which they disbelieve, and the more delicate learning of which they are able to avail themselves, constitute features formerly lacking in the works of even the most serious-minded deists,[1] and require a difference in the spirit, if not in the mode, in which Christians must seek to refute them."[2] A general description like the foregoing is, of course, liable to much exception and qualification when it is applied to particular individ-

[1] Such as Herbert and Morgan.

[2] Farrar's Bampton Lectures, Am. Ed., p. 307.

uals. Yet the drift of it will be recognized as correct by those who regard with a penetrative eye the skeptical literature of the day. In contrast with the past, unbelief is oftener now an infection than a willful attack. There are more at present who can be truly said to be *afflicted* with doubt. In the refinement and learning exhibited by the antagonists of Revelation, a decided superiority belongs to the present. Just place Paine's *Age of Reason* by the side of Renan's newly published *Life of Christ!* The difference of the old infidelity from the new, is instantly felt by the dullest observer. The spirit of the one is coarse and bitterly hostile to Christianity; the dependence is more on railing than reasoning; and the warfare is waged without the aid of historical knowledge. The Deistical writers were, to be sure, frequently above Paine in the character of the weapons they employed, and in the temper with which they wielded them; and yet the name of Paine fairly suggests the general character of the movement, at least in its later stages. The work of Renan is the production of a scholar possessed of abundant philological and historical learning; it is dedicated to a departed sister who aided in its composition; it abounds in expressions of sentiment; it knows how to value much that is sacred to the Christian believer; it is founded upon laborious studies and upon travels in the land of the Bible. Skepticism has without doubt improved immensely in its general tone. And yet the sketch which we have quoted above, in order to be full, would require to be qualified by a distinct mention of the fact that there is witnessed on the side of skeptical writers even of the more refined school, in our own times, the occasional development of an animosity toward the Christian faith, that ill accords with their habitual tone, and seems to imply that after all there lies deep down in the heart an unwholesome fountain of bitter feeling with reference to the doctrines and restraints of religion.

For the reason that the peculiar traits of the modern skepticism, and the peculiar character of the class who are affected by it, are not clearly discerned, the comparative strength of the infidel party in our times is underrated by not a few even of Christian teachers. When the present is compared with the past, they begin at once to take a census of the known or avowed opposers of Christianity, and to put the result of this count of heads by the side of a similar reckoning made for an earlier epoch. They are not awake to the subtler form which skepticism has assumed. They fail to see that, though it be often less tangible and pugnacious, it is more diffused like an atmosphere. They are not aware how widely the seeds of unbelief are scattered through books and journals which find a hospitable reception even in Christian families. And they do not appreciate the significance of the fact that so large a number of the leaders of opinion on matters outside of the sphere of religion, are adherents, more or less outspoken, of the skeptical school. Infidelity appears in better dress and in better company than of old; it takes on the function of the educator and social reformer; it prefers a compromise with Christianity to a noisy crusade against it; but the half-friendly attitude it assumes may render the task of exposing and withstanding it all the more difficult. This ambiguous, fluctuating tone of the skepticism of our day, renders the analysis of its fundamental position the more incumbent; and this we attempt in the present Essay.

We begin with remarking that the principal question at issue is *not* the Inspiration of the Scriptures. There is one point of view, as we shall shortly explain, from which the importance of this question is not exaggerated. But the mere question of the relation of human agency to divine agency in the production of the Scriptures is, in itself considered, of not so great moment. The fact of Inspiration is chiefly important as containing a guaranty for the authority of the Bible. If the Bible were exclusively the work of men, and yet came to us attended with a divine attestation to the truth of its contents, the main end for which Inspiration is desired and thought necessary, would be attained. The authority of the Scriptures as a Rule of Faith and Practice is the doctrine of prime value; and Inspiration is required as a shield against the liabilities to hurtful error, which pertain to every exertion of the human mind without the aid of a higher light. Something is gained, in our view, in the discussion of these topics, when we steadily keep in mind the great object to be secured (if it can be consistently with truth), which is none other than the Protestant principle of the Authority of the Bible as a guide to the knowledge of duty and salvation. Whether he proceed from a scientific or a practical motive, the inquirer for religious truth has first to settle the question, where shall this truth be found. This is obviously the first step. Until this point is determined, there is no criterion of truth, no "judge to end the strife" of diverse opinions. The Roman Catholic considers the Church, through the voice of its clergy and their head, the infallible expounder of truth. In every doubt, he has an arbiter at his side whose verdict, being the direct result of divine illumination, is held to be conclusive. The Protestant agrees with the Roman Catholic in holding to an objective standard, but the standard with him is the Bible, which he feels authorized to interpret for himself. Denying that the Church is either the unerring interpreter of Scripture, or the infallible guardian of oral teaching of Christ and the Apostles, which tradition has handed down, he falls back upon the Bible itself. The Bible alone is his Rule of Faith. This we take to be the fundamental position of Protestantism on the question which, as we have said, stands at the threshold of all profitable religious inquiry. On the contrary, the Rationalist differs from both the Roman Catholic and

Protestant, first in setting aside every objective Authority, every Authority exterior to the mind itself, in matters of religion, and then in positively maintaining the sufficiency of Reason. Nothing is allowed to stand which cannot justify itself at this tribunal of his own understanding. There is no divine testimony which is separate from the thoughts and deductions of the human mind, and entitled to regulate belief. We may stop to observe that an ingenious German writer[1] has not improperly classified the Mystic with the Rationalist, so far as the former takes his own feeling for a source and criterion of truth, superior to any external Rule. The Mystic and the Rationalist meet on the common ground of a renunciation of objective Authority, the one relying ultimately upon subjective reason, the other upon subjective feeling, for all his convictions of religious truth. And hence the Mystic is found to pass over, not unfrequently, by a natural and easy transition, to the position of the Rationalist, the difference between them often depending for the most part on a diversity of temperament and education. Now the Protestant principle which is thus distinguished from that of the Romanist and of the Rationalist, is of vital moment; and it stands in close connection with the other doctrine of Biblical Inspiration. Give up the principle of the Normative Authority of the Bible, and we are driven upon the alternative of either abjectly surren-

[1] Kliefoth, *Einleitung in die Dogmengeschichte.*

dering ourselves to the Church, or of being set adrift, with the Rationalist, upon a sea of conjectures and uncertified reasonings of men. When, for example, I open an Epistle of St. Paul, and find there a passage upon the design and effect of the Saviour's death, and when I have ascertained the sense of the passage by a fair exegesis, may I then be sure of its truth? Or when I meet on the page of Scripture with practical injunctions pertaining to the duties of life, may I depend upon them as strictly conformed to the truth, and shape my conduct in accordance with them? Here is the practical question concerning the Bible; and the fact of Inspiration, or of supernatural aid enjoyed by the writers, owes its value chiefly to the assurance it may afford upon this primary question. It is interesting to observe that the most discerning of those theologians at the present day who are dissatisfied with the old formulas concerning Inspiration, feel the necessity of still abiding by the cardinal Protestant principle of the Normative Authority of the Scriptures. The Bible is still held to be the safe and sufficient Rule of Faith, upon which the Christian may cast himself without misgiving. Thus Dr. Arnold, holding that the apostles in the New Testament predict the speedy Advent of Christ to judgment, is, nevertheless, careful to remark, that by the recorded words of Christ which declare this point not to be a subject of Revelation, and by the circumstance that those injunctions of St. Paul which were founded in his own mind on this expectation, are expressly given as not having divine authority, but as counsel, the error of the apostles is prevented from having the effect to weaken in our estimation their general authority. That is to say, this anticipation was an error, but an error into which they do not profess that Inspiration led them, and from the misleading influence of which all are saved who attend to the words of Christ in the passage above referred to. Another witness to the importance of upholding the Protestant view upon this subject is the learned and brilliant theologian of Heidelberg, Dr. Rothe. In the essays[1] which he put forth a few years ago, and which he has since collected in a little volume, the old theological definitions in regard to Inspiration are frankly discarded for the reason that, in the opinion of the author, they were constructed from a mistaken conception of the nature and method of Divine Revelation. Not only does he extend the influence of the human element, or factor, in the composition of the Scriptures so far as to admit of the introduction of errors in physical science and in history, but he does not hesitate to allow that the Apostles fell into mistakes in reasoning and in their method of interpreting the Old Testament, and to distinguish between the doctrines they set forth, and the arguments

[1] First published in the Studien u. Kritiken. They are collected by the Author under the title, *Zur Dogmatik*.

to which they resort in confuting adversaries, and which are more or less the result of their own fallible reflection. In these and other particulars, Rothe departs widely from the accepted formulas of doctrine. And yet he maintains, and feels it necessary to maintain, the Normative Authority of the Scriptures. This he endeavors to save by his view that the Bible is not only a self-explaining, but, to some extent, also a self-correcting, book. If we are able to discern the imperfection of an ethical sentence, or ethical judgment, in one portion of the Scriptures—for example in the Psalms—we do this only by means of a more advanced ethical standard which the Gospel, or the Scriptures as a whole, has given us, so that the Rule of Faith—the source of knowledge—still remains an objective one. We are still moving in the sphere of the Bible, seeing in the Bible's own teaching, judging by the Bible's own standard. A view not dissimilar from that of Rothe is suggested in various passages of the celebrated Letters of Coleridge on the subject of Inspiration. "Is it not a fact," he asks, "that the books of the New Testament were tried by their consonance with the rule, and according to the analogy, of faith? Does not the universally admitted canon—that each part of the Scripture must be interpreted by the spirit of the whole—lead to the same practical conclusion as that for which I am now contending; namely, that it is the spirit of the Bible, and not the detached words and sentences, that is infallible and absolute?"[1] It is foreign to our present purpose to criticise these views of Rothe, which have evidently made a strong impression in Germany, or the somewhat similar, though less guarded, declarations of Coleridge. We advert to them both, simply to illustrate wherein lies the importance of the doctrine of Inspiration, and how essential it is, even in the opinion of profound theologians who are counted among the most liberal of the adherents of the Evangelical system, to uphold the Protestant doctrine of an objective and *on the whole* unerring standard of religious truth and duty.

Yet the subject of the Normative Authority of Scripture is of subordinate interest when compared with the debate that has arisen upon the historical reality of the Scriptural miracles. The attention of thoughtful men, everywhere, is concentrated upon the question of the verity of those parts of Scriptural history which describe miraculous events. If this be established, the speculative objections to the doctrinal system of Christianity at once fall to the ground. All opposition of this sort is then silenced, if not satisfied. On the other hand, if the miracles are disproved, Christianity is stripped of its essential peculiarity. The central fact of a Supernatural Interposition having for its end the restoration of

[1] Coleridge, *Confessions of an Inquiring Spirit*, in his Works, Am. Ed. vol. v. p. 612.

man to communion with God, is lost. The Christian system of doctrine is reduced to a mere product of the human mind, having no divine sanction, and mixed, we know not how largely, with error. That this question of the historical reality of the Scriptural miracles involves the whole claim of Christianity to be a Revelation, is plain, for Revelation and Miracle are inseparable from each other. In fact, the ablest skeptical writers of the present day have set themselves to the work of undermining the evidence for the Scriptural miracles. To explain the origin of Christianity, and the origin also of the New Testament narratives of supernatural events, on some hypothesis that shall dispense with the need of putting faith in the latter, is the problem which they are struggling to solve. The Life of Christ by Strauss, in both the earlier and the recent form, is simply an elaborate attempt to set aside miracles, by propounding some hypothesis more plausible than the old exploded theory of a wilful deception on the part of the early disciples. The Life of Christ by Renan is likewise little more than an effort to account for Christ and Christianity and the Christian Scriptures, without giving credence to miraculous events. The recent criticism of the New Testament canon, embracing the attempt to impeach the genuineness of various books, is only a part of the great discussion of the historical truth of the New Testament miracles; for it is difficult to attack the credibility of the Gospel histories without first disproving their genuineness. This main issue is never withdrawn from the mind of writer or reader. The resources of learning and skill which are expended by the Tübingen school of critics with Baur at their head, and in turn by their antagonists, in reference to the authorship and date of the Gospels and of other portions of the New Testament, are only a chapter in the controversy to which we allude. The spectacle presented is that of a conflict for the possession of a place not so much valued for itself, as for being the key that carries with it another position on which all thoughts centre. Thus the real issue between the believer and the unbeliever has become distinct and conspicuous. Did Christ do the works which none other men could do? This is the vital question—we might almost say, the only question. The case of Christianity rests upon the decision of it. Its claim to a rank essentially different from that of other religions and philosophies, stands or falls according as this question is answered. Is the doctrine of God, or does Christ speak of himself, uttering a human wisdom which, however rare, is only human, bearing upon it no loftier sanction, and even mixed with an amalgam of error?

This being a question so momentous, we have a right to expect of every one who enters into the discussion of the character of the Scriptures, especially if he be understood to represent the Christian cause, that he shall declare himself in regard to it without ambiguity. Whatever view he may take upon special questions, upon this cardinal proposition of supernaturalism he has no right to appear to halt or to oscillate between two opinions. The volume of *Essays and Reviews* which lately kindled so great an excitement in the English Church, appears to us to be liable to this charge. In several of the dissertations that compose it, there is manifest an evasiveness and indecision, a disposition to pare down the supernatural in the Scriptures to a minimum, if not to doubt its existence altogether. An explicit, unshrinking avowal of a belief in the historical reality of the Christian miracles, would have redeemed that book, in our judgment, from its gravest fault. We remember that a critic of the *Essays,* in one of the English literary journals, cited from the book one skeptical insinuation after another, appending to each the question: "but what of the Resurrection?" This or that stricture may be just, or may not be—such was the purport of criticism—*but what of the Resurrection of Christ from the dead?* On what ground do these authors stand? Is it the design to shake the faith of men in supernatural Christianity and recommend a naturalistic theory? If not, why this hesitation to commit themselves to a bold avowal on the subject of miracles, and to let their readers see how much is implied in the fact of the Resurrection of Christ? The concession that a single miracle took place in connection with Christianity imparts to this religion an unspeakable elevation and awfulness in the view of every considerate mind. Although in these remarks we have chiefly in mind the New Testament, yet we should be inclined to bring a similar accusation against Stanley, for the ambiguous tone of his recent History of the Jewish Church, did he not expressly disclaim the ability to sever, in his own mind, in many cases, the natural and the supernatural. We are continually left afloat in regard to this most interesting and most important question. Now an event appears to be represented as miraculous, and in the next sentence it is resolved into a merely natural occurrence. Were it not for the distinct avowal of the author, to which we have adverted, his work would be justly chargeable with being written in a jesuitical tone—a tone least of all corresponding with the author's character. For ourselves we must acknowledge our preference for a single page of severe scientific criticism, over a library of volumes like this of Dr. Stanley, where so little is decided and settled. What men crave in these days, is satisfaction upon the difficult questions which meet them in the early portions of the Old Testament, and, if at all in earnest, they will not be content to be put off with pleasant description. In striking contrast with the censurable uncertainty of the *Essays and Reviews* upon the subject of miracles, is the tone of Rothe in the little work to which we have already alluded. Starting with the avowed design to oppose the views more commonly taken of the Scriptures, he is careful at the outset to avow his undoubting faith in miracles and in the supernatural character of Christianity. He desires it to be distinctly understood that on this subject he is full and clear. On this platform he will stand in the prosecution of the further inquiries to which he invites attention. Such a course alone is worthy of a theologian who has a nobler aim than merely to instill doubts concerning the justice of received views.

Thus, the principal question in the controversy with unbelief is an historical one. Hardly a worse mistake can be committed in dealing with most skeptics at the present day, than to *begin* by insisting upon the inspiration of the Bible. We should rather place ourselves back in the position which the apostles occupied in preaching to the Gentiles, before the New Testament Scriptures were written. We should make it our first aim to substantiate the great facts which are recorded in the New Testament, and which formed the pith and marrow of the apostles' testimony. We must meet the skeptic on the ordinary level of historical investigation, and bring before him the proof that the Gospel miracles were actually performed, substantially as these histories of the New Testament narrate. There is no other common ground on which he and we can stand. Unless he can be satisfied of the credibility of the Gospels in these main particulars, it is useless to go farther and attempt to convince him that this body of writings is the product of Divine inspiration—much less that they contain no sort of error. The first and the great proposition to be established is, that God has made a supernatural revelation; and this done, other points of truth may follow in their proper place. In this controversy, it behooves us to keep in mind the order of things to be believed. First comes the leading, the commanding truth, of a miraculous attestation to the mission of Jesus. Let this once become a firm conviction, and the next step is to ascertain his teaching and the contents of his religion. Every earnest mind will be ready to take this step; will immediately look about for some authentic source of knowledge on this subject; and then the peculiar character and claims of the Bible will be made a theme of investigation.

While we hold that the direct question at issue with the skeptic and unbeliever is an historical one, we think that Apologists fall into a mischievous error in defining the nature of the evidence for Christian Revelation. This evidence, it is frequently said, being historical, is of a moral or probable kind, as distinguished from demonstrative. The appreciation of it, therefore, it is added, depends in no small degree upon the spirit of the individual by whom it is weighed. So far we fully agree with the ordinary Apologist, and could say with him that the force which the historical proofs will actually have in persuading the mind, differs with the tempers of feeling which are brought to the consideration of them. Only we say, it is a fatal error to confine the inward qualification for judging of this evidence, to the virtues of candor, simplicity, and honesty. On the contrary, we freely concede and contend that these virtues may exist up to the ordinary measure, and even beyond it, and yet this evidence fail of leading the mind to conviction. We freely grant that unbelievers have lived in the past, and some live to-day, whose ability for historical investigation is of an unusually high order. In the treatment of secular history, they evince no want of candor and no excessive incredulity. And although they withhold their belief from the supernatural facts of Christianity, we cannot charge them with any marked disposition to pervert, conceal, or disparage the evidence by which these facts are supported. We would not for a moment deny that great names are on the roll of infidelity; names of men who, to say the least, are not *peculiarly* liable to the charge of being uncandid and prejudiced in their investigation of any important subject. The Christian Apologist, as we think, is entitled and required to take higher ground, and to extend this qualification for appreciating the proofs of revelation beyond the common virtues of fairness and honesty. We are called upon distinctly to recognize the truth, that in the consideration of this subject we find ourselves in a sphere where the deep alienation of the human heart from God and Divine things exerts a powerful influence upon the judgment.[1] When we are called to determine the truth or falsehood of any historical statement, our judgment will be affected inevitably by the view we take of the conditions and causes at work in connection with the event which is alleged to have occurred. The same law is applicable to the Gospel history. Were these events ordinary, or unmiraculous events, the evidence for them would not only be convincing, but, for all thorough students, overwhelming. But another element may come in to arrest the judgment and defeat the natural effect of the proof; the circumstance, namely, that the events are thought to be either out of the range of possibility, or in the highest degree unlikely to occur. The evidence may be felt to be all that could be asked, and more than could be required, in the case of any natural event, but the event being, if it occurred, a miracle, there is a positive incredulity beforehand, which, it may be, no amount of historical proof can overcome. This *variable element*, which *may* neutralize the strongest array of historical evidence, lies in the general habit of feeling with reference to supernatural things. At the bottom of unbelief is a rationalistic or unreligious temper. This truth is admirably set forth in one of the sermons of Arnold. "The clearest notion,"

[1] It may be well to compare here what the New Testament itself has to say of the prerequisites of faith. See Matt. xi. 25; 1 Cor. i. 19–27; and like passages.

he says, "which can be given of Rationalism would, I think, be this: that it is the abuse of the understanding in subjects where the divine and human, so to speak, are intermingled. Of human things the understanding can judge, of divine things it cannot; and thus, where the two are mixed together, its inability to judge of the one part makes it derange the proportions of both, and the judgment of the whole is vitiated. For example, the understanding examines a miraculous history: it judges truly of what I may call the human part of the case; that is to say, of the rarity of miracles, of the fallibility of human testimony, of the proneness of most minds to exaggeration, and of the critical arguments affecting the genuineness or date of the narrative itself. But it forgets the divine part, namely, the power and providence of God, that He is really ever present amongst us, and that the spiritual world, which exists invisibly all around us, may conceivably and by no means impossibly exist, at some times and to some persons, even visibly." This Rationalism, however, is a thing of degrees. Where not including an absolute disbelief in the realities of a higher world, it may still involve a practical insensibility to their influence. They are left out of the account in determining the question of the truth or falsehood of the New Testament history. We would make this variable element still more comprehensive, including within it the soul's sense of sin and discernment of the beauty of holiness. The judgment which the mind forms in respect to the proofs of Christian Revelation, is greatly affected by the presence or absence of certain experiences of the heart, which are rational and just, but which belong in a very unequal degree to different men. An illustration of the general truth contained in Arnold's remark may be taken from another, but, in some respects, a kindred department. Let us suppose that a painting is discovered in some Italian town, which, it is claimed, is a work of Raphael. Now for the settlement of this question there are two sources of proof. There is, in the first place, all that bears on the outward authentication of the claim; as the consideration of the place where the painting is found, the integrity of those who had it in charge, the historical circumstances which are said to connect it with the artist to whom it is ascribed, the known facts in his life which tend to prove or disprove the truth of the pretension. As far as this kind of proof is concerned, any discriminating person may be pronounced competent to appreciate the degree of force that belongs to it, and, if the settlement of the point depended exclusively upon this branch of the evidence, to come to a just conclusion. But there is obviously another sort of evidence to be considered and weighed. The character and merits of the painting, as a work of art, in comparison with the high and peculiar excellence of Raphael, must enter into the case, as a part of the proof. But how many are the acute and pains-taking men who are here disabled from estimating —from *feeling*, we might rather say, the force of this branch of the evidence! They can examine the documents, they can question the witnesses, they can scrutinize all the outward testimony; but they are destitute of the perceptions and feelings which are the indispensable qualification of a critic of art! The analogy holds true in this particular, that in the question of the verity of the Gospel histories, one great part of the evidence lies in a province beyond the reach of the faculty of understanding, in the sense in which Arnold uses the term. The whole mode of thought and feeling concerning God, and His Providence, and His character, concerning human sin and human need, has a decisive influence in determining the judgment to give or refuse credit to the historical proof. Possibly God has so arranged it, that while this proof is sufficient to satisfy one whose spiritual eye is open to these realities, it is yet endued with no power to create conviction where such is not the fact. He who magnifies the presumption against supernatural interposition, not allowing for the moral emergency that calls for it, and hardly recognizing the Power from whom it must come, puts on a coat-of-mail which is proof against all the arguments for Revelation. He is shut up to unbelief by a logical necessity. The effect of the internal argument for the supernatural origin of the Gospel is directly dependent upon that habit of feeling, either rationalistic or the opposite, the operation of which we have described. The various particulars of this argument, at least the most important of them, are lost upon an unreligious nature. The painful consciousness of sin, for example, is the medium through which is discerned the correspondence of the Gospel method of salvation with the necessities and yearnings of the soul. An experience of the disease opens the eye to the true nature and the value of the remedy. Such an impression of the evil of sin and of personal guilt, as men like Luther and Pascal have had, uncovers the deep things of the Gospel. In the Gospel system alone is the situation of the soul, which is slowly learned by the soul itself, understood and met. Another eye has looked through the heart before us, and anticipated the discovery, which we make, imperfectly and by degrees, of its guilt and want. We might point out how the same self-knowledge will find in the spotless character of Christ a glory and impressiveness undiscernible by such as think not how great a thing it is to be free from sin. And so the tremendous power exerted by Christianity to reform the world—to move men to forsake their sins—will be estimated aright. It is no part of our present purpose to exhibit in detail the blinding effect of the rationalistic temper. Whoever carefully surveys the more recent literature of skepticism, will not fail to see the source from which it springs. It was by ignoring the existence and character of God that Hume constructed a plausible argument against the possibility of proving a miracle. The moment that the truth concerning God and the motives of His government is taken into view, the fallacy of Hume's reasoning is laid bare. The first canon which Strauss lays at the foundation of his criticism is the impossibility that a miracle should occur. Any and every other hypothesis, he takes for granted, is sooner to be allowed than the admission of a miraculous event. He assumes, from beginning to end, that "a relation is not historical, that the thing narrated could not have so occurred," when "it is irreconcilable with known, and elsewhere universally prevailing, laws." By this circumstance, before all others, the unhistorical character of a narrative is ascertained.[1] So M. Renan, at the outset of his late work, remarks: "That the Gospels are in part legendary is evident, since they are full of miracles and the supernatural."[2] Afterward, though he does not with Strauss openly affirm the strict impossibility of a miracle, he lays down "this principle of historical criticism, that a supernatural relation cannot be accepted as such, that it always implies credulity or imposture, that the duty of the

[1] Strauss's *Leben Jesu*, B. I., S. 100.

[2] Renan's *Vie de Jésus*, p. xv.

historian is to interpret it, and to seek what portion of truth and what portion of error it may contain." But how futile is the attempt to convince one that an event has occurred, which he professes to know is either impossible, or never to be believed! In other words, how futile to argue with one who begs the question in dispute!

The foregoing observations upon the reception that is given by skeptics at the present day to the proof of Christian miracles, bring us to the deeper and more general cause of unbelief, which is none other than the weakening or total destruction of faith in the supernatural. It is not the supernatural in the Scriptures alone, but the supernatural altogether, which in our day is the object of disbelief. At the root of the most respectable and formidable attack upon Christianity—that which emanates from the Tübingen school of historical critics—is an avowed Pantheism. The doctrine of a God to be distinguished from the World, and competent to produce events not provided for by natural causes, is cast away. The apotheosis of Nature or the World, of course, leaves no room for anything supernatural, and a miracle becomes an absurdity. Indeed, the tacit assumption that a miracle is impossible, which we find in so many quarters, can only flow from an Atheistic or Pantheistic view of the Universe. The Deist can consistently take no such position. He professes to believe in a living and personal God, however he may be disposed to set Him at a distance and to curtail His agency. He must therefore acknowledge the existence of a Power who is able at any moment to bring to pass an event over and beyond the capacity of natural causes. Nay, if his Deism be earnestly meant, he must himself believe in a miracle of the most stupendous character—in the creation of the world by the omnipotent agency of God. Holding thus to the miracle of creation as an historical event, he cannot, without a palpable inconsistency, deny that miracles are conceivable or longer possible. For no sincere Deist can suppose that the Creator has chained Himself up by physical laws of His own making, and thereby cut Himself off from new exertions of His power, even within the sphere where natural forces usually operate according to a fixed rule. One of the marked characteristics of our time, therefore, is the loose manner in which Deism is held even by those who profess it, as shown in their reluctance to take the consequences of their creed and their readiness to proceed in their treatment of the subject of miracles upon Pantheistic principles. The theories and arguments of Strauss and the Tübingen skeptics, which are the offshoot of their Pantheistic system, are adopted, for example, by Theodore Parker, who professes to believe in the personality of God. But though entertaining this different belief, it is plain that he generally brings to the discussion of miracles the feeling and the postulates of a Pantheist. His Deism is so far from being thorough and consistent, that he not only, here and there, falls into the Pantheistic notion of sin, as a necessary stage of development and step in human progress, but also habitually regards a miracle as equivalent to an absurdity. A gifted female writer has lately put forth a plea in behalf of a Christless Theism which she wishes to see organized into a practical, working system.[1] Anxious respecting the possible fate of the truths of Natural Religion in the crisis occasioned by the supposed downfall of faith in Revelation, she forgets that skepticism as to the supernatural origin of Christianity generally results from a prior adoption of an Atheistic or Pantheistic philosophy. The evil she dreads is not an accidental consequence, but an effective cause, of disbelief in the claims of the Gospel. At least, faith in Revelation and faith in the verities of Natural Religion sink together. The same writer forgets also that the doctrine of Theism, however supported by the light of Nature, came to us, in point of fact, from the Bible. The nations learned it from the Bible. It is a truth which we practically owe to Revelation. And as this is the case, so it is natural that with the denial of Revelation, that doctrine should be discarded. The result

[1] Frances Power Cobbe, *Broken Lights.*

of previous experiments should warn against the indulgence of the hope that Natural Religion can succeed in the effort to embody itself in a practical system of worship. The Theophilanthropists of the French Revolution, who espoused the three principles —God, Virtue, Immortality—tried to maintain religious worship. In Paris alone their assemblies at one time numbered not less than twenty thousand persons, and occupied ten churches. But there was not vitality enough in the system to keep it alive, and this apparently promising sect quickly melted away. In the ancient world, among thinking men, skepticism as to the supernatural on the one hand, and the Christian faith on the other, were the two combatants, and so it will be now. As far as this class are alienated from Christianity, they are more commonly alienated in an almost equal degree from all religious faith. Signs of such an obscuration of faith appear in various quarters. Not a few ill-supported speculations of physical science, which have been lately brought before the public, have their real motive in a desperate reluctance to admit a supernatural cause. The most unfounded conjectures are furnished in the room of argument, so earnest is the desire of some minds to create the belief that the worlds were *not* framed by the word of God, and that things which are seen *were* made of things which do appear. To this we must refer the ambition of some philosophers to establish their descent from the inferior animals—a wild theory, only to be compared with the old mythologic doctrine of transmigration. The disposition to remove God from any active connection with the world, or to transport Him as far back as possible into the remote past, is the real motive of this attempt, which can plead no evidence in its favor, to invalidate absolutely the distinction of species and discredit our own feeling of personal identity and separateness of being. There can be no doubt that a powerful tendency to Pantheistic modes of thought is rife at the present day. The popular literature, even in our country, is far more widely infected in this way than unobservant readers are aware. The laws of Nature are hypostatized—spoken of as if they were a self-active being. And not unfrequently the same tendency leads to the virtual, if not explicit, denial of the free and responsible nature of man. History is resolved by a class of writers into the movement of a great machine—into the evolution of events with which the free-will neither of God nor of man has any connection.[1]

We are thus brought back, in our analysis of the controversy with the existing unbelief, to the postulates of Natural Religion. On these the Chris-

[1] The tendencies to Naturalism, at work at the present day, are forcibly and comprehensively touched upon in Chapter I. of Bushnell's "Nature and the Supernatural"—a work which, in its main parts, is equally profound and inspiring.

tian Apologist founds the presumption, or anterior probability, that a Revelation will be given. These, together with the intrinsic excellence of Christianity, he employs to rebut and remove the presumption, which, however philosophers may differ as to the exact source and strength of it, undoubtedly lies against the occurrence of a miracle. The antecedent improbability that a miracle will occur, disappears in the case of Christianity. The issue relates to the miracles; but the ultimate source of the conflict is a false or feeble view, on the part of the unbeliever, of the primitive truths of religion. This will explain how a new awakening of conscience, or of religious sensibility, has been known to dispel the incredulity with which he had looked upon the claims of Revelation.

It is more and more apparent that the cause of Natural Religion, and that of Revealed Religion, are bound up together. But the native convictions of the human mind concerning God and duty cannot be permanently dislodged. Atheism is an affront alike to the inquiring reason and the uplooking soul of man. Pantheism mocks his religious nature. It is inconsistent with religion—with prayer, with worship—with that communion with a higher Being, which *is* religion. It is inconsistent, also, with morality, in any earnest meaning of the term; for it empties free-will and responsibility, holiness and sin, of their meaning. Every one who acknowledges the feeling of guilt to be a reality and to represent the truth, and every one who blames the conduct of another, in the very act denies the Pantheistic theory. Conscience must prove, in the long run, stronger than any speculation, no matter how plausible. In the soul itself, then, in its aspiration after the living God and its conviction of freedom and of sin, there is erected an everlasting barrier against the inroads of false philosophy, and one that will be found to embrace within the shelter of its walls the cause of Christianity itself.

ESSAY II.

THE GENUINENESS OF THE FOURTH GOSPEL.

The Gospel that bears the name of John is one of the main pillars of historical Christianity. Christianity would indeed remain were the apostolic authorship and the credibility of this Gospel disproved; for before it was written, Jesus and the resurrection had been preached by faithful witnesses over a large part of the Roman world. Christianity would remain; but our conception of Christianity and of Christ would be materially altered. The profoundest minds in the Church, from Clement of Alexandria to Luther, and from Luther to Niebuhr, have expressed their sense of the singular charm and surpassing value of this Gospel. In recent times, however, the genuineness of the fourth Gospel has been impugned. It was denied to be the work of John by individual skeptics at the close of the last century; but their attack was not of a nature either to excite or to merit much attention. Not until Bretschneider published (in 1820) his *Probabilia* did the question become the subject of serious discussion. But the assault which has been renewed by the critics of the Tübingen school, with Baur at their head, has more lately given rise to a most earnest and important controversy. The rejection of John's Gospel by these critics is a part of their attempted reconstruction of early Christian history. Starting with the assertion of a radical difference and hostility between the Jewish and the Gentile types of Christianity,—between the party of the Church that adhered to Peter and the original disciples, and the party that adhered to Paul and his doctrine,—they ascribe several books of the New Testament to the effort, made at a later day, to bridge over this gulf. The Acts of the Apostles proceeds from this motive, and is a designed distortion and misrepresentation of events connected with the conflict about the rights of the Gentile converts. And the fourth Gospel is a product of the same pacifying tendency. It was written, they say, about the middle of the second century, by a Christian of Gentile birth, who assumed the name of John in order to give an apostolic sanction to his higher theological platform, in which love takes the place of faith, and the Jewish system is shown to be fulfilled, and so abolished, by the offering of Christ, the true paschal Lamb. We hold that the fundamental proposition, which affirms a radical hostility between Pauline and Petrine Christianity, can be proved to be false, even by the documents which are acknowledged by the Tübingen school to be genuine and trustworthy; and that the superstructure which is reared upon this foundation can be proved, in all its main timbers, to be equally unsubstantial. In the present Essay, however, we shall take up the single subject of the authorship of the fourth Gospel, and shall make it a part of our plan to refute the arguments which are brought forward by the skeptical critics on this question — the most important critical question connected with the New Testament canon. But while we propose fairly to consider these arguments, we have no doubt that the attack upon the genuineness of John has its root in a determined unwillingness to admit the historical reality of the miracles which that Gospel records. This feeling, which sways the mind of the critics of whom we speak, is the ultimate and real ground of their refusal to believe that this narrative proceeds from an eyewitness of the life of Jesus. And were there nothing in Christianity to remove this natural incredulity, and to overturn the presumption against the occurrence of miracles, the ground taken by the Tübingen critics in reference to this question might be reasonable. It is right to observe that behind all their reasoning there lies this deep-seated, and, in our opinion, unwarrantable prejudice.

We have recorded below the titles of some of the more recent defences of the Johannean authorship:[1] Bleek's Introduction, in which the author discusses

[1] Bleek's *Einleitung in das N. T.*, 1862, and *Beiträge zur Evangelien-Kritik*, 1846. Meyer's *Kom. über das Evang. des Johannes*, 3^e^ A., 1856. De Wette's *Kom. über das Evang. des Johannes*, 4^e^ ed. (edited by Brückner), 1852. Schneider's *Aechtheit des Johann. Evang.*, 1854. Mayer's *Aechtheit des Evang. nach Johann.*, 1854. Ebrard's *Wissenchaftl. Kritik der Evangel. Geschichte*, 2^e^ A., 1850, pp.

the question at length, with his wonted clearness and golden candor, and his Contributions to the Criticism of the Gospels, in which some important points are treated more fully; Meyer's Introduction to his Commentary on John, which contains a brief, condensed exhibition of the principal points of argument; Brückner's edition of De Wette's Commentary on John, in which the later editor has presented the internal proofs with much force, and has noticed in detail the interpretations of Baur; Schneider's little tract, which handles with ability certain parts of the external evidence, but falls far short of being a complete view; Ewald's Essays, which contribute fresh and original thoughts upon the subject, but are not without faults in opinion as well as temper; Ebrard's Critical Examination of the Evangelical History, which, notwithstanding an occasional flippancy of style and tendency to overstatement, contains many valuable suggestions; and Mayer's copious treatise, in which the external testimonies are ably considered, though too much in the temper of a contro-

828-952. Ewald's Jahrb., III. s. 146 seq., V. s. 178 seq., X. s. 83 seq. —The following are among the most important Essays in opposition to the Genuineness of John: Baur, *Kritische Untersuchungen über die Kanon. Evangelien* (1847), and *Die Johanneische Frage u. ihre neuesten Beantwortungen*, in Baur and Zeller's *Theologische Jahrbücher*, 1854, pp. 196-287; Zeller, *Die äussern Zeugnisse über das Daseyn und den Ursprung des vierten Evangeliums*, in his *Theol. Jahrb.* 1845, pp. 579-656, comp. 1847, pp. 136-174; Hilgenfeld, *Die Evangelien* u. s. w. (1854); Strauss, *Das Leben Jesu für das deutsche Volk* (1864), p. 62 seq.

versialist, and with occasional passages not adapted to convince any save members of the Roman Catholic church, of which the author is one. We intend to present our readers with a summary of the arguments, most of which are touched upon in one or another of these writers; although we lay claim at least to independence in weighing, verifying, and combining the various considerations which we have to bring forward.

That the apostle John spent the latter part of his life in Proconsular Asia, in particular at Ephesus, is a fact fully established by trustworthy testimony of ancient ecclesiastical writers. At the conference of Paul with the other apostles in Jerusalem (Gal. ii. 1 seq.; Acts xv.), which occurred about twenty years after the death of Christ, John is mentioned, in connection with Peter and James, as one of the pillars of the Jerusalem church. Whether he was in Jerusalem on the occasion of Paul's last visit, we are not informed. It is in the highest degree probable that John's residence at Ephesus began after the period of Paul's activity there, and either after or not long before the destruction of Jerusalem. Among the witnesses to the fact of his living at Ephesus in the latter part of the second century, Polycrates and Irenaeus are of especial importance. Polycrates was himself a bishop of Ephesus near the end of the second century, who had become a Christian as early as A. D. 131, and seven of whose kinsmen had previously been bishops or presbyters. In his letter to Victor, he expressly says that John died and was buried at Ephesus.[1] Irenaeus, who was born in Asia, says of the old presbyters, immediate disciples of the apostles, whom he had known, that they had been personally conversant with John, and that he had remained among them up to the times of Trajan (whose reign was from the year 98 to 117). Some of them, he says, had not only seen John, but other apostles also.[2] Whether the ancient stories be true or not, of his fleeing from the bath on seeing there the heretic Cerinthus, of his recovering the young man who joined a company of robbers, or the more probable story, found in Jerome, of his being carried in his old age into the Christian assemblies, to which he addressed the simple exhortation: "Love one another," they show a general knowledge of the fact of his residing at Ephesus, and of his living to an extreme old age.[3] His Gospel, also, according to the testimony of Irenaeus, Clement, and others, and the general belief, was the last written of the four, and the tradition places its composition near the close of his life.

[1] Euseb., Lib. V. c. 24; cf. Lib. III. c. 31.

[2] *Adv. Haer.*, Lib. II. c. 22, al. 39. § 5.

[3] Iren. *adv. Haer.*, Lib. III. c. 3. § 4. (Euseb., Lib. IV. c. 14)—Clem. Alex., *Quis dives salvetur*, c. 42. (Euseb., Lib. III. c. 23.)—Hieron. in *Ep. ad Galat.* VI. 10.

The External Evidence.

Mayer begins his argument by an appeal to Jerome and Eusebius; the one writing in the later, and the other in the early, part of the fourth century; both having in their hands the literature of the Church before them; both diligent in their researches and inquiries; both knowing how to discriminate between books which had been received without contradiction, and those whose authority had either been disputed or might fairly be questioned; and yet neither having any knowledge or suspicion that the fourth Gospel was not known to the writers of the first half of the second century, with whom they were familiar. This appeal is not without force; but instead of dwelling on the inference which it appears to warrant, we choose to begin with the unquestioned fact of the universal reception of the fourth Gospel as genuine in the last quarter of the second century. At that time we find that it is held in every part of Christendom to be the work of the Apostle John. The prominent witnesses are Tertullian in North Africa, Clement in Alexandria, and Irenaeus in Gaul. Though the date of Tertullian's birth is uncertain, a considerable portion of his life fell within the second century, and his book against Marcion, from which his fullest testimony is drawn, was composed in 207 or 208. His language proves the universal reception of our four Gospels, and of John among them. These together, and these exclusively, were considered the authentic histories of the life of Christ, being composed either by apostles themselves or by their companions.[1] The testimony of Clement is the more important from his scholarly character and his wide acquaintance with the Church. He became the head of the Catechetical school at Alexandria about the year 190. Having been previously a pupil of various philosophers, he had in his mature years sought instruction from Christian teachers in Greece, in Lower Italy, in Syria, in Palestine, as well as in Egypt; and his works which remain prove his extensive learning. Not only is the genuineness of the fourth Gospel an undisputed fact with Clement, but, not to speak of other testimony from him, he gave in his lost work, the Institutions, quoted by Eusebius, "a tradition concerning the order of the Gospels which he had received from presbyters of more ancient times;" that is, concerning the chronological order of their composition.[2] But of these three witnesses, Irenaeus, from the circumstances of his life as well as the peculiar charac-

[1] *Adv. Marcion.*, Lib. IV. c. 2; also c. 5. He says in this last place: "In summa, si constat id verius quod prius, id prius quod et ab initio, id ab initio quod ab apostolis; pariter utique constabit, id esse ab apostolis traditum, quod apud ecclesias apostolorum fuerit sacrosanctum." Then shortly after: "eadem auctoritas ecclesiarum apostolicarum caeteris quoque patrocinabitur evangeliis, quae proinde per illas, et secundum illas habemus:" here follows the enumeration of the four. It is historical evidence—the knowledge possessed by the churches founded by the apostles,—on which Tertullian builds.

[2] Euseb., Lib. VI. c. 14. That the four Gospels alone were regarded as possessed of canonical authority is evident from other

ter of his testimony, is the most important. A Greek, born in Asia Minor about the year 140, coming to Lyons and holding there first the office of presbyter, and then, in 178, that of bishop, he was familiar with the Church in both the East and the West. Moreover, he had in his youth known and conversed with the aged Polycarp of Smyrna, the immediate disciple of John, and retained a vivid recollection of the person and the words of this remarkable man. Now Irenaeus not only testifies to the universal acceptance in the Church of the fourth Gospel, but also argues fancifully that there *must* be four and only four Gospels to stand as pillars of the truth; thus showing how firmly settled was his faith, and that of others, in the exclusive authority of the canonical Gospels.[1] To the value of

places in Clement. In reference to an alleged conversation between Salome and Jesus, Clement says: "We have not this saying in *the four Gospels which have been handed down to us*, but in that according to the Egyptians,—ἐν τοῖς παραδεδομένοις ἡμῖν τέτταρσιν εὐαγγελίοις οὐκ ἔχομεν τὸ ῥητόν, ἀλλ' ἐν τῷ κατ' Αἰγυπτίους. *Strom.*, Lib. III. c. 13. (See Lardner, Vol. II. pp. 236 and 251).

[1] *Adv. Haer.*, Lib. III. c. 1. § 1. This noted passage on the four Gospels thus begins: "Non enim per alios dispositionem salutis nostrae cognovimus, quam per eos, per quos evangelium pervenit ad nos; quod quidem tunc praeconaverunt, postea vero per Dei voluntatem in scripturis nobis tradiderunt, fundamentum et columnam fidei nostrae futurum." Like Tertullian, he makes his appeal to sure historical evidence. In speaking of Polycarp and the men who followed him, he says of the former (III. 3. 4): "qui vir multo majoris auctoritatis et fidelior veritatis est testis, quam Valentinus et Marcion et reliqui, qui sunt perversae sententiae." The curious attempt to show that there could not be more or fewer than four authoritative Gospels is in Lib. III. c. 11. § 8.

his testimony we shall have occasion again to refer. We simply ask here if it was possible for Irenaeus to express himself in this way—to affirm not merely the genuineness of the four Gospels, but the metaphysical necessity that there should be four—if John's Gospel had been made known for the first time during his lifetime, or shortly before. With these noteworthy witnesses, we associate the great name of Origen, the successor of Clement at Alexandria, although Origen's theological career is later, terminating near the middle of the third century, he having been born but fifteen years before the end of the second; for his extensive journeys through the Eastern Church, and as far as Rome, and especially his critical curiosity and erudition, together with the fact that he was born of Christian parents, give extraordinary weight to the evidence he affords of the universal reception of John's Gospel. In the same category with Irenaeus, Clement, and Tertullian, belong the Canon of Muratori, or the list of canonical books which Muratori found in an old manuscript in the Milan library, and which is certainly not later than the end of the second century; and the ancient Syriac version of the New Testament, the Peshito, having a like antiquity. In both these monuments the Gospel of John is found in its proper place. Nor should we omit to mention here Polycrates, the bishop of Ephesus, who, as we have said, represented the Asia Minor churches in the controversy concerning the celebration of Easter in the year 196, and in his letter to Victor, the Roman bishop, alludes to John, who, he says, "leaned upon the Lord's breast," *ὁ ἐπὶ τὸ στῆθος τοῦ κυρίου ἀναπεσών.*[1] Even Hilgenfeld, one of the most forward of the Tübingen critics, does not longer deny that the expression is drawn by Polycrates from John xiii. 25 (xxi. 20). It proves the acceptance of John's Gospel by the Christians of Asia Minor.

Looking about among the fragments of Christian literature that have come down to us from the second half of the second century, we meet with Tatian, supposed to have been a pupil of Justin Martyr, though after the master's death the disciple swerved from his teaching. It is now conceded by Baur and Zeller that in his apologetic treatise, the Oratio ad Graecos, composed not far from the year 170, he quotes repeatedly from the Gospel of John.[2] There is also no reason to doubt that his work entitled Diatessaron—a sort of exegetical Harmony—was composed upon the basis of our four Gospels. Eusebius says that Tatian "having formed a certain body and collection of Gospels, I know not how, has given this the title Diatessaron, that is, the Gospel by the four, or the Gospel formed of the four, which is in the possession of some even now."[3]

[1] Euseb., Lib. V. c. 24.

[2] The following are examples,—*Oratio*, c. 13: καὶ τοῦτο ἔστιν ἄρα τὸ εἰρημένον· ἡ σκοτία τὸ φῶς οὐ καταλαμβάνει. c. 19: πάντα ὑπ' αὐτοῦ, καὶ χωρὶς αὐτοῦ γέγονεν οὐδὲ ἕν. c. 5: ὁ λόγος ἐν ἀρχῇ γεννηθείς. c. 4: πνεῦμα ὁ θεός. See Bleek, s. 229.

[3] Lib. IV. c. 29.

Precisely how the work was constructed from the four Gospels, Eusebius appears not to have known. He testifies, however, to the fact of its being in the hands of catholic Christians. At the beginning of the fifth century Theodoret tells us that he had found two hundred copies of Tatian's work in circulation, and had taken them away, substituting for them the four Gospels.[1] A Syriac translation of this work began, according to a later Syrian writer, Bar Salibi, with the opening words of the Gospel of John: "In the beginning was the Word." To this Syriac edition, Ephraem Syrus, who died in 378, wrote a commentary, as Syriac writers inform us; and this translation must therefore have been early made. The attempt of Credner to invalidate this evidence on the ground that the Syrians confounded Tatian with Ammonius, the author of a Harmony in the early part of the third century, is overthrown by the fact that Bar Salibi distinguishes the two authors and their works.[2] Considering all the evidence in the case, together with the fact that Tatian is known to have quoted the Gospel of John in his Oratio, there is no room for doubting that this Gospel was one of the four at the foundation of the Diatessaron. Contemporary with Tatian was Theophilus, who became bishop of Antioch in 169. In his work Ad Autolycum, he describes John's Gospel as a part of the Holy Scriptures, and John himself as a writer guided

[1] Theodoret, *Haeret. Fab.*, I. 20, as cited by Bleek, s. 230.

[2] See Meyer's *Einl.*, s. 9. Lardner, Vol. II. p. 445. Bleek, s. 230.

by the Holy Spirit.[1] This explicit statement is a most weighty item of evidence. In addition to this, Jerome states that Theophilus composed a commentary upon the Gospels, in which he handled their contents synoptically: "quatuor evangelistarum in unum opus dicta compingens."[2] There is no good reason for questioning the statement of Jerome respecting a work with which he appears to have been himself acquainted. A contemporary of Theophilus is Athenagoras. His acquaintance with the Prologue of John's Gospel may be inferred with a high degree of probability from his frequent designation of Christ as the Word. "Through him," he says, "all things were made, the Father and Son being one; and the Son being in the Father, and the Father in the Son;"[3]—language obviously founded on John i. 3; x. 30, 38; xiv. 11. Another contemporary of Theophilus, Apollinaris, bishop of Hierapolis in Phrygia, in a fragment found in the Paschal Chronicle, makes a reference to the pouring out of water and blood from the side of Jesus (John xix. 34), and in another passage clearly implies the existence and authority of the fourth Gospel.[4] The Epistle of the churches of Vienne and Lyons, written in 177,

[1] Ὅθεν διδάσκουσιν ἡμᾶς αἱ ἅγιαι γραφαὶ καὶ πάντες οἱ πνευματοφόροι, ἐξ ὧν Ἰωάννης λέγει· ἐν ἀρχῇ, κ.τ.λ., quoting John i. 1, 3 (Lib. II. c. 22).

[2] *Hieron. de viris ill.*, 25, and *Ep.*, 151. Bleek, s. 230.

[3] *Suppl. pro Christianis*, c. 10.

[4] *Chron. Pasch.*, pp. 13, 14, ed. Dindorf, or Routh's *Reliq. Sacrae*, I. 160, 161, 2d edit. See Meyer's *Einl.*, s. 9. There appears to be no

and presenting an account of the sufferings of their martyrs in their great persecution under Marcus Aurelius, an epistle from which Eusebius gives copious extracts,[1] contains a clear reference to John xvi. 2, in the passage where they say: "Then was fulfilled that which was spoken by our Lord, that the time will come when whosoever killeth you will think that he doeth God service." The same epistle, applying the thought of 1 John iii. 16 (comp. John xv. 12, 13), praises the love of one of their martyrs who "was willing in defense of the brethren to lay down his own life."[2] But every testimony to the first epistle is, for reasons to which we shall advert hereafter, virtually a testimony for the Gospel.

We go back now to the first half of the second century, and among the remnants of early Christian literature which remain, where so much has irrecoverably perished, the writer who is most entitled to consideration is Justin Martyr. He was born about the year 89, and his life extended at least ten years beyond the middle of the next century. A native of Flavia Neapolis, near the ancient Sichem, he had visited various countries, having been at Alexandria and Ephesus before he came to Rome. He had, therefore, an extensive acquaintance with the Church. It is well known

sufficient reason for questioning the genuineness of these fragments, as is done by Lardner (Vol. II. p. 315), and Neander (*Church Hist.*, Vol. I. p. 298, N. 2). See Schneider, s. 52.

[1] Euseb., Lib. V. c. 1.

[2] *Epist. Eccl. Vien. et Lugd.*, cc. 3,4. Routh. *Reliq. Sacrae*, I. 298, 300.

that Justin in different places refers to works which are styled by him the Records or Memoirs by the Apostles and their Followers or Companions, and which, as he observes, "are called Gospels."[1] He quotes from these as the authentic and recognized sources of knowledge respecting the Saviour's life and teaching. He further states that they are read on Sundays in the Christian assemblies, where "all who live in cities or in country districts" meet together for worship. They are read, he says, in connection with the writings of the Old Testament prophets: and when the reader concludes, the people are instructed and exhorted "to the imitation of these excellent things."[2] The evangelical histories which he has in mind, then, were used in the public worship of Christians everywhere. What were these Records or Memoirs? This title, we may observe, was probably given to the gospel histories, partly for the reason that in Justin's view they bore a character analogous to Xenophon's Memorabilia of Socrates, and also because it was a designation intelligible to those for whose benefit he was writing. Of the

[1] τὰ ἀπομνημονεύματα τῶν ἀποστόλων. *Apol.*, I. c. 67. ἀπομνημονεύμασι, ἅ φημι ὑπὸ τῶν ἀποστόλων αὐτοῦ καὶ τῶν ἐκείνοις παρακολουθησάντων συντετάχθαι. *Dial. c. Tryph.*, c. 103. οἱ γὰρ ἀπόστολοι ἐν τοῖς γενομένοις ὑπ' αὐτῶν ἀπομνημονεύμασιν, ἃ καλεῖται εὐαγγέλια, οὕτως παρέδωκαν. *Apol.*, I. c. 66. Justin twice uses the term τὸ εὐαγγέλιον, as the later fathers often do, to denote the Gospels collectively. (*Dial. c. Tryph.*, cc. 10, 100.) This designation implies that the Gospels to which he refers—the collection of Gospels—were possessed of an established authority.

[2] *Apol.*, I. c. 67.

direct citations from these Gospel Memoirs in Justin, and of the numerous allusions to sayings of Christ and events in his life, nearly all plainly correspond to passages in our canonical Gospels. That the quotations are inexact as to phraseology, is not a peculiarity of Justin. He probably quotes from memory; and for his purpose it was not requisite that he should be verbally accurate.

Before we proceed to speak of his use of John in particular, we will advert to the question which has been warmly discussed, whether he quotes from *other* gospel histories than those in our canon. Considering that the cases of an allusion to sayings or transactions not recorded in the canonical Gospels, are so very few, and that of these not one is explicitly referred by Justin to the Memoirs,[1] it is not at all improbable that the source of his knowledge in these exceptional cases was oral tradition. Living so near the time of the apostles, when, as we know, some unrecorded sayings of Christ and circumstances in his life were orally reported from one to another, this supposition is by no means unnatural. Yet as written narratives, besides the four of our canon, were extant, and had a local circulation—especially the Gospel of the He-

[1] Such a reference to the Memoirs has been supposed in *Dial.c. Tryph.*, c. 103 (p. 352 ed. Otto), but erroneously. Nor is there a reference to the Memoirs in *Dial. c. Tryph.*, c. 88 (p. 306 ed. of Otto), where ἔγραψαν οἱ ἀπόστολοι αὐτοῦ refers grammatically only to the last part of the sentence. *There is no citation by Justin from the Memoirs, which is not found in the canonical Gospels.*

brews among the Ebionite Christians—Justin may have been acquainted with one or more of these, and thence derived the exceptional passages which we are considering. That either of these, however, was generally read in the churches (as were the Memoirs of which Justin speaks) is extremely improbable; for how could any Gospel which had been thus made familiar and dear to a multitude of Christians by being read in their assemblies, be suddenly thrown out and discarded without an audible word of opposition? How can such an hypothesis stand in view of the fact that by the time Justin died Irenaeus had already reached his manhood? It is clearly established that Justin had in view the same Gospels which we read in our Bibles, although, as we have said, he may have been acquainted with other less trustworthy narratives of the life of Christ.[1] If we suppose, as there is no necessity for doing, that he derived a few facts or sayings from such a source, it by no means follows that he put these writings on a level with the authoritative Memoirs—the *ἀπομνημονεύματα*. Be it observed, that in the multitude of his

[1] That by the ἀπομνημονεύματα Justin had in mind solely the four Gospels, is earnestly maintained by Semisch, and by Professor Norton in his very able work on the Genuineness of the Gospels. Bleek holds that he had these mainly, if not exclusively, in view. Ewald, without any just reason, thinks that because the records are said to emanate from the apostles and their followers, he had reference to many such writings, which were in his hands. *Jahrb. d. Bibl. Wis.* VI. 60.

allusions to the evangelical history, those which cannot be distinctly traced to the canonical Gospels do not exceed six in number.

The evidence that the fourth Gospel formed one of Justin's authoritative Records or Memoirs cannot be gainsaid. In a long list of passages collected from Justin by Semisch and other writers, there is a marked resemblance in language and thought to places in the fourth Gospel.[1] In regard to many of these, to be sure, we are not absolutely obliged to trace them to this source. They may have been derived from unwritten tradition. But we are authorized to find the origin of this class of expressions in John, when we have assured ourselves, from other passages which admit of no doubt, that Justin made use of the fourth Gospel. And from this conviction there is no escape. We mention here only one, but perhaps the most obvious and striking, of the special quotations which Justin has drawn from this Gospel. Having described with some detail the method of Christian baptism, Justin adds: "For indeed Christ also said: 'except ye be born again, ye shall not enter into the kingdom of heaven.' And that it is impossible for those who are once born to enter into their mother's womb, is plain to all."[2] Here is a

[1] The work of Semisch to which we refer—*Die Denkwürdigkeiten des Märtyrers Justinus*—is a thorough examination of the question: What Gospels were made use of by Justin?

[2] Apol., I. c. 61: Καὶ γὰρ ὁ χριστὸς εἶπεν· Ἂν μὴ ἀναγεννηθῆτε, οὐ μὴ εἰσέλθητε εἰς τὴν βασιλείαν τῶν οὐρανῶν. Ὅτι δὲ καὶ ἀδύνατον εἰς τὰς

passage so peculiar, so characteristic of John's Gospel, that we are precluded from attributing it to any other source. Is it credible that Justin drew this passage from some other gospel, which suddenly perished and was supplanted by that bearing the name of John? Writers of the Tübingen school have suggested that this, as well as other passages seeming to be from John, were taken by Justin from the Gospel of the Hebrews. Aside from the entire absence of proof in support of this assertion, all the information we have concerning the Gospel of the Hebrews warrants the declaration that it contained no such passages. The Gospel of the Hebrews bore a great resemblance in its contents to our Gospel of Matthew. It was the product of a translation and mutilation of our Greek Matthew. There is much to be said in favor of the opinion, for which Bleek argues, that the known fact of its resemblance to Matthew first gave rise to the impression that Matthew originally wrote his Gospel in the Hebrew tongue.[1]

μήτρας τῶν τεκουσῶν τοὺς ἅπαξ γεννωμένους ἐμβῆναι, φανερὸν πᾶσίν ἐστι. There is no reasonable doubt that the quotation in *Dial. c. Tryph.*, c. 88, *οὐκ εἰμὶ ὁ χριστός, ἐγὼ φωνὴ βοῶντος*, is from John i. 20, 23: *οὐκ εἰμὶ ἐγὼ ὁ χριστός . . . . ἐγὼ φωνὴ βοῶντος ἐν τῇ ἐρήμῳ.*

[1] The occurrence of this passage relative to regeneration in the Pseudo-Clementine Homilies (Hom. xi. 26), with the same deviations from John that are found in Justin's quotation, was made an argument to prove that both writers must have taken it from some other Gospel —the Gospel of the Hebrews. But the *additions* to the passage in the Homilies, and the omission of the part concerning the impossibility of a second physical birth,—points of difference between Justin and

The fact of Justin's acquaintance with John's Gospel, however, does not rest solely upon the evidence afforded by the citation of isolated passages.

the Homilies,—are quite as marked as the points of resemblance, which may be an accidental coincidence. The deviations in Justin's citation from the original in John are easily explained. They are chiefly due to the confusion of the phraseology of this passage with that of John iii. 5 and Matt. xviii. 3,—than which nothing was more natural. Similar inaccuracies, and from a similar cause, in quoting John iii. 3, are not uncommon now. That Justin uses the compound verb ἀναγεννάω, is because he had found occasion to use the same verb just before in the context, and because this had become the current term to designate regeneration.

Baur in one place adduces John iii. 4 as an instance of the fictitious ascription to the Jews, on the part of the author of this Gospel, of incredible misunderstandings of the words of Jesus. If this be so, surely Justin must be indebted to John for the passage. Anxious to avoid this conclusion, and apparently forgetting what he had said before, Baur, in another passage *of the same work* affirms that this same expression is borrowed alike by the author of John and by Justin from the Gospel of the Hebrews! See Baur's *Kanonische Evangelien*, pp. 290, 300, compared with pp. 352, 353. There were two or three other citations, however, in the Homilies, in which it was claimed that the same deviations are found as in corresponding citations in Justin. But if this circumstance lent any plausibility to the pretence that these passages in Justin were drawn from some other document than the canonical John, this plausibility vanishes and the question is set at rest by the publication of Dressel's ed. of the Homilies. This edition gives the concluding portion, not found in Cotelerius, and we are thus furnished (Hom. xix. 22, comp. John ix. 2, 3) with an undenied and undeniable quotation from John. This makes it evident that Hom. iii. 52 is a citation of John x. 9, 27, and also removes all doubt as to the source whence the quotation of John iii. 3 was derived. The similarity of the Homilies to Justin, in the few quotations referred to above, is probably accidental; if not, it

In his doctrine of the Logos and of the Incarnation, and in the terms under which the person of the Saviour is characterized, are indubitable marks of a familiarity with John. This peculiar type of thought and expression pervades the whole theology of Justin. We can hardly doubt that it was derived by him from an authoritative source. In one passage, Justin directly attributes the truth of the Incarnation, "that Christ became man by the Virgin," to the Memoirs.[1] Are we to believe that this whole Johannean type of doctrine was found in some unknown Gospel, which in Justin's day was read in the Christian congregations in city and country, but was suddenly displaced by *another* Gospel having just the same doctrinal peculiarity; a change which, if it took place at all, must have occurred in the later years of Justin's life, and in the youth of Irenaeus? And yet Irenaeus knew nothing of it, had no suspicion that the fourth Gos-

simply proves that Justin was in the hands of their author. This may easily be supposed. The date of the Homilies is in the neighborhood of 170. See on these points Meyer's *Einl.*, s. 10. Bleek, s. 228. Semisch, 193 seq.

[1] *Dial. c. Tryph.*, c. 105. The explicit reference to the Memoirs is grammatically connected only with the clause which we have cited above, and not with the entire sentence, as has been frequently supposed. Yet, it is scarcely doubtful that the whole conception of Christ, of which this clause was a part, was derived from the same source. "For I have proved," says Justin, "that he [Christ] was the only-begotten of the Father of all things, being properly begotten by Him as his Word and Power,"—here follows the clause, with the reference to the Memoirs, which is quoted above.

pel had any author but John, or that the fixed and sacred number four was made up by so recent an intruder!

The value of this testimony of Justin is evinced by the various and incongruous hypotheses which have been resorted to, for the purpose of undermining it.[1] But all now admit (what ought never to have been disputed) that under the name of Memoirs he refers to no single Gospel exclusively, but to a number of Gospels. It is admitted, also, that among them were the Gospels of Matthew, Mark, and Luke. But the Memoirs were by "Apostles and their Companions." Besides Matthew, Justin's collection must necessarily have embraced one other apostle. Whose work was this but that of John? No other work which pretended to emanate from an apostle can supply the vacant place. No evidence which is worth consideration points to any other; no other ever had the currency which Justin ascribes to the documents to

[1] We have not thought it necessary to refute Hilgenfeld's hypothesis, that one of Justin's principal authorities was the apocryphal Gospel of Peter. (See Hilgenfeld, *Die Evangelien Justin's*, 1850, s. 259 seq.) This Gospel Hilgenfeld assumes to have been the basis of the canonical Gospel of Mark,—a groundless assumption, resting upon a misinterpretation of Papias, who refers to the canonical Gospel itself, and not to any unknown work out of which this Gospel is thought to have grown. The idea that the Gospel of Peter, a book so insignificant and so little known in the early church, was one of the authoritative documents of Justin! The proofs which Hilgenfeld adduces, are, in our judgment, far-fetched and destitute of force.

which he refers. When we find in Justin, therefore, the same designation of the authors of his Gospels,—"Apostles and their Companions,"—which Irenaeus and Tertullian use to denote the four canonical writers, how can we resist the conviction that these are the writers to whom he, as well as they, refer? "The manner," says Norton, "in which Justin speaks of the character and authority of the books to which he appeals, proves these books to have been the Gospels. They carried with them the authority of the Apostles. They were those writings from which he and other Christians derived their knowledge of the history and doctrines of Christ. They were relied upon by him as primary and decisive evidence in his explanations of the character of Christianity. They were regarded as sacred books. They were read in the assemblies of Christians on the Lord's Day, in connection with the Prophets of the Old Testament. Let us now consider the manner in which the Gospels were regarded by the contemporaries of Justin. Irenaeus was in the vigor of life before Justin's death; and the same was true of many thousands of Christians living when Irenaeus wrote. But he tells us that the four Gospels are the four pillars of the church, the foundation of Christian faith, written by those who had first orally preached the gospel, by two apostles and two companions of apostles. It is incredible that Irenaeus and Justin should have spoken of different books." When "we find Irenaeus, the contemporary of Justin, ascribing the same character, the same authority, and the same authors, as are ascribed by Justin, to the Memoirs quoted by him, which were called Gospels, there can be no reasonable doubt that the Memoirs of Justin were the Gospels of Irenaeus."[1]

But we have testimonies to the genuineness of the fourth Gospel prior even to Justin. The first of these we have to mention is Papias, who flourished in the first quarter of the second century. He wrote a work in five books entitled "An Explication of the Oracles of the Lord," in the composition of which he depended mainly on unwritten traditions which he gathered up in conversation with those who had heard the apostles. Eusebius states that "he made use of testimonies from the First Epistle of John."[2] That this Epistle and the fourth Gospel are from the same author, has been, it is true, called in question by the Tübingen critics. But if internal evidence *has any weight*, is ever entitled to any regard, we must conclude, in agreement with the established, universal opinion, that both these writings have a common author. In style, in language, in spirit, in tone, they have the closest resemblance; and to ascribe this resemblance in either case to the imitation of a counterfeiter, is to give him credit for an unequalled

[1] *Gen. of the Gospels*, Vol. I. pp. 237–239.

[2] Euseb., Lib. III. c. 39.

refinement of cunning.[1] So that the testimony of Papias to the first Epistle is likewise evidence of the genuineness of the Gospel. The attempt is made, indeed, to invalidate this testimony by the suggestion that possibly Eusebius gives, in this instance, simply an inference of his own from passages in Papias which that author himself may not have found in John. But this suggestion rests upon no proof, and has not the force of a probability, in view of the explicit assertion of Eusebius. The Tübingen critics make much of the circumstance that Papias is not said by Eusebius to have made use of John's Gospel; but until we know what particular end Papias had in view in his allusions to New Testament books, this silence is of no weight. That he did acknowledge the First Epistle of John, indicates that he also knew and acknowledged the Gospel. Turning to the Apostolic Fathers, we find not a few expressions, especially in the Ignatian Epistles, which remind us of passages peculiar to John; but in general we cannot be certain that these expressions were not drawn from oral tradition. Yet in some cases they are much more naturally attributed to the fourth Gospel, and in one instance this can hardly be avoided. Polycarp, in his epistle to the Philippians, says: "for every one who does not confess that Jesus

[1] On the certainty that the first Epistle was written by the author of the Gospel, see De Wette's *Einl. in das N. Testament.* § 177 a.

Christ is come in the flesh is antichrist."[1] The resemblance of language to 1 John iv. 3 is striking; but a thought which in that form is so peculiar to this canonical epistle, being, as it were, the core of the type of doctrine which it presents, can hardly, when found in Polycarp, an immediate pupil of John, be referred to any other author.[2] Another and still earlier testimony is attached to the fourth Gospel itself (John xxi. 24). This passage purports to come from another hand than that of the author, of whom it says: "*we* know that his testimony is true." It has been attached to the Gospel, as far as we are able to determine, from the time when it was first put in circulation. If it be not part and parcel of a flagrant imposition, it proves the work to have been written by the beloved disciple.

An important part of the external evidence for the genuineness of the fourth Gospel, is the tacit or express acknowledgment of the fact by the various heretical parties of the second century. Significant, in connection with this point, is the circumstance that the Artemonites, the party of Unitarians who came forward in Rome near the end of the second century, did not think of disputing the apostolical origin of that Gospel to which their opponents were indebted for their strongest weapons. Had the fourth Gospel

[1] πᾶς γὰρ ὃς ἂν μὴ ὁμολογῇ Ἰησοῦν Χριστὸν ἐν σαρκὶ ἐληλυθέναι ἀντίχριστος ἐστι. Ad Phil. 7.

[2] Meyer's *Einl.*, s. 5.

first been heard of within the lifetime of the old men then living in the Roman church, we should look for an attack from this Unitarian party, who did not lack ability, upon its authority. But no doubt of this kind was expressed. From the disputes which agitated the middle part of the century, however, the argument we have to present is mainly derived. If the fourth Gospel was acknowledged to be the work of John by Marcion, the Valentinian Gnostics as well as their opponents, and at the epoch of the Montanistic controversy, the most skeptical must give up the attempt to bring down into the second or third quarter of the second century the date of its authorship.

We begin with Marcion. Marcion was a native of Pontus, and came to Rome about the year 130. In his enthusiastic and one-sided attachment to Paul's doctrine, he exaggerated the contrast of law and gospel into an absolute repugnance and contrariety, rejected the Old Testament, regarding the God of the Old Testament as an inferior Divinity, hostile to the Supreme Being, and consequently was led to make up a canon of New Testament writings to suit himself. His Gospel, as the church Fathers testify, was a mutilated copy of Luke, so altered as to answer to his peculiar tenets. The priority of our Luke to Marcion's Gospel is now generally allowed, even by the Tübingen critics who had previously taken the opposite ground. There is, indeed, no room for doubt in reference to this fact. Not only is Marcion known to have altered the Pauline Epistles to conform them to his opinions, but the fragments of his Gospel which have been preserved, are plainly the product of an alteration of corresponding passages in our third Gospel. But our present inquiry relates to John. Was Marcion acquainted with the fourth Gospel? The negative has been stoutly maintained by the school of Baur, in opposition, however, to decided proof. We learn from Tertullian that Marcion rejected John's Gospel—a fact which implies its existence and general reception; and Tertullian explains his motive in this procedure. Tertullian says: "But Marcion having got the Epistle of Paul to the Galatians, who blames the apostles themselves, as not walking uprightly, according to the truth of the gospel, and also charges some false apostles with perverting the gospel of Christ, *sets himself to weaken the credit of those Gospels which are truly such*, and are published under the name of apostles, or likewise of apostolical men."[1] That is to say, conceiving, like the

[1] Sed enim Marcion nactus epistolam Pauli ad Galatas, etiam ipsos apostolos suggillantis ut non recto pede incedentes ad veritatem evangelii, simul et accusantis pseudapostolos quosdam pervertentes evangelium Christi, connititur ad destruendum statum eorum evangeliorum quae propria et sub apostolorum nomine eduntur, vel etiam apostolicorum, ut scilicet fidem, quam illis adimit, suo conferat. *Adv. Marcion.*, Lib. IV. c. 3. This accounts for his not selecting John's Gospel instead of Luke. His zeal for Paul, which was attended with hostility to the other Apostles, was his prime characteristic.

modern school of Baur, that there was a hostility between Peter, James, and John on the one hand, and Paul on the other, and making himself a partisan of Paul, he rejected everything that came from them. Tertullian makes it clear that by "the Gospels published under the name of apostles or likewise of apostolical men," he intends the four of our canon.[1] Hence the Gospels which he says were rejected by Marcion must be Matthew, Mark, and John. Again, Tertullian, speaking of the adoption by Marcion of Luke's Gospel alone, says: "Now, since it is known that these (Matthew, Mark, and John) have also (as well as Luke) been in the churches, why has Marcion not laid hands on these also, to be corrected if they were corrupt, or received if incorrupt?"[2] Tertullian would convict Marcion of an inconsistency in laying aside the other Gospels,[3] not pretending to purge them of fancied corruptions, and yet not receiving them. Once more, in regard to a certain opinion of Marcion, Tertullian says, addressing Marcion, that if he did not *reject some* and *corrupt others* of the scriptures which contradict his opinion, the

[1] *Adv. Marcion.*, Lib. IV. c. 2. "Denique nobis fidem ex apostolis Ioannes et Matthaeus insinuant, ex apostolicis Lucas et Marcus instaurant," etc.

[2] *Adv. Marcion.*, Lib. IV. c. 5. "Igitur dum constet haec quoque apud ecclesias fuisse, cur non haec quoque Marcion attigit aut emendanda, si adulterata, aut agnoscenda, si integra?" etc.

[3] "Quod omissis eis Lucae potius institerit." *Ibid.*

Gospel of John would convict him of error.[1] The correctness of Tertullian in these statements has been impeached, but he had taken pains to inform himself concerning the life and opinions of Marcion, and there is no good ground for charging him here with error. His accuracy is confirmed by the explanation he gives of the origin of Marcion's hostility to the apostles, as proceeding from his wrong view of the passage in Galatians. We must conclude, therefore, that when Marcion brought forward his doctrine, the fourth Gospel was extant, the acknowledged work of John.

The general reception of John as an apostolic work preceded the Valentinian Gnosticism. Valentinus, the author of the most vast and complete of all the fabrics of Gnostic speculation, came to Rome about the year 140. That the Gospel of John was admitted to be genuine, and used as such, by his party, is well known. Irenaeus speaks of the Valentinians as making the most abundant use of John's Gospel: eo quod est secundum Johannem plenissime utentes.[2] Heracleon, one of the followers of Valentinus, wrote a commentary upon John's Gospel, from which Origen in his work upon John frequently

[1] "Si scripturas opinioni tuae resistentes non de industria alias reiecisses, alias corrupisses, confudisset te in hac specie evangelium Ioannis," etc. *De Carne Christi*, c. 3. For other passages to the same effect from Irenaeus and Tertullian, see De Wette's *Einl. in d. N. T.* § 72 c. Anm. d.

[2] *Adv. Haer.*, Lib. III. c. 11. § 7.

quotes.[1] Ptolemaeus, another follower, expressly designates the Prologue of John as the work of the apostle, and puts his own forced explanation upon its contents.[2] The precise date of Heracleon and Ptolemaeus we cannot determine, but they must have written not far from the middle of the century. But did Valentinus himself know and acknowledge the fourth Gospel as the work of John? This we might infer with great probability from its acceptance by Heracleon and his other followers. We should draw the same conclusion from the silence of Irenaeus as to any rejection of John's Gospel by Valentinus, and from his statement as to the use of it by the school in general. Moreover, Tertullian contrasts Valentinus and Marcion in this very particular, that whereas the latter rejected the Scriptures, the former built up his system upon perverse inter-

[1] The passages in Heracleon referred to by Origen are collected in Grabe's *Spicilegium*, Vol. II., and in Stieren's ed. of Irenaeus, I. 938–971.

[2] *Epist. ad Floram*, c. 1, ap. *Epiph. Haer.*, xxxiii. 3. See Grabe's *Spicilegium*, II. 70, 2d ed., or Stieren's *Irenaeus*, I. 924.

The work which passes under the name of *Excerpta Theodoti*, or *Doctrina Orientalis*, a compilation from the writings of Theodotus and other Gnostics of the second century, contains numerous extracts from one or more writers of the Valentinian school, in which the Gospel of John is quoted and commented upon as the work of the apostle. See particularly cc. 6, 7. These Excerpta are commonly printed with the works of Clement of Alexandria; they are also found in Fabricius, *Bibl. Graeca*, Vol. V., and in Bunsen's *Analecta Ante-Nicaena*, Vol. I.

pretation. Valentinus, he says, did not adjust the Scriptures to his material—his doctrine—but his material to the Scriptures.[1] Marcion made havoc of the Scriptures; Valentinus *autem pepercit*. And Tertullian says, directly, that Valentinus makes use of the whole instrument, *i. e.* canonical Gospels. Tertullian's phraseology has been sometimes erroneously supposed to indicate doubt upon this point. He has been translated as follows: "for if Valentinus appears (videtur) to make use of the entire instrument (*i. e.* our Scriptures), he has done violence to the truth with a not less artful spirit than Marcion."[2] Were this the exact sense of the passage, the *videtur* might naturally be considered the concession of an adversary, Tertullian not being able to charge his opponent with the actual rejection of any of the Gospels, however tempted by polemical feeling to throw out such an imputation. But the term *videri* is frequently used in the writings of Tertullian, not in the sense of "seem," but "to be seen," "to be fully apparent;" and such we are persuaded is its meaning in the present passage.[3] But aside from

[1] "Valentinus autem pepercit, quoniam non ad materiam scripturas excogitavit . . . . . auferens proprietates singulorum quoque verborum." *De Praescript. Haeret.*, c. 38.

[2] "Neque enim si Valentinus integro instrumento uti videtur, non callidiore ingenio quam Marcion manus intulit veritati." *De Praescript.*, c. 38.

[3] Comp. *Tert. Adv. Prax.*, c. 26, 29; *Adv. Marc.*, iv. 2; *De Orat.*, c. 21; *Apol.*, c. 19; *Adv. Jud.*, c. 5, quoted from Is. i. 12.

this evidence, we are furnished with direct proof of the fact that Valentinus used and acknowledged the Gospel of John, through the lately-found work of Hippolytus. Hippolytus wrote the "Refutation of all Heresies" in the earlier part of the third century. He devotes considerable space to the systems of Valentinus and the Valentinians, which he traces to the mathematical speculations of Pythagoras and Plato. In the course of his discussion, referring to Valentinus, he writes as follows: "All the prophets and the law spoke from the demiurg, a foolish god, he says—fools, knowing nothing. On this account it is, he (Valentinus) says, that the Saviour says: 'all that came before me are thieves and robbers.'"[1] The passage is obviously taken from John x. 8. The pretension of the Tübingen critics that the author here ascribes to the master what belongs to his pupils, is improbable; since Hippolytus, while coupling Valentinus and his followers together in cases where their tenets agree, knows how carefully to distinguish the different phases of belief in the schools. The peculiarities of the Italian Valentinians, Heracleon and Ptolemaeus, of the oriental Valentinians, Axionikus and Ardesianes, and the special opinions of other individuals of the party, are definitely characterized. We have in their disposition of this case a specimen of the method of

[1] Hippolytus (Duncker and Schneidewin's ed.), Lib. VI. c. 35.

reasoning adopted by Baur and his followers. Hippolytus, we are told, may have attributed to Valentinus what belongs only to his pupils. Granted, he may have done so. The supposition is possible. But what is the evidence that in this instance he did so? We are to assume that he is right until he is proved to be wrong. We are not arguing about what is possible or impossible; but we are discussing points where probable reasoning alone is applicable. So, these critics tell us it is *possible* that Polycarp quoted an anonymous sentence current at the time, which is also taken up into the first epistle bearing the name of John. It is *possible* that this or that writer drew his passage from some lost apocryphal work. The possibility we grant, for in these matters demonstration is of course precluded. But the suggestion of a mere possibility on the opposite side against a presumptive, natural, and probable inference, cannot pass for argument.

When we look at the interior structure of the system of Valentinus, we find that the characteristic terms employed by John are wrought into it, some of them being attached as names to the aeons which, in a long series of pairs, constitute the celestial hierarchy. Among these pairs are such as *μονογενής* and *ἀλήθεια*, *λόγος* and *ζωή*. The artificial and fantastic scheme of Valentinus, so in contrast with the simplicity of John, wears the character of a copy and caricature of the latter. That it has this relation to John we cannot, to be sure, demonstrate; for it may be contended that both the Gnostic and the author of the fourth Gospel took up current terms and conceptions, each writer applying them to suit his own purpose. But the freshness and apparent originality of John's use of this language, not to speak of the other proofs in the case, are decidedly against this theory of Baur. When we bring together all the items of evidence which bear on the point, we feel warranted to conclude with confidence that not only Ptolemaeus and the other disciples of Valentinus, but also their master, alike with his opponents, acknowledge the apostolic authorship of the Gospel.[1] Through Hippolytus we are provided with another most important witness in the person of Basilides, the other prominent Gnostic leader, who taught at Alexandria in the second quarter of the second century. Among the proof-texts which Hippolytus states that Basilides employed, are John i. 9: "This was the true light that lighteth every man that cometh into the world;" and John ii. 4: "My hour is not yet come."[2] In the passage in Hippolytus containing these quotations ascribed to Basilides, and in the closest connection with them, stand his essential principles and characteristic expressions; so that the suggestion of a confounding of master and pupils on the part of Hippolytus has

[1] See Schneider, s. 35.

[2] Hippol., Lib. VII. cc. 22, 27.

not the shadow of a support. In connection with this piece of evidence, we may advert to the statement of Agrippa Castor, a contemporary of Basilides, that he wrote "twenty-four books on *the Gospel*."[1] It has been rendered highly probable that this denotes a commentary on the four Gospels.[2] The same expression—"the Gospel"—it will be remembered, is used by Justin Martyr, as well as by the Fathers subsequent to him, for the Gospels collectively.

How widely extended was the knowledge and use of the fourth Gospel among the heretics of the second century, is further illustrated by the numerous quotations that were made from it by the Ophites or Naasseni, and the Peratae, which are preserved by Hippolytus.[3]

We have to touch upon one other movement in the second century, the controversies connected with Montanism. The main features of Montanism were the Chiliasm, or expectation of the Saviour's millennial reign and speedy advent, and the prophecy or ecstatic inspiration. In the millennial doctrine, as well as in the belief in the continued miraculous gifts of the Spirit, there is a striking resemblance between the Montanists and the followers of Edward Irving. We cannot say how far Montanism professed to found itself on John's Gospel, because we know not

[1] Euseb., Lib. IV. c. 7.

[2] See Norton's *Gen. of the Gospels*, Vol. III. p 238.

[3] Hippol., Lib. V. cc. 7, 8, 9, 12, 16, 17.

precisely when in the development of the sect the claim to the presence of the Paraclete, in this form, was set up. We allude to Montanism, therefore, to speak of a certain party that opposed it. Irenaeus speaks of some who, in their opposition to the recent effusions of the Divine Spirit upon men, do not accept of the Gospel of John, "in which the Lord promised that he would send the Paraclete, but at the same time reject both the Gospel and the prophetic Spirit."[1] Shortly before, he had spoken of some who would fain exhibit themselves in the character of searchers for truth, possibly referring to this same class. Epiphanius describes a class of zealous opponents of Montanism, who were probably the same mentioned by Irenaeus. Epiphanius styles them Alogi, as opposing the Logos Gospel. They maintained that the Gospel of John did not agree with the other three Gospels, in regard to various points in the life of Christ,—as in the omission of the forty days' temptation, and in the number of passovers he is said to have kept.[2] Their opposition,

[1] Irenaeus, Lib. III. 11. 9. Let the reader mark that this is the only allusion to a rejection of the fourth Gospel, as not by John, which we find in any writer before the latter part of the fourth century. The party to which Irenaeus refers consisted probably of a few eccentric individuals, who attracted no attention, and none of whose names are preserved. Moreover, as we have remarked above, any slight weight which their opposition could be conceived to have, is neutralized by their equal opposition to the Apocalypse.

[2] For a full explication of the character of the Alogi as they are described by Epiphanius and Irenaeus, see Schneider, s. 38 et seq.

however, is really an argument for the genuineness of John. It shows the general acknowledgment of this Gospel at the time when they made their opposition, which was not long after the middle of the second century. It proves that their opponents, the Montanists, and the Church generally, received it. Moreover, their groundless ascription of the Gospel to Cerinthus is a valuable testimony from them to its age; for Cerinthus was a contemporary of John. Baur's unfounded praise of the critical spirit of this insignificant party, is strange, considering that they also rejected the Apocalypse, which he holds to be the genuine work of John, and that they ascribed both the Apocalypse and the Gospel to the same author. It seems probable that the Alogi were led by their strong hostility to the Montanistic enthusiasm to dislike the fourth Gospel when Montanism claimed to find a warrant for itself in the promise of the Spirit, and on this doctrinal ground, making use also of the apparent historical differences between the fourth Gospel and the other three, they rejected it. Precisely what was the nature and reason of their opposition to the doctrine of the Logos we know not; but their feeling on this subject accords with their rationalistic turn of mind. The circumstances of their opposition, as we see, are a strong indirect argument for the antiquity and genuineness of the Gospel they rejected.[1]

[1] We are also entitled to cite Celsus as a witness to the fourth

Before we leave this topic—the use of the fourth Gospel by the heretics—we ask our readers to consider the full weight of the argument that is founded upon it. The great doctrinal battle of the Church in the second century was with Gnosticism. The struggle with this first heresy of a Gentile origin had its beginnings early. The germs of it are distinctly perceived in the Apostolic Age. At the middle of the second century, the conflict with these elaborate systems of error was raging. By Justin, the Valentinians, the Basilideans, the Marcionites (followers either of Marcus or of Marcion), and other Gnostic sects, are denounced as warmly as by

Gospel. The date of Celsus is about the middle of the second century. He professed to derive his statements concerning the evangelical history from the writings of the disciples of Christ. The great body of his statements are plainly founded on passages in our canonical Gospels, especially in Matthew. But Celsus speaks of Christ being called by his disciples the Word. He speaks of the blood which flowed from the body of Jesus,—a circumstance peculiar to John's narrative. He also says: "To the sepulchre of Jesus there came two angels, as is said by some, or, as by others, one only." Matthew and Mark mention one only, Luke and John two. Again, Celsus gives the Christian narrative of the Resurrection as containing the fact that Christ, "after he was dead, arose, and showed the marks of his punishment, and how his hands had been pierced." This circumstance is recorded only in John xx. 27. It is indeed "possible," as Meyer suggests, that Celsus found these things in apocryphal gospels, but the probability is the other way. Meyer should not have so lightly valued the testimony afforded by Celsus. These passages from Origen against Celsus may be found in Lardner, Vol. VII. pp. 220, 221 and 239. To the testimony of the Clementine Homilies we have before adverted.

Irenaeus and his contemporaries.[1] And by both of the parties in this wide-spread conflict, by the Gnostics and the church theologians, the fourth Gospel is accepted as the work of John, without a lisp of opposition or of doubt. If the fourth Gospel originated as the Tübingen school pretend, it appeared in the midst of this distracted period; it was cast into the midst of this tumult of controversy. With what incredible skill must this anonymous writer have proceeded, to be able to frame a system which should not immediately excite hostility and cause his false pretensions to be challenged! How can we suppose that a book, appearing for the first time at such an epoch, having of necessity so close a bearing on the great themes of controversy, and claiming to be the production of an apostle, would encounter no denial? The acknowledgment of this Gospel, both by the Gnostic who was obliged to pervert its teachings through forced interpretations, and by the orthodox theologian, furnishes an irresistible argument for its genuineness.

Thus far we have dealt, for the most part, with those isolated passages of the early writers wherein the existence and authoritative standing of John's Gospel are presupposed. Not all these separate items of evidence are of equal strength. Together they constitute an irrefragable argument. And yet

[1] *Dial. c. Tryph.*, c. 32.

the main, most convincing argument for the genuineness of this Gospel, is drawn from the moral impossibility of discrediting, in such a case, the tradition of the early Church. Let us consider for a moment the character of this argument.

We begin with observing that, on matters of fact in which men are interested, and to which, therefore, their attention is drawn, and in regard to which there are no causes strongly operating to blind the judgment, the evidence of tradition is, within reasonable limits of time, conclusive. An individual may perpetuate his testimony through the instrumentality of one who long survives him. The testimony of a generation may in like manner be transmitted to, and through, the generation that comes after. Next to the testimony of one's own senses is the testimony of another person whom we know to be trustworthy. And where, instead of one individual handing over his knowledge to a single successor, there is a multitude holding this relation to an equal or greater number after them, the force of this kind of evidence is proportionably augmented. Moreover, the several generations do not pass away, like the successive platoons of a marching army, but the young and the old, the youth and octogenarian, are found together in every community; so that upon any transaction of public importance that has occurred during a long period in the past, witnesses are always at hand who can either speak from personal knowledge or from testimony directly given them by individuals with whom they were in early life familiar.

Few persons who have not specially attended to the subject, are aware how long a period is sometimes covered by a very few links of traditional testimony. Lord Campbell, in his Lives of the Chancellors, remarks of himself, that he had seen a person who had seen a spectator of the execution of Charles I., in 1649. A single link separated Lord Campbell from the eyewitness of an event occurring upwards of two hundred years before. Suppose this intervening witness to be known by Lord Campbell to be a discriminating and trustworthy person, and we have testimony that is fully credible. We borrow two examples from Mr. Palfrey's excellent History of New England. The first relates to the preservation of the knowledge of the landing-place of the Pilgrims. Plymouth Rock, says the Historian, "is now imbedded in a wharf. When this was about to be built, in 1741, Elder Thomas Faunce, then ninety-one years old, came to visit the rock, and to remonstrate against its being exposed to injury; and he repeated what he had heard of it from the first planters. Elder Faunce's testimony was transmitted through Mrs. White, who died in 1810, ninety-five years old, and Deacon Ephraim Spooner, who died in 1818, at the age of eighty-three."[1] In another place, Mr. Palfrey

[1] Palfrey's *Hist. of N. England*, Vol. I. p. 171. N. 3.

has occasion to observe: "When Josiah Quincy, of Boston, was twelve or thirteen years old, Nathanael Appleton was still minister of Cambridge, and a preacher in the Boston pulpits; Appleton, born in Ipswich in 1693, had often sat, it is likely, on the knees of Governor Bradstreet, who was his father's neighbor; and Bradstreet came from England, in John Winthrop's company, in 1630. Eyes that had seen men who had seen the founders of a cisatlantic England, have looked also on New England as she presents herself to-day."[1] Mr. Quincy died in 1864. Every man of seventy who can unite his memory with the memories of the individuals who had attained the same age when he was young, can go back through a period of more than a hundred years. He can state what was recollected fifty years ago concerning events that took place a half century before. If, in reference to a particular fact, we fix the earliest age of trustworthy recollection at fifteen, and suppose each of those, whose memories are thus united, to give their report at the age of eighty, there is covered a period of one hundred and thirty years. We can easily think of cases where, from the character of both the witnesses, the evidence thus derived would be entirely conclusive.

But traditionary evidence had a special security and a special strength in the case of the early Christian

[1] Palfrey's *Hist.*, Vol. III. p. vi. of the preface.

Church. The Church, as Mayer forcibly observes, had a physical and spiritual continuity of life. There was a close connection of its members one with another. "Like a stream of water, such a stream of youths, adults, and old men is an unbroken whole." The Church was a community—an association. A body of this kind, says Mayer, recognizes that which is new as new. It is protected from imposition. How would it be possible, he inquires, for a new Augsburg Confession to be palmed upon the Lutheran churches as a document that had long been generally accepted?

In estimating the force of this reasoning, we must take notice of the number of the early Christians. We must remember that at the close of the first century Christianity was planted in all the principal cities of the Roman Empire. It was in the great cities and centres of intercourse, as Jerusalem, Antioch, Ephesus, Corinth, Alexandria, Rome, that Christianity was earliest established. As early as Nero's persecution (A. D. 64) the Christians who were condemned, constituted, according to Tacitus, a "great multitude."[1] In Asia Minor, in the time of Trajan, or at the close of the century, they had become so numerous that, according to Pliny, the heathen temples were almost deserted. A century later, making due allowance for the rhetorical exaggeration of Tertullian, and not depending on him alone, we are certain that the number of the Christians had vastly multiplied. In

[1] *Ann.*, I. xv. c. 44.

every part of the Roman Empire, in all places of consideration, and even in rural districts, Christian assemblies regularly met for worship. And in all these weekly meetings the writings of the apostles were publicly read, as we learn from so early a writer as Justin Martyr.

Now we have to look at the Christian churches in the second century, and ask if it was possible for a history of Christ, falsely pretending to be from the pen of the Apostle John, to be brought forward twenty, thirty, or forty years after his death, be introduced into all the churches east and west, taking its place everywhere in the public services of Sunday? Was there no one to ask where this new Gospel came from, and where it had lain concealed? Was there no one, of the many who had personally known John, to expose the gigantic imposture, or even to raise a note of surprise at the unexpected appearance of so important a document, of which they had never heard before? How was the populous church at Ephesus brought to accept this work on the very spot where John had lived and died?

The difficulty, nay the moral impossibility, of supposing that this Gospel first saw the light in 160 or 140 or 120, or at any of the dates which are assigned by the Tübingen critics, will be rendered apparent, if we candidly look at the subject.[1] We have spoken of

[1] The latest assailant of the Genuineness of John, Schenkel, in his work, *Das Charakterbild Jesu*, places the date of the Gospel from

Irenaeus and of his testimony to the undisputed, undoubting reception, by all the churches, of the fourth Gospel. If this Gospel first appeared as late as or later than 120, how does it happen that he had not learned the fact from the aged presbyters whom he had known in Asia Minor? Irenaeus, before becoming bishop, was the colleague of Pothinus at Lyons, who perished as a martyr, having, as the letter of his church states, passed his ninetieth year. Here was a man whose active life extended back well-nigh to the very beginning of the century, who was born before John died. Supposing John's Gospel to have appeared as late as 120, the earliest date admitted by any part of the skeptical school, Pothinus was then upwards of thirty years old. Did this man, who loved Christianity so well that he submitted to torture and death for its sake, never think to mention to Irenaeus an event of so great consequence as was this late discovery of a life of the Lord from the pen of his most beloved disciple, and of its reception by the churches? Polycrates, bishop of Ephesus, at the time of his controversy with Victor, describes himself as being "sixty-five years of age in the Lord," as having "conferred

A. D. 110–120. This indicates progress in the right direction among the skeptical critics. But as they push back the date, they have to encounter a new source of difficulty. The nearer they approach to the time of the Apostle, the greater the number of persons who were familiar with him and his circumstances, and the greater the obstacle, from this cause, to a successful imposture. It may here be observed that Schenkel contributes nothing new on the question before us.

with the brethren throughout the world, and studied the whole of the Sacred Scriptures;" as being also of a family, seven of whose members had held the office of bishop or presbyter. According to his statement, his own life began as early at least as the year 125, while through his family he was directly connected with the contemporaries of John. How is it that Polycrates appears to have known nothing about this late appearance of the wonderful Gospel which bore the name of John, but was the work of a great unknown? How is it that the family of Polycrates either knew nothing of so startling an event, or if they knew anything of it preserved an absolute silence? Clement of Alexandria had sat at the feet of venerable teachers in different countries, of whom he says that they "have lived by the blessing of God to our time, to lodge in our minds the seeds of the ancient and apostolic doctrine." From none of these had he derived any information of that event, so remarkable, if we suppose it to have occurred—the sudden discovery of a gospel history by the Apostle John, of which the Christian world had not before heard. Justin says that in the churches there are many men and women of sixty and seventy years of age, who have been Christians from their youth; and he is speaking only of the unmarried class.[1]

So at every preceding and subsequent moment in the first half of the second century, there were many

[1] *Apol.*, I. c. 15.

old persons in every larger church whose memory went back far into the apostolic age. Now if the statement of Irenaeus and his contemporaries as to the composition of the fourth Gospel by the Apostle John was false, and this work in reality saw the light not till long after his death, when some forger offered it for acceptance, how is it possible that there should be none to investigate its origin when it first appeared, and none afterwards to correct the prevalent opinion concerning it?

There is no way for the skeptical critic to meet this positive argument, founded on the unanimous voice of tradition, and this negative argument *ab silentio* in refutation of his theory, unless he can prove that the Christians of the second century were so indifferent as to the origin of their scriptures that they received whatever might offer itself to their acceptance, provided the contents were agreeable to their doctrines and prepossessions. If there were few or none who were either inquisitive or competent to judge of the real claims of a book that professed to be an authentic and apostolic history of Christ, then an imposture of this magnitude might be successful, provided a person were found shrewd and unscrupulous enough to undertake it. But how stands the fact? The greater portion of the early Christians were undoubtedly from the poorer class. Even these must have been deeply interested in obtaining authentic accounts of that Master for whom they were offering up life itself. But they had among them trained, inquisitive scholars — men educated in the schools of philosophy. Justin Martyr and the Greek Apologists are not liable to the charge of illiteracy. It was a time when Christianity had to answer for itself, as well in treatises addressed to the public magistrate as before the civil tribunals. It is, moreover, a noteworthy fact that the writers bring to the Scriptures the test of historical inquiry. They do not ask what book is doctrinally acceptable, but what book bears the stamp of an apostolic approval. Referring to a saying of Christ adduced from an apocryphal Gospel of the Egyptians, Clement's first remark is, that it is not contained in the four Gospels which "have been handed down to us." Irenaeus and Tertullian insist only upon the historical evidence that the canonical Scriptures are apostolic. Nothing but authentic tradition is of any weight with them on the question. It is true that Schwegler, Strauss, and some other writers are in the habit of asserting that the Christians of the first ages were wholly uncritical, and were satisfied with the claim of any book to be apostolic, if it seemed edifying. But scholars need not be told that sweeping representations of this nature are not sustained by proof and are grossly exaggerated. Origen, that most learned and inquisitive scholar, was born when Irenaeus was still in the midst of his activity. The earlier conflicts with Judaizing and Gnostic heresy which carry us far back of Irenaeus towards the commencement

6

of the century, stimulated Christians to the exercise of discrimination in respect to writings which claimed an apostolic sanction. Appeal is made to the instance of the partial acceptance, at the end of the second or early in the third century, of the Pseudo-Clementine Homilies. This work, however, was accompanied with pretended documents in attestation of its apostolic authorship, and with an explanation of the reason why it did not sooner appear;[1] and was hence supposed to be a genuine work which had been altered and interpolated by heretics. A few facts of this nature are no more sufficient to convict the contemporaries of Origen, Irenaeus, and Justin of utter indifference or heedlessness in respect to the authorship of books, than the acceptance of Ossian or the credence given to the Shaksperian forgeries of Ireland suffice to convict the contemporaries of Porson and Johnson of a like stupidity. Moreover, the incomparably greater importance which belonged to the histories of the life and teachings of Christ, in the estimation of the early Christians, by the side of such works as the Clementine Homilies and Recognitions, destroys the parallel. The latter might be accepted, in certain circles at least, with little inquiry; that a deception should be successful, and universally successful, in the case of the former, is inconceivable. All the knowledge we have relative to the formation of the New Testament canon goes to disprove the imputation of carelessness or incompetency

[1] See Gieseler's *K. G.*, B. I. 285. N. 21.

brought against the Christians of the second century. There is proof that the four Gospels of our canon were distinguished, as having preëminent authority, from all other evangelical histories in the early part of the second century. All other narratives of the life of Christ, including those of the many writers of whom Luke speaks in the introduction to his Gospel, as well as those of subsequent authors, were discarded, and, if used at all, were explicitly treated as not endued with authority. Four, and only the four, in the time of Irenaeus and Tertullian, were regarded as apostolic and canonical. Lechler[1] mentions an example from Eusebius illustrating the feeling of church teachers at that time. Serapion, who was bishop of Antioch about 190, found in circulation at Rhosse (Orossus), a town of Cilicia, an apocryphal gospel called the Gospel of Peter. He says in regard to it: "We, brethren, receive Peter and the other apostles as Christ himself. But those writings which falsely go under their name, as we are well acquainted with them, we reject, and know also *that we have not received such handed down to us*."[2] This is one expression; but it falls in with the whole current of the evidence in relation to the temper of Irenaeus and his contemporaries.

Having thus surveyed the external proofs of the genuineness of John, we pass to consider

[1] *Studien u. Krit.*, 1856. 4. s. 871.

[2] Euseb., Lib. VI. c. 12.

The Internal Evidence.

1. The fourth Gospel claims to be the work of the Apostle John; and the manner of this claim is a testimony to its truth. The author explicitly declares himself an eyewitness of the transactions recorded by him (i. 14, compared with 1 John i. 1–3, iv. 14; John xix. 35; compare also xxi. 24.) In the course of his narrative, one of the disciples, instead of being referred to by name, is characterized as that "disciple whom Jesus loved" (xiii. 23; xix. 26; xx. 2 seq.; xxi. 7). In the appendix to the Gospel (xxi. 24; compare ver. 20) this disciple is declared to be its author. And we cannot well explain this circumlocution, except on the supposition that the author resorts to it in order to avoid the mention of his own name. Now, who of the disciples most intimate with Jesus is referred to under this description? Not Peter; for Peter is not only repeatedly spoken of by his own name, but is expressly distinguished from the disciple in question (xiii. 24; xx. 2 seq.; xxi. 7; 20 seq.). Not James; for besides the proof derived from the universal supposition of the ancient Church, that James was not the person denoted, we know that he was put to death early in the apostolic age (Acts xii. 2), while we may infer from John xxi. 23, which is otherwise confirmed, that the disciple in question must have reached an advanced age. If it be granted that the author, whoever he may have been, was one of the original disciples, James is excluded,

because the Gospel was evidently written later than his death, and out of Palestine. But if the disciple whom Jesus loved is not Peter or James, who can it be but John? That the author would represent himself to be John, is also strongly suggested by his omitting to attach to the name of John (the Baptist) the usual appellation ὁ βαπτιστής, especially when we observe that he is elsewhere careful, as in the case of Peter and of Judas, to designate precisely the person meant. Supposing the writer to be himself John the *Evangelist*, and moreover to have stood, as a disciple, in an intimate relation with the Baptist, we have a double reason for his omitting in the case of the latter this usual title. The connection of the beloved disciple with Peter (xx. 2 seq.; xxi. 7; and also xviii. 15 seq., where the ἄλλος μαθητής is none other than the beloved disciple) is another argument tending to show that John is meant; since we find afterwards, in the Acts, that John and Peter are closely associated.[1]

Indeed, it is held by Baur that the design is to lead the reader to the inference that John is the author. Now, if we suppose that this inference is the simple fact, we have in the modest suppression of his name by John the manifestation of a certain delicacy of feeling, which is consonant with the spirit of the work. It would be connected with its real author by those to whom he gave it, without any

[1] See also Luke xxii. 8.

proclamation on his part of his relation to it; as in truth it was ascribed to John from the outset. On the contrary, supposing the Gospel not to be genuine, we are obliged to attribute to the author a refinement in fraud, an outlay of skill in deception, wholly inconsistent with the simplicity and pure tone of this Gospel, and not likely to exist in a literary forger. Judging from other known specimens of apocryphal literature, and from the intrinsic probabilities in the case, we should expect of such a fraudulent writer, that he would boldly and openly assume the name and apostolic authority of John, instead of leaving the authorship to be ascertained in the manner we have indicated, by a careful inspection and combination of passages. The indirect, modest way, then, in which the author discovers himself, carries with it the unmistakable character of truth.

2. The truth of this claim of the fourth Gospel to have John for its author, is confirmed by the graphic character of the narrative, the many touches characteristic of an eyewitness, and by other indications of an immediate knowledge, on the part of the writer, of the things he relates.

In respect to these points, which mark the narrative as the product of an eyewitness and of one directly cognizant of the facts, none of the other Gospels can be compared with the fourth. We have not in mind here the general plan and outline of the history, which will be considered under another head, but rather the style in which the various incidents are presented. Of this pervading peculiarity of the fourth Gospel our readers will be reminded by a few examples. As one instance, we may refer to John i. 35 seq., where an account is given of the calling of the disciples: "again the next day after"—the day is thus definitely given—" John stood and two of his disciples; and looking upon Jesus as he walked,"—here we have the position of both John and Jesus,—" he saith, 'Behold the Lamb of God!' And the two disciples heard him speak, and they followed Jesus. Then Jesus *turned and saw them following*, and saith," etc. In reply to their question, "'Where dwellest thou?' He saith unto them, 'Come and see.' They came and saw where he dwelt, and abode with him that day, *for it was about the tenth hour*." Supposing the writer to have been one of these two disciples, speaking of an event that would be indelibly stamped upon his memory, this minuteness of description would be natural. If we have not an eyewitness, we have a subtle and painstaking deceiver. For another example of vivid recollection we may refer to John xiii. 21 seq., in the description of the last supper. We are told that Jesus was troubled in spirit, "and said, 'Verily, verily I say unto you that one of you shall betray me.' Then the disciples *looked one on another*, doubting of whom he spake." There is first an interval of silence, and looks of inquiry and fear cast from one to another; but who would venture to ask the question, which of their number was to be faithless? "Now there was leaning on Jesus' bosom one of his disciples whom Jesus loved. Simon Peter therefore *beckoned to him*"—he signified his wish by a motion of the hand—"that he should ask who it should be of whom he spake. He then lying on Jesus' breast, saith unto him, 'Lord, who is it?'" Jesus replies that he will point out the individual by handing him the sop. This silent act, understood by John, was followed by the remark of Jesus to Judas: "That thou doest, do quickly. Now no man at the table knew for what intent he spake this unto him." Some of them, we are told, thought that Judas was directed to buy those things that they "had need of against the feast, or to give something to the poor." Who can avoid feeling that the writer is here presenting a scene that was pictured on his memory? How unnatural, as well as painful, is the supposition of a carefully contrived fiction! Another instance of particular recollection is found in John xviii. 15 seq., where, in connection with the account of the bringing of Christ before Caiaphas, we read: "And Simon Peter followed Jesus, and so did another disciple; that disciple *was known unto the high priest*, and went in with Jesus into the palace of the high priest. *But Peter stood at the door without.*" Peter had no such means of admission. "Then went out that other disciple which was known unto the high priest, and *spake unto her that kept the door,* and brought in Peter." There the inquiry of this door-keeper drew from Peter his first denial of a connection with Christ; and we read further: "The servants and officers stood there, *who had made a fire of coals; for it was cold:* and they warmed themselves, and Peter stood with them and warmed himself." The circumstance of there being a fire is mentioned by Luke, but in the manner of stating it in John, as well as in the preceding circumstances that are peculiar to him, we find the clearest signs of a personal recollection. The record of the inward conflict and vacillation of Pilate as displayed in his conduct (ch. xix.), is characterized by the same features, which show it to be a vivid recollection of circumstances witnessed by the writer. So there is much in the narrative of the crucifixion having the same peculiarity. Thus we read (vs. 26, 27): "When Jesus therefore saw his mother, and the disciple standing by whom he loved, he saith unto his mother, 'Woman, behold thy son.' Then saith he to the disciple, 'Behold thy mother.' And from that hour that disciple took her to his own home." And again we read (vs. 34, 35): "One of the soldiers with a spear pierced his side, and forthwith came there out blood and water. *And he that saw it bare record,* and his record is true; and he knoweth that he saith true, that ye might believe." Is this too a fiction, which the author sought to commend to credence by a solemn asseveration, or is it a simple, faithful reminiscence?

What a life-like description, and how true to the conception elsewhere gained of the respective characters, is the account of the running of Peter and John to the empty sepulchre! They "ran both together;" but the other disciple, outrunning Peter and arriving first at the sepulchre, pauses, and, *stooping down* to look in, sees "the linen clothes lying;" yet struck, perhaps, with a feeling of awe, enters not. "Then cometh Simon Peter following him;" but not sharing in the hesitation of his companion, with characteristic impetuosity, at once goes in, "and seeth the linen clothes lie, and *the napkin that was about his head not lying with the linen clothes,* but wrapped together in a place by itself. Then," encouraged by the example of his more forward associate, "went in also that *other disciple,* which came first to the sepulchre, and he saw and believed" (xx. 3–9). The same freshness and naturalness which belong to the record of outward events are found in the portrayal of mental experiences. We mention, as an example, the notice of the refusal of Thomas to believe without seeing, and of the reaction of his mind on being shown the print of the nails (John xx. 24–29); and the refusal of Peter to have his feet washed by the Master, followed by the request: "Not my feet only, but also my hands and my head" (John xiii. 9). The ninth chapter, which describes the healing of a man who had been blind from his birth, and the eleventh chapter, containing the narrative of the raising of Lazarus, in their naturalness, vividness, and fulness of detail, cannot fail to impress the candid reader with the conviction that the writer was personally cognizant of the circumstances he relates. In how simple, unartificial a strain does the narrative, in each case, proceed! And in how life-like a way are the circumstances linked together! Observe, in the first narrative, the exclamation of the neighbors on seeing the man's sight restored: "Is not this he that sat and begged?" the different voices: "some said, 'this is he;' others said, 'he is like him;' but he said, 'I am he;'" the evident perplexity of the Pharisees; the parents' way of prudently evading a direct answer to their interrogatóries by referring them to the man himself: "he is of age, ask him;" the *naïf* energy with which he confronted the Pharisees' queries. In reading this passage of the fourth Gospel, it is difficult to resist the impression that the writer is stating, in a perfectly artless manner, circumstances that fell within his own immediate knowledge. Not less strongly is this impression made of the writer's immediate knowledge, as well as fidelity, in reading the eleventh chapter. Notice, for example, this passage in the conversation of Jesus with his disciples before he started for Bethany: "after that he saith unto them, 'Our friend Lazarus sleepeth; but I go that I may awake him out of sleep.' Then said his disciples, 'Lord, if he sleep, he shall do well.' Howbeit Jesus spake of his death; but they thought that he had spoken of taking of rest in sleep. Then said Jesus unto them plainly, 'Lazarus is dead.'" This conversation was surely remembered. What motive would lead one to invent such a conversation? Observe, also, the graphic minuteness of the following statements (vs. 28 seq.): Martha, who had gone out to meet Jesus, when she had spoken with him, "went her way and *called Mary her sister secretly*, saying, 'the Master is come and calleth for thee.' As soon as she heard that, she arose quickly and came unto him. Now Jesus was not yet come into the town, but was in that place where Martha met him. The Jews then which were with her in the house, when they saw Mary that she rose up hastily and went out, followed her, saying, 'she goeth unto the grave to weep there.'" We must suppose here either an accurate knowledge on the part of the writer, or an elaborate and gratuitous skill in contriving falsehood. Who can follow this narrative through, and note the expressions of deep-felt human feeling,—including the reference, in a single word, to the tears of Jesus,—and not be struck with the obvious truthfulness of the writer? Or are there no marks by which sincerity and truth can be distinguished from fraud? [1]

[1] Among the illustrations of the present topic referred to by

There are many passages which show incontestibly that the author of the fourth Gospel wrote from an interest in the history as such.[1] There are numerous uncontrived and unmistakable signs that he is writing from recollection, and not from invention. Among the examples of this peculiarity are the allusions to Nicodemus in three places, which are widely apart from each other (John iii. 2; vii. 50; xix. 39), and which imply *an increasing faith* in his mind. The particular mention of the time of the occurrence of different events, as on this or that day, is not important to the narrative, and simply indicates that the writer brings out facts as they lie in memory: see John ii. 13; iv. 6, 40, 43; v. i.; vi. 4, 22; vii. 2, 14; xii. 1, 12; xviii. 27 seq.; xix. 14. The name of the servant whose ear was cut off by Peter is given: John xviii. 10. Localities are designated, where no other than a historical interest can prompt the writer to do so. For example, it is said (c. iii. 23) that John was baptizing "in Aenon near to Salim:" the Evangelist describes a pool at Jerusalem (John v.

De Wette (*Einl. in das N. T.* § 105, *a*), and which we have not especially noticed, are John v. 10 seq. (the circumstances that followed the cure wrought at the pool of Bethesda; the questions put to the man who had been healed, by the Jews; his not knowing who it was that had healed him; his subsequent meeting with Jesus in the temple); vii. 1 seq. (the secret journey of Christ to the feast of Tabernacles, after the conversation with his unbelieving relatives); xii. The whole of chap. iv. (the interview of Christ with the woman of Samaria), is a striking example of vivid, detailed narration.

[1] See Brückner's De Wette, *Einl.*, s. xv.

2), as being by the sheep-gate—*gate* and not *market* should have been supplied by the English translators —and "called in the Hebrew tongue, Bethesda, having five porches:" in c. viii. 1, we read that "Jesus went unto the mount of Olives, and early in the morning he came again into the temple;" so that the fact of his going at night to the mount of Olives is simply recorded, with no mention of anything that he did, or that occurred there—a striking instance of historical recollection, since no significance attached to the bare fact of his going to the mount: Philip is designated (c. xii. 21) as "of Bethsaida of Galilee," although this has no apparent connection with the incident there recorded of him: it is narrated that Pilate sat down in his judgment-seat "that is called the Pavement, but in the Hebrew, Gabbatha;" a description of no moment in itself, but involved in the writer's recollection of the spot.

A similar mark of historical faithfulness is contained in the incidental allusions to features of the gospel history which yet the Evangelist does not record, but which were preserved either by the Synoptics or in oral tradition. These things, it is assumed, are known to his readers. We have in John iii. 24, in the allusion to John's being cast into prison, a signal instance of this sort. Jesus is spoken of as from Nazareth (John i. 45, 46), although no explicit statement about his residence there had been given. He is designated by the people of

Nazareth as "the son of Joseph, whose father and mother" were known to them (John vi. 42; comp. i. 45). For the first time, in c. vi. 67, "the twelve" are incidentally mentioned. Didymus, the Greek name of Thomas, is associated with the Hebrew designation of this apostle in John xi. 16, xx. 24, xxi. 2. In c. xi. 2, the Evangelist explains parenthetically that Mary, the sister of Martha, was the same Mary which anointed the Lord with ointment, and wiped his feet with her hair. This incident, which is given in Matthew xxvi. 6–13, Mark xiv. 19, is assumed by the Evangelist to be well known, although he had not himself recorded it, and it appears in his narrative at a later point (c. xii. 3).

We have no need to pursue the topic further. We find everywhere in this Gospel the air and manner of an eyewitness and participant in the scenes recorded.

3. The general structure and contents of the fourth Gospel, considered as a biography of Christ, are a convincing argument for its historical truth and genuineness.

We come now to the decisive point in the conflict between the advocates and the opponents of the genuineness of this Gospel. It is contended by the latter that the representation which is found in the fourth Gospel, both of the course of events in the life of Christ and of the character of his teachings, is not only "divergent from that of the other Gospels, but absolutely incompatible with it;" and that since these Gospels in this respect are right, the fourth cannot be the work of an apostle.

The difference between the fourth Gospel and the other three, in the particulars referred to, is in truth very palpable and very important. The impression made by the first three, or synoptical Gospels, regarded by themselves, is that Jesus, after his baptism and temptation, repaired to Galilee, and remained there until shortly before his death, when he went up to Jerusalem to the passover. They record his teachings and miracles in Galilee and on this journey to Jerusalem, but say nothing of any intermediate visits to that city, and nothing of any prior labors there. From the synoptical Gospels alone, the impression would be gathered that the period of his ministry was only a year. On the other hand, John distinctly mentions not less than two journeys of Jesus from Galilee to Jerusalem previous to the last (ii. 13; v. 1), and seems to justify the conclusion that in each of these visits he remained a considerable time either in the city or in its neighborhood. The duration of his ministry, according to the fourth Gospel, cannot be less than two years and a half, and may possibly exceed three years. Not less remarkable is the difference in the style of the Saviour's teaching in this Gospel, compared with the representations found in the other three. In the synoptical Gospels, Christ utters either brief, sententious apothegms, or parables;

while in the fourth Gospel we have extended dialogues and long discourses in quite a different vein. Other minor points of difference might be mentioned, but these which we have named are of chief importance.

Before we proceed to consider in detail the bearing of these peculiarities of John upon the main question before us, we offer one preliminary remark. The more serious the difference between the contents of the synoptical Gospels and of John, the greater is the difficulty to be met by the opponents of the genuineness of the latter. For how could a Gospel which so runs athwart the accepted views of the life and teaching of Christ, be brought forward and gain credence unless it were *known* to have the sanction of an apostle? The later the date assigned to the Gospel, the greater is the difficulty. What *motive* for a forger, fabricating his work long after the apostolic age, to depart from the traditional and certified conception of Christ's life and teaching? And supposing him to have a motive to do this, how could he succeed? These are questions to which the opponents of the genuineness of the Gospel find it impossible to give any satisfactory answer. Even if they were to show that the contrast between John and the synoptical histories almost amounts to an incompatibility, they only increase thereby the difficulty of solving the problem we have suggested. What inducement had a writer of the second century to deviate, without necessity, and to so extraordinary an extent, from the long prevalent and authorized view of the Saviour's life? And how was the Church persuaded to accept this new version of his career? Such is the hard problem presented to the skeptical critic. On the contrary, if it can be made to appear on a careful investigation, that, in these very particulars which are made the ground of objection, the fourth Gospel unquestionably presents historical truth; that incidentally it supplements the other three just where they need explanation; and especially that this Gospel alone presents a consecutive and connected view of the life of Christ, we have gone far toward establishing its apostolic authorship. We have not only obviated the principal objection; we have also furnished a positive and convincing argument on the other side. Its historical peculiarities, so far from being a fatal objection against, will be seen to be a conclusive argument for, its genuineness. Only an apostle could have thrown this flood of light upon the course of events in the life of Christ. Only an apostle could have brought to the support of his narrative an authority sufficient to obtain for it credence. We shall be obliged to notice with brevity the various considerations connected with the present topic.

1. The journeys of Christ to Jerusalem and his ministry there. For reasons which we cannot with certainty determine, the synoptical Gospels confine themselves to the Galilean ministry. The ques-

tion is: Have we ground for concluding, independently of John, that Jesus had repeatedly visited that city and labored there? The synoptical Gospels say nothing inconsistent with his having done so; they are simply silent upon the subject. It would certainly be more natural to suppose that Jesus who claimed to be the Messiah, even if his ministry had continued but a year, would during this time have gone up to Jerusalem, both as an act of compliance with the law and as a means of gaining access to such a multitude as the festivals brought together. It is not easy to account for the fanatical hatred of the Pharisees in Jerusalem towards him, if we suppose that he had never crossed their path, save in casual encounters with them away from Jerusalem, in Galilee.

Various facts mentioned in the synoptical Gospels seem to presuppose such previous labors on his part in the capital. Thus Joseph of Arimathea, a member of the Sanhedrim, is said, in the synoptical Gospels, to be a disciple of Jesus (Matt. xxvii. 57 seq.; Luke xxiii. 50 seq.; Mark xv. 42 seq.); but Joseph was a resident of Jerusalem, having, as we are told, a tomb there. There, it is probable, he became acquainted with Christ. Again, we learn from Luke (x. 38 seq.) that Jesus stood in such intimate relations with the family of Martha and Mary, as imply a previous stay in that neighborhood prior to this last visit. But we are happily furnished with a conclusive proof of the Saviour's repeated visits to Jerusalem, in the lamentation he uttered over the city, as recorded by both Matthew and Luke (Luke xiii. 34 seq.; Matt. xxiii. 37 seq.): *Ἱερουσαλὴμ, Ἱερουσαλὴμ . . . . ποσάκις ἠθέλησα ἐπισυνάξαι τὰ τέκνα σου . . . . καὶ οὐκ ἠθελήσατε, κ.τ.λ.*

Baur would make it out that the whole Jewish people are apostrophized under the term "Jerusalem," as the centre and home of the nation. This interpretation seems improbable, when we remember that when the Saviour uttered these words he was gazing upon the city. It is demonstrated to be false by the context in Luke. Immediately before, in the preceding verse, the Saviour says: "for it cannot be *that a prophet perish out of Jerusalem*."

It may be well to notice the last device of interpretation, by which Strauss struggles to avoid the inevitable inference to be drawn from this passage.[1] We notice his new hypothesis more willingly, because it offers so fair an illustration of his general method of criticism. "This expression," says Strauss, "can Jesus least of all have used where Luke puts it, on his journey to Jerusalem, and before he had once during the period of his public activity seen that city. But even in Jerusalem itself, after a single stay there of only a few days, he cannot have pointed out how *often* he had attempted in vain to draw its inhabitants to himself. Here *all shifts*"—such as

[1] *Leben Jesu für das deutsche Volk*, s. 249.

that of Baur, noticed above—"*are futile,* and it must be confessed: if these are really the words of Christ, he must have labored in Jerusalem *oftener and longer* than would appear from the synoptical reports." Now, the reader will ask, how is this conclusion to be escaped? Nothing more easy. "These are *not* his words," says Strauss. It is true that Matthew gives them as such, in connection with the other declaration: "wherefore, behold, I send unto you prophets, and wise men, and scribes, and some of them ye shall kill and crucify," etc. But this last expression, as quoted by (Luke xi. 49 seq.), is disconnected from the apostrophe to Jerusalem, which is found later, in c. xiii. 34, 35. And that expression concerning the rejection of the divine messengers, though occurring in the midst of a discourse of Christ, is introduced by Luke with the words: "therefore also said the wisdom of God." On these data, Strauss sets up the theory that the whole passage, as found in Matthew, is a quotation from some lost christian book written about the time of the destruction of Jerusalem, in which the personified wisdom of God was represented as speaking! It is interesting to mark the process by which he arrives at this conclusion. Matthew is held to be right in conjoining the two expressions, and Luke wrong in separating them. But Matthew is wrong in leaving out the introductory words: "therefore also saith the wisdom of God." Luke, again, is wrong in not connecting *both* expressions with this formula, and in making the apostrophe to Jerusalem to be the words of Christ himself. Why Matthew, whom Strauss elsewhere pronounces altogether the best authority, especially in regard to the discourses of Christ,[1] should *leave out* the formula of citation, and attribute to Jesus words extracted from the supposed lost book, is indeed a difficulty. Strauss says that it was owing to the singularity—*seltsamkeit*—of this formula! Why Luke should attribute to Christ himself the words of lamentation over Jerusalem, when they stood connected with the passage relative to divine messengers *in a book that did not purport to be a record of the words of Christ*, is another unexplained circumstance. It is plain that Strauss credits, or discredits, each evangelist, in an entirely arbitrary manner, in order to meet the exigencies of a theory. The apostrophe to Jerusalem *must* be regarded as the outpouring of Christ's own feeling and as uttered by him. Both evangelists explicitly declare this. And apart from the considerations already mentioned, the conclusion of the passage has no propriety unless it were spoken by Jesus: "for I say unto you, ye shall not see me henceforth, till ye say, Blessed is he that cometh in the name of the Lord." In the passage (Luke xi. 49): "therefore also saith the wisdom of God," the last phrase probably denotes Jesus himself, and may have been attached in current speech to this cita-

[1] *Leben Jesu für d. deutsche Volk*, s. 115.

tion of his words. Hence Luke takes it up into his report.[1]

The apostrophe to Jerusalem proves, therefore, that Jesus had again and again preached in that city and labored to convert its inhabitants. The fourth Gospel is incidentally but convincingly sustained in attributing a prolonged ministry to Christ and repeated labors at Jerusalem, by the synoptical Gospels themselves. But suppose a writer in the second century to have set himself to the work of composing a fictitious gospel for the purpose of indirectly inculcating a dogmatic system of his own; how certain that he would have adhered to the traditional view of the course of the Saviour's ministry! By giving it a longer duration, and introducing visits to Jerusalem and labors there not mentioned by the received Gospels, he would only invite suspicion and expose himself to detection. No advantage could be conceived to follow such a wide departure from the prevalent conception, which would not be immeasurably outweighed by the certain disadvantages and perils

[1] This is the opinion of Neander and Meyer. Strauss is not so original as he claims to be, in this piece of interpretation. Baur, after suggesting his own explanation, of which we have spoken above, remarks in a note that if this interpretation is unacceptable, then the lament over Jerusalem may be taken as the words of some (unknown) prophet, which in this definite form were (fictitiously) put into the mouth of Christ. See Baur's *Kanon. Evang.*, s. 127. In plainer language: if you cannot explain away the meaning of the passage, deny that Christ said it!

attending it. It must have been, then, from a regard to historical truth and from a knowledge of the facts, that the author of the fourth Gospel has so constructed his history. And this author, whoever he was, had an authority with Christians so great as to enable him to vary thus widely, without the imputation of error, from the prevalent tradition.

The more the general plan of the fourth Gospel is examined, the more is it seen to rest upon the solid foundation of historical verity. The progress of events in the life of Jesus, from the beginning onward to the final result, is clearly understood from this Gospel. We see how it came to pass that though "he came to his own, his own received him not." The vacillation of the people, now turning in his favor, and now, as he disappointed their expectations, turning against him, together with the origin and growth of the implacable hostility of the Jewish leaders, are made entirely comprehensible.

And the fourth Gospel alone gives an adequate explanation of the way in which the catastrophe was brought on. We see how the consequences of the raising of Lazarus obliged the Pharisees to proceed at once to the most decisive measures against Jesus. It was this event, and the effect of it upon the minds of the people, that precipitated the result. In regard to this closing portion of Christ's life, we have in John the clue to the solution of what is left, in part, unsolved in the other Gospels. Even Renan finds that "the last months of the life of Jesus in particular are explained only by John."[1] A narrative is commended to credence by being thus consistent and intelligible. The same distinction, the same verisimilitude, belongs to the account of the Saviour's resurrection, a section of the history in which the synoptical Gospels are especially fragmentary. In John we have a view, as clear and coherent as it is artless and natural, of the transactions that followed his reappearance from the tomb.

2. In considering the credibility of the fourth Gospel, as this question is affected by a comparison of its matter with the contents of the other three, we have to notice the difficulty and apparent discrepancy upon the date of the crucifixion, and also the paschal controversies of the second century, in their bearing upon this point of chronology.

It is well known to every student of the Gospels that there is difficulty in reconciling the statement of the first three, respecting the date of the last supper, and consequently respecting the date of the death of Christ, with the statement of John. All the evangelists agree as to the day of the week—that the supper was on Thursday evening, and the crucifixion on the next or Friday morning. The synoptical Gospels, however, appear to place the last supper in the evening when the Jews ate the passover-meal; i. e. on the evening of the 14th Nisan, or, according to the Jewish reckon-

[1] Renan, *Vie de Jésus*, p. xxxiii.

ing, the beginning of the 15th Nisan. The fourth Gospel, on the other hand, appears to place the last meal of Jesus with the disciples on the evening before the passover-supper of the Jews; i. e. on the 13th, or, according to the Jewish reckoning, the 14th, Nisan, and the crucifixion on the morning immediately before, instead of after, this Jewish festival.

The Tübingen critics regard the two representations as really inconsistent and irreconcilable; and on this ground, as they hold that the fourth Gospel is incorrect, they maintain that it could not have proceeded from John. If the two representations can be fairly harmonized with each other, of course their argument vanishes with the foundation on which it is built. Without pronouncing judgment on the various modes which have been proposed by Dr. Robinson and other harmonists for reconciling the two accounts, let us consider the effect, as regards the credibility and genuineness of the fourth Gospel, of admitting that the discrepancy is real and irremovable. The diversity of the principles of criticism which are adopted by the major part of the able defenders of supernatural Christianity and evangelical doctrine in Germany, from those in vogue among us, is remarkably exemplified by their treatment of the particular question before us. Not only do Neander, Bleek, Meyer, and others hardly less distinguished, coincide with their adversaries in admitting that the discrepancy is irremovable; but Bleek builds upon it an earnest argument for the credibility and apostolic authorship of John.[1] He insists, with much force, upon the improbability that a writer in the second century, who wished to be considered an apostle, would contradict the three Gospels and the accepted tradition of the Church, on such a point as the date of the last supper and of the crucifixion. Who but an apostle, or one thoroughly acquainted with the facts, would think of making himself responsible for such a deviation? Who, but an apostle, could hope to be believed? In a word, how extremely unnatural that a forger should think of assigning another date to these leading facts in the evangelical history! Bleek, also, endeavors to show that the supposition that the crucifixion took place on the morning *before* the passover-lamb was eaten, is corroborated by incidental statements in the synoptical Gospels themselves,[2] as well as by all the probabilities in the case; so that the accuracy of the fourth Gospel, in this particular, is established, and thus a strong argument is furnished for its general credibility.[3]

[1] It should be stated that these critics do not consider the first Gospel, in its present form, to emanate from the Apostle Matthew. See Neander's *Leben Jesu*, s. 10. Bleek's *Einl.*, s. 88 seq. The first Gospel is held to stand in substantially the same relation to the apostles as the other two; and the historical position of all three is indicated in Luke i. 1, 2; i. e. they record the things which were *delivered to their writers* by eyewitnesses. It is not the eyewitnesses themselves, but those to whom they spoke.

[2] Matt. xxvi. 5, xxvii. 59 seq.; Mark xv. 42, 46; Luke xxiii. 56.

[3] Ellicott, in his *Life of Christ* (Am. Ed. p. 292, N. 3) considers

The opponents of the genuineness of John attempt to draw a support for their cause from the paschal controversies of the second century. These arose from a difference in practice in regard to a certain festival celebrated about the time of the Jewish passover. There was discussion on this difference, in which the churches of Asia Minor were opposed by the church of Rome, on the occasion of Polycarp's visit to Anicetus of Rome about the year 160; then ten years later, in which Claudius Apollinaris, bishop of Hierapolis, and Melito of Sardes, took part; and especially at the end of the second century, when Victor, bishop of Rome, proposed to break off fellowship with the Asia Minor bishops on account of their refusal to abandon their ancient custom. In these controversies, and in the defence of their practice, the Asia Minor bishops were in the habit of appealing to the authority of the Apostle John, who had lived in the midst of them.

Everything turns upon ascertaining the real point of difference and the real character of the Asia Minor observance. So much is certain, that this observance, whatever may have been its origin or significance, occurred on the evening of the 14th, or, in the Jewish reckoning, the beginning of the 15th, Nisan. Baur

that no other interpretation of John is admissible but that which places the last supper on the evening before the usual passover-meal of the Jews. "The statements," says Ellicott, "are so clear, that to attempt, with Wieseler (*Chron. Synops.*), Robinson (*Bib. Sacra* for Aug. 1845), to explain them away, must be regarded as arbitrary and hopeless." See John xiii. 1, 29, xviii. 28, xix. 31.

holds that it was established as a commemoration of the last supper, the passover-meal of Jesus with his disciples; and hence infers that John, whose authority supported the Asia Minor observance, could not have written the account of the last supper in our fourth Gospel.

But Baur's argument is on a foundation of sand. It is clear, from the earliest discussions on the subject, that the difference did not consist in a diverse mode of observing the same festival; but that in Asia Minor *there was a festival which did not exist at Rome.* This commemoration was on the 14th Nisan, on whatever day of the week it might fall; whence the adherents of the Asia Minor custom were called Quartodecimani, while Occidental Christians observed Friday and Sunday of each week as the days, respectively, of the Lord's death and resurrection. A day was observed by the Asia Minor Christians which was not observed at Rome. Nor is there any probability that the Asia Minor festival was established as a commemoration of the last supper.

There are two views as to the origin of their festival. It was the final view of Neander, and is the opinion of Meyer and Schneider, that it commemorated the death of Christ—the sacrifice of the true paschal Lamb, of which the Mosaic paschal lamb was the type (1 Cor. v. 7; John xix. 36). If this be the fact, the festival accords with the supposed chronology of John's Gospel. The fragment of Apollinaris has been supposed to connect the Asia Minor festival with the last supper, and to defend the correctness of the day of its observance by an appeal to Matthew. But Schneider forcibly argues that Apollinaris is reporting, not his own view, which was that of the Quartodecimani, but the view of a smaller party of Judaizers, from which he dissents; so that Apollinaris (as also the fragment of Hippolytus) is really a witness to the agreement of the Quartodecimani with the chronology of the fourth Gospel. The other hypothesis concerning the design of the Asia Minor festival, is that of Bleek, De Wette, and others, who consider this festival to have been originally the Jewish passover, which the Jewish converts at Ephesus and elsewhere had continued to observe, and with which in their minds Christian ideas and associations were more and more connected. In particular, there was naturally associated with it the recollection of the last supper of Jesus with the disciples. There was no such reference originally connected with the festival, nor did this association of it with the last supper grow up until long after the death of John. This apostle did not interfere with a commemoration which he found established in Ephesus and other places in that region. Bleek shows that the theory of an original reference of the Asia Minor festival to the last supper would imply an earlier origin of the yearly Christian festivals than we have any reason to think belonged to them. It is not inconsistent with Bleek's general view, to adopt Schneider's interpretation of Apollinaris, in which case even this writer affords no proof of an association by the Quartodecimani of their festival with the Saviour's last supper. This hypothesis relative to the character of their commemoration, that it was at the outset simply the Jewish passover, which in Rome, and in other churches where the Gentiles were more predominant, was not kept up, appears to us to be best supported. In any case, the charge that a contradiction exists between the early Asia Minor tradition concerning John's testimony and the chronology of the fourth Gospel is without foundation.

4. The discourses of Christ in the fourth Gospel. These have been used as an argument against the apostolic origin of this Gospel: an argument founded on their inherent character; their relation, both as to form and matter, to the teaching of Christ recorded by the synoptical evangelists; the portraiture of Christ which they convey; their fitness to the circumstances under which they are alleged to have been spoken; their uniformity, both with each other and with the expressions of other characters in the Gospel, as well as with those of the author himself.[1]

Under this head we shall chiefly follow Bleek, regretting, however, that we are under the necessity of abridging his excellent suggestions.

That the discourses of Christ in John stand in contrast, in important respects, with his teaching in the

[1] Bleek, s. 194.

other Gospels, is not denied. The first question is, whether the contrast is so great that both styles of teaching could not belong to the same person. Here Bleek pertinently refers to the case of Socrates, and to the opinion that is coming to prevail, that the representation in Plato has much more of truth than was formerly supposed; an opinion held by such men as Schleiermacher, Brandis, and Ritter, and commended by the apparent necessity of supposing a more speculative element in the teaching of Socrates than Xenophon exhibits, if we would account for the schools of speculative philosophy that took their rise from him. He must have had another side than that which we discern in Xenophon's record.[1] How much easier is this to be supposed in the case of Him who was to act effectually upon every variety of mind and character! How natural and inevitable that each of his disciples should apprehend Christ from his own point of view, according to the measure of his own individuality; so that for the understanding of Christ in his fulness, we have to combine these various, but not incongruous, representations of him.

But, as in a former instance, we find in the synoptical writers proof that the fourth Gospel, in the

[1] Whoever will examine cc. ix. and x. of the fourth Book of the Memorabilia, will see that these are fragmentary specimens from another vein than that which furnishes to Xenophon most of his reports. A like feeling is produced when we compare the last chapter of the Mem. with Plato. Socrates *must* have said much more, in this closing period, than Xenophon has recorded.

character of the discourses attributed to Christ, does not depart from historical truth. As to their form, we are told, especially in Matt. xiii. 10 seq., that the Saviour, at least in discoursing to the disciples, did not confine himself to the gnomes and parables; that he spake thus to the people on account of the dulness of their understanding, while to the disciples it was "given to know the mysteries of the kingdom of heaven." The statements (Matt. xiii. 34; Mark iv. 34) that he never spake to the people save in parables, are of course of a general character, and, fairly interpreted, are not inconsistent with his addressing the people at times in accordance with the reports of John. Occasionally in the synoptical Gospels, moreover, we meet with expressions of Jesus in striking consonance with his style in the Johannean discourses, and thus giving us a glimpse of another manner of teaching which the synoptical writers sparingly report. The most remarkable example is Matt. xi. 25 seq. (compare Luke xi. 21 seq.), the ejaculation of Jesus, beginning: "I thank thee, O Father, Lord of heaven and earth, because thou hast hid these things from the wise and prudent, and hast revealed them unto babes. Even so, Father, for so it seemed good in thy sight." How perfectly in harmony with the style of Jesus in the latter part of John![1]

[1] In John, also, examples of the aphoristic style, such as prevails in the synoptical reports of the teaching of Christ, are not wanting. See John xii. 24, 26; xiii. 16, 20.

As to the contents of the fourth Gospel, it is freely granted that the higher nature of Christ and the relation of the Son to the Father are here a much more predominant theme. Essentially the same conception of Christ, however, is found in the first three Gospels. In them he is the Son of God, in a higher than any official sense: he is the judge of the world. And in several passages, we find him claiming the lofty attributes given him in John, and in the same style. Thus in Matt. xi. 27 he says: "All things are delivered to me of my Father; and *no man knoweth the Son but the Father; neither knoweth any man the Father save the Son, and he to whom the Son will reveal him.*" This mutual knowledge, exclusive, superhuman, and perfect, on the part of the Son and the Father, is affirmed here in the peculiar manner of the fourth Gospel. In Matt. xxii. 41 seq. (compare Mark xii. 35 seq.; Luke xx. 41 seq.) we have a plain suggestion of the fact of his pre-existence.

The objection that the discourses of Christ in John have a close resemblance to the style of the evangelist himself and to that of his first Epistle, is obviated when we remember that, as a result of his peculiar relation to Christ, the Saviour's mode of expression would naturally be taken up; that we are under no necessity of supposing that he aimed to give a verbally accurate report of the Master's teaching; and that some freedom as to style is unavoidable in abbreviating and selecting the portions of his discourse for which there was a place in so brief a work. All this, as well as that thorough inward digestion and assimilation, on the part of the evangelist, of the Saviour's discourses, which were consequent on the length of time that had elapsed since they were heard, will account for the peculiarity in question, without impairing in the slightest degree the historical truth and substantial accuracy of the Johannean reports.

The falsehood of the assertion that these discourses are fictitious and put into the mouth of Jesus by the writer, after the manner of ancient Greek and Roman historians, is evinced in particular by certain briefer expressions which are interspersed in them, and which admit of no explanation except on the supposition that the reports are faithful A signal example is John xiv. 31, where, in the midst of a long discourse to the disciples, occur the words: "Arise, let us go hence!"[1] They are not followed by any intimation that the company actually arose and left the place where they were. On the contrary, the discourse goes on, in the words: "I am the true vine," etc. But if we suppose what follows to have been spoken by the way; or, which is perhaps more natural, if we suppose that having spoken the words first quoted which summoned the disciples to quit the place where they were, the Saviour's

[1] ἐγείρεσθε, ἄγωμεν ἐντεῦθεν.

interest in his theme and love for them led him to go on still longer, while, it may be, they all remained standing, then these words have a proper place and meaning. The circumstance would imprint itself on the recollection of John, and it affords an impressive proof of his fidelity in reporting his Master's discourses. But no reason can be given why a forger should have introduced this fragmentary, unexplained phrase. Had he chosen to interrupt the discourse by such a phrase, he would infallibly have added some other statement, such as: then they arose and went. This little phrase, to a candid reader, is a most convincing item of evidence. Bleek also dwells upon the character of the prophetic utterances of Christ in John, especially of the predictions relative to his own death. The fact that they are in the form of intimations, rather than distinct declarations, will better account, in the view of Bleek, for the misunderstanding of them on the part of the disciples. The form in which they appear in John wears, in his opinion, the stamp of historical truth, since it is altogether probable that in this form they were actually spoken. Especially, as Bleek thinks, is the historical fidelity of the evangelist shown by those passages from Christ upon which the evangelist puts his own interpretation, drawn from an observation of the subsequent event. Such are John ii. 19: "destroy this temple, and in three days I will raise it again," where we are told that the obscure reference to the temple of his body was discerned by his disciples not till after the resurrection; and John xii. 32: "and I, if I be lifted up from the earth, will draw all men unto me," to which the evangelist appends a similar explanation. There can be no doubt in these instances that the apostle has faithfully reported the sayings of Jesus; and this fact must be even more evident to those critics who do not hesitate to question, in these cases, the perfect correctness of the disciples' interpretation.

5. The Hellenic culture and the theological point of view of the author of the fourth Gospel are made an objection to the Johannean authorship. They prove, it is maintained, that the work does not belong to the apostolic age, was not written either by a Palestinian or by any other Jew, but by a Gentile Christian of the second century. In the notice of these several points we principally follow Bleek.

(1) Was the author of the fourth Gospel a Jew? It is objected that his manner of referring to the Jews proves him not to be of their number. Thus we read of the "Jews' Passover," "the Jews' feast of tabernacles," the "feast of the Jews," the "preparation of the Jews," the "ruler of the Jews" (ii. 6, 13; iii. 1; v. 1; vi. 4; vii. 2; xi. 55); and frequently the author, alluding to the adversaries of Jesus and those with whom he came in contact, speaks of them in general as *οἱ Ἰουδαῖοι*. This style is capable of explanation only on the hypothesis

that the Gospel was written late in the apostolic age, when the Christian Church had come to be fully independent of the Jewish, and by a writer who was himself outside of Palestine, and addressed his work not only to Jews, but also, and still more, to Gentiles and Gentile Christians. And this supposition, which removes the difficulty, is itself the church tradition concerning the composition of John.[1] But independently of this tradition, there can be no doubt that the author was of Jewish extraction. In proof of this, Bleek refers to the writer's familiarity with the Jewish laws and customs, which is so manifest in his account of the events connected with the Saviour's death; to the pragmatical character of the Gospel, so far as the fulfilment of Old Testament predictions and promises is frequently pointed out; and to the fact that a portion of these citations are translated directly from the Hebrew, instead of being taken from the Septuagint,—a fact that is conclusive in favor of his Jewish, and strongly in favor of his Palestinian, origin. It occurs to us, also, that Baur, in conceding that the author professes to be the Apostle John, may be himself challenged to explain why he is so negligent in affording evidence of a Jewish extraction. Surely, so expert a counterfeiter would not have forgotten a point so essential

[1] Even Paul speaks of his "former conversation *in the Jews' religion;*" of his profiting "in the *Jews' religion,*" Gal. i. 13, 14.

to a successful attempt to personate the Apostle. The charge that errors are found in John inconsistent with the hypothesis that the author was a Palestinian Jew, is without foundation. That Bethany (the true reading for "*Bethabara* beyond Jordan," in John i. 28) was either the name of a place in Peraea, or was a slip of the pen for Bethabara; that, at any rate, the writer did not misplace the Bethany where Lazarus dwelt, is demonstrated by John xi. 18, where this town is expressly said to be fifteen stadia from Jerusalem. The assertion that in the designation of Caiaphas as high priest for that year, *ἀρχιερεὺς τοῦ ἐνιαυτοῦ ἐκείνου* (xi. 51; xviii. 13,) the author implies a belief that the high priest was changed every year, is entirely unwarranted by anything in the text. The term "Sychar" for the old city Sichem, instead of being a blunder, may be an old pronunciation of the Jews and Samaritans of that time. As used by the Jews there may lurk under it a reference to the hated character of the Samaritans; or, finally, it may be simply an error of transcription.[1]

[1] See Bleek, s. 209. The supposition that it is really the name of a town distinct from Sichem, though near it, agrees with the oldest traditions, and on several accounts seems more probable. So Hug (*Introd.* Part II., sec. 59), Ewald (*Die Johan. Schriften*, I. 181), Brückner, Bäumlein, Thomson, (*The Land and the Book*, II. 206), and others. Comp. Grove's art. in Smith's *Bible Dict.* The explanations given above (from Bleek) rest purely on conjecture; this rests on historical and topographical arguments, confirmed by the existence at the present day of a place with a similar name ('Askar) near the site of Jacob's well. Lightfoot (*Chorog. Enquiry*,

(2) The objection is made that a Galilean fisherman, like John, could not be possessed of so much Greek culture as the fourth Gospel discovers. But the family of John were neither in a low station, nor in straitened circumstances. He was certainly trained by his pious mother in the knowledge of the Old Testament. He may have been early taught the Greek language, which was then so widely diffused. The report which the members of the Sanhedrim had heard, that Peter and John were unlearned and uncultivated men (Acts iv. 13) can only signify that they were not educated in the schools of the Rabbis. Had John not attained some mastery of the Greek language, it is not so likely that he would have taken up his residence in the midst of Asia, where only Greek was spoken, even by the Jews. And during his prolonged residence there his familiarity with the language would doubtless increase.

(3) The type of doctrine in the fourth Gospel, and especially its Christology, have been thought to be an argument against its composition by John, the Palestinian Jew. In particular, the Logos idea in John, it is said, was an Alexandrian notion, borrowed from the Greek philosophy, and introduced into Christian theology at a later period. We cannot

prefixed to John, ch. iv. sec. 5) finds "the valley of the well of Sokar" spoken of in the Talmud as at a great distance from Jerusalem. He also suggests, as does Hug, that the name סוכר may denote a *burial-place.*

enter at length into the discussion of this point. We simply say that, as regards the language or the *form* of the doctrine, it may have been derived from the book of Proverbs and from Sirach, and not improbably was derived from this source, though further developed, by Philo himself. Elsewhere and earlier in the New Testament itself, if not in the Epistle to the Hebrews, yet undeniably in the Apocalypse, we meet with the Johannean terminology. But, even if the language pertaining to the Logos came at first from the Greek philosophy, it may have been taken up by John, as a fit designation of the pre-existent Christ. Properly qualified, it became a vehicle for conveying his conception of the Son in his relation to the Father. In the use of this term, John enters upon no speculation. He would rather turn away the mind from vain speculations, from the unprofitable discussions about the Logos that may have been current, to the living, historic Revealer of God, the actual manifestation of the Invisible One, the Word made flesh, which had "dwelt among us." Accordingly, after the first few verses, we hear no more of the Logos. No allusion to the Logos is introduced into his report of the discourses of Jesus. As to the matter of the conception, we utterly deny the theory of the school of Baur, that the early church was Ebionite, regarding Christ as a mere man. We hold that this theory is abundantly refuted by passages in the synoptical Gospels and Pauline Epistles, and is proved to be false by a fair view of the early history of the Church. The theology of Philo, it deserves to be remarked, contains nothing more than the vaguest conception of the Messiah, and is throughout far more speculative than ethical; affording, therefore, no materials for that conception of Jesus Christ which is found in John, and which only an intuition of the living person of Christ could have awakened. The conception of Christ in John is the product of the impression made by Christ himself upon the soul of the disciple.

(4) We have to notice another objection emanating from the school of Baur, that the free and liberal spirit of the fourth Gospel toward the Gentiles is inconsistent with the position attributed to John in Galatians ii. 9. But this objection proceeds from the assumption, underlying the whole system of the Tübingen school, that Peter and the other Jerusalem apostles were radically opposed to the doctrine of Paul relative to the rights of the Gentiles; that they were, in short, Judaizers. We hold this assumption to be demonstrably false, and the fabric of historical construction reared upon it to be a mere castle in the air. There is nothing improbable in the circumstance of the inquiry for Jesus made by the devout Greeks (John xii. 20) at which Baur stumbles. Even in Matthew, which Baur regards as preëminently a Jewish-Christian Gospel, is recorded the Saviour's emphatic commendation of the Centurion's faith (viii.

10 seq.); the distinct prediction that the kingdom should be taken from the Jews, and given to another people (xxi. 43); the injunction to preach the gospel to every creature (xxviii. 19); the prophecy that it should be preached to all nations (xxiv. 14); and the parables describing the universal spread of the gospel (ch. xiii.). We are not to leave out of view, in considering the spirit of the fourth Gospel with reference to Gentile Christianity, the inevitable effect of great providential events, of which the destruction of Jerusalem was one, and of the long interval of time during which the distinct character of the Christian Church and the broad design of Christianity had become more and more plain. In this objection of Baur, the attempt is made to uphold one false proposition by another that is equally false.

There is one objection not to be separated entirely from the one last considered, but which is more serious and plausible than any we have named. The other difficulties which we have noticed, though not unworthy of consideration, vanish, and in most cases even turn into arguments for the contrary side. But the difficulty we have now to speak of, is urged with especial emphasis. It is strongly maintained by those who impugn the genuineness of John, that the Apocalypse, which they hold to be his work, cannot come from the same author as the fourth Gospel. It cannot be denied that there exists a degree of disparity, both in language and thought, between the

Apocalypse and this Gospel. "The language [of the Apocalypse] is incomparably rougher, harder, more disconnected, and exhibits greater errors than is true of any other book in the New Testament, while the language of the Gospel, though not pure Greek, is in a grammatical view incomparably more correct."[1] This contrast between the style of the two books was stated as long ago as the middle of the third century, by Dionysius of Alexandria.[2] So there are various special peculiarities of language in the Gospel which are missed in the Apocalypse. "A still greater and more essential difference is discovered when we look at the contents, spirit, and whole character of these writings."[3] Under this head Bleek refers, in particular, to the different position of the Apocalypse with reference to the Jewish people, so opposite to that of the Gospel, where *οἱ Ἰουδαῖοι* is often, without qualification, the designation of the opposers of Christ; to the definite expectation of the second advent and millennium, together with the conception of anti-Christ as a particular individual, which is unlike the conception found in 1 John ii. 18 seq.; iv. 3. We have to weigh the objection to the genuineness of the Gospel which these differences have suggested.

1. The impossibility that both books should have the same author is far from being established. The

[1] Bleek, s. 626.

[2] Euseb., Lib. VII. c. 25. [3] Bleek, s. 626.

Apocalypse was written shortly after the death of Nero and shortly before the destruction of Jerusalem. The interval prior to the composition of the Gospel was not far from twenty years,—a period giving room for important changes in the style and habits of thought of any writer; an era, too, most eventful, as concerns the development of the plan of providence relative to the Jewish nation. That they were destined, as a body, to reject the gospel, and to be rejected of God, was made manifest. It must be confessed that the force of our remark, so far as it pertains to the change in style and modes of thought, is weakened by the fact that, when the Apocalypse was written, John must have been sixty years old; a period of life after which important changes of this character are less likely to occur. But another consideration is to be taken into the account,—that the mood of mind and feeling out of which the Apocalypse was written was altogether peculiar and extraordinary, as was the state of things in the midst of which the author wrote. The same author, at such a time, when his soul was stirred to its depths by the terrible events, either present or "shortly to come to pass," and writing under the impulse of prophetic inspiration, would fall into quite a different style from one that would be natural in a calmer mood, when his only object was to set down recollections of Christ and his teaching. Moreover, there are not wanting various points of resemblance, both in language and matter, between the two works. To prove this relationship, we have the authority of Baur himself, from whom we translate the following passage: "We cannot ignore the fact that the evangelist put himself in thought in the place of the Apocalypsist, and designed to make use, for the ends aimed at in his Gospel, of the consideration enjoyed by the Apostle John, who, as apostle, as author of the Apocalypse, and as having been for so many years the principal head of their churches, had become the highest authority with the Asia Minor Christians. Nay, it is not merely the borrowing of the external support of so distinguished a name; there are not wanting, also, internal points of affinity between the Gospel and Apocalypse; and one cannot forbear to wonder at the deep geniality, the fine art, with which the Evangelist, in order to transmute spiritually the Apocalypse into the Gospel [um die Apokalypse zum Evangelium zu vergeistigen], has taken up the elements which, from the point of view of the Apocalypse, led to the freer and higher point of view of the Gospel."[1] Now, admitting that so close an inward relationship connects the Gospel with the Apocalypse, why not refer this to the natural development of the author's own mind and the progress of his views, rather than ascribe it to a hateful fraud and lie? If the art of the forger was so clever and admirable, how can we accept Baur's further view, that he has palpably and obviously betrayed

[1] Baur's "*Das Christenthum,*" etc., s. 147, 2d Ed.

himself? Whatever opinion is entertained of the authorship of the Apocalypse, the Tübingen theory is convicted of a gross inconsistency. That both works, the Apocalypse as well as the Gospel, come from the Apostle, is the judgment of Gieseler; and as far as authority is concerned, the confident assertions made on the other side are more than balanced by the calm opinion of this deeply-learned and impartial scholar. Says Gieseler: "the internal difference, in language and modes of thought, between the Apocalypse which John wrote before he had passed beyond the Hebrew training and the Palestinian Jewish Christianity, and the Gospel and the Epistles which he wrote after living from twenty to thirty years among the Greeks, is so inevitable a consequence of the circumstances in which he was placed, that, had this effect not occurred, the fact would have awakened suspicion. And yet there exist in the two works many points of resemblance, and evidences of the continuity of the author's development and culture."[1]

2. But even if it were established that the Apocalypse and the fourth Gospel are not from one author, the verdict must still be given in favor of the genuineness of the Gospel. Bleek agrees, on the whole, with De Wette and Baur in supposing that we are compelled to reject the Johannean authorship of one or the other, and, in common with Neander and many other critics of the evangelical as well as the unbelieving

[1] Gieseler's *K. G.*, B. I. s. 127. N. 8.

school, holds the opinion that the Apocalypse is not the work of John. As we have said, *provided the dilemma can be made out to exist,* this is the reasonable opinion. The Apocalypse has no doubt been in the church since the date we have assigned for its composition. As early as Justin Martyr it was quoted as the work of the Apostle John; but its genuineness was also early questioned. It was questioned not only by the Alogi, but also by the Roman presbyter Caius (circa 200) who likewise ascribed it to Cerinthus.[1] Dionysius of Alexandria, the pupil and successor of Origen, to whose opinion on the style of the Apocalypse we have adverted, endeavors to prove from internal evidence that the Apostle John did not write the work, and is inclined to attribute it to a contemporary of the Apostle at Ephesus, John the presbyter. Eusebius leans to the same opinion. He, also, hesitates about placing it among the Homologoumena, or New Testament writings which were universally received as apostolical.[2] It was not included in the ancient Syrian version. Long after it was received universally in the Western church, doubts concerning its genuineness continued in the East. If written by John the presbyter, "a holy and inspired man," as Dionysius supposes him to be, the later habit of ascribing it to the Apostle, may have been a mistake for which the real author was not respon-

[1] Euseb., Lib. III. c. 28. [2] Euseb., Lib. III. c. 25.

sible. And if the denial of its genuineness sprang from the great reaction of the Church in the second century against Chiliastic views, it was supported, as we have seen in the case of Dionysius, by critical arguments. The evidence for the apostolic authorship of the Apocalypse is far from being equal to the accumulated weight of evidence for the Johannean authorship of the fourth Gospel. For the former, the main proofs of a composition by the Apostle are external. In the case of the fourth Gospel, besides having all that can be asked in the way of external evidence, we are able to add the most impressive internal proofs of its genuineness.

In giving the internal evidence for the genuineness of John, it would be a great oversight to omit a notice of the proof afforded by the last chapter. Every reader of the Gospel will observe that in the last verses of the twentieth chapter the author appears to be concluding his work. It was held by Grotius, with whom agree many living critics on the evangelical side, as well as Zeller and other disciples of the Tübingen school, that the entire twenty-first chapter is from another hand. Others are of opinion that this is true of the last two verses alone. That such is the fact respecting the last verse and the last half of the verse preceding, from the words, "and we know that his testimony is true,"—admits of no rational doubt. The remainder of the chapter bears strong marks of genuineness, although it is not improbable that John added the chapter to his Gospel as a sort of supplement. In any case, it is obvious that the conversation upon the question whether John was to survive until the advent of Christ, would possess no interest and have no pertinency at any time long subsequent to his death. But the concluding verses, regarded, as they must be, in the light of a testimony to the genuineness of the Gospel on the part of the person or persons by whom it was issued, constitute an impressive proof. The fact that this attestation is anonymous indicates that he or they who made it, were well known to those for whom it was designed; it is utterly inconsistent with the supposition of fraud. What meaning or value would an attestation wholly anonymous have possessed, at the first appearance of the Gospel, unless the source whence this testimony proceeded were well known? An impostor would have named the church of Ephesus or its bishop, if he had intended to give a factitious credit to his forgery, by claiming their sanction for it. Suppose this conclusion to have been written by friends to whom John had delivered his Gospel, and from whom it went forth to the world, and the whole phenomenon is explained.

In the preceding pages, various objections from the side of disbelievers in the genuineness of this Gospel have been incidentally considered. Yet the aim has been positively to establish our proposition, with the introduction of no more of polemical matter than seemed indispensable to this end. We now propose to subject the theory of Baur to a more detailed examination.

Baur's Theory Respecting the Authorship of the Fourth Gospel.

To reduce the observations of Baur to a self-consistent hypothesis is not an easy task. In general, however, he holds that the main idea of this Gospel is the development of the unbelief of the Jews in its conflict with the self-manifestation of Christ, until that unbelief culminates in the taking of his life. Baur is not original in supposing this to be a leading thought in the writer's mind. But nothing is thereby proved against the verity of the history, since the actual course of Christ's life *was* attended with the development of a spirit of disbelief, which finally broke out in the great act of violence. But Baur goes farther. He pretends that the history is fictitious and is artificially contrived as a vestment for the idea. This, however, is not the sole idea for which, as it is claimed, the writer weaves a fictitious dress. That faith, in order to be real and of any value, must be self-sustained by an inward power of its own, with no help from outward proof through miracles, is supposed to be another leading thought of the writer; and this, it is pretended, he illustrates by means of invented narrative. Besides, Baur professes to find the traces of Gnostic Dualism in the antithesis of light and darkness, to which the Gospel writer more than once adverts.[1] Sometimes the language of Baur would seem to imply that the Evangelist, misled by the vividness of his own conceptions, actually confounds them with reality. But, notwithstanding an occasional vague expression of this kind, it is Baur's real meaning, as he abundantly explains, that the narratives of the fourth Gospel are intentional fictions composed to embody certain ideas and recommend them to acceptance.

This remarkable hypothesis Baur undertakes to support by exegesis. The character of his interpretations we shall now exhibit to the reader. We should observe that in this department of our inquiry we have derived essential aid from the acute observations of Brückner.

1. There is no truth in the charge that a Dualistic theory is taught in John's Gospel. In connection with every passage which Baur cites, the distinction between light and darkness is declared to be ethical. It is not a physical or metaphysical separation, but is founded in voluntary character. Men remain in darkness "because their deeds are evil;" they *will not* come to the light for fear of being rebuked. See John iii. 19–21; also, compare John viii. 47 with viii. 34, and John xii. 35, 36 with John xii. 43. It is said that "*all things* were made by" the Word, and that

[1] Baur, *Die Kanon. Evangelien*, s. 88, 89.

He "came unto *His own*," i. e., to the Jews (John i. 3, 11). How baseless then is the imputation of a Gnostic Dualism to the Evangelist, in which the Jews, or most of them, are destitute of "the light-nature!"

2. Baur's exposition of the passages relative to John the Baptist is most unnatural. In c. i. 32, 33 there is given the testimony of John the Baptist to the descent of the Spirit, as a dove, upon Jesus. This sign, he said, had been appointed "by Him who sent me to baptize with water." How plain, especially with the narrative of the Synoptics before us, that the recognition of Jesus was at his baptism, which the Evangelist notices here, though it had taken place earlier than the events just before recorded! Yet Baur denies this, and even denies that the passage implies that Jesus was baptized by John! Baur attempts to establish the existence of an artificial chronology—a double trias of days, beginning with c. i. 29 and terminating with c. ii. 12; but we need say no more than that the double trias is made out by assuming a new day, falsely and without the slightest support from the text, at ver. 41. Had the Evangelist contrived the chronological scheme which his critic imputes to him, he would not have omitted to make the division of time at ver. 41, which the critic interpolates.

Baur's treatment of the narrative of the miracle in Cana is extraordinary. Why a circumstantial account of this kind should be deliberately fabricated by such a writer as the Evangelist, is a question not easy to answer. Baur sees in it an allegorical representation of the position of John the Baptist (which is indicated by the water), and the transition to the higher position of Jesus (which is denoted by the wine); together with a further reference to Jesus under the symbol of the bridegroom. Not that the Evangelist means that his readers should regard his narrative as a fiction; he would palm it off on them as fact. But it is the force of "the idea" in his own mind, which moves him to the invention of the story. It is hardly necessary to say that the notion of an allegory is favored by not so much as a hint in the narrative itself; nay, it is excluded by the declaration (in ver. 11) that the end of the miracle was the manifestation of the glory of Christ.

A good illustration of the style of Baur's exegesis is afforded by his comments on John iii. 22, where Jesus is said to have tarried with his disciples and baptized. In the next chapter (John iv. 2), it is incidentally explained that Jesus himself baptized not, but his disciples. That this explanation, omitted in the first passage, should be thrown in afterwards, is nothing strange. But Baur sees in the two passages the proofs of a deep design. The Evangelist, he thinks, would elevate Jesus above John, but would do it gradually, with a kind of artful rhetoric. First, he equalizes the former with the latter, by stating that

Jesus baptized; then, after an interval, he advances a step by adding that Jesus did not (like John) himself baptize, but caused this rite to be performed by his disciples. Such a puerile device is gravely imputed to the artless writer of this Gospel!

3. On other points in the earlier chapters of John, Baur's interpretation will not bear examination. It is represented that the author of the Gospel makes Judæa "the country" of Jesus (John iv. 44); although it is perfectly evident from the context that such is not his meaning, but that he ascribes the increasing admiration of Jesus on the part of the Galileans, his countrymen, to the commotion which he had occasioned at Jerusalem. Nicodemus is pronounced a fictitious character, introduced as a representative of the unbelieving Jews who require miracles, while the woman of Samaria is said to represent the susceptible Gentiles who believe without the need of miracles. Unfortunately for Baur's theory, Nicodemus is *not* described as an unbeliever, but as having some degree of faith, and the Samaritan woman believes in consequence of the evidence which she had of the miraculous knowledge of Christ, by whom she was told all things that ever she did (John iv. 29).

4. The effort of Baur to destroy the credibility of the seventh chapter, a portion of the Gospel which is stamped with irresistible evidence of truth, leads him into still more perverse interpretation. Jesus (ver. 10) went up to the feast, not with his brethren, not openly,

"but as it were in secret"—ὡς ἐν κρυπτῷ. This plain statement, Baur not only twists into a declaration that Jesus made himself, after a Docetic fashion, invisible, but, also, that he presented himself before the Jews in a form different from his own. And this is only one of the misinterpretations which the seventh chapter is made to suffer. Of this misrepresentation of the sense of ὡς ἐν κρυπτῷ, Brückner says: "it is not sustained by the words themselves, it rests upon the false interpretation of vs. 15 and 20, and it is fully refuted by ver. 14, where the public appearance of Christ without any such Docetic transformation is related, as well as by ver. 25, where Jesus is actually recognized by some at the same moment when others do not know him,—so that, if Baur's view were right, he must have taken on a shape which veiled the identity of his person from some, while it was disclosed to others." Baur's treatment of the entire chapter, Brückner has well exposed. "According to Baur," says this able critic, "the theological end (tendency) to be accomplished by the seventh chapter is to show how the dialectics into which unbelief enters carry their own dialectical refutation; and in this way, that Jesus in three different sorts of self-manifestation confronts the unbelief of the Jews: in the first, ἐν κρυπτῷ; in the second, at ver. 28; in the third, at vs. 37 seq. This whole arrangement by Baur breaks to pieces on the correct interpretation of ver. 10, which refers to no appearance of Christ before the Jews, such as Baur pretends to be referred to by the ἐν κρυπτῷ; it, also, clashes with the fact that the favorable inclination of the *people* to Jesus (vs. 12, 31, 40, 41) is just as often brought forward, as is the unbelief of the Jews; it ignores the distinction between "the people" (ὄχλος) and the Rulers, which runs through the whole chapter, and which greatly influences the words of Christ, as well as the replies to him and the judgment concerning them; it robs the narrative, in which the Evangelist is much more concerned with things done than with things said, of its life; and it imputes to the Evangelist purposes which are nowhere indicated, and have no more plausibility than a great many others which might be suggested with an equal or greater show of justice."[1] If we could reasonably ascribe to the author of the Gospel any "tendency," it would be more rational to say that he designed to set forth the schism between the people and the rulers, and even among the rulers themselves, than to exhibit the unbelief of the Jews as a body. And Baur's exegesis of this chapter may serve as a touchstone of his theory. He is under the necessity of finding in this, as in every other narrative in the Gospel, some occult design, "the idea," which sways the writer in the contrivance of his alleged fiction. To explain the narrative in detail conformably to this theory is found quite impossible, without a resort to the most fanciful and violent interpretation.

[1] Brückner's De Wette, s. 139, 140.

5. Baur would have us believe that the Evangelist has made up various tales and conversations in order to exhibit a particular conception of faith and of unbelief. Thus, the belief of the Samaritans and the belief of the nobleman (John iv. 39, 50) are designed, we are assured, to commend a faith which is founded on the words of Christ, instead of on miracles. It is impossible not to see the difference of the two cases. The faith of the Samaritans was first awakened by the saying—*διὰ τὸν λόγον*—of the woman: "He told me all that ever I did." It rested on belief in her testimony to the exhibition of miraculous knowledge. The nobleman, on the contrary, believed the word—*τῷ λόγῳ*—of Jesus; that is, credited a particular declaration; and he "believed," at least was assured in his faith, after the miracle and in consequence of it, ver. 53. Equally fanciful is Baur's notion that the design of the sixth chapter is to depict the manner in which a faith that is produced by miracles, shows itself a mere semblance of faith; that the allusion to Judas (vi. 64) is to show how a perverse will becomes likewise the mere counterfeit of faith; that the inquiry, "have any of the Rulers or the Pharisees believed on him," is put into the mouth of the Pharisees and Priests for the purpose of presenting the climax of unbelief, when it rests upon no grounds at all! The case of Thomas is considered by Baur to be a fiction to illustrate the doctrine that faith, when based on sight, is no faith. But Jesus does not say that

Thomas has *no* faith; he says the opposite. He says, "because thou hast seen, *thou hast believed*," and then exalts the faith of those who have not seen. But these last are not those who believe without evidence, but who believe on the evidence of testimony, which Thomas (ver. 25) had refused to do. That Baur's interpretation of the Evangelist's design is false, the verses immediately following the account of the skepticism of Thomas decisively prove: "Many other signs truly did Jesus.... but these are written, *that ye might believe that Jesus is the Christ, the Son of God.*"

6. Certain circumstances in the narrative of John which to an unprejudiced reader afford irresistible evidence of its historical truth, are construed by this hostile and suspicious criticism into proofs of sinister, mendacious contrivance. For example, the anointing of the eyes of the blind man with clay (c. ix. 6) is pronounced an invention to make the breaking of the Sabbath more marked; and the delays and reluctance of Pilate, which are so true to nature, are fabricated to enhance the guilt of the Jews in condemning him. In the same spirit Baur charges that the hearing of Jesus before Annas is a fabrication to heighten the guilt of the Jews; although John does not stop to record the actual condemnation of Jesus by either Annas or Caiaphas, and a careful examination of his narrative (comp. John xviii. 24 with vs. 18, 25, 28) shows that the denials of Peter took place after Jesus was led away from Annas to Caiaphas, so that nothing

that occurred in the interview with the former is recorded. One of the most extravagant specimens of the Tübingen method of criticism is the notion that in this Gospel there is a studied depreciation of Peter.[1] The honor put upon Peter by his Master's solemn charge (John xxi. 15, 18), an incident recorded by no other evangelist, would seem to be a sufficient refutation of a charge which rests on trivial grounds. It is even affirmed by these critics that in John xviii. 26, where one of the servants who interrogated Peter is characterized as a kinsman of the person "whose ear Peter cut off," the Evangelist goes out of his way to bring in an act discreditable to Peter; an act, too, which these critics also say is falsely attributed to him. A double falsification is thus laid to the charge of the Evangelist, and in one instance, at least, a very cunning falsification. Our readers must judge whether thoughts like these really had their birth in the mind of the Evangelist, or only in the mind of his critic.

7. Baur dwells with much emphasis on the account of the piercing of the side of the crucified Jesus by a soldier's lance, as a passage fully sustaining his hypothesis respecting the general character of the Gospel, and in particular his theory that the author dates the crucifixion on the morning before the occurrence of the Jewish passover-meal, in order to make that event coincide chronologically with the slaying of the passover-lamb. Having said that the soldiers did not

[1] Baur, s. 323.

break the legs of Christ, but that one of them pierced his side, probably in order to assure himself that he was dead, as he appeared to be, the Evangelist adds (John xix. 36, 37): "these things were done that the scripture should be fulfilled, 'a bone of him shall not be broken.' And again another scripture saith, 'they shall look on him whom they pierced.'" Now this passage is *all* that the Gospel says which can be thought to imply a similitude between Christ and the slain lamb of the passover.[1] We are willing to concede that such an analogy is here implied, in the circumstance that the bones of Christ were not broken. But the attention of the Evangelist is more drawn to the fact that predictions are fulfilled (see ver. 37), irrespective of the thought that thereby Jesus was exhibited as the Passover-Lamb; and his interest is still greater in the surprising fact that water with blood flowed from the wound in his side. Had it been a leading purpose on his part to set forth a parallelism between the crucifixion and the slaying of the lamb, a purpose so prominent in his mind as to lead him to contradict the received authorities by misdating Christ's death, it is impossible that the analogy should have been suggested in so cursory and incidental a way. He would infallibly have made his theological idea clear and conspicuous. The Apostle Paul himself,

[1] The exclamation of the Baptist (John i. 29) refers to the conception of the Messiah which was drawn from Isaiah liii., and not to the lamb of the passover.

who, according to Baur, undoubtedly placed the death of Jesus on the morning *after* the Jewish passover-meal, brings forward even more explicitly the same analogy which John is supposed to suggest, and probably does suggest, in the passage on which we are commenting. Paul says (1 Cor. v. 7): "for even Christ, our Passover, is sacrificed for us." It is worthy of note that the same thought which is innocent when suggested by Paul, is made to bear so tremendous a burden of consequences when suggested by the Evangelist. The reader will not forget that this passage in John in respect to the piercing of the body of Christ by the soldier's lance, is accompanied by a solemn asseveration of its truth, the Evangelist—for it is of himself that the writer speaks—professing to have been an eyewitness (c. xix. 35). It is curious to inquire how Baur disposes of this passage, which if it be false, must be held to resemble very closely wilful lying, notwithstanding the disquisitions of the Tübingen critics about anonymity, the license allowed to literary forgery in the old time, and "the power of the idea." Baur's language, in commenting on this asseveration of the Evangelist, is unusually hazy. He appears to say that it is only the truth of the intuition that Christ in dying opened the fulness of spiritual life for the believing world, which "the Evangelist testifies to with the immediate certainty of his Christian consciousness." It cannot be Baur's intention to say that the Evangelist does not design to make his readers believe in the objective facts which he here records; and yet the critic shrinks, with a somewhat commendable feeling, from distinctly charging him with conscious mendacity. It will be plain to every unsophisticated mind that what is called "the might of the idea," granting that such a force was operative in the Evangelist's mind, would lead no one but a liar deliberately to affirm that he had seen a certain person struck with a lance by a soldier, when he had not.

8. It would be easy to multiply from Baur's treatise examples of what we cannot but consider a wholly improbable, and even forced, exegesis of passages in this Gospel. For the present discussion, however, it is only essential to notice his interpretations so far as they are employed to sustain his leading hypothesis. Yet, we cannot forbear to mention one or two additional instances of this unnatural construction of the Evangelist's words. The critic finds in the reply of the risen Jesus to the salutation of Mary: "go unto my brethren, and say unto them, I ascend unto my Father," an expression of the purpose of Christ to ascend on the instant; and, according to Baur, that he *did* then and there ascend, is the Evangelist's idea. It is hardly necessary to say that the present tense of the verb does not at all confine us to this strange inference, which is contradicted by vs. 26, 27. It is obviously the idea of the Evangelist that Christ had been on the earth up to the time of his meeting Mary (vs. 1–17), which of itself overthrows

Baur's notion that he is represented as ascending immediately on his rising from the dead. A signal instance of a similar style of exegesis, as well as illustration of the embarrassment in which Baur involves himself in his arraignment of the Evangelist, is the explanation he gives of John xiv. 31, a passage which we have adduced in proof of the fidelity of the Evangelist's report of the discourses of Christ: "Arise, let us go hence" (*ἐγείρεσθε, ἄγωμεν*). These words, which were doubtless a current phrase, happen to be used by Christ, according to Matt. xxvi. 46, in another connection. The author of John, says Baur, found them in the Synoptics and introduced them at this place, in order *to make a pause!* It happens that a pause is made without this phrase, which in any event would be perfectly inapposite to the purpose. As far as we can see, the Evangelist might as well be conceived to introduce the fragment of a genealogy for the sake of making a transition to a new topic, as a phrase like this.

These curiosities of interpretation remind us of the incongruous representations of the Tübingen criticism in regard to the relation of the Evangelist to the synoptical writers. All concede that the fourth Gospel, in structure and contents, has the character of an independent narrative. This independence the Tübingen critics, in many instances, exaggerate into an intended contradiction, and a seemingly needless contradiction on essential points. Yet they affirm, in the same breath, that even on these points where the Evangelist wantonly breaks loose from the synoptical authorities, he slavishly borrows from them. It is in imitation of the synoptical writers that John makes Jesus visit Jerusalem to attend festivals; yet he does not scruple to contradict them in multiplying the number of these visits: he takes from the other Gospels the circumstance of the scourging in the temple, but transfers it from the end to the beginning of his ministry: he is dependent on the same writers for much that is said of John's baptism "with water," and his recognition of Jesus (John i. 31, 35), and yet implies that Jesus was not baptized. For these and numerous other supposed deviations from the Synoptics, the critics are able to assign no sufficient reasons. The Synoptics might have been followed, and the ends attributed to the Evangelist equally well secured. The Tübingen pretension is most inconsistent when single words and scraps of sentences are alleged to be borrowed from the first three Gospels, although the passages where they are found in the Evangelist are, in their matter, original and wholly independent of those Gospels. A good example is the passage, "Arise, let us go hence" (John xiv. 31), which has already been referred to. Sometimes Baur is obliged to fall back on hypotheses more characteristic of Strauss, in order to provide his readers with some explanation of the narratives of miracles. Thus, the raising of Lazarus is to present an exertion of miraculous power, which is a grade above the case, in the Synoptics, of the raising of the son of the widow of Nain. Of course, not a particle of proof is vouchsafed in support of this empty conjecture. Again, Baur contends that the narrative of the healing of the nobleman's son (John iv. 46 seq.) is a copy or imitation of the narrative in Matt. viii. 5 seq. of the cure of the centurion's servant. Baur supposes that the former narrative was to prove the superiority, in the judgment of Christ, of a faith which rests on his word alone; and he further supposes that a constant aim of the fourth Gospel is to covertly extol the susceptibility of the Gentiles, in contrast with the unbelief of the Jews. Now in Matthew's narrative (Matt. viii.), Jesus is represented to have marvelled at the centurion's faith, and to have said: "Verily I say unto you, I have not found so great faith, no, not in Israel!" If the author of John were following Matthew's narrative, this would be the most welcome and the most apposite passage in the whole of it. Yet he omits it altogether! Can a hypothesis receive a more complete overthrow than is experienced by that of Baur concerning this portion of John?

We have judged it desirable thus to sift the interpretations of the Tübingen critics, for the sake of thoroughly acquainting our readers with the character of the arguments which are relied upon in the assault upon the genuineness of this Gospel. Be it remembered that all this unsound, artificial interpretation is indispensable to the success of their cause. A correspondence must be found between the various incidents, conversations, discourses, in John and the theological "tendency" which has the credit of fabricating them. A failure to detect this correspondence, in the detailed investigation of the Gospel, and by a fair exegesis of it, is the downfall of the entire theory, even if there were nothing else to be said against it. That such a failure is justly attributable to the critic, the foregoing examination has sufficiently evinced.

In a previous part of this Essay, we have remarked upon the proofs of an interest in the history as such—a genuine historical feeling—on the part of the author of this Gospel. These are proofs which, being obviously undesigned features in the narrative, are peculiarly impressive. And since the variations in John from the synoptical Gospels can be accounted for on no such theory as that of the Tübingen critics, we are authorized in pronouncing them evidences of the faithful recollection of the Evangelist. Let the reader examine his account of the baptism of Jesus and the testimony to Jesus by the Baptist (John i. 19–37); his record of the calling of the apostles (John i. 35–43); his description of the designation of the traitor, at the last supper (John xiii. 21–30); his narrative of the denials of Peter (John xviii. 15

seq.); his specification of the dates of the supper and the crucifixion; his relation of the circumstances attending the last journey of Jesus to Jerusalem. Let the reader compare the Evangelist in these places with corresponding passages in the Synoptics, and he will feel that he has in his hands an independent and accurately informed historian.

When Baur, leaving the special criticism of the Gospel, proceeds to state his conception of the character and motives of the author of this extraordinary composition, he betrays, if we mistake not, in his lowered, apologetic tone, some feeling of embarrassment. What conception have the Tübingen critics of the writer of this Gospel? He was a man, as Baur says, of remarkable mind, of an elevated spirit, and penetrated with a warm, adoring faith in Christ as the Son of God and Saviour of the world. That faith must have been founded on the evangelical history. At least, it must have involved a reverential sense of the sacredness of that history. How could such a man *fabricate* a life of his Master, as a substitute for the authentic lives with which he was acquainted? How could he pervert, distort, falsify transactions, with the reality of which his holiest feelings were bound up; artfully assuming to be an apostle and confidant of the Lord, for the sake of ascribing to him discourses that he never uttered and deeds that he never performed! Baur compares the

Evangelist with the Apostle Paul.[1] He, says Baur, was not one of the original disciples. It was only through visions that he personally knew Christ. And Baur draws a deliberate parallel between the Apostle to the Gentiles, and the unknown but gifted and ardently believing author of this Gospel. The comparison is an unhappy one for his theory. Imagine the Apostle Paul sitting down to fabricate a fictitious history of the Saviour! Imagine him casting away the authentic deeds and words of Christ and inventing in the room of them a fictitious tale of his life! The thought of so sacrilegious an act could never occur to his earnest soul. Had it been suggested by another, with what indignation and horror would he have repelled the proposal! No reader of the Pauline Epistles will have a doubt on this point. Yet an imposture even more flagrant is attributed to the author of the fourth Gospel, for he claims to be a companion of Christ; while at the same time his accusers associate him with Paul, as a counterpart in intellectual and moral qualities, and in the depth and ardor of his faith in the Lord. The religionists, weak-minded and of obscure moral perceptions, who are responsible for the clumsy fabrications found in the apocryphal Gospels, for the most part confined themselves to those periods of Christ's life where the canonical authors are silent, such as the infancy of the Lord. They sought to connect with the authentic narratives

[1] Baur's *Kan. Evangelien*, s. 384.

their silly inventions. It was reserved for the writer of the fourth Gospel to attain to that pitch of audacity, or that confusion as to the distinction between truth and falsehood, which qualified him to extend his cleverly executed fraud over the whole contents of the evangelical history. And yet he was one fit to be placed in the same category with Paul!

It is incredible that a work of the power and loftiness of the fourth Gospel should have sprung up in the second century. Let any one who would understand the difference between the apostolic and the next following age undertake to read the Apostolic Fathers. He will be conscious at once that he has passed into another atmosphere. He has descended from the heights of inspiration to the level of ordinary, and often feeble, thinking. In the first half of the second century there is no writer of marked originality; none who can be called fresh or suggestive. To set a work like the fourth Gospel in that age is a literary anachronism. That a writer, towering so above all his contemporaries, should stoop to wear a mask, and gain his end by a hateful, jesuitical contrivance, is a supposition burdened with difficulties. The irrational character of this hypothesis, Neander has well shown in a passage which is valuable alike for its thoughts and for the source whence they come, and with which we conclude the present Essay.

"The whole development of the Church from Justin Martyr onward testifies to the presence of such a Gospel, which operated powerfully on men's minds. It cannot be explained from any single mental tendency in the following age, nor from the amalgamation of several. To be sure, this production existed as a representation of a higher unity, as a reconciling element with reference to the contrarieties of that age, and could exert an attractive power over minds of so opposite a kind as a Heracleon, a Clement of Alexandria, an Irenæus, and a Tertullian. Where should we be able to find in that age a man who was elevated above its contrarieties of opinion [Gegensätze], by which everything is more or less swayed? And a man of so superior a Christian soul, must needs skulk in the dark, avail himself of such a mask, instead of appearing openly in the consciousness of all-conquering truth and in the feeling of his mental preëminence! Such a man, so exalted above all the church Fathers of that century, had no need, forsooth, to shrink from the conflict. He must certainly have put more confidence in the might of truth than in these arts of darkness and falsehood. And how can it be shown that such a man, when he is contemplated from the point of view of his own age, would have been restrained by no reverence for sacred history, by no scruples, from falsifying a history, the contents of which were holy to him, through arbitrary fictions, manufactured in the interest of a given dogmatic tendency,—through lies, in fact, which were to find their justification in the end to be attained by means of them? And how unskilfully would he have proceeded if, in order to attain his end, he presented the history of Christ in a way that was in absolute contrast with the universally accepted tradition? Nay, only from such an apostle, who stood in such a relation to Christ as a John stood, who had thus taken up into his own being the impression and image of that unique personality, could proceed a work which stands in such a relation to the contrarieties of the post-apostolic age. It is a work out of one gush, original throughout. The Divine in its own nature has this power of composing differences, but never could a product so fresh, so original in its power [urkräftiges], proceed from a contrived, shrewdly planned, reconciliation of differences. This Gospel, if it do not emanate from the Apostle John and point to that Christ, the intuition of whom, on the part of the writer, gave birth to it, is the greatest of enigmas."[1]

[1] Neander's *Geschichte d. Pflanz. u. Leit. der Kirche*, 4 A. B. 2, s. 637

ESSAY III.

RECENT DISCUSSIONS UPON THE ORIGIN OF THE FIRST THREE GOSPELS.

THE characteristics which belong in common to the first three Gospels, and distinguish them from the Gospel of John, we suppose to be familiar to the reader. The first three Gospels—the Synoptics—dwell chiefly upon the Galilean ministry of Jesus. Compared with John, they are less heedful of the chronological order. In truth, the chronological outline of the Saviour's ministry can be gathered from the fourth Gospel alone. The Synoptics not only have a large amount of matter in common, but their consonance in phraseology extends too far to be the result of accident; at the same time that the divergences, existing side by side with this resemblance, equally demand an explanation. This mingled divergence and coincidence have put to the test the ingenuity of critics. One general theory is that of an original Gospel, existing prior to the three, but revised or enlarged by each historian independently. But this theory has two branches, there being some who hold that the original Gospel was a written work, whilst others consider it a mass of oral tradition which had acquired a fixed form. The other general theory is that of a priority on the part of one of the evangelists, the use of whose work by a successor gives occasion to the peculiarity in question. But the various hypotheses which have been brought forward under this theory, or the different views as to the order in which the Gospels were written, exhaust the possibilities of supposition. They form, in fact, an example in permutation. Matthew, Luke, and Mark, was the series in the hypothesis of Griesbach, which has been extensively followed. Another set of critics are equally confident that the precedence in age belongs to Mark.[1] Others, again, are satisfied with neither of these views. The long-continued diversity of opinion on the subject is a sign of the difficulty of the problem. This problem we do not propose to discuss in the present Essay. We might even waive the question whether these three narratives were composed by the persons to whom they are respectively ascribed, were it not that this question cannot be wholly disconnected from the proposition which we deem to be of prime importance. Could it be shown, as is maintained by some critics who accept the narrative as substantially historical and credible, that the first Gospel was not written by Matthew, the proposition with which we are at present concerned, would

[1] For a full classification of critical opinions on this subject, see Meyer's *Einleitung* to the first volume of his commentary on the N. T., or Holtzmann's recent work, *Die Synoptische Evangelien.*

not be seriously affected. What, then, *is* the question of fundamental importance, on which the credibility of the Gospel history turns?

The main thing which the skeptical school seeks to accomplish, as far as the first three Gospels are concerned, is to bring down their date into the post-apostolic age. History is testimony. The credibility of testimony depends—supposing that those who give it wish to tell the truth—on their means of information. The credibility of the Gospels is conditioned on the fact that they emanate either from actual witnesses of the events recorded, or from well-informed contemporaries. If it could be established that these narratives were drawn up long after the actors in the events, and the generation contemporaneous with them, had passed away—that they comprise floating stories and traditions which were gathered up at or after the end of the century in which Christ and his immediate disciples, and those who heard their teaching, lived—their historical value might well be called in question. To support some hypothesis of this kind, or at least to throw a mist of uncertainty over the whole question of the origin and date of the Gospels, is the end and aim of skeptical criticism. We, on our part, maintain that nothing has been brought forward in behalf of the skeptical cause, which tends to weaken the established view that the Gospels belong to the apostolic age, embody the testimony of the eyewitnesses and earwitnesses of the life of Christ, and come down to us with the seal and sanction of the apostolic Church.

We are not required to review in detail the proofs of the early date of these histories. It will be sufficient to examine the grounds on which the received view is sought to be impugned. It may be well, however, to remind the reader, in a few words, of the nature of the proof which has been relied on for establishing the early origin of the first three Gospels —as it is these which we are now to consider. Every fair and discerning reader must feel how well the whole tone and style of these writings comport with the belief that they emanate from the first age of Christianity. Galilee is reflected in them in a thousand indefinable touches. *Christ*—to mention a single peculiarity—has not come to be an habitual name of the Saviour, as it begins to be even in the Epistles and in John, but is purely an official title. In these Gospels he is simply called Jesus. For the early date of the first three Gospels, we have the unanimous voice of Christian antiquity. They are considered and declared by the early Church to be authoritative productions handed down from the apostolic age. We find in the writers of the post-apostolic period no other conception of the life and ministry of Christ than is presented in the canonical Gospels. We meet here and there with a saying of Christ or an incident in his life which they would seem to have derived from some other source of knowledge; but these exceptions are so very few and unimportant as to render the prevailing fact of the coincidence between the representation of the Fathers and that of the Gospels the more striking. The apostolic Fathers do not formally state the sources whence their quotations are drawn. They commonly bring forward a fact of the Saviour's life or a passage of his teaching, without formal reference to the authority from which they derived it. Nor do they evince any care for verbal accuracy. But the apostolic Fathers, the contemporaries and survivors of the apostles, contain many passages which are unmistakably drawn from the synoptical Gospels. The peculiar method of introducing New Testament passages favors the supposition that they quote from recognized documents. At least in one important passage, an authoritative written source is expressly referred to. Barnabas remarks:[1] "Let us therefore beware, lest it should happen to us *as it is written:* there are many called, few chosen." This quotation, which is found in Matt. xx. 16 and xxii. 14, is introduced by the same phrase which the Jews made use of in citing from their sacred books. Barnabas referred to some book having a like authority among Christians, and in no other book of this class except our Matthew is the passage found. The value of this quotation as a decisive proof that, when it was made, the Gospel of Matthew

[1] c. iv. Whether the Epistle of Barnabas be genuine or not, it is certainly very early.

was clothed with canonical authority, has been fully established by the recent discovery of the Greek text of Barnabas in the Codex Sinaiticus. By this document the phrase, *it is written,* is proved to be a part of the original, and not an addition of the Latin translator, as Credner and others had been inclined to maintain. The Epistle of Barnabas belongs in the early part of the second century. That a canon of the New Testament had begun to be formed, is also clearly indicated by this manner of quotation. That Matthew did not stand as the sole Gospel in this canon, Tischendorf has argued on good grounds.[1] The drift of the evidence points to the conclusion that the four Gospels enjoyed then the preëminence which they bear in Justin and the writers that follow him. This we know, that the long scrutiny which has been directed to the quotations in Justin has established, beyond all reasonable doubt, the fact of a use by him of all of our canonical Gospels. And Justin was born a little more than ten years before the end of the first century, and less than twenty years after the capture of Jerusalem, and at a time when the Apostle John was probably still living. From Matthew and Luke especially, his citations are very numerous.

Let us now take up the Synoptics in their order, commencing with

[1] See Tischendorf, *Wann wurden die Evangelien verfasst?* p. 42 seq.

MATTHEW.

I. We begin with an examination of the testimony of Papias, which, in respect to both Matthew and Mark, is most valuable, and has properly attracted the earnest attention of modern critics. Renan builds upon this testimony, or rather upon his misconception of it, his theory respecting the origin of the Gospels. Scholars of every school unite in their estimate of the importance to be attached to this piece of evidence.

Papias was bishop of Hierapolis, in Phrygia, in the first half of the second century. He is described by Irenaeus[1] as "an ancient man," a contemporary and friend of Polycarp, who was a disciple of John the Evangelist. Irenaeus also states that Papias had himself heard the Apostle John, but Eusebius considers that Irenaeus errs in this particular by wrongly interpreting the language of Papias. But Papias says of himself that he made inquiries of many persons who had been familiar with the apostles, and he was certainly acquainted with John the Presbyter, who was a contemporary of John the Apostle at Ephesus. Partly, but not wholly, on account of his millenarian views, so offensive to Eusebius, Papias is pronounced by the latter a man of inferior talents. But however moderate his intellectual powers, he was justly regarded as an honest witness or reporter of what he

[1] Quoted in Euseb., *H. E.*, Lib. iii. c. 39.

had seen and heard.[1] He reports what he had received from companions of the apostles. He busied himself with gathering up from oral tradition the declarations of the apostles, which he published, with comments of his own, in a work consisting of five books. From this work, Eusebius presents us with the following extract:

"And John the Presbyter said this: 'Mark being the interpreter of Peter wrote accurately whatever he remembered, though indeed not [setting down] in order what was said or done by Christ, for he did not hear the Lord, nor did he follow him: but afterwards, as I said, [he followed] Peter, who adapted his discourses to the necessities of the occasion, but not so as to furnish a systematic account of the oracles of the Lord (*κυριακῶν λογίων* or *λόγων*); so that Mark committed no fault when he wrote some things as he recollected them. For of one thing he took care—to pass by nothing which he heard, and not to falsify in anything.'" "Such," adds Eusebius, "is the relation in Papias concerning Mark. But of Matthew this is said: 'Matthew wrote the oracles (*τὰ λόγια*) in the Hebrew tongue; and every one interpreted them as he was able.'"

[1] The often-quoted passage in Papias relative to the colossal grapes to be expected in the Millennial age awakens no doubt as to his veracity. It only shows that apocryphal sayings of Christ were early set in circulation, and by its contrast with the style of the canonical Gospels, confirms their veracity.

The passage had always been considered, up to a recent date, as referring to our Gospels of Matthew and Mark. It was suggested, however, by Schleiermacher that the *logia*, which we have rendered oracles, signifies only *discourses;* and hence a number of critics, including the distinguished commentator, Meyer, have founded upon this testimony of Papias the opinion that at the basis of our first Gospel, and prior to it, was a collection by Matthew of the teachings of Christ, and that the canonical Gospel was the product of a subsequent addition of narrative matter to that earlier work.

We believe this restriction of the sense of *logia*, in the passage, to be unauthorized and erroneous, and that the old interpretation of Papias, the interpretation which Eusebius evidently gave the passage, is the true one. It is well, however, to see how the case stands, provided the term receives the limited meaning which these critics affix to it. Papias, in what he says of Matthew, does not quote the Presbyter; yet it may safely be concluded that he derived this information from the same earlier authorities whence the rest of his work was drawn.

The principal remark we have to make here is, that even supposing *logia* to mean *discourses* simply, yet Papias is speaking, as Meyer concedes and maintains, aoristically—of something that had occurred at a former time, but was no longer the fact. That is, when he says that "every one interpreted the

Hebrew Matthew as he could"—ἡρμήνευσε δʼ αὐτὰ ὡς ἠδύνατο ἕκαστος—he means, and implies in his language, that the necessity of rendering the Hebrew into the Greek *had* once existed, to be sure, but existed no longer. Why not? Evidently because the *Greek* Matthew was now in the hands of Christians. This Greek Matthew which Papias and his contemporaries used, was unquestionably our first Gospel in its present form. Our Greek Matthew is represented by the Fathers to be a *translation* of a Hebrew Gospel. If we admit the correctness of the tradition, then, as Meyer shows, the Hebrew Matthew must have received its supplement of narrative matter, and in its complete form been generally connected with the name of this apostle, before the Greek version was made. The hypothesis that this Gospel received essential changes or additions of matter, subsequent to the time of Papias, is excluded by an overwhelming weight of evidence. There is, indeed, other and sufficient proof that our Matthew existed in its present form within thirty or forty years of the Saviour's death. But independently of this proof, and even when the sense of *logia* is limited, the testimony of Papias himself—still more, if that testimony emanates, as is probably the fact, from pupils of apostles whom he had consulted—carries back the date of our Matthew, in its present form, into the apostolic age.

But if *logia* cover the narrative matter as well as the discourses, and if Papias thus refers to the Gospel of Matthew as we have it, the early origin of the Gospel is explicitly attested.

That such is the real purport of the *logia* is apparent from the following considerations:

1. The word is capable of this more extended import. It denotes *sacred words—oracles;* and with its kindred terms has this meaning not only in ecclesiastical writers, but also in the New Testament. It is probably used in Heb. v. 12 as an equivalent for the whole *Christian revelation.* The restriction of its meaning by Meyer, in this place, is opposed by other good critics, including Bleek.[1] We have a clear example in Luke i. 4: "that thou mightest know the certainty of those things—λόγων—wherein thou hast been instructed." Luke writes a consecutive history of the life and ministry of Jesus in order to assure Theophilus of the certainty of the things which were believed among Christians, and had been taught him. The contents of the Gospel of Luke which follows,

[1] λόγια is used for the Old Testament—the whole revelation of God—in Romans iii. 2. Other passages where the word is found, are Wisdom xvi. 11 (comp. v. 5); Acts vii. 38; 1 Peter iv. 11. For the sense of the word in ecclesiastical writers, see Suidas *sub voce;* also Wettstein, T. ii. p. 36. Important illustrative passages are Ignatius ad Smyr. c. iii, and the classification of the Scriptures by Ephraem Syrus (in Photius). In this last place, τὰ κυριακὰ λόγια seems to be plainly a designation of the Gospels. We may observe here, that even if the sense of *logia* in Papias were, philologically considered, doubtful, the existence of another work than our Matthew, for which there is not a particle of evidence from any other source, could not be inferred from a single doubtful expression.

constitute the *logoi.* Even Meyer allows that the narrative matter is included in the word, though indirectly. The objection of Credner, that the application of the term *logia,* in the sense of divine words, to the New Testament writings, presupposes a view of their inspiration which was not prevalent so early as the time of Papias, has, in our judgment, no validity. The reverence of Papias for the declarations of the apostles, which breathes through the whole passage in Eusebius, accords well with such a mode of characterizing them. The form of the quotation from Matthew in Barnabas, on which we have commented above, shows the error of Credner's opinion. The whole of the apostles' testimony in regard to the teachings and works of Christ, constituted the *logia*—the oracles of the Lord, or the oracles pertaining to the Lord.[1]

2. It is well-nigh certain that in the account which Papias gives of *Mark's* Gospel, the *logia* includes the works as well as words of Christ. Papias attributes a want of order to Mark's record of the words and works of Christ—the things "said or done" by Him. He then proceeds to explain the reason of this peculiarity. Mark had derived his information from listening to the discourses of Peter. But Peter was in the habit

[1] It has been thought by some that the works and words of Christ were termed the "*logia* of the Lord," as being the total expression which He made of Himself. But this is less natural. Nor do we think that other critics are right in referring the *logia* to the discourses, as being the *predominant feature* of the gospel, or the feature with which Papias was chiefly concerned.

of selecting his matter to suit the occasion, and therefore did not furnish a systematic statement of the *logia* of the Lord.[1] How can the *logia* here denote anything less than "the things said *or done?*" Papias adds, that in writing some things according to his recollection, Mark committed no fault. Even here Meyer's lexical scrupulosity would fain limit the *logia* to the discourses of Christ, and then make the "some things," which Mark set down without following the chronological order, relate only to this part of his reports. But this interpretation is obviously strained, and appears to be directly overthrown by the circumstance that Papias attributes the absence of order to Mark's reports of the *deeds* as well as the words of Christ. Why should Peter observe the chronological order more carefully in referring to incidents in the life of Christ, than in recalling his discourses? That *logia* has the comprehensive meaning in the description of Matthew, is thus proved by the extended sense which we are under the necessity of attributing to it in the passage that follows respecting Mark.

3. If the *logia* do not embrace the whole of Matthew, then Papias furnishes no account of the origin of the Gospel, with the exception of that part of it which includes the discourses of Christ. He had in his hands, as Meyer and all sound critics admit, our complete Gospel of Matthew. It would be natural for him, if he began to give an account of its origin,

[1] The reading of Heinichen here is λόγων; but λογίων is the reading adopted by other good critics. See Meyer and Bleek.

to explain how the *narrative* portions of the Gospel were brought into it. Eusebius takes it for granted that Papias is explaining the origin of the canonical Gospel of Matthew, and for this reason cites the passage. Neither Eusebius nor any writer before him, nor any writer for fifteen centuries after him, knew anything of a collection of discourses of Matthew, or of any work of Matthew, save the entire canonical Gospel which bears his name.

4. Irenaeus, whom Meyer elsewhere[1] pronounces an independent witness on the subject, says that Matthew wrote his Gospel in the Hebrew. Irenaeus gives the same tradition which is given by Papias, who was an old man when Irenaeus was a youth. Irenaeus knows nothing of a composition of a report of the Saviour's discourses by the Apostle Matthew, which received a narrative supplement from some later hand. The other writers of the second century are equally ignorant of a fact which, if it be contained in the testimony of Papias, must have been generally known.

5. The work of Papias himself was entitled an Exposition of the Oracles (λογίων) of the Lord. But, as we know from the fragments that remain, it was partly made up of narrative matter. Incidents in the life of Christ, and teachings of Christ, equally found a place in this work. Meyer, unjustifiably as we think, would make the narrative matter in Papias a part, not of the *logia*, but of the Exposition attached to the *logia*. The truth seems to be that Papias gathered up

[1] Meyer's *Einl. z. Matthaus*, s. 5.

all that he could hear of what the disciples of Christ had reported of him, and accompanied this record with observations of his own.

We are persuaded, and we trust that the considerations above presented will convince our readers, that this restriction of the sense of *logia*, which goes no farther back than Schleiermacher, and is a subtlety that escaped Eusebius and Irenaeus, is without any good foundation. And we are brought to the conclusion that the testimony of Papias, that "ancient man," who had been conversant with many of the disciples of the apostles, establishes the fact of the origin of the first Gospel in the apostolic age.

II. The relation of the Gospel of Matthew to the uncanonical Gospel of the Hebrews, affords proof of the early date of the former.

The Gospel of the Hebrews, written in the Aramaic dialect, was the most widely known of all the uncanonical Gospels. It was the Gospel in use among the Hebrew Christian sects, which were separated from the general Church. It existed, however, in varying forms. Thus, the stricter Ebionites had cut off the first two chapters, in which the circumstances attending the miraculous birth of the Saviour were related. The numerous allusions in the Fathers to the Gospel of the Hebrews—the *εὐαγγέλιον καθ' Ἑβραίους*—make it clear that it had a close resemblance to the canonical Matthew. A careful comparison demonstrates that it was our Matthew, altered and amplified. That the priority belongs to the canonical Gospel—whether it existed originally in the Hebrew or the Greek, we will not now inquire—is established. For example, in the Latin translation of Origen's commentary on Matthew, there is quoted from the Gospel of the Hebrews a narrative of the conversation of the young man with Jesus, a passage corresponding to Matthew xix. 16 seq. The young man, as in Matthew, comes to Jesus with his question as to the method of attaining eternal life. Jesus tells him to obey the law *and the prophets.* "He replies, 'I have done so.' Jesus said unto him, 'come, sell all that thou hast and divide among the poor, and come, follow me.' But the rich man *began to scratch his head*, and was not pleased," etc. No one can doubt in regard to such a passage, that it springs from the amplification of the simple narrative in Matthew. The narrative is spun out with apocryphal details.[1]

We are concerned to ascertain, next, the age of the Gospel of the Hebrews. It was certainly known to Hegesippus, before the middle part of the second century. And there is no reason to think that it was then new. Himself a Hebrew Christian by birth, he had probably been long acquainted with it. But we will not indulge in conjecture. It is safe to affirm that the Church received no evangelical history from the

[1] The priority of Matthew has been convincingly shown by various writers; among them by Franck, in a thorough Article in the *Studien u. Kritiken*, 1848, 2.

judaizing Christians after the latter had become separated. The existence of the Gospel of Matthew among them—for the Gospel of the Hebrews was an altered Matthew—requires us to conclude that it enjoyed a general acceptance before the Jewish-Christian parties were formed. But these acquired a distinct existence, according to the trustworthy testimony of Hegesippus, at the beginning, or about the beginning, of the second century. Before this, however, and from the time of the destruction of Jerusalem, the movement towards separation began. The judaizing Christians looked with growing jealousy and hostility upon the Gentile believers and their churches. To our mind, it is altogether improbable that the Gospel of Matthew could have been composed, and have been accepted by both classes of Christians, at any time subsequent—to say the least, long subsequent—to the destruction of Jerusalem by Titus. Besides the difficulty of accounting for its acceptance on both sides, on the supposition of a later date, the partisan feelings of the judaizing Christian would infallibly have been reflected on its pages. But in this artless chronicle there is not the slightest trace of judaizing bitterness.

III. We have to consider now the prophecies of the second advent of Christ, which are contained in Matthew, in their bearing on the date of the Gospel.

In touching upon this topic, we are brought in contact, indeed, with the principal exegetical difficulty in the New Testament. The final advent of Christ to judgment, and the destruction of Jerusalem, appear to have been connected together in time, as if the former were to follow immediately upon the latter. After what seems clearly to be a prediction of the downfall of Jerusalem (Matthew xxiv. 1–29), we read that "*immediately* (εὐθέως) after the tribulation of those days," the Son of Man will come in the clouds of heaven, in the sight of "all the tribes" on earth, and "gather together his elect from the four winds, from one end of heaven to the other" (vs. 29–32, comp. c. xxv. 31 seq. and Luke xxi. 27, 31). And we read (in ver. 34): "this generation (γενεά) shall not pass, till all these things be fulfilled."

We are not called upon, in this place, to consider the difficulty that is presented by these passages. The paramount question of the origin and date of the Gospel is the question which we have in hand. That our Saviour did not predict that the world would come to an end instantly on the destruction of Jerusalem, is shown by other parts of his own teaching. He is represented in the synoptical Gospels as declaring that the time when the end would occur was not a subject of Revelation, but a secret of the Father. In a more comprehensive way, he said to the disciples (Acts i. 7): "It is not for you to know the *times or seasons*, which the Father hath put in his own power." And the apostles, though hoping and looking for the end, did not claim in their Epistles to be taught by Inspiration when the end would come. Moreover, there are various teachings of the Saviour in regard to His kingdom, which imply a slow progress and a long operation of the gospel in the world. It is like leaven. It is like a grain of mustard-seed. It is the salt of the earth. It is to be preached to all nations. He compares Himself, as to the moral effect of His death, to the corn of wheat which, if it do not fall into the earth and die, "abideth alone; but if it die, it bringeth forth much fruit."

We can afford, in the present discussion, to waive the inquiry how these predictions as they are set down in the first Gospel (and so substantially in Mark and Luke), are reconcilable with these other teachings of Christ and with historical fact. It is enough that skeptics, almost with one voice, have maintained that here is really a distinct prediction that the end of the world would occur in connection with the destruction of Jerusalem and within the lifetime of the generation then on the stage. Theodore Parker has expressed this view. Gibbon makes the supposed prediction a theme of his elaborate satire. Now, if this be their interpretation, they are compelled to acknowledge that the Gospel which contains this erroneous prophecy appeared in its present form before Jerusalem was captured by Titus, or before the year 70. It must have been written as early as thirty or forty years after the Saviour's death. No Gospel-writer would set forth without explanation a prediction of a mighty event, which all his readers would know had not been verified.

No writer in the year 80, or 90, or 100, would fix the date of the end of the world at the destruction of Jerusalem, in a document which he wished to be believed.

We may even take a step farther. If some interpretations of the passages in Matthew be adopted, which recognize an infallible accuracy in the synoptical reports of the Saviour's teaching, yet it may be safely held that had the Evangelist been writing at a later time, some explanation would have been thrown in to remove the *seeming* discrepancy between prophecy and fulfilment. If it be supposed, for example, that in the perspective opened to the prophetic vision, two grand events, though parted in reality by a long interval, were brought together—as distant mountain-peaks when approached are found to be far apart—yet it would be natural to expect that when the interval had actually disclosed itself to the observer, some intimation of the fact would be dropped. So that even on the orthodox, as well as on the skeptical, interpretation of the eschatology in the Synoptics, their early date is manifest.

It remains for us to notice the Tübingen hypothesis concerning Matthew. Baur's general theory is not the mythical theory, but "the tendency-theory." He has discussed and pointed out the weakness of the procedure of Strauss in his attempt to disprove the statements of the fourth Gospel by opposing to them the authority of the Synoptics, and at the same time to contradict the Synoptics by quoting the fourth

Gospel against them. If there is to be any positive construction of the evangelical history, as Baur perceived, there must be gained somewhere a firm standing-place. This he finds in the first Gospel. Not that even this Gospel is fully authentic and historical. Yet there is in Matthew a substantial kernel of historical truth. All the Gospels are, more or less, the product of a theological *tendency;* that is, they result from the artificial recasting and amplifying of the veritable history in order to suit the views of some theological party or interest in the primitive church. In Matthew, the Jewish-Christian side is the prevailing motive determining the cast and tone of the narrative. Luke represents the opposite, or Gentile, party. But the first Gospel is less inspired by a definite, dogmatical interest, which leads in the other Gospels to the conscious alteration and fabrication of history; and Baur is disposed to concede to Strauss that there is a larger admixture of the myth or the *unconscious* creations of feeling in Matthew, than is true of the remaining Gospels.

When we come to inquire for a precise explanation of the origin of the first Gospel, we are met with very divergent responses from the various choir-leaders of the Tübingen school. In fact, with respect to the whole of the special criticism by which they seek to convict the Gospels of being *tendenz-schriften,* they are hardly less at variance with each other than with the Christian world generally. Passages that are confidently quoted by one critic in proof of a certain "tendency," are alleged by another as illustrations of a "tendency" exactly opposite. With regard to Matthew, Hilgenfeld, who agrees, in this particular, with Strauss, does not limit the sense of the *logia* of Papias so as to exclude narrative matter; yet he pretends to be able to dissect the first Gospel and to separate a primitive Matthew—an *Ur-Matthäus*—from later accretions. We are absolved from the necessity of following him in the baseless and arbitrary division which he seeks to run through the contents of Matthew, since his construction has gained so little applause even from his master. But we may attend for a moment to Baur's own view. He appears to take the *logia* in the restricted meaning, and to attach some importance to the supposed tradition of a collection of *logia*, forming the basis of our Matthew. This hypothesis we have already examined. Baur's effort to bring down the date of the Gospel into the second century is a bad failure. Desirous of holding that the second advent is foretold as immediately subsequent to the predicted destruction of Jerusalem, he is obliged to refer the latter prediction to some other war than that of Titus. Accordingly, he interprets it as applying to the war of Hadrian in the year 131 or 132, and therefore fixes the date of the composition of the Gospel between 130 and 134! It is unfortunate for this bold assertion, that our Matthew was an authoritative writing among Christians, and read as such in their assemblies "in city and country," in the time of Justin Martyr, who was born near the end of the first century. But aside from this historical testimony, which it is vain to attempt to invalidate, Baur's interpretation can be easily proved to be palpably false. In the destruction of Jerusalem foretold in Matthew (xxiv. 1–4) the temple was to be laid in ruins. This was accomplished by Titus, and not by Hadrian. With what face then can the prophecy be referred to the war of Hadrian? It is doubtful, indeed, whether, in this last war, there was even a destruction of the city. The parallel passages in the other evangelists (see Luke xxi. 5–7, 12, 20), determine the reference of the prediction to the war of Titus, beyond the possibility of doubt. Moreover, "this generation" was not to pass away before this event was to occur. Baur claims that this phrase—ἡ γενεὰ αὕτη—may cover a period as long as a century. But this claim is void of truth. The phrase everywhere in the New Testament signifies the average term of human life, and was held, according to the Greek usage, to be equivalent to a third of a century. Besides, explanatory expressions occur in the prophetic passages of Matthew, which define the meaning of the phrase in the way we have stated.[1] The difficulty presented by these passages, we are firmly convinced, is not to be escaped by affixing another than the proper and uniform meaning to this phrase.

[1] See Matthew xvi. 27, 28.

The forced and manifestly false interpretation of Baur, which has been noticed above, is due to the straits into which he is brought by his untenable theory. Confronted by unimpeachable historical witnesses, he is not only obliged to ignore, or unjustifiably to disparage, their testimony, but also to resort to shifts in interpretation which only mark the desperation of his cause. There is absolutely nothing to conflict with the supposition that our first Gospel comes down, in its integrity, from the apostolic Church; while the positive evidence, both direct and corroborative, fully establishes the fact.

MARK.

The ancient testimonies, of which that of Papias is the first, to the genuineness and early date of the second Gospel, would seem to preclude the possibility of a question on these points. Mark is declared to have been an attendant of Peter and to have derived his knowledge of the life and ministry of Jesus from the discourses of that apostle. This is substantially the declaration of all the writers in the second half of the second century; and it has been thought by some good critics that even as early as Justin Martyr, and in one passage of Justin himself, the Gospel of Mark was styled Peter's Gospel.

But it has been contended of late that the description of Papias does not answer for our Mark and must refer to some other work. In the later form of the theory, Papias is made to describe an earlier Mark —an *Ur-Markus*—which is the germ of our present Gospel.

Now of the existence of this earlier work there is no intimation in any of the Fathers. How did the fact of its existence escape the knowledge of Irenaeus and his contemporaries? When did all the manuscripts of it disappear? In truth, the theory in this form is preposterous, and even Baur is driven to a different hypothesis. Before attending to this, however, let us revert to the statements of Papias and see how far they are from lending support to the notion that he had in mind any other work than our Mark.

Papias, or John the Presbyter, his informant, represents that Mark, though a careful and accurate writer, depended on the oral discourses of Peter for his knowledge and therefore did not dispose his matter—*ἐν τάξει*—in the chronological order. This is all the evidence on which the theory of an earlier Mark is founded! But, in any event, this remark is only the impression of an individual as to the character of the second Gospel. He doubtless compared Mark with the more consecutive narrative of Matthew. Moreover, it is plain that he had in mind the lack of completeness in Mark, which begins abruptly with the preaching of John. For he afterwards explains that Mark wrote down "*some* things"—whatever he recollected; though it is added that he left out nothing that he heard. The necessary gaps and omissions constituted in part the want of order—*τάξις*—which he noticed in Mark.[1] The second Gospel did not seem tc be a full, systematical digest—a *σύνταξις*—of the words and deeds of Christ, like Matthew, but had a more irregular, fragmentary structure. Not that Mark neglected arrangement altogether and simply pasted together the reports of Peter in the order in which he heard them. This is not at all implied; but only that he had not the means of exactly arranging and filling out his history. To call into existence another work, different from our Mark, on no other ground than this observation of Papias, is a folly of criticism.

The Tübingen writers have set up the wholly unsupported assertion, that our Mark is the amplification of an earlier "Gospel of Peter;" but, as might be expected, they have little agreement with each other in the forms which they give to their theory. Hilgenfeld is persuaded that Mark is the product of a recasting, in the Petrine interest and that of the Roman Church, of the Gospel of Matthew.[2] Marvellous that this Petrine, Roman Catholic partisan should

[1] Meyer is plainly wrong in making the "some things"—*ἔνια*—cover only a *portion* of what Mark set down. The meaning is that only a part of the teachings and works of Christ find a place in his Gospel. The want of order, as we have said before, is predicated as much of the record of the "things done," as of the "things said."

[2] Hilgenfeld's *Die Evangelien*, s. 148.

have left out of his work the passage: "Thou art Peter, and on this rock will I build my church!" Strange that he should have stricken out the passage which, above all others, was suited to his purpose! Baur, seeing that the supposition of an earlier Gospel of Mark is incredible, on account of the absence of all traces of such a work and all allusions to it, has invented a new hypothesis which is, if possible, more irrational than Hilgenfeld's. Papias has mixed up, we are told, things that have no connection—the existence of the Gospel of Mark, with which he was perhaps not even acquainted, and the legend of discourses which were thought to have been delivered by Peter on his missionary journeys. But of what weight is this naked conjecture in opposition to the distinct testimony of Papias? If a witness is to be set aside on so flimsy a pretext, there is an end of historical investigation. Besides, it is not Papias alone who testifies to the Gospel of Mark and the connection of Mark with Peter. Irenaeus, Clement, Eusebius, say the same; and there is no reason to suppose that they simply reëcho the statement of Papias. All these writers represent what was unquestionably the general belief at the time when Papias wrote.

These assaults upon the integrity of the Gospel of Mark, by critics who do not stick to any one hypothesis as long as it takes the seasons to revolve, have not weakened in the slightest degree that argument in behalf of the Gospel on which the Church has rested from the apostolic age until now. Are historical testimonies to be blown away by the empty guess of a theorist?

LUKE.

The school of Baur have been especially confident in asserting that Luke's Gospel was written to further a certain theological interest. It is a *tendenz-schrift,* they are sure, which emanates from the Pauline side, and represents the gospel history in a way to favor the Gentile claims and privileges.

Now, every historian who is not a mere story-teller, writes from his own point of view. Every historian will disclose in the complexion of his work his own character and situation. Certain aspects of the subject which have for one writer a peculiar interest, are thrown by a writer of a different cast more into the background. The position and character of an historian affect his selection and disposition of the matter. But the question is whether he is betrayed into inveracity and perversion by the bent of his mind and his party connections. It is clear that Luke, a disciple of Paul and writing for a heathen convert, is more interested in the intention of the author of the gospel to provide salvation equally for the Gentiles. But is he thereby led to indulge in misstatement and invention? Does he omit important facts because they would clash with a view which he wishes to make out? And does he not scruple to fabricate incidents for the sake of helping forward a party interest? This is charged by Baur—charged, as we believe, without proof, and falsely. There is no inconsistency between the representation of the life and teachings of Christ in Matthew, and that made in Luke. The design of Christianity to embrace the Gentiles, even to bring to them an advantage above the unbelieving nation to whom the gospel first comes, is abundantly attested in Matthew. What are the proofs by which Baur would sustain his impeachment of Luke? They are, one and all, destitute of weight. Luke omits to mention the distinction put upon Peter when he was styled the Rock; but so does Mark. It is charged that Luke contrives to disparage the twelve disciples, in order to pave the way for an inference to the honor of Paul. This is pure fancy, and has against it such passages as Luke xxii. 29, 30, where the Lord declares that a kingdom is appointed for this band of disciples, even as the Father had appointed for him; and that they should "sit on twelve thrones, judging the twelve tribes of Israel." Hilgenfeld is acute enough to find in this promise a designed *depression* of the twelve, since they are to judge Israel *alone!* What, then, is the purport of the same promise in "judaizing" Matthew?[1] That the kingdom is preached in Samaria, according

[1] Matt. xix. 25.

to Luke, is also, if we are to believe Baur, a fiction designed as a typical prelude to Paul's free offer of salvation to the heathen, and to pacify objectors to this last procedure. Especially is the mission of the Seventy (Luke x. 10) discredited, and ascribed partly to the desire to diminish the consideration of the twelve, and partly to the wish to furnish a justifying parallel or preparation, in the manner just mentioned, for the Pauline liberality to the Gentiles and for the missions among them. But in sending out the Seventy, Christ did not organize them into a permanent body. There is no trace of such a body of disciples in the Acts, as there certainly would be if they had been a permanent body, or if the narrative in Luke had been a doctrinal fiction. The Seventy were provisionally employed, in the course of this last journey of Jesus to Jerusalem, when He was desirous of making Himself more widely known to the people. The number was fixed at seventy, not because the Jews reckoned the languages of the world at seventy, which is Baur's explanation, but more likely in allusion to the seventy elders appointed by Moses, just as the twelve disciples corresponded with the number of tribes. Nor did the Seventy go to the heathen. It does not appear that they went to the Samaritans even; and Luke himself records that by the Samaritans Jesus himself had been inhospitably received.[1] It has been properly suggested, in reply to Baur, that

[1] Luke ix. 51 seq.

were this incident a wilful fiction, it would be so contrived as to present a greater resemblance to the later apostolic history, than the occult, remote, far-fetched analogy which Baur imagines himself to discern. So slender are the principal grounds on which important portions of the third Gospel are pronounced a fabrication! They illustrate the morbid suspicion of these critics, and their slavish subjection to a preconceived, indefensible theory concerning the original character of Christianity.

One of the most important topics connected with modern discussions relative to the origin of the third Gospel, is the relation of that Gospel to the Gospel of Marcion. In the genial portraiture which Neander has drawn of this noted heresiarch, it appears that the love and compassion of Christ had struck into his soul. Not discerning that this love and compassion presuppose and require the feelings of justice, he conceived that the representations of the character of God in the Old Testament are inconsistent with the image he had formed of Christ. Moreover, the apostles, with the exception of Paul, seemed to him to be entangled in Old Testament views and to have perverted the pure doctrine of Jesus. On the contrary, the expressions in Paul about the Christian's emancipation from the law and about free grace, being imperfectly understood by Marcion, fell in with the current of his feeling. Hence, though starting from a practical and not a speculative point of view, he developed a gnostical theory, according to which the God of the Old Testament was a Demiurg, inferior to the Father of Jesus. He shaped his scriptural canon to suit his doctrinal belief. The Gospel of Luke, as written by a companion of Paul, and as bringing out the Pauline doctrine, he regarded with favor; but, according to the unanimous testimony of the Fathers, he mutilated and abridged this Gospel in order to conform it to his own system. Similar liberties he took with the Pauline Epistles, which he also received. He may have fancied that the changes which he made in all these documents were a restoration of them to their original form. Yet there is no indication whatever that these changes were made on any other authority than his *a-priori* theory of what Christ and the apostles must have taught.

A native of Pontus in Asia Minor, Marcion came to Rome about the year 140—possibly ten years later. Hence, if the statement of Tertullian and the rest of the Fathers is correct, respecting the relation of his Gospel to that of Luke, he is a most important witness to the early and general reception of Luke's Gospel in its present form. It would seem to be well-nigh impossible to call in question this early testimony. It is true that Marcion did not succeed in removing from Luke all features not in keeping with his system. But this is only to say that he did not do his work with entire thoroughness and consistency. Irenaeus and Tertullian and their contemporaries, be it observed, lived shortly after Marcion. Irenaeus had grown to be a young man before Marcion died. Tertullian had taken great pains to collect information concerning Marcion's career and system. But, independently of their testimony in itself considered, how can it be supposed that a Gospel which Marcion and the Marcionites alone received, was taken up by Catholic Christians, and enlarged and improved for their own use? What possible motive could prompt them to appropriate to themselves this heretical, spurious Gospel, and add it to those which they knew to be authentic? How did the churches drop out the work which Marcion used—supposed to be the real Luke—and substitute for it the new-fangled Gospel which was fabricated on the basis of it? How is it that we have no notice of this exchange—no traces of a previous use of the curtailed Luke of Marcion, on the part of the churches? And such a procedure would bring down the date of the canonical Gospel to 130 or 140!

The first to dispute the received view as to Marcion's Gospel, was the founder of German rationalism, Semler. He suggested that our Luke and Marcion's Luke are different recensions, or editions, of the same work. Others after him assigned the priority to the Luke of Marcion. Opinion swayed from one side to the other on this question, until Baur strenuously contended that Marcion's Gospel is first and the canonical Luke was made on the basis of it. This hypothesis he defended at length in his work on the *Canonical Gospels*.[1] But a careful comparison of the numerous passages of Marcion's Luke, which are found in the Fathers, made it impossible longer to dispute the priority of the canonical Gospel. And after the publication of the work of Volkmar on this subject, Baur himself retracted his previous hypothesis and came on to the same ground. In his work on Mark's Gospel, he says: "It is no longer to be denied, as I have become convinced by a repeated examination, that most of the variations between Marcion's Gospel and our own are, with a prevailing likelihood, to be regarded as arbitrary alterations in the interest of a given system." The priority of our Luke is now an established, uncontradicted fact. See how much this fact involves! Marcion took an accepted, generally received Gospel, and applied to it his pruning-knife. Our Luke, then, was most certainly an authoritative document in the churches early in the second century. But a more valuable deduction may be made with entire confidence. Marcion selected a work which he regarded, and others regarded, as the composition of a disciple of Paul, and deriving its authority and value from this circumstance. We may safely infer that our Gospel was generally considered at the beginning of the second century, or about thirty years after we suppose it to have been written, to be the work of an

[1] Baur's *Kanonische Evangelien*, s. 393 seq. (1847).

earlier writer, an associate of the apostles. As concerns the argument from tradition for the genuineness and early date of Luke, we could ask for nothing more.

Baur's whole theory concerning Luke was, in reality, shattered by the demolition of the false and most improbable hypothesis of a priority of Marcion's Gospel. Yet, in his later works, he does not wholly abandon his erroneous construction. The canonical Luke, he still holds, was originally composed by a strictly Pauline and anti-Petrine Christian. Various passages which are plainly and palpably irreconcilable with such a theory, he declares to be interpolated by a subsequent writer whose position is "mediatory," or half-way between the two parties, into which Baur falsely supposes the early Church to have been split. For this theory of a later editor, there is not an iota of historical evidence. It is, like so many other hypotheses, spun out of the bowels of the critic. The dissection of the Gospel, which is attempted, is from beginning to end a purely arbitrary proceeding, and has no better foundation than had the mutilation attempted by Marcion. To illustrate the groundless and arbitrary character of Baur's criticism of Luke, we bring forward a single instance. In Luke xvi. 16, there is recorded the saying of the Saviour: "It is easier for heaven and earth to pass, than one tittle of the law to fail." In place of "the law"—*τοῦ νόμου*—there was found in Marcion's Gospel—*τῶν λόγων μου*—

"my words." The existence of this declaration in Luke concerning the perpetuity of the law, is at war with Baur's idea of the anti-Jewish character of the Gospel. It is one of the clearest proofs of the unfounded nature of his theory. Hence, he puts forward the assertion that Marcion has the true reading. For the reading of Marcion there is no manuscript support whatever. It comports, moreover, with the character of all the rest of his alterations. He aims to erase whatever gives a sanction to the Old Testament law. Yet we are expected to accept the wholly unsupported and groundless doctrine of that oracular personage styled *Die Kritik*, who reverses his own decision with every new moon!

Much of the mistaken and mischievous speculation adverse to the genuineness of the third Gospel, has sprung from Schleiermacher's hypothesis of the composite character of this Gospel and of the Acts. He proposed the theory that the Gospel of Luke is a series of earlier documents linked together, the task of Luke being merely that of a compiler. This view was ingeniously advocated. A similar hypothesis was held concerning the Acts, the second work of the same author. But this hypothesis, both in respect to the Gospel and the Acts, has been proved to be unfounded. Whatever written materials were in the hands of Luke, neither of his works is a mere compilation. Each of them has a coherent outline, and is pervaded by qualities of style peculiar to the evangelist. One of the ablest refutations of the Schleiermacherian theory is contained in the work of Lekebusch upon the Acts. The prologue of Luke's Gospel evinces the error of that theory. Luke avows his intention to prepare an orderly, a systematic and connected, narrative of the life and ministry of Jesus. And the impression made by the prologue that he designs to fuse his materials into a regular composition, is sustained by an inspection of the contents of the work.

This prologue of Luke's Gospel is chiefly valuable as a testimony to its genuineness and credibility. As such, it well deserves examination. Many before him had written accounts, more or less full, of the life and ministry of Jesus. He has carefully followed down the course of the Saviour's history from the beginning —for this is the meaning of the passage rendered: "having had perfect understanding of all things from the very first." But how did he, and "the many" to whom he refers, ascertain the facts "most surely believed among us?" He answers that "they delivered them unto us—*παρέδοσαν ἡμῖν*—which from the beginning" of the Saviour's career "were eyewitnesses and ministers of the word." Two things are here affirmed: first, that Luke's knowledge came from the apostles and other immediate disciples of Christ; and, secondly, that it came to him *directly* from them, without the intervention of third persons.

This last is implied in the phrase "delivered to us"—παρέδοσαν ἡμῖν—as may be seen by an examination of other passages where the same phrase occurs; as, for example, 1 Cor. xi. 23. The informants of Luke were eyewitnesses of the history which he undertakes to record. He was contemporary with them. The early date of his work is verified by his own distinct statement.

THE RELATION OF THE APOCRYPHAL TO THE CANONICAL GOSPELS.

The fact of the existence of apocryphal Gospels has given occasion, among those who have not studied the subject, to erroneous impressions. It has been supposed by some that a considerable number of Gospels, besides the four of the canon, were in the hands of the early Church, and that, for reasons which may not have been fully sufficient, these last were selected, and clothed with authority. This belief, or conjecture, is unfounded, as we shall soon point out. And a careful attention to the subject of the apocryphal Gospels has the effect to set forth in a clearer light the antiquity and authority of the received Gospels. A few remarks will bring before the reader the more important considerations.[1]

[1] The old and standard work on the subject of the apocryphal literature is that of Fabricius. "A New and Full Method of Settling the Canonical Authority of the New Testament, etc.," by Rev. J. Jones (Oxford, 1798), is Fabricius with English translations. The

1. None of the works now extant under the name of apocryphal Gospels, have any claim to be considered authentic histories of Christ, or to be regarded, in the remotest degree, as rivals or competitors of the canonical Gospels.

It is the fashion of writers like Strauss to quote from these apocryphal Gospels as well as from the Gospels of the canon, for the sake of creating an impression that both belong to the same category, which no person pretending to be a scholar would venture to assert. The apocryphal Gospels are at a world-wide remove from the canonical Gospels, in the character of their contents. They relate almost exclusively to the nativity and infancy of Jesus and the glories of his mother, or to circumstances attending and following his death. They are chiefly made up of silly tales, which are too plainly fabulous to merit any attention. Nor have they any title to attention on

remarks and deductions of Jones are sometimes good, but often ill-judged. Thilo began to edit the apocryphal Gospels in a most scholarly manner, but only published a first volume. Tischendorf, besides his critical edition of the *Evangelia Apocrypha* (1853), has discussed the bearing of the apocryphal Gospels upon the question of the genuineness and credibility of the Gospels of the canon, in his prize essay *de Evangeliorum apoc. origine et usu* (1851), and in his recent dissertation, *Wann wurden die Evangelien verfasst* (1865). Norton's chapter (*Genuineness of the Gospels*, Vol. iii. ch. xii.) is lucid and instructive. He goes farther than most scholars would approve, in discrediting the *existence* of apocryphal books which ecclesiastical writers mention by their titles. But his skepticism in this particular is a healthy antidote to extravagances in the opposite direction.

the score of age. All of them are demonstrably later than our Gospels. Most of them are even centuries later. It is supposed by Tischendorf that three of these are alluded to by early Fathers, but of this we cannot be certain. Justin Martyr twice mentions the Acts (ἄκτα) of Pilate, as a document where could be found an attestation of the Saviour's history. Tertullian has a similar reference. A book called *Gesta Pilati*, or Acts of Pilate, forms a part of the so-called Gospel of Nicodemus. But the Acts of a Roman governor—such a work as Justin designates—was his official Report to the Emperor, which was deposited in the archives at Rome. Whether in the time of Justin there was any *published* narrative of that sort, purporting to be Pilate's report of the judicial proceeding in the case of Jesus, we are unable to say.[1] But the *Gesta Pilati* which we possess is a narrative of Christ's life on the basis of our Gospels, which it is pretended that Nicodemus wrote and the Emperor Theodosius (which Emperor of that name, we are not told) found among the public records in the hall of Pontius Pilate, at Jerusalem. This Gospel of Nicodemus is unquestionably a composite work, and the part embraced in the *Acta Pilati* may be, as Tischendorf thinks, as old as Justin. Yet there has

[1] Perhaps Justin refers to no writing which he had seen, but to a public document which he supposes to exist. In the same way (*Apol.*, I. 34) he says: "As you may learn from the lists of the taxing, which were made in the time of Cyrenius, the first governor of yours in Judea."

been confessedly great license in altering the text; and after all, the opinion of Norton that this production is of a later date, is not conclusively disproved. Origen, in the first half of the third century, once refers to a book of James, as containing the statement that the brothers of Jesus were children of Joseph by a former marriage; and the apocryphal Protevangelion of James contains a similar statement. But there is no other allusion to such a work until near the end of the fourth century. The work now extant is a silly legend concerning the birth of Mary and the birth of Jesus, and is thought by Norton to be of much later date than the likewise unimportant book which Origen casually notices, and to which he attributes no authority. Tischendorf, however, is convinced that some traces of an acquaintance with the Protevangelion are found in Justin and in Clement of Alexandria, and that the manuscripts now extant substantially correspond to the work which was in their hands. But the first of these points must still be considered doubtful, and the conclusion of Tischendorf as to the antiquity of the work is therefore equally uncertain. Origen, also, alludes to a spurious Gospel of Thomas. A passage in Irenaeus is thought to indicate that it was in use among the heretical Marcosii, and Hippolytus states that a Gospel of Thomas was received by the Naasseni.[1] An apocryphal work professing to emanate

[1] Iren. *Adv. Haer.*, Lib. i. c. 20; Hippol. (Duncker and Schneid. Ed.) pp. 140, 142.

from Thomas, is now extant (though in very divergent forms), of which the work alluded to by Origen may have served as the basis. It is composed of fabulous tales of the boyhood of Jesus. But Norton even doubts whether the Gospel of Thomas, which is mentioned by Origen, was a narrative. He thinks that, like other spurious works bearing the name of Gospel, it may have been a doctrinal homily.

Tischendorf is of the opinion that the *Acta* and the *Protevangelion* were composed somewhere in the first decades of the second century. From the evident dependence of these works on the Gospels of the canon, he infers that the latter were in general use at an earlier day. This conclusion stands or falls, according to the judgment which is formed as to the correctness of the date assigned to the *Acta* and the *Protevangelion*.[1] At all events, these and the other apocryphal Gospels now extant show what sort of works would have been produced, had the canonical writers followed their own fancy and invention. In this aspect, the apocryphal Gospels afford an impressive confirmation of the verity of the canonical histories. The sobriety and simplicity of the latter, together with their distinct statement that no miracles were performed by Jesus prior to his baptism, are in wonderful contrast with the fanciful and fan-

[1] Tischendorf supposes that the *Descensus Christi ad inferos* in the Evangelium Nicodemi is also as old as the middle of the second century.

tastic complexion of the spurious Gospels. The clumsiness of the counterfeit sets off the perfection of the original.

2. The apocryphal Gospels which are mentioned by the early Fathers, and most if not all of which have perished, had only a local circulation, had no authority save with minor heretical parties, and had no effect on that generally prevailing conception of the life and teaching of Christ, which was founded exclusively on the four authentic and canonical narratives unanimously received by the early Church.

We must explain that we do not include in this statement the Gospel of the Hebrews and Marcion's Gospel, for the reason that both of these works were produced by the alteration of canonical Gospels. The Gospel of the Hebrews existed in many varying forms, and under different titles. The Gospel of the Twelve Apostles, for example, and other books the titles of which have come down to us, were different editions of the Gospel of the Hebrews. This work, as we have said, was our Matthew altered.[1] The Gospel

[1] That the Gospel of the Hebrews was never put by the church and church writers on a level with the canonical Gospels, has been fully proved. See, for example, the Article of Franck (*Stud. u. Krit.*, 1848, 2), to which we have before referred. As to the use of it by Hegesippus, Eusebius merely says that he brought forward some things from the Gospel of the Hebrews, as he did from unwritten Hebrew traditions. Origen and Jerome were too intelligent to rank it with the canonical Gospels. Eusebius places it among the Antilegomena, it being the Gospel used by the Hebrew Christians. Euseb., III. 25.

of Marcion was our Luke abridged and otherwise changed.

The truth which we wish to convey is, that *there were no Gospel histories* in the second century which were contending for acceptance by the side of the Four; none which had come into general use and were discarded; none having any claims to be authentic, which required to be seriously weighed. As far as we can ascertain, there were no other Gospels which had a consideration sufficient to render them candidates for public favor in the Church. It should be remarked that the first attempts at evangelical writing which Luke mentions in his preface, were early supplanted by the canonical histories, so that none of the former, as far as we can discover, were known to the ecclesiastical writers of the second century.

The Gnostics were the falsifiers and fabricators of Scripture, according to the statement of the Fathers. In the controversy of Irenaeus and Tertullian with the Gnostics, both sides take for granted a life and teaching of Christ, which, with wholly insignificant exceptions, is identical with the representation of our canonical Gospels. He is assumed to have done and said just what they record. The leading sects of the Gnostics were therefore governed in their conception of the career and ministry of Christ, by the authority and the representations of the canonical histories.

Tertullian, who has so much to say of the falsification of Luke by Marcion and of his rejection of the rest of the Gospels on dogmatic grounds, does not mention any apocryphal Gospels as in use among the Valentinians, the principal gnostical sect, and the rest of his opponents. In one place only, Irenaeus speaks of a gospel as used by the Valentinians, bearing the title of the *True Gospel* or the *Gospel of Truth*. We know not whether this was narrative or homily. We know not whether Irenaeus had ever seen the work. We know not whether it really existed, or whether Irenaeus did not mistake the claim on their part to be possessed of the true Gospel, or the true interpretation of the Gospel, for an allusion to a book. But of this we are certain, that he, and, as far as we know, they, brought forward no passage from it. The Gospel of Basilides is another work which, if indeed such a work existed, was probably not a narrative. It was little known; and not a sentence from it is quoted by the ancient writers. Origen says that Basilides wrote a Gospel and prefixed his own name to it; a statement which is repeated by Ambrose and Jerome. But the refutations of Basilides take notice of nothing drawn from such a work. He is said by Eusebius (quoting from Agrippa Castor) to have written a work in twenty-four books "upon the Gospel"—apparently an exegetical work; and this fact may not improbably have given rise to the supposition that he had fabricated a new Gospel.

In order to show how obscure, comparatively, these apocryphal Gospels were, and how far the existence of them is from weakening, in the least degree, the evidence for the antiquity and verity of the canonical four, we will state all that is known concerning the two most prominent of these fictions —the Gospel of Peter and the Gospel of the Egyptians.

The Gospel of Peter has been made to figure conspicuously in the manifold hypotheses of the skeptical school of critics. It is instructive to see just how much is *known* concerning this work, which, from the ado made about it by the critics in question, one would infer to be a document of great notoriety and importance in the early Church. It has been said that Justin Martyr, in a passage of his Dialogue with Trypho, makes reference to a Gospel of Peter; but this is a mistake.[1] The first notice of the Gospel of Peter is from Serapion, near the end of the second century. Serapion, bishop of Antioch, had, as we learn from Eusebius, found that some disturbance

[1] The passage is in *Tryph.*, c. 106. See Otto's excellent note, (Otto's Ed. of Justin, Vol. II. p. 361). There may be an omission of *ἀποστόλων* before *αὐτοῦ*, as Otto supposes; or the *αὐτοῦ* may refer to *Christ;* or, again, the allusion may be to Mark, which was known as Peter's Gospel. We think that the context (see c. 105) renders it in the highest degree probable (as Otto thinks) that Justin, according to his usual custom, refers in this place to the *ἀπομνημονεύματα* collectively and in the plural—that is, to our four Gospels.

had been created in the church at Rhosse, a town in Cilicia, by a so-called Gospel of Peter which was in the hands of some of the church-members. At first, thinking that the book was harmless, he deemed the affair undeserving of notice. But afterwards he procured a copy of the book from some of the Docetae, who used it, and found it to contain objectionable matter. Origen has a single allusion to this Gospel, as containing, like the book of James, the statement that the brothers of Jesus were children of Joseph by a former marriage. It is afterwards barely mentioned, as an apocryphal book, by Jerome. This is *all* that we know of the apocryphal Gospel of Peter! It is not clear that Origen had ever seen it. The bishop of what was then the principal See in the East had never heard of the book until he met with it at Rhosse; and when he wished to examine it, he was obliged to borrow a copy of some heretical Docetae by whom it was used! Moreover, there is nothing to show that it was a narrative. The way in which Serapion speaks of it would rather suggest the inference that its contents were of a doctrinal nature. Eusebius reckons it among the evidently spurious works "which were never esteemed valuable enough to be cited by any ecclesiastical writer."[1]

The Gospel of the Egyptians is first mentioned by Clement of Alexandria near the end of the second century. He notices a fabulous conversation of

[1] Euseb., III. 25.

Jesus with Salome, cited from it by certain heretics, but expressly characterizes the book as apocryphal. A passage similar to that referred to by Clement of Alexandria is found in the spurious fragment entitled the Second Epistle of Clement (of Rome) to the Corinthians, which was not written earlier than the time of Clement of Alexandria; and it is possible that the forger of the last work was acquainted with this fictitious Gospel. It is enumerated by Origen and Jerome among the titles of apocryphal Gospels, which they furnish. Epiphanius says that the Sabellians made use of it; but his statement needs confirmation. So much, and so much only, is known of the Gospel of the Egyptians. Some have considered it one form of the Gospel of the Hebrews. Others, including Norton, have held it to be, not a narrative, but a doctrinal work. It was written in an obscure and mystical vein, and probably presented the ascetic notions of Egyptian gnostical sectaries, among whom it originated. It must have had a limited circulation. No Christian writer has ever attributed to it any historical authority.

We might proceed to notice other spurious gospels, or books called by the name of gospels, which are the subject of casual allusion in ecclesiastical writers of the first centuries. But we have said enough to give our readers a fair impression of their insignificant importance. Reminding the reader of what we have said of the Gospel of the Hebrews, which was framed on the basis of our Matthew, we may distinctly affirm, not only that the four Gospels of the canon were universally accepted by the Christians of the second century, but also that no other gospel narratives can properly be said to have divided their honors with them. It may be affirmed, with hardly any qualification, that they stood without competitors. The spurious gospels secured little or no recognition outside of heretical parties or coteries from which they emanated. On the contrary, if not wholly unknown, they were rejected by the church teachers everywhere, and by the great body of Christian people.[1]

It has been already remarked that the principal anti-gnostical writers of the second century, and their adversaries, alike proceed on a conception of the life and ministry of Jesus, which is identical with that of the canonical Gospels. That is to say, both parties assume that the history of Christ which we find in our Gospels, is alone authentic. A like confirmation of the authority of the canonical Gospels is obtained from Justin Martyr. They were undeniably the Gospels to which he refers as being authoritative—the writings of the Apostles and their Companions.

[1] For an enumeration of these apocryphal writings, see De Wette's *Einl. in d. N. Testament*, § 73 a; also Hofmann's Art.—Pseudepigraphen, etc.—in Herzog's *Real-Encyc.* This last Article, however, refers to the real and *supposed* allusions in the ecclesiastical writers to the uncanonical gospels; and the references require much sifting.

But, apart from this, in the multitude of Justin's allusions to the life and teachings of Christ, there are only six which cannot be at once traced to the Gospels of the canon. Among these there is only one, or at most two, sayings of Christ. Both of these are found, also, in Clement of Alexandria, who regards the four Gospels alone as authoritative. The other four cases of deviation from our Gospels in Justin, are of trivial consequence—slight details added to the canonical narrative. With these unimportant exceptions, the whole representation of the history of Jesus in this Father, coincides with that of the accepted evangelists.[1] Now Justin lived through the half century that followed the death of John. He had travelled extensively. He was held in honor by his contemporaries and successors. He gives proof, therefore, that the prevailing conception of the life and teachings of Christ in his time, was identical with that of the canonical historians, and was derived from them. There was *only one tradition* in the Church from the beginning.

We subjoin brief remarks on the probable mode in which the earliest records of the life of Jesus originated. Jesus himself wrote nothing. He acted with quickening and renovating power upon the world's life. But for Him to become an author would

[1] Semisch, *Denkwürdigkeiten des Justin*, s. 344. The statement of Semisch we have verified by a careful and repeated perusal of Justin's writings.

violate a subtle feeling of propriety of which all of us are sensible. At first, the fresh recollections of the men and women who had known him, especially of the disciples who had composed, as it were, his family, were the unwritten book which all, who desired, could consult. But in that age, and when the gospel soon found numerous adherents among Greeks, both foreign Jews and heathen, it was impossible that the teachings of Christ and the events of his life should long remain unrecorded. At the outset, it is probable that isolated memoranda were made of particular events or discourses. These rudimental records first came into being in Galilee and about Capernaum. In this way, a cluster of traditions would easily come to exist. Then, and before long, followed the combination of them, and the earliest efforts at framing a connected history. Such were the essays which Luke notices in his prologue. At length, within thirty or forty years of the death of Christ, there were efforts at more regular composition, of which the works of Luke are the maturest specimen. The first three Gospels present indubitable traces of such an origin as we have indicated. We are not to look for chronological precision in narratives thus constructed. We are not to look for light on all parts and points of the Saviour's earthly life. The Gospel of John, an original composition, emanating from the mind and heart of the loved disciple, is the document to be first consulted in the *scientific* construction of the Saviour's history. The four together enable us to gain a knowledge of Jesus, not so full as we crave, yet sufficient for every practical need.

ESSAY IV.

BAUR ON PARTIES IN THE APOSTOLIC CHURCH AND THE CHARACTER OF THE BOOK OF ACTS.[1]

THE great question which the Church in the apostolic age was required to consider and determine, was the relation of Christianity to the ritual law of the Old Testament. Was that law still binding? Or rather—for in this form, as was natural, the question first came up—was that law binding on the Gentile believers? In short, could a man be a Christian without first becoming a Jew? It cannot be denied that the full extent of the commotion which this question stirred up, is better understood in the light of recent discussions than was the case formerly. Discounting very much, as we shall, from the extravagant representation of the Tübingen critical school, we still feel that the sound of this great conflict reverberates through no inconsiderable portion of the New Testament Scriptures. The Epistle to the Galatians is a

[1] *Das Christenthum u. die Christliche Kirche der drei ersten Jahrhunderte*, von Dr. Ferdinand Christian Baur. Tübingen, 1853. (Author's last Ed., 1860.)

Die Composition u. Entstehung der Apostelgeschichte, von Eduard Lekebusch. Gotha, 1854.

fervid argument on this one theme. The Epistle to the Romans, though not devoted—the opinion of Baur to the contrary notwithstanding—to this distinctive subject, gives to the matter of the relation of the Jew to the Gentile, a prominent place. The two Epistles to the Corinthians bear witness to the dissension which the same question had provoked. The Epistle to the Hebrews is an argument designed to reconcile the Jewish believer to the abrogation of the old ordinances, and to keep him from lapsing, out of love to them, from the faith in Christ. The book of Acts, and most of the other monuments of the apostolic age, contain more or less of allusion to the grand question we have described.

For it *was* a grand question. It was not simply the question—which of itself to a Jew could not fail to have the deepest interest—of the transitory or perpetual validity of the Mosaic laws and institutions. But it was, also, the question whether Christianity was, in its real nature, a spiritual, and so a universal, religion, or only an improved sect or phase of Judaism. In this transitional era, when the kingdom of God was breaking through and casting off its rudimental and provisional form, and assuming the permanent features of a religion of the spirit and a religion for mankind—in that crisis of history, it was inevitable that such commotion and controversy should arise. It was one illustration of the truth that the Son of Man did not come to bring peace, but a sword. As new chemical changes and combinations are attended with heat and combustion, so is it with every such revolution and new beginning in the course of history. And we may add that even to the present day, the Protestant definitions of the essential nature of the gospel and of the method of salvation, are sought especially in those fervent declarations against bondage to rites and ceremonies, and in favor of the sufficiency of Christ, which were elicited from the Apostle Paul in the progress of this momentous controversy.

The history of this controversy, and of the question and parties involved in it, has lately acquired a new importance, from the place which it is made to fill in the historical theory of Baur and his school. Strauss, in his Life of Christ, had said little of the book of Acts, and that little of not much weight. This book remained a bulwark of faith for any who were disturbed by the skeptical criticism to which the evangelical histories had been subjected. Here, at least, was the testimony of a contemporary of the apostles, and a companion of one of them, which established the fact of a miraculous dispensation, and afforded proof of the prior miracles of the gospel. But things could not be left by the Tübingen critics in this unsatisfactory state. The book of Acts was next made the object of attack; and, what we have now specially to observe, this attack was a part of a systematic theory, by which the origin of catholic Christianity, or of Christianity in the form we have it, and of the larger part of the canonical writings of the New Testament, is explained in a naturalistic way, through a peculiar view of the character of the conflict to which we have adverted, and of the consequences to which it led. This attempted reconstruction of the history of the apostolic age, on account of the extraordinary learning and ability with which it has been defended, especially by Baur; on account, also, of the light which it incidentally throws on the condition of the apostolic church; and, above all, on account of that increased confidence in the strength of the Christian cause which the failure of this assault upon it is fitted to inspire, deserves a fair examination.

Before engaging in this task, it may be well to say a word in answer to an inquiry that is likely to occur to the mind of a reader not conversant with the early history of the Church. How, it may naturally be asked, can such a theory as that of the modern Tübingen school, denying as it does the accepted views respecting the origin of most of the canonical books of the New Testament, have even a show of plausibility? How can it keep the field for a moment in the face of the testimony of the early Church? Such theories are possible, we reply, for the reason that so scanty and fragmentary remains of literature have come down to us from the period immediately following the apostolic age. After the death of the leading apostles and the destruction of Jerusalem, there succeeds an interval which may be properly styled a *saeculum obscurum.* We have the writings of John which appeared in the latter part of the first century. Then we have the apostolic Fathers. But these writings are not of a nature to satisfy many of the most important inquiries in regard to the state of the Church. The early Greek Apologists, if we possessed them intact, would be invaluable; but the first copious works emanating from this class of writers are the treatises of Justin Martyr, whose earliest extant production falls into the second quarter of the second century. Precious, from a historical point of view, as these works of Justin are, they consist of Apologies to the Pagan and to the Jew, and leave unnoticed many points on which light might have been thrown, had their author been writing, for example, on some subject of doctrinal theology. In brief, so far as this very interesting era is concerned, we have peculiar occasion to lament—to borrow the language of Grote when speaking of Greek literature in general—that "we possess only what has drifted ashore from the wreck of a stranded vessel." [1] We do not mean that the internal evidence of the New Testament documents, the numerous items of proof gathered from relics of the literature of the next period, and the testimony of the great writers of the second half of the second century, are insufficient. They do constitute a body of evidence which effectually refutes the main positions of the Tübingen school.

[1] Grote's Preface to the *History of Greece.*

But for the reasons we have stated, there is room for the essays of conjectural criticism. A picture of the state of things in the early Church may be drawn, a theory ingeniously framed, whose inconsistency with the truth is not, at the first blush, so patent as to preclude the need of a careful refutation. Not until such a theory is thoroughly probed and compared with the multiform evidence pertaining to the subject, is it clearly seen to be untenable.

The following are the essential points in Baur's theory.[1] The doctrine of Christ was, in principle, an abolishment of the Old Testament ritual and of the distinction, as to religious rights and privileges, between the Jew and the Gentile. But the original disciples did not advance to the conclusion which lay impliedly in the religious ideas of the Master. On the contrary, they persisted to the end in the traditional persuasion that the way of salvation was through Judaism; that the Gentile must enter the Church by that door, and that the uncircumcised had no part in the Messiah's kingdom. The Apostle Paul alone was

[1] We have drawn our representations of the Tübingen views chiefly from the work of Baur, the title of which is given at the beginning of this Essay. This work is the final, condensed presentation of his theory relative to the origin and early history of Christianity. The work of Lekebusch (the title of which is also given above) is the ablest refutation, with which we are acquainted, of Baur's theory in its bearing on the Acts of the Apostles. In this branch of the discussion, especially, we have frequently availed ourselves of his suggestions.

so enlightened as to perceive that the old rites were abrogated by the nature of the new religion, and that the Gentile stood on an equality with the Jew, faith being the sole requirement. Nay, he held that circumcision and the ritual were no longer admissible, since they implied some other object of reliance than Christ, some other condition of salvation besides faith. Hence, there was a radical difference in doctrine between Peter and the Jerusalem Christians on the one hand, and Paul and his followers on the other, which led to a personal disagreement and estrangement between these two apostolic leaders. There grew up two antagonistic types of Christianity, two divisions of the Church, separate and unfriendly to each other. Such was the state of things at the end of the apostolic age. Then followed attempts to reconcile the difference and to bridge the gulf that separated Gentile from Jewish, Pauline from Petrine Christianity. To this end, various irenical and compromising books were written in the name of the apostles and their helpers. The only Epistles of Paul which are counted as genuine are that to the Romans, that to the Galatians, and the two Epistles to the Corinthians. But the most important monument of this pacifying effort is the book of Acts, written in the earlier part of the second century by a Pauline Christian who, by making Paul something of a Judaizer and then representing Peter as agreeing with him in the recognition of the rights of the Gentiles, hoped, not in vain, to produce a mutual friendliness between the respective partisans of the rival apostles. The Acts is a fiction founded on facts, and written for a specific doctrinal purpose. The narrative of the council or conference of the apostles, for example (Acts xv.), is pronounced a pure invention of the writer, and such a representation of the condition of things as is inconsistent with Paul's own statements, and, for this and other reasons, plainly false. The same ground is taken in respect to the conversion of Cornelius and the vision of Peter attending it.

Before we directly examine these views, let us observe the main facts in the history of the reception of the Gentiles into the Church, assuming, for the present, that the documents are trustworthy. We shall show hereafter, especially in regard to the Acts, that the impeachment of their genuineness and credibility cannot be sustained.

Without doubt, Christ himself observed, during his life, the ceremonial law.[1] Until that law should be supplanted by his finished work—by the act of God who gave it—he considered it obligatory. As a faithful servant, he came under the law. He rejected, indeed, the traditions of the elders, the ascetic, superstitious practices which the Pharisees had appended to the Old Testament legislation. So he signified the

[1] On the position of Christ in reference to the law, we have little difference with Baur. Baur's observations on this topic are marked

authority that belonged to him to modify the law by fulfilling it, or carrying it forward to a form answering fully to the idea underlying it—as when he declared himself the Lord of the Sabbath (Mark ii. 28).[1] It is true, however, that complying with the ritual himself, he also bade others comply with it, even with its minute provisions. At the same time, both by implication and explicitly, he authorized the conclusion that in the new era which he was introducing, the ceremonies of the law would have no longer any place, nor would they be required. They belonged to another, a rudimental, preparatory system, that was passing away. The barrier between Jew and Gentile was about to fall down. The sublime declaration of Jesus at the well of Sychem respecting the nature of acceptable worship and the abolishment of all restrictions of place, as well as many other passages hardly less significant, will readily occur to the reader. We will accommodate ourselves to the predilection of the Tübingen critics for the Gospel of Matthew, and draw some illustrations from that source. First, the spiritual character of the doctrines and precepts of Jesus is a most impressive characteristic. Righteousness and piety, as described in the Sermon on the Mount, belong to the tempers of the heart. The inwardness of true religion was never so thoroughly and sublimely laid down as in this teach-

by his usual perspicuity and force. See *Das Christenthum*, etc., s. 25 seq.

[1] So De Wette and Meyer.

ing. For him who thus taught, what value could forms, in themselves considered, possess? The love of God and man is the sum and substance of duty; to be perfect as the Father in Heaven is perfect, the sole aspiration. Secondly, in his direct opposition to the Pharisees, the real character of the principles of Christ comes out. It is formalism—a trust in forms—which calls forth his reprobation. "Not that which goeth into the mouth defileth a man; but that which cometh out of the mouth." "Those things which proceed out of the mouth *come forth from the heart;* and they defile the man" "But to eat with unwashen hands defileth not a man." (Matt. xv. 11, 18, 20). What a simple and luminous exposition of the nature of good and evil! How clear that in the eyes of Jesus, forms had no inherent value, no abiding existence! The abrogation of the former system he affirmed and explained by saying that new wine must not be put in old bottles, or new cloth patched into an old garment. How could he more pointedly affirm that he was establishing a system so far different from the old, that the features of the two could not be blended? To cling to the old ritual, as something essential, would have the effect to destroy the fundamental peculiarity of the new system. Attempt it not, "lest the bottles should break and the wine be spilled" (Matt. ix. 17 paral.). This, be it remembered, was in reply to the question, why his disciples abstained from fasting. Thirdly, Christ forewarned his Jewish hearers that the

Gentiles would even take their place in gaining possession of the blessings of the new kingdom. In connection with the centurion's exhibition of faith in the power of Jesus to heal his absent servant, he said that many would come from the east and west, many Gentiles, and sit down with the Patriarchs in the kingdom of Heaven, whilst the children of the kingdom—the natural expectants of the inheritance—would be cast out (Matt. viii. 11, 12). In the parable of the vineyard and the rebellious husbandmen, who stand for the Jews, their crime in slaying the messengers of the owner, and finally his son and heir, leads to their destruction and to the letting out of "the vineyard unto other husbandmen." The Jews, rejecting the Messiah, are to be supplanted by the Gentiles. In keeping with such teaching are the predictions uttered by Christ concerning the destruction of Jerusalem and the downfall of the temple. Looking down upon the city, he said: "Behold your house is left unto you desolate!" But the disciples were commanded to carry the gospel to the Gentiles—to disciple the nations. That the Gentiles were to be embraced in the Messianic kingdom was a familiar part of prophecy. As to how the kingdom was to be extended over them, was a point in regard to which the prevalent anticipations were colored by the mistaken ideas and unspiritual ambition of the people. But the incorporation of the Gentiles, in some way, into the Messiah's kingdom, all the Jews expected. Christ commanded that the same gospel which the disciples had received themselves should be offered to their acceptance—adding the direction that the believer should be baptized, and the promise that he should be saved. All other points he left to be settled in the light of providential events and under the subsequent teaching of the Holy Spirit. In accordance with that reserve which adapted the disclosure of truth to the recipiency of the learner, Christ went no farther than to throw out the great principles, the command and the intimations which have been adverted to, not defining precisely either what course the heathen were to take with reference to the Mosaic ritual, or what was to become of ceremonial Judaism. These things the apostles were left to learn, in the prosecution of their work, by the outward instruction of providential events and the inward illumination by the Spirit. This reserve on the part of Christ is a characteristic and impressive example of the divine method of teaching. Instead of tearing up the old institutions—sweeping them away by a peremptory edict, before the mind was prepared for the change by perceiving that they had become superfluous, he left the Church to be first educated up to the requisite point. The dropping of the old forms was to result, as a logical and necessary consequence, from the expansive force of the new system. The logic of events—the full comprehension of the gospel—the distinct understanding of the offices of Christ—would undermine and supplant the ritual law. How much better for the revolution to take place thus, than to be precipitated by an abrupt decree, enforced as a law from without upon minds which had gained no insight into the ground and reason for a seeming repeal of divinely given statutes!

Let us now proceed to note the manner in which the great lesson was learned. The apostles, and the infant church at Jerusalem under their guidance, continue to observe the ceremonies of the law as of old. They have no thought of dispensing with circumcision and the other requirements of the ritual. They are Jews, believing in the Messiah. The first murmur of difference in that young community, of which the opening part of Acts presents so delightful a picture, is the complaint of the Hellenists—the foreign, Greek-speaking Jews—that their poor are neglected in the distribution of alms. This little incident, apart from its immediate consequence, is significant as bringing before us the two classes of Jews, which, though closely and cordially united by a common descent and common creed, are yet in some respects dissimilar, as subsequent events prove. Of the deacons chosen, one is said to have been a proselyte of righteousness; that is, a heathen admitted by circumcision to a full participation in the privileges of the Jew. The persecution attending the martyrdom of Stephen[1] disperses the Church and leads to the

[1] Stephen was a Hellenist. He was charged by "false witnesses" with blaspheming the temple and the law, and with saying that

first effective preaching of the word beyond Jerusalem. The vision of Peter, and the baptism of Cornelius, are the earliest recognition of Gentile Christianity. Whether Cornelius was, or was not, a proselyte of the gate, cannot be determined, nor is the question very material. The previous feeling of Peter and the Jerusalem Christians, as to the qualifications for admission to the Christian Church, is seen in his remark on the occasion of his interview with Cornelius: "Ye know how that it is an unlawful thing for a man that is a Jew to keep company or come unto one of another nation."[2] Moreover, on his return to Jerusalem, "they that were of the circumcision"—the Jewish Christians—call him to account for having eaten with Gentiles (Acts xi. 2, 3). His defence is a recapitulation of the circumstances of his vision and a statement of the fact that the gifts of

Jesus of Nazareth would "destroy this place," and "change the customs" delivered by Moses (Acts vi. 13, 14). The witnesses were "false," since doubtless they maliciously perverted what Stephen had said. Yet it is evident from the tone of his speech—see especially Acts vii. 47–50, and the denunciation he was uttering when he was interrupted—that the charge was not a pure invention, but was built up on what Stephen had said. See Neander's *Gesch. d. Pflanz. u. Leitung.* u. s. w.

[2] Abstinence to this extent from intercourse with the heathen was not enjoined in the Pentateuch. But Peter's remark represents the feeling and usual practice of the later Jews. The proselyte of the gate was uncircumcised, so that there was a like repugnance to intercourse with him—at least to sitting at the table with him.

the Spirit had been exhibited by the new converts. "Forasmuch," he says, "then, as God gave them the like gift as he did unto us who believed on the Lord Jesus Christ, what was I that I could withstand God?" This explanation for the time appeases the discontent. But the principal event is the establishment of a Gentile church, or a church made up partly of converted and baptized heathen, at Antioch. We read that those who were scattered abroad by the persecution following the death of Stephen "travelled as far as Phenice, and Cyprus, and Antioch, *preaching the word unto none but unto Jews only.* And some of them were men of Cyprus and Cyrene, which when they were come to Antioch spake unto the *Grecians,*" not Hellenists but Hellenes, "preaching the Lord Jesus." A great number of the Grecians—uncircumcised Gentiles—moved by that sense of spiritual necessities which prevailed so extensively among the heathen throughout the Roman world, believed in Christ. Observe it was men of Cyprus and Cyrene—Hellenists—who laid the foundation of this Gentile church. Barnabas, himself a Jew by birth, but a native of Cyprus, is sent from Jerusalem to visit this rising church so strangely composed. Seeing the reality of the work of grace which had been effected, he rejoiced in it, and having brought Paul—who was also, by birth a Hellenist—from Tarsus, whither he had retired, the two labored together for a year, "and taught much people." Paul is now fairly embarked upon the grand work of his life. Partly on account of the peculiarity of his inward experience and partly on account of the depth and logical force of his mind—not to speak of special enlightenment from above—he discerned most clearly that faith, and faith alone, is the condition of salvation; that to make the soul depend for pardon upon legal observances along with faith, is to set the ground of salvation, partially at least, outside of Christ, and to found the Christian hope upon self-righteousness instead of his merits. He went straight to the unavoidable inference that the ritual system is not to be observed as a means of salvation, and is in no sense obligatory upon the Gentiles. Thus Paul stands forth, in this part of the apostolic age, the glorious champion of the freedom and universality of the gospel. It is a religion for the world—not for the Jew alone, but for the Gentile equally. The wall that divided the two classes of mankind, "the hand-writing of ordinances" being now blotted out, has been levelled to the ground. The missionary journey of Paul and Barnabas greatly enlarged the number of heathen converts; for when they had first preached to the Jews in the places they visited, they then turned to the Gentiles. After their return they continued their labors at Antioch, now the parent-of churches among the heathen, and the second metropolis, as it were, of Christianity. But the church of Antioch is disturbed by certain men which came down from Judea—judaizers—who declared the necessity of circumcision for salvation. As the result of the "no small dissension and disputation with them," it is determined to send Paul and Barnabas at the head of a deputation to Jerusalem to confer with the apostles and elders upon this question. Of this visit, besides the narrative in the Acts, we have the advantage of an invaluable notice from the pen of Paul himself (Gal. ii.). Waiving for the present the consideration of this last passage, we see from the account of Luke, that when the messengers from Antioch had been received by their brethren at Jerusalem, "*certain of the sect of the Pharisees which believed*" brought forward their demand, that the Gentile converts should be circumcised and required to observe the Mosaic law. It is interesting to notice that the zealous judaizers were converted Pharisees. After much disputing, Peter and James interpose; the former referring to the events connected with the baptism of Cornelius, and both rejecting the proposition of the judaizers. Their judgment and that of the church was, that certain statutes which the Jew deemed most essential, should be complied with by the heathen converts. They were to abstain "from meats offered to idols, and from blood, and from things strangled, and from fornication." The fact of the reading of the law of Moses in the synagogues of every city on the Sabbath, is set forth as a reason for the propriety of this requirement.[1] Thus, so far as the influence of the apostles went, this great question was put to rest,

[1] The precise significance of this reason has been a mooted point among commentators. Of the various interpretations which have been suggested, it appears to us that the choice lies between two. Some would paraphrase the passage thus: "as to the Jews, *they* need no prescription, since they will of course follow the law which is read on the Sabbath." This was the interpretation of Chrysostom, and is adopted by Neander. Others, including Meyer and Lekebusch, make the passage a statement of the reason why the Gentiles were to conform in these particulars to the Jewish law; the reason, namely, that the reading of the law in the synagogues every Sabbath, rendered it more offensive to the Jews to see that law, in these conspicuous points, disregarded. This appears to us to be the true sense of the passage. Gieseler, and also Baur, would make the passage signify by implication, that "the Jewish law had proved itself ineffectual for the conversion of the Gentiles, whilst the opposite result in connection with the preaching of Paul and his associates, had shown the ceremonial law to be the only hindrance to the spread of the true religion." Ewald suggests that the reason was advanced to pacify the fear of those who thought that the Mosaic law would fall into disuse if this indulgence were extended to the Gentile converts. Both these interpretations seem to us much less natural than the one we have approved. The view we adopt is supported by the authority of Professor Hackett in his scholarly work on the Acts.

As to the decision itself, it consists of four particulars. The heathen converts were to abstain from the flesh of animals slain as a sacrifice to idols, from using the blood of animals for food, from fornication, and from eating animals who had been strangled or put to death by any other mode than by shedding their blood. The first of these was in compliance with Ex. xxxiv. 15. The second and the fourth were Levitical statutes, and founded on the sacredness of blood. The third, a moral prohibition, was joined with these *adiaphora*, because in the progress of heathen corruption it had come to be regarded as almost an *adiaphoron*—a thing morally

and on grounds satisfactory to Paul and his coadjutors. But the judaizing party was far from resting satisfied under this most Christian arrangement. As all know, they pursued the Apostle Paul wherever he went, sowing division in the churches he planted and striving to destroy the esteem in which he was held by his converts. They seem to have sometimes made use of the name of Peter, and to have pretended to be his followers, and we find a self-styled party of Peter among the opponents of Paul in the Corinthian church.

After the conference at Jerusalem, there are two occurrences that deserve special notice. The one is the controversy of Paul and Peter, or, rather, the rebuke of Peter by Paul at Antioch. Peter had associated freely with the Gentile converts—had eaten with them. But on the arrival of certain judaizing Christians from Jerusalem, he changed his course out of a timid regard to their prejudice, and withdrew from the Gentile believers. Even Barnabas was led to follow his example. Paul publicly "withstood" Peter, saying: "If thou then, being a Jew, livest after the manner of the Gentiles (ἐϑνικῶς), why compellest thou the Gentiles to live as do the Jews (ἰουδαΐζειν)?" We shall hereafter consider this controversy more at length. Here we merely call

indifferent. See on this point, Winer's *Realworterb.*, Art. *Hure*, and Meyer on Acts xv. 20.

attention to the ground of Paul's complaint, which was a dereliction from his own principles, or hypocritical conduct, on the part of Peter. The charge was that "he walked not uprightly." It was not an error of opinion, but a moral error, which Paul censured.

The other occurrence requiring special notice, is the last visit of Paul to Jerusalem. The narrative of Luke gives us a clear view of the state of things in the church there. Paul and his associates were cordially received. But when he had recounted to the apostles the fruits of his ministry among the Gentiles, and they had welcomed the intelligence, James informs him of a prejudice against him in the minds of many, owing to a report which had gained credence. He had been charged, doubtless by Jews and Judaizers from Asia and the west, with having urged the foreign, Greek-speaking Jews—the Hellenists—to forsake the Mosaic law and abstain from circumcising their children. This accusation was false. The Jewish-Christian members of the Gentile churches were, not unlikely, as Ewald conjectures, falling away from the observance of the ritual. And this might have given occasion to the charge against Paul. But there is not a particle of evidence tending to show that he ever sought to dissuade Jews from complying with the ritual. He rejected the doctrine that the observance of the law is essential to salvation. He rejected the doctrine that the observance of it was obligatory upon Gentile converts; and the adoption by them of the Jewish ritual under the idea that salvation was contingent upon observing it, he regarded as a fatal error—as a dishonor to the sufficiency of Christ, and a method of self-righteousness. But his opposition to the law extended no farther. On the contrary, as he himself said, to the Jews he made himself a Jew. He respected their national feelings and customs. Hence he found no difficulty in taking upon him the vow which James recommended, as a visible proof that the charges against him were false, and that he was no renegade from the religion of his fathers.[1] But this act did not save him from the fanatical hatred of the Jews from Asia—the unbelieving Jews who had so often stirred up tumults against him in the towns where he had preached. However he may have pacified the *believing* Jews by showing respect for the national customs, he did not secure himself from the violence of the Asian Jews who were present in the city in large numbers, and in addition to their old enmity were exasperated by the erroneous impression that Paul had taken Trophimus, an Ephesian Gentile whom they had seen with him, into the temple. Hence the mob, which had for its final consequence the journey of the apostle to Rome.

From this survey we are brought to the conclusion

[1] The feeling of James respecting the propriety of observing the law is plainly discovered in Acts xxi. 24.

that while it is true that the Apostle Paul understood the relations of the new and the old dispensation with peculiar clearness, and vindicated the liberty of the Gentiles with a singular depth of conviction and an unvarying consistency, it is nevertheless true, also, that Peter and the original apostles, and the church of Jerusalem, as far as its public action is concerned, were in cordial fellowship with Paul and willingly tolerated the Gentile branch of the church, not imposing upon it the yoke of the law, with the exception of the few prudential regulations recommended by the apostolic convention.

Baur and his followers maintain an opposite opinion. There existed, they hold, a radical opposition in principle between these two branches of the church, which involved a mutual antagonism on the part of their apostolic leaders. The proof of this position Baur professes to find chiefly in certain expressions of the Apostle Paul in his Epistles, which are alleged to be inconsistent with many of the representations found in the Acts. From the two Epistles to the Corinthians and the Epistle to the Galatians, Baur draws most of the arguments on which he relies to establish his position. There was in the Corinthian church, we are told, a party which denied that Paul had a right to consider himself an apostle, and sought to supplant him by setting up the superior authority of Peter and the rest of the original disciples of Christ. This party was stirred up by Jewish Christians who brought the letters of recommendation from Jerusalem, to which Paul sarcastically alludes.[1] In the Epistle to the Galatians, it is said, the radical diversity of principles between the two types of Christianity, already developed in the Epistles to the Corinthians, is attended with the record of a personal alienation between Peter and Paul, which, so far as we know, was never healed. In the Epistle to the Romans, Paul is supposed to write in a milder and more conciliatory spirit; announcing his intention to carry the contribution of money to Jerusalem, and in other ways manifesting a disposition to overcome the hostility which, it is pretended, existed against him and his doctrine on the side of the mother-church. Especially does Baur dwell upon the account in the Acts of the circumcision of Timothy, asserting that such an act would be absolutely incompatible with the doctrine laid down by Paul (Gal. v. 2): "If ye be circumcised, Christ shall profit you nothing." Other instances of conformity to the Jewish law, which are attributed to Paul in the Acts, he pronounces to be equally unhistorical. The entire representation given there of the personal relations of Paul to Peter and his associates, Baur affirms to be contrary to the intimations and assertions of Paul, and to be contradicted, in particular, by Paul's narrative of his

[1] Such letters might be taken, probably, by any Christian who was *rectus in ecclesia*, in case he wished to travel.

conference with the apostles, in the second chapter of Galatians.

We believe that these propositions of the Tübingen critics are not sustained by the evidence to which they appeal, but are flatly contradicted by it, and that their positions are contrary to the truth. What evidence is there, in the Epistle to the Corinthians, of such a division and hostility as Baur affirms to have existed? There was a faction which claimed to be the disciples of Peter. But what proof is there that *he* gave them any countenance? There was also, among the opponents of Paul, a party claiming to follow Apollos—himself a disciple of the Pauline doctrine. Who pretends that Apollos encouraged such a movement? To our mind, all the language of Paul in reference to the other apostles which is found in these Epistles, proves the opposite of Baur's proposition. The apostles are spoken of as one body of fellow-laborers. In vindicating his authority against the aspersions cast upon him, Paul asserts, to be sure, that "he is not a whit behind the very chiefest apostles" (2 Cor. xi. 5). But he does not say or insinuate that "the chiefest apostles" are *no* apostles, or that they are perverters of the truth. The opposite of this is everywhere implied. He says: "God has set forth *us the apostles* last, as it were appointed to death;" and in the record of hardship that follows, he associates with himself his fellow-apostles. Witness also his appeal to the testimony of the other apostles—of Peter, James, and the rest—in proof of the Resurrection of Christ, and the coupling of their testimony with the reference to the appearance of Christ to himself: "For *I am the least of the apostles* and not worthy to be called an apostle, because I persecuted the Church of God." He compares himself with the other apostles and takes the lowest place among them! But a more striking refutation of Baur's view is contained in the remarks of Paul upon the contribution he was collecting for the poor brethren at Jerusalem. In the First Epistle he exhorts the Corinthians to aid in making up this "contribution for the saints"—*saints* it appears they were, notwithstanding their supposed heresy and hostility! And in the Second Epistle he speaks of the matter more at length. He had long been engaged in this charitable service (ix. 2). He says that the conveyance, by his instrumentality, of this contribution, will not only relieve "the wants of the saints," but will call forth at Jerusalem "thanksgiving unto God;" that the church at Jerusalem will find occasion to glorify God for the faithfulness of the Corinthians in thus practically carrying out their Christian profession, and for the genuineness of their Christian fellowship (*κοινωνίας*) manifested in this liberality. He adds that the saints at Jerusalem with prayer "will long after you" on account of the abounding grace of God vouchsafed to you. A deep, yearning, prayerful interest will be excited towards the Corinthian Christians in the hearts of their brethren at Jerusalem. Who can believe that this contribution is going to a church which is considered by Paul to be made up of Judaizers—professors of what he calls another gospel? If the Corinthians had understood Paul's letter to them as Baur does, what must have been their surprise at these incongruous exhortations and expressions of fraternal regard for the Jerusalem believers! Turn we now to the Epistle to the Romans, written not long after. There we find the apostle pouring out his love and compassion for his kinsmen according to the flesh—explaining that the apparent rejection of them by Divine Providence is temporary. Of the contribution he says: "Now I go unto Jerusalem to minister unto the saints. For it hath pleased them of Macedonia and Achaia to make a certain contribution for the poor saints which are at Jerusalem. It hath pleased them verily, and their debtors they are. For if the Gentiles have been made partakers of their spiritual things"—for Jerusalem was the mother-church whence Christianity with all its blessings flowed out to the Gentiles —"their duty is also to minister unto them in carnal things" (Rom. xv. 25 seq.).[1] Here the Apostle Paul honors the Jerusalem church as the fountain whence the Gentiles have derived their Christianity. Are these expressions compatible with the notion that this

[1] Principally on account of its alleged complaisance towards the Jewish Christians, the xvth chapter (as well as the xvith) of this

church had no fellowship with the uncircumcised converts of Christianity, and that its leaders were hostile to Paul, and in turn considered by him to be involved in fundamental error? The assertion or insinuation by Baur, that there was any essential change in Paul's feeling between the writing of the Epistles to the Corinthians and Galatians, and that to the Romans, is without foundation. During the whole period in which the composition of the first-named Epistles occurred, Paul was interested in the business of gathering the contribution which he afterwards carried to Jerusalem.

But the main reliance of Baur is on Paul's narrative, in the second chapter of Galatians, of his conference with the apostles and his subsequent conflict with Peter at Antioch. But an examination of this interesting passage, instead of confirming Baur's theory, will, as we think, demonstrate its falsity. Be it remembered that Paul is writing to a church which the Judaizers had tried to turn away both from his

Epistle is declared by Baur—without the shadow of external proof and contrary to the internal evidence of both style and thought—to be an interpolation. His argument is a mere *petitio principii.* The arbitrary attempt to cast these inconvenient passages out of the Epistle, is well answered by Meyer in his Commentary on the Romans (K. xv.). Bleek, a cautious and unprejudiced critic, says, in reference to the denial by Baur and Schwegler of the genuineness of the last two chapters of the Epistle: "The grounds for this denial are wholly false and untenable, and the genuineness of these chapters, as well as the fact of their belonging to our Epistle, is to be regarded as certain." *Einl. in d. N. T.*, s. 416.

doctrine and from their esteem and respect for his person and apostolic authority. He is placed under the necessity of explaining his relations to the other apostles; and this he does by showing, on the one hand, his own independence and equality with them, and, on the other, the full recognition and fellowship which they had accorded to him. He is speaking of the same visit which Luke describes in the fifteenth chapter of the Acts. Fourteen years after his first visit to Jerusalem, when he had spent a fortnight with Peter (i. 18), he went there in company with Barnabas and Titus. He communicated "privately to them which were of reputation" (*τοῖς δοκοῦσι*), the gospel which he was in the habit of preaching.[1] His motive in taking this course is set forth in the following words: "lest by any means I should run, or had run, in vain." That is to say, he explained his method of preaching in order that he might be rightly judged and appreciated by his fellow-apostles. We shall see, as we proceed, whether or not he was successful. Before stating the result of his conference, he describes the ineffectual attempt of "false brethren unawares brought in" to procure the circumcision of Titus, and his own prompt and effectual resistance

[1] This account by Paul, and the narrative in the xvth of Acts, supplement each other. The latter relates to the *public* transaction, including the decision which was reached; the former, as above stated, refers to a conference of a more private nature. But the phraseology in Gal. ii. 2 *implies* that there was a *public* conference also. See Ellicott and Meyer on the passage.

to their endeavor. The "false brethren" are judaizing reactionists having no right in the Christian brotherhood, but having crept in, as it were—intruded where they do not belong. They made it their business "to spy out the liberty" of the Gentile converts; that is, they watched with an inimical intent, designing to bring these converts to accept the yoke of the Mosaic law. Here the difference between such false brethren and the apostles is palpable. Would Paul have undertaken to explain his gospel to these "false brethren," lest he should run in vain? Rather would he, as he did, sternly resist them. But the refusal of Paul to circumcise Titus is used as an argument to disprove the historical truth of the circumcision of Timothy. It is said that Paul would not have done at one time what he absolutely refused to do at another. But why did he refuse to circumcise Titus? First, because he was a heathen by birth, and secondly, because his circumcision was demanded on doctrinal grounds, so that to yield would have been to give up at once the rights of the Gentiles and justification by faith. But Timothy was the son of a Jewish mother, and he was circumcised for a totally different reason from that for which the circumcision of Titus was demanded. Timothy was circumcised out of respect to unconverted Jews, not converted Judaizers. His circumcision neither imperilled the rights of the Gentiles, nor clashed with the doctrine of Justification. In this act, Paul simply made himself "a Jew unto the Jew," on his maxim of making himself all things to all men—so far as no principle was violated.[1] There is, then, no inconsistency such as is charged by the Tübingen critics. The circumcision of Timothy as truly accords with the principles of Paul, as the circumcision of Titus would have contradicted them. Having mentioned the circumstances concerning Titus, Paul now returns to his conference with the apostles: "But of those"—from those—"who seemed to be somewhat,"—that is, were regarded with most respect—here Paul breaks off the sentence by throwing in this parenthetical remark: "whatsoever they were, it maketh no matter to me; God accepteth no man's person;" and then he adds: "for they who seemed to be somewhat, in conference added nothing to me." The mode of characterizing the apostles as "those who seem to be somewhat," is misinterpreted when it is supposed to contain a tinge of irony. Nothing of that sort belongs to the phraseology. It is the equivalent of the earlier expression—"them which were of reputation." And as to the parenthetical clause, it must be remembered that Paul's enemies were endeavoring to disprove his claim to be an apostle, and to represent that the older apostles were possessed of superior authority. His purpose is to express, as against this disparagement, his consciousness of a perfect equality in respect to rights and claims, with the other apostles. And

[1] 1 Cor. ix. 20 seq.

having been led to allude to the high estimation in which they stood, he adds a cautionary explanation which would exclude the inference that he considered himself in any degree subordinate to them. "Whatever they were—however high may be the standing of men, God is not thereby rendered partial towards them." The last clause in the quotation above, is, however, the most important. Paul says of the apostles, that in conference they added nothing—*οὐδὲν προσανέθεντο*—to him. He had shortly before said that on his arrival in Jerusalem he "communicated"—*ἀνεθέμην* is the word—to the apostles the gospel he had preached. And now he says that *they*—*οὐδὲν προσανέθεντο*—had nothing to add to that gospel by way of correction or supplement. They had no fault to find with it, no new principles to suggest; "*but contrariwise*" they—what? for everything turns on the statement that is to follow—"*they gave to me and Barnabas the right hands of fellowship.*" Seeing that Paul had been successful in converting the Gentiles as Peter had been successful in converting the Jews, and heeding this instruction of Providence; seeing, moreover, the "grace that was given" to Paul, the other apostles—who seemed to be pillars, or, rather, were esteemed as the leaders and supporters, of the Jerusalem church—Peter, James, and John, gave the hand of fraternity and fellowship, it being understood that in accordance with the plain suggestions of Providence, Paul and Barnabas should labor in heathen countries, whilst the other apostles should "go unto the circumcision." These statements, instead of supporting, utterly demolish Baur's theory. To say as he does, in effect, that this union was on the outside—was, in fact, a peaceable division and schism in the church, in which those who affirmed the necessity of circumcision and those who denied it, being unable to walk together, concluded to divide without an open quarrel, is to offer as gross a misinterpretation of a Scriptural passage as can well be conceived. The Apostle Paul expressly says that the other apostles had nothing to add to the principles which governed him in his preaching. He implies, and intends to convey the idea, that Peter, James, and John, were satisfied with the gospel which he preached. The imputation that Paul gave the right hand of fellowship to those who maintained, to use his own language, "another gospel," when neither he nor they *felt* that they were brethren, holding a common faith and engaged in a common work, is wholly inconsistent with his known character, and would reflect upon him and them the deepest dishonor. That the fellowship was cordially meant is proved in a manner which no audacity of denial can gainsay, by the *reasons* which Paul assigns for the act,—the perception, namely, that a great work of God had been done among the Gentiles, and that Paul was himself endued with heavenly grace for the work of an apostle. The same thing is rendered still more evident by the circumstance that the Jerusalem apostles requested Paul and Barnabas to remember the poor at Jerusalem and collect for them contributions—to which request they willingly agreed. Of the zeal with which Paul addressed himself to this work of charity and fellowship, we have abundant evidence.[1] Did Peter, James, and John, seek for the money of heretics and heretical teachers? Did Paul and Barnabas labor to minister to the wants of Judaizers—"dogs," as Paul plainly calls them in the Epistle to the Philippians? No! the fellowship of the Jewish and Gentile teachers was genuine and cordial: and so the underpinning of the whole Tübingen theory falls away.

It would argue, however, not only an ignorance of the subsequent history, but also an ignorance of human nature, to suppose that this friendly and fraternal interview and the decisions of the apostolic convention would avail either to define, in all points, the relation of the two branches of the church, or to suppress permanently the judaizing faction. That

[1] It had been a custom of the Jews scattered in foreign lands to send up gifts to the capital, expressing thus their sense of the pre-eminence of the Judaean church gathered about the centre of their religion. Ewald associates this old custom with the record of the repeated contributions sent from the Gentile churches to the mother-church at Jerusalem. These were, to be sure, only voluntary tokens of love. Yet the Jewish Christian would naturally be reminded of the old custom we have mentioned. Hence the fact of the sending of these contributions would be a peculiar sign of respect as well as fellowship. See Ewald's *Geschichte*, &c., B. VI. s. 438.

this faction was still alive and influential, was shown by the transactions at Antioch which Paul proceeds to explain. Peter had not hesitated to eat with the Gentile converts there; to break over thus the restriction which the Jew placed upon himself, as to intercourse with the heathen.[1] But on the arrival of certain Jewish Christians from Jerusalem, he changed his course and withdrew from them; the other Jewish converts and even Barnabas following his example.[2] This conduct of Peter roused the indignation and called forth the plain and earnest rebuke of Paul. In mingling freely with the Gentile Christians, Peter acted in keeping with the liberal views which he had acquired in connection with the conversion of Cornelius and had expressed at the apostolic convention. This convention had not defined what course the Jewish Christians were to take on the point in question. We cannot say, therefore, that Peter, in case he had abstained from eating with the Gentiles, would have violated the terms of that arrangement. It is not remarkable that in the conference at Jerusalem

[1] See Luke xv. 2; 1 Cor. v. 11.

[2] These Christians from Jerusalem are said (ver. 12) to have come ἀπὸ Ἰακώβου—that is, to have been sent by James. The business on which they were sent, we know not, just as we know not the particular object of Peter's visit. There is no intimation that James had given any sanction to the course which they chose to take with respect to the Gentile believers. To suppose that he had, would be as unwarrantable as to infer, from the course which Peter had first taken, that he had been sent, or had come, expressly to eat with the Gentiles and live as one of them.

this particular question was not settled or considered; and although this freedom of intercourse which swept down all the old barriers between Jew and heathen might be a logical deduction from the spirit of that agreement, it is not remarkable that Jewish believers —even those of a liberal turn and in favor of the fellowship concluded upon at the convention—should fail to perceive at once the propriety of such a practice. Peculiar embarrassments, as we shall hereafter more fully point out, lay in the way of such a concession. We must not forget the force of a life-long, hereditary prejudice which is intrenched among religious beliefs. Simple abstinence from this kind of fellowship with the Gentile Christians could not, therefore, be regarded as an absolute breach of the covenant which secured to them their rights and the recognition of their Christian standing. There were still two branches of the church. But the offence which Paul charged upon Peter was threefold. He was guilty of an inconsistency in departing from the course which he had pursued before the arrival of the Jewish Christians; of hypocrisy, since in thus altering his conduct, he acted against his real convictions and from fear; and of the virtual attempt to lead the Gentile converts to judaize, or to make them feel that they ought to be circumcised. Peter was not accused of an error of doctrine, but of an error in conduct. He behaved in a manner inconsistent with his real views, just as Barnabas did, and there is just as little ground for imputing to Peter a judaizing principle on account of his conduct on this occasion, as there is for imputing the same principle to Barnabas. Peter acted from the same cowardly feeling which had once moved him to deny his Master. If Paul had complained that Peter held a false principle, that he did not understand the rights of the Gentiles, this controversy might be urged in support of Baur's theory. But inasmuch as the censure of Paul presupposes an essential agreement between himself and Peter in their views upon the matter in question, Baur's theory not only gains no foothold, but is effectually overthrown by the record of this conflict. We simply add that Paul's reasoning on this occasion is a most forcible exposition of the principal ground of his unflinching opposition to the laying of the ceremonial law upon the Gentiles. Such an act would derogate from the sufficiency of Christ as a Saviour, and imply that when a man believed on him, he had not secured his salvation, but was still in his sins. "If righteousness come by the law, then Christ is dead in vain."[1]

The continuance of a judaizing party after all these events, and notwithstanding the fellowship between the apostle to the heathen and "the pillars" at Jerusalem, is not to us a cause of wonder. Remember how ingrained was the prejudice that must be removed before the requirement of circumcision

[1] Gal. ii. 16–21.

could be dispensed with! And how inveterate was the obstinacy of the pharisaical Jew, who had been so trained as hardly to distinguish between the moral and ceremonial precept, in respect either to sacredness or perpetuity, and who had accepted the Messiah, having no thought that the law or any portion of it was to pass away! And the rapid spread of Gentile Christianity, a fact which threatened to reduce ultimately the party of the ritual to a hopeless minority, would naturally rouse them to adhere more zealously to their position, and to put forth fresh efforts to obtain for it a triumph.

The objections of Baur to the narrative of Luke disappear in the light of the preceding review. As to Peter, the fellowship he extended to Paul (Gal. ii. 9), and his liberality in reference to the Gentile Christians at Antioch—with the exception of the temporary infidelity to his real convictions—were the proper sequel of his vision in the case of Cornelius. There is nothing in Peter's course, which throws the least doubt upon the record of that event. We must suppose, indeed, that in the interval of about fifteen years, between the affair of Cornelius and the apostolic convention, the judaizing spirit had grown stronger, rather than weaker, in the Jerusalem church. This was natural. Pharisees (Acts xv. 5) had become convinced of the Messiahship of Jesus, and had brought into the church their zeal in behalf of a strict adherence to the Mosaic ritual. And we have only to imagine the situation of that church, to perceive the difficulties that beset this whole subject. The Jewish Christians themselves kept up the observance of the old forms. They frequented the temple, like other devout Israelites. That *they* should give up the ceremonial law had not been claimed or suggested. As patriotic Jews, they could not break away from the national customs. But a religious motive bound them to the old observances until these should be repealed, or until they should discern that the gospel had virtually supplanted them. Luther's doctrine of justification carried with it logically the abolition of a great part of the existing ritual of the church. But it was only by degrees that the Wittenberg reformers felt the incongruity, and shook themselves clear, so to speak, of forms whose vitality was gone. And yet these forms were of merely human institution. But if the Jewish Christians would observe the law, how could they break over it in their intercourse with the Gentiles? How should they adjust their relations to the heathen converts? The state of things, as we gather it from Luke, is just what we should expect to result from this anomalous situation. On the one hand, there is rejoicing in the mother-church at the conversion of the Gentiles. It is seen that they have become recipients of the Spirit. There is a thankful acknowledgment of them as fellow-believers. Yet the question of freely mingling with them—of treating them in all respects as *Jewish* brethren were treated—was encumbered with the difficulties we have mentioned. A bigoted but influential faction strenuously contended against the lawfulness of eating with heathen converts, and sought to impose on *them* circumcision and the other points of the ritual. The apostles, and the church acting as a body, refused this last demand, and shook hands with Paul, the determined defender of the rights of the Gentiles. Peter, enlightened by the teaching of the Spirit, could not refuse to eat with his Gentile brethren; yet yielded for a time at Antioch to the pressure of judaizing opinion. The affair of Cornelius, if it excited discontent at Jerusalem, and had no permanent effect on the judaizing element which rather grew than declined in strength, left a lasting impression on his mind, and led him at the apostolic convention to take the side of the Gentiles.[1]

It is easy to understand, we observe further, how there might be many who had no sympathy with the Judaizers in their requirement that the heathen convert should be circumcised, but were still unprepared for that degree of liberality in intercourse with their Gentile brethren which Peter had exhibited at

[1] For good remarks on the topics touched upon in the paragraph above, see Ewald's *Ges. d. Volkes Israel*, B. vi. s. 226 seq., 426 seq. We may add that the narrative of the conversion of Cornelius in the Acts is full of graphic details. Persons, places, and times, are exactly designated. If it be a fiction, it is an example of the "lie circumstantial."

Antioch. We have among us a numerous and respectable body of Christians—a friend has suggested the illustration—who believe that baptism is an essential prerequisite of communion, and that immersion alone is baptism; who, therefore, decline to sit at the Lord's table with those whom they cordially love as fellow-Christians, and whose labors in spreading the gospel they look upon with heartfelt sympathy. The Baptist does not deny the name of Christian brother to those from whom he is obliged to withhold certain forms of fellowship. So it was, we doubt not, with many Jewish Christians.[1]

As concerns Paul, the narrative of Luke is equally relieved of difficulties. That Paul, in Galatians ii., does not mention the *public* conference, which Luke describes, is easily explained. It was no part of his purpose to give a complete history of the proceedings at Jerusalem. The particular point to which his mind was directed, was his relation to the other apostles. Had the public transaction modified, in any essential particular, the result of his private interview with them, he might have been called upon to speak of it. Such, however, was not the fact. He could conscientiously say that nothing was added—*οὐδὲν προσανέθεντο*—to his gospel. The conclusions of the convention, founded as they were on a desire to

[1] It hardly need be said that we imply here no judgment as to the justice or injustice of the position which the Baptist takes. The illustration is pertinent, whether he be right or wrong.

put no needless obstruction in the way of the spread of the gospel among the Jews, and accompanied by an express acknowledgment of the rightful exemption of the Gentiles from the yoke of the law, were fully consistent with Paul's position. But if Paul was not called upon to allude, in Gal. ii., to the public proceeding on the occasion of his visit to Jerusalem, the purpose he had in view rendered it inappropriate that he should do so. His immediate purpose was to guard against the impression that he stood, in any sense, in a subordinate position with reference to the other apostles. An allusion to the arrangement of the convention might have furnished his enemies with a pretext for the unfounded charge of a dependence on his part upon "the pillars" at Jerusalem.

It is objected to Luke's narrative of the convention, that the decision which is said to have been made there would infallibly have been referred to by Paul in 1 Cor. viii., where the matter of eating flesh offered to idols is considered. In answer to this objection, we remark that the apostle in this passage *does* oppose the practice referred to, and on the same *general* ground as that assigned in the Jerusalem letter; namely, a regard for those who thought the practice wrong (comp. Acts xv. 21 and 1 Cor. viii. 9 seq.). His aim was to instil a right feeling into the minds of the Corinthians, and to inculcate a principle on which they could act intelligently. An appeal to authority—or what would be taken for authority—would have defeated this design. Besides, it was not the danger of giving needless offence to the Jews, but it was the consciences of weak Gentile brethren which Paul had to consider. Moreover, the arrangement at the conference applied to the churches of Syria and Cilicia, in particular to Antioch and to the dissension that had broken out there. After Gentile Christianity had become widely prevalent, after Paul had fully entered, as an independent laborer, into his own peculiar field, and when, especially, the Jewish Christians (of the Judaizing type) kept up their mischievous efforts to deprive the Gentiles of their liberty, it may well be assumed that the arrangement in question, based, as it was, on a prudential consideration, had become obsolete. It had been made to meet an emergency. When Paul had founded numerous churches, and churches, too, made up chiefly of Gentile converts, that recommendation, adopted for the sake of sparing the feelings of the Jews and of preventing the inference that the Gentiles were enemies of the Old Testament religion, would cease to have any validity. It had no resemblance to the decree of a later council. It was a fraternal recommendation sent to Antioch, through Silas and Judas Barsabas (Acts xv. 22), the substance of it being also put into a letter which they carried. There was not a judicial proceeding, but a consultation of brethren.[1] They did not come together to

[1] See, on this subject, Neander's *Pflanz. u. Leit. d. Kirche*, B. I.,

give law to the Church, but to quiet a particular disturbance.

We are now prepared to consider the question of the genuineness of the Acts. If we have shown that the representation which is there given of the respective positions of Paul and Peter, and of the mutual relations of the Jewish and Gentile Christians, is *not* discordant either with the statements of Paul or with the probabilities in the case, we have destroyed the sole argument of any weight against the genuineness of the book. For on this imaginary discordance the objection to the early composition of the Acts is founded. But, in our judgment, the genuineness of this book can be fully established, and the attack which has been made upon it shown to be groundless.

1. The testimony of the author, direct and incidental, when we consider the form in which it is given, is a strong proof of the genuineness of the book, and in the absence of counteracting evidence, a convincing proof.

We assume, what is now a conceded fact, that the third Gospel and the Acts have the same author. Independently of the evidence afforded by the preface to the Acts, the resemblance of the two books in language and style is conclusive. Now the third Gospel purports to be written by one personally

s. 422 seq., Lekebusch, s. 314 seq., Bleek's *Einl. in d. N. T.*, s. 371 seq., Meyer, *Gal. Einl.* § 3, *Apostelgeschichte*, s. 280.

acquainted with the apostles. He records what he had received from "eyewitnesses and ministers of the word" (Luke i. 2). The Acts, addressed to the same Theophilus, and referring in its preface back to the Gospel, is the sequel of the latter work. The author of the Acts, therefore, claims to be an acquaintance of the apostles. And we may observe—though the remark might properly be made a special topic of evidence—that, since all the proof of the early date of the Gospel tends equally to establish the early date of the Acts, and since we have internal proof that the Gospel was written not later than about the date of the destruction of Jerusalem, the genuineness of the Acts is a necessary inference. Proving that Luke wrote the Gospel, we have proved that he wrote the Acts also. And the phraseology in the prologue of the Gospel obliges us to suppose either that the writer is a conscientious and well-informed historian, or consciously and basely false. He declares that he writes in order that Theophilus may be assured of the *certainty*, the unassailable reality—*τὴν ἀσφάλειαν*—of the truths of Christianity in which he had been instructed. But not to dwell on the connection of the Gospel with the Acts, and considering this last book by itself, we are happily provided with an incidental testimony of the most convincing character. We allude to the passages in which the writer speaks in the first person plural, thus including himself among the participants in the events he records. This use of the "we" begins with Paul's leaving Troas (xvi. 11), and continues in the account of his stay at Philippi. It is resumed on the return of Paul to Philippi (xx. 5–15) —thus raising the presumption that the author of these passages had in the interval tarried at that place. The remaining passages in which this peculiarity appears, are xxi. 1–18, xxvii. 1—xxviii. 17. Now, what is the explanation of this phenomenon? Only two hypotheses are open to discussion among those who ascribe the book to Luke. The first is the old, generally received, and, as we think, well sustained view that Luke was himself, in these places, the attendant of Paul. The second is the hypothesis of Schleiermacher, variously modified by other writers, that Luke here introduces, without formal notice, a document emanating, as they commonly suppose, from Timothy, or, as some have thought, from Silas. This last form of the hypothesis, that Silas wrote the passages in question, is supported by no argument worthy of attention, and is fully refuted by the circumstance that in connection with at least one of the passages (see Acts xvi. 19–25), Silas is mentioned in the third person. But the theory that Timothy is the author of these passages, though adopted by so able and candid a writer as Bleek, has been, as we believe, effectually disproved.[1] This theory does not, to be

[1] The examination of the "Timothy-hypothesis" by Lekebusch (s. 140–167), is one of the finest parts of his excellent treatise. We present the more prominent considerations bearing on the topic.

sure, shake the general credibility of the book, or the fact of its being composed by Luke. But how stands the evidence in regard to it? We read (in Acts xx. 4, 5): "And there accompanied him [Paul] into Asia, Sopater of Berea; and of the Thessalonians, Aristarchus and Secundus; and Gaius of Derbe, *and Timotheus;* and of Asia, Tychicus and Trophimus. *These* going before tarried *for us* at Troas." If, under the term "these," all who are named before are referred to—which is the most natural interpretation[1] —the so-called Timothy-hypothesis falls to the ground. In connection with this piece of evidence, it deserves remark that the absence of all detail—the summary style of the narrative—in passages directly connected with those under consideration, and covering a portion of Paul's career in which Timothy bore an equal part, is against the supposition that Luke had at his command a diary of this apostolic helper. But the decisive argument against the Schleiermacherian hypothesis, is the wrong view of the general structure and character of the book which that theory implies. Were it true that the book presents the appearance of being a compilation of documents imperfectly fused together—left in a good degree in their original state —it might not unreasonably be assumed that the author had taken up a document from another's pen, without taking care to alter the pronominal feature which we are discussing. This idea of the book was

[1] See Meyer, *ad loc.*

a part of Schleiermacher's theory. But a more thorough examination of the Acts has made it clear that, from whatever sources the author draws his information, it is one production, coherent in plan; its different parts connected by references forward and backward; uniform in style; and flowing from a single pen. If Luke took up into his work a document of Timothy, he could not have given it the complete harmony with his own style which it exhibits, without changing its form and phraseology *to such an extent as renders it impossible to suppose the retention of the "we" to be artless or accidental.* Memoranda of Timothy, if Luke had such, were *rewritten by him;* but this leaves the retaining of the "we," with no explanation, an insoluble fact. We infer, then, with confidence, that Luke, in these passages, *professes* to speak in his own person.[1] This fact Zeller and the other Tübingen critics admit; and their conclusion is, that whilst the author of the Acts, writing in the second century, used a previously written document, he intentionally left the "we" as it stood—although the document in other parts was materially wrought

[1] There remains, to be sure, the unanswered question, why Luke does not more expressly state the fact of his joining Paul, but leaves it to be gathered from this use of the pronoun. But this difficulty is, to say the least, not greater than the difficulty of supposing him to introduce a document of this sort without notice and without altering the pronominal form. The book was written for a private individual. Of the circumstances of Luke's companionship with Paul, Theophilus may have known something before.

over by him—in order to produce the false impression that he was the contemporary and associate of Paul! This refined fraud is attributed, and it is thought necessary to attribute, to the author of the Acts! But if we are not prepared to adopt this theory, we have no alternative but to accept the testimony of the author concerning himself; that is, to ascribe his work to a contemporary and companion of the apostles.

2. The assumption that the book of Acts is spurious, and its contents in great part fictitious, is irreconcilable with the moral spirit that characterizes the work. The presumption adverse to Baur's theory, which is raised by the author's own testimony respecting himself, is confirmed by the moral tone of the book. It is true that every well-meaning book is not thereby proved to come from the writer from whom it pretends to emanate. Nor would we contend that the ideas of antiquity, and of Jewish antiquity in particular, in regard to this matter of authorship accorded in all respects with the ethical feeling of a modern day.[1] Apocryphal and other ancient works are extant, which bore the name of some revered person of an earlier time, and which, notwithstanding this groundless pretension, were designed to promote the cause of religion. But an elaborate outlay of cunning for the purpose of creating a false impression in respect to the real author of a book, especially when the motive is to promote the interests of a party,

[1] This Lekebusch frankly allows.

deserves reprobation, whether the book be ancient or recent. An effort of this kind must always have been considered a piece of knavery. Where there is plainly discovered an earnest regard for the law of veracity, we are cut off from supposing anything like a pious fraud. In this case, we must give credit to the testimony which the book itself offers respecting its author. Much more are we precluded, in that case, from considering a large part of the narrative a deliberate fiction. Now there is manifest throughout the book of Acts a penetrating discernment of the sacredness of truth and the obligation of veracity. He who set down the record of the sin and punishment of Ananias and Sapphira was incapable of palming off, as a veritable history of the apostles and of the manner in which they were guided by the Holy Spirit, a series of fictitious stories invented by himself. Dropping for the moment the question of the general verity of the narrative, let us observe the amount of duplicity which the above-described theory of Zeller imputes to the author of the Acts. The retention of the "we" in a document which he has recast and recomposed—a retention deliberately resolved upon, we are told, for the sake of deceiving the reader into the belief that the author lived long before—is certainly equivalent, in a moral point of view, to the *insertion* of this pronoun by the writer for the same end.[1] If the author, writing, it is supposed, in the second century,

[1] See Lekebusch.

were charged with *inserting* this word, here and there, in his own composition, the duplicity would not be worse. How foreign this refined method of self-advertisement is from the universal habit of apocryphal writers, who are apt to blazon their assumed names on the front of their works, will strike all who are acquainted with this species of literature. A writer capable of such a trick as is charged upon the author of the Acts, would almost infallibly have introduced the passages which contain the "we" with an explicit declaration that here he joined Paul, or became a participant in the events that follow. But the particular point on which we now insist is the incompatibility of such detestable deceit with the pure and truthful air of the historian, and his recognition of the law of veracity.

3. An irrefragable argument for the genuineness and credibility of Acts is afforded by the relation in which it stands to the Pauline Epistles.

The coincidences and diversities are each an impressive proof of the correctness of the old and accepted view concerning the book. As to the former, the peculiarity of them, as Paley, in the *Horæ Paulinæ*, has very ingeniously shown, is that they are undesigned. There are such correspondences with the data furnished by the Epistles as could not have been contrived, for they can only be detected by searching. The omissions in the Acts are an equally remarkable feature. We learn from the Epistles various facts of importance respecting Paul, which a writer of the second century would certainly have worked into a history or historical romance in which the Apostle was to figure so prominently. Thus, for example, we have no notice in the Acts of the sojourn of Paul in Arabia, shortly after his conversion, which he himself mentions (Gal. i. 17). Luke describes him as preaching in Damascus, and, "after that many days were fulfilled," as flying from the machinations of the Jews to Jerusalem. For aught that appears, the author of the Acts is ignorant of the fact of his visiting Arabia. But a later writer, with the Epistle to the Galatians in his hand, would not have failed to show, at least, his knowledge of an event so distinctly stated by the Apostle himself. The three shipwrecks, and most of the other hardships which Paul had endured (2 Cor. xi. 24 seq.), are not mentioned in the Acts.[1] And if we look at what is actually narrated by Luke, although Baur's theory of an inconsistency between the general representations of the Acts and the Epistles is false, yet the former shows itself an independent narrative. It is not built up on the basis of information derived from the writings of Paul. These are not made use of in its composition. Now, this fact demonstrates the early date of the Acts. Suppose that a Gentile Christian of the second century had conceived the plan of writing a work for the purpose which Baur attrib-

[1] The shipwreck recorded in the Acts was subsequent to the writing of this Epistle.

utes to the author of this book: his very first act would have been to resort to the Epistles for the materials out of which to construct his work. Conscious that a comparison of his production with these well-known documents would be inevitable, he would guard against the semblance of contradiction. He would seek throughout to dovetail his work with the authentic records of the apostolic age. Hence, in laboring to swell their list of discrepancies between the Acts and Paul, the Tübingen critics are unconsciously beating down their own theory.

4. Baur's theory is not sustained, but is overthrown, by a candid view of the contents of the Acts. Lekebusch has shown that the alleged parallelism in the career of Peter and of Paul is chiefly in the imagination of the critics, and that the differences in their respective deeds and fortunes are vastly more numerous and more conspicuous than the points of resemblance. In truth, there are no such resemblances which are not accidental and to be expected in the case of the two leading apostles, both of whom were engaged in the same work and exposed to like perils. That, in the Acts, Paul is said to have addressed himself, in the places he visited, first to the Jews and then to the heathen, rather confirms than weakens the authority of Luke; for such was unquestionably the historical fact. An opposite course would have been in the highest degree unnatural. The gospel was a means of salvation "to the Jew *first*,

and also to the Greek" (Rom. i. 16); and if Paul was the Apostle to the Gentiles, this meant simply that his field of labor was in Gentile countries. But there are passages in the Acts which a writer having the end in view which Baur imputes to the author of the book would never have admitted. He is, by the supposition, a Pauline Christian, and designs to make it appear that Paul was a recognized apostle, on a footing of perfect equality with the original disciples. Yet he begins, in the very first chapter, by describing the choice of an apostle, at the instance of Peter, to fill up the number of the twelve. He must be, said Peter, one who "has companied with us" through the whole life of Christ, from the baptism of John, and be ordained "to be a witness with us of his resurrection" (Acts i. 21, 22). In treating of the Apocalypse, Baur—without reason, as we think—regards the allusions to "the twelve" apostles as an indirect thrust at the Apostle Paul, and a sign of the judaizing character of the book. Yet here we have a Pauline Christian falling into a similar style! A partisan of Paul, inventing history for the purpose of exalting his equal apostolic claims, it is safe to say, would never have introduced the passage in question.

But let us turn to the narrative of the last visit of the Apostle Paul to Jerusalem—that visit which was so important in its results, and is so fully described by the author of the Acts. It is one main design, they say, of this author to extenuate and hide from view the mutual opposition of the two branches of the Church, and to produce the impression that the body of Jewish Christians agree on the ritual question with Paul. Now, what do we find in the midst of this very passage in which Paul is brought into contact with the church at Jerusalem and the Jewish Christians who thronged the city? Why, James and the elders at Jerusalem are reported as saying to Paul: "Thou seest, brother, how *many thousands*"—literally myriads, μυριάδες—"of Jews there are which believe; and they are *all zealous of the law;*" and they were all jealous of Paul on account of the information they had received that he was in the habit of dissuading Jews from observing the Mosaic law and circumcising their children. That is, a writer, who is inventing and altering history for the purpose of hiding a fact, gives to that fact a conspicuous place in his narrative! Baur has no other solution than the remark that the writer here "forgets the *rôle* he is playing." But the answer is, that supposing so shrewd a writer as he is represented to be, to forget *anywhere* the design he had in view, he could not forget it in the crisis of the whole history, when Paul met the Jewish-Christian Church for the last time, and when this very point of the authority of the ritual, and the views and feelings of the Jewish believers, is the theme of the narrative.[1]

[1] Baur more than insinuates that the Jewish *Christians* took part in this violent attack upon Paul, and that Luke is at pains to

We have adverted above to the manner in which the author of the Acts begins his work. Not less incompatible with the Tübingen theory is the manner in which he concludes. The reader must bear in mind that, according to Baur and Zeller, a main aim of the writer is to represent the Apostle in a friendly attitude towards his Jewish countrymen. A Gentile Christian holds out the olive-branch to the Jew. But how ends this "reconciling" and "pacifying" production? It winds up with a denunciation from Paul against the unbelief of the Jews, in which, using the stern words of the prophet Isaiah, he charges upon them a judicial blindness, and adds: "Be it known therefore unto you, that the salvation of God *is sent unto the Gentiles*, and that *they will hear it*." That is, the divine rejection of the Jews and choice of the Gentiles is the last word from Paul which the reader hears! How would that sound in the ear of the zealous Judaizer whom this book was to conciliate, and win to the esteem of Paul and of his type of doctrine? Is it not plain that the "tendency" ascribed to this work is read into it by the critics? Their interpretation is not drawn from an unprejudiced examination of the contents of the book, which are flatly inconsistent with it, but from the demands of a

suppress the fact. If we are to believe Baur, then, the same writer who so flagrantly "forgets his part" as to make mention of the zeal of "many thousands" of believers for the law, recovers his memory so fully as to falsify in the very next breath!

preconceived, and, we believe, unfounded historical theory of their own contriving.

The neglect of the writer to avail himself of the most natural means of promoting his alleged purpose, is, also, a proof that this purpose belongs only to the critic's brain. A single example of this negligence, unaccountable on Baur's theory of the design of the book, is the omission of the writer to bring Paul and Peter together in Rome, where, according to a belief then current, they both perished as martyrs in the Neronian persecution.[1] What would the writer of an irenical fiction lay hold of so soon, as the supposed conjunction of the two apostles in the capital of the world, and their common fate? How easily might a tale be spun out of this meeting of the leaders of the two branches of the Church, which would effectually promote the author's plan! Yet the book closes abruptly—the author seeming at last to hasten to the conclusion—with no mention of Peter's visit to Rome, connection with the Gentile capital, or interview with Paul.

5. The unfitness of such a work as the book of Acts to secure the end for which, according to Baur,

[1] For proof that the report of Peter having suffered martyrdom at Rome is met with prior to the date assigned by the Tübingen critics to the Acts, see Gieseler's *Church History*, B. I. s. 27, N. 6. In truth, there is no sufficient reason for disbelieving the tradition so early and widely current. For a full examination of the point, see Dr. Schaff's *History of the Apostolic Church*, p. 372 seq. See also Bleek's *Einl.*, s. 563.

it was composed, stands in the way of the acceptance of his theory.

Here, if we are to believe the Tübingen critics, was a great division in the Church. Jewish Christians, on the one hand, following the doctrine of Peter, required circumcision and a compliance with the ritual as a condition of fellowship with the Gentile Christians. The latter, on the contrary, following the authority of Paul, as decidedly refused to yield to this demand. Efforts are at length made from different sides to bring about an accommodation. And this writer composes an historical romance for the purpose of spreading such a conception of the apostolic history as shall remove, especially, the Jewish-Christian prejudice against communion with the heathen believers. To this end he represents Peter as tolerating the Gentiles in their uncircumcision, as taking part in the reception of Cornelius into the Church, and as resisting the imposition of the yoke of ritual observances upon the Gentiles. But how would the judaizing party relish this representation of their great Apostle? Were they so little wedded to their principles as to abandon them the moment they were told by some writer, pretending to be an associate of Paul, that their views relative to the course taken by Peter and in respect to his doctrine were contrary to the truth? Had they only to be told, in a book falsely purporting to come from a Pauline Christian of a former day, that Peter really fraternized with Paul and was in favor of the immunity of the Gentile converts? And similar inquiries are pertinent when we consider how such a work would be received by the followers of Paul. If this great Apostle had, in truth, forbidden circumcision altogether, as the Baur school pretend, and if his disciples were rooted in their attachment to his principles, as they were certainly familiar with his writings, how would they be satisfied with the narrative of the circumcision of Timothy and the other examples of conformity to the law, recorded in the Acts? Would they not have spurned this misrepresentation of the principles and conduct of their great leader, and made their appeal to the very passages in his Epistles on which the Tübingen critics found their thesis as to his real position? It is unaccountable that a work which flies in the face of the cherished opinions and traditions of the two rival parties, should pass uncontradicted, and even contribute to secure a most important change in the platforms on which they respectively stand. Yet this unknown writer in the first quarter of the second century, audaciously perverting the facts of history and adding incidents which sprung from his own invention, succeeded, if we are to believe the Tübingen critics, in this unexampled imposture. To this extent do these critics task our credulity.

To what desperate shifts the Tübingen critics are driven, in their effort to read into the Acts a deep-laid plot which has no existence outside of their own suspicious fancy, may be seen from one or two examples. Luke records a contention between Paul and Barnabas which led to their separation from each other. Will it be believed that he is charged by Baur with making this record of a comparatively "unimportant" dispute, in order to divert the thoughts of his readers from the more serious quarrel with Peter, which he is desirous of covering up? As if his readers, with the Epistle to the Galatians in their hand, could be kept in ignorance of this dispute with Peter! As if the allusion to one conflict could suppress the recollection of another! Why, as Lekebusch inquires, should he not rather pass over in silence the minor quarrel also, provided his aim were such as Baur imagines? The earlier prominent record of the friendship of Paul with Barnabas, that "distinguished and meritorious member of the Jerusalem church," is attributed to the apologetic or conciliatory design of the author of the Acts. Yet the same author now describes a sharp controversy between them! The simple truth is, that the conflict with Barnabas is mentioned because it had an influence on the history of the missions to the Gentiles and of the spread of Christianity among them, which it is the leading purpose of Luke to narrate. The controversy with Peter had no such influence. It was merely an example of the inconsistency of Peter, which Luke, if he was informed of it, had no occasion to record.[1]

[1] See Lekebusch, s. 305.

Another illustration of that strange, morbid suspicion which is a prime quality of the Tübingen criticism, is the charge that the journey of Paul to Jerusalem (Acts xi.), which the Apostle in Gal. ii. does not mention, was invented by Luke for the purpose of bringing Paul as often as possible into intercourse with the Jerusalem apostles! Now if we look at Luke's narrative, we find that all he says of that journey is in one verse (v. 30): "and they sent it [a contribution for the poor] to the elders by the hands of Barnabas and Saul." If Luke had the purpose of which he is accused, why should he confine himself to a bare mention of the fact of the journey? Would he not infallibly have given details of the interview? Would he not, at least, have stated that Paul met the other apostles and conferred with them? Would he, as he does, make it known that Peter, the Jewish-Christian leader, was at that time in prison, so that he and Paul could not have met? Luke describes, with some detail, the occasion of the contribution. Agabus, one of the prophets who had come from Jerusalem, predicted a dearth, and the Antioch Christians accordingly determined to send relief to their brethren in Judea. We are required, then, to suppose that Luke took pains to invent all this to serve as a preface to the bare, solitary remark that Saul was sent to Jerusalem with the money. This, says Lekebusch, is to make Luke build up mountains that a mouse may come forth. We have no warrant for supposing that Paul intended to record in Galatians all the visits he had made to Jerusalem.[1] In fact, we do not know that on the occasion referred to by Luke, in Acts xi., Paul entered Jerusalem. He was indeed sent with Silas, but, as Luke says nothing further, it is not improbable that he was prevented, for some reason, from going so far as the city. In any event, the treatment of this topic by Baur and his followers is a fair example of that hyper-criticism which finds an occult, and generally a bad, motive underneath the simplest historical statement.

The historical discrepancies alleged to exist between Luke and the other authorities, whether sacred or secular—which discrepancies, were they made out, cannot be shown to imply any design, any *tendency*, on the part of the author—afford no help to the Tübingen cause. The consideration of them, in case the subject of inquiry were the nature and extent and the proper formula of *inspiration*, would be pertinent; but admitting them to be insoluble, they are not sufficient to affect the general *credibility* of the historian, which is the question under discussion. Take, for example, the reference to Theudas (Acts v. 36), and suppose him to be the same Theudas whom Josephus refers to (Antiq. xx. 5, 1), and that Luke is therefore guilty of an anachronism; or, suppose an error in the reference in the Gospel to a taxing under Cyrenius

[1] πάλιν (again, another time), not δεύτερον, is the word he uses (ii. 1).

(Luke ii. 1), and that the cause which drew Joseph and the mother of Jesus to Bethlehem is mistakenly given—that their visit to Bethlehem was occasioned by some other tax, and that Luke's chronology on this point is at fault: would his general credibility as a historian be impaired? If so, there is no secular historian who does not fall under a like condemnation. There was a traditional belief that Martin Luther was born during a visit of his mother to a fair in Eisleben. The statement is found in so good an authority as Seckendorf, who doubtless derived it from what he considered an authentic source; and after him it is found in a multitude of writers. It is now known, however, that the parents of Luther had removed their abode to Eisleben before the birth of Luther, and that no fair was held in the place at that time! Shall the former historians of Luther be for this reason convicted of carelessness or wilful falsification? Or will it be denied, on account of their discrepancy with later biographies, that Luther was born in Eisleben? This would be parallel to the course taken by Strauss and his friends, even if the chronological difficulty in Luke were proved to be insoluble. Macaulay attributes the epithet *Silent*, attached to the name of William, the founder of the Dutch Commonwealth, to his taciturn habit;[1] although the truth is that he had no such habit, and acquired this title from his prudent reticence on a single occasion. The same historian probably con-

[1] Macaulay's Life of William Pitt, in the *Encyclopaedia Britannica*.

founded George Penn, a pardon-broker, with William Penn the Quaker. This may, perhaps, suggest the possibility of there being more than one Theudas. But however this may be, who will charge the English historian with being careless in his researches and uninformed in the matters whereof he writes? It may be said that in Luke the difficulty is enhanced by the occurrence of the reference to Theudas in a speech of Gamaliel. But—on the supposition, again, that an error here were proved—is absolute correctness in the report of a public speech, and in all the historical references it may contain, so very common? Suppose that Gamaliel was known to have referred, in his address to the Sanhedrim, to various factions which had all proved to be short-lived, and that in the version of the speech which reached Luke, the name of Theudas had erroneously crept in, owing possibly to the circumstance that his name was often linked, in common speech, with that of Judas of Galilee, whom Gamaliel had really mentioned: we affirm that analogous examples of inaccuracy can be found in the most approved and trustworthy historians. These alleged discrepancies, and all others, should, each by itself, be made the subject of fair and searching investigation. But the apologist and the skeptic both err when the latter claims, and the former consents, to stake the credibility of the New Testament, much more the cause of supernatural Christianity itself, upon the possibility of harmonizing all minor diversities. To the antagonist of revelation we say, Grant that it cannot be done; even grant that the sacred historians stand in all respects upon a level with uninspired writers of equal qualifications for ascertaining the truth and of equal integrity in communicating it; yet you are as far as ever from succeeding in your attack upon revelation. Were it our purpose, in this Essay, to go beyond the special objections characteristic of the Tübingen school, we might dwell upon the numberless allusions in the Acts to points of geography and history, to existing features of law and government, to customs and manners, most of which are incidental and such as only a contemporary writer could weave into a narrative. It is not too much to say that the general correctness of Luke in these manifold particulars has been positively established. The passage, for example, relating to the voyage and shipwreck of St. Paul, has been subjected to a most thorough scrutiny, and the pathway of the ship followed from point to point. The result is a striking verification of Luke's narrative. He is shown to be, by this passage in his narrative, an observing and truthful writer.[1]

[1] See Smith's *Voyage and Shipwreck of St. Paul;* also the excellent Life of St. Paul by Conybeare and Howson. A beautiful instance of Luke's *candor* is Acts xxi. 29. Describing the rage of the fanatical Jews from Asia, and their cry that Paul had introduced Greeks into the temple, he adds, parenthetically: "For they had seen before with him in the city, Trophimus, an Ephesian, *whom they supposed that Paul had brought into the temple.*" The effect of this remark of Luke is to palliate their guilt in offering violence to Paul.

The speeches recorded by Luke in the Acts have been a favorite subject of skeptical attack. But the force of this attack is broken when it is conceded that the language in which the speeches are presented, is, generally speaking, that of the historian. Some of them were not made in the Greek, but in another tongue; and in regard to the rest, it must be in fairness, and may be with safety, allowed that the form in which they are recorded is given them by Luke. This accounts for their resemblance in phraseology to the ordinary style of Luke's narrative. Ancient historians, as all scholars know, were in the habit of throwing into the direct form—the *oratio directa*—or the form of quotation, what a modern writer presents in form as well as in fact in his own language. But when we look at the contents of the speeches in the Acts, they are found to harmonize with the known characters of the various persons to whom they are ascribed, and with the circumstances in which they were severally uttered. As an offset to the complaint that Paul's peculiar doctrine is missing from his speeches, and from the book generally, we may put the judgment of Luther that the principal purpose for which the book was written was to "teach all Christendom the great

They had drawn a false inference from seeing Trophimus with Paul in another place. With his usual felicity, Bengel points out the accordance of this circumstance of Paul's association with Trophimus with the Apostle's character: "Paulus Trophimum non introduxit in templum: neque eum tamen plane vitavit Judaeorum causa." *Gnomon* (Acts xxi. 29).

fundamental Christian doctrine" of justification by faith alone.[1] The reader has only to recall such passages as the direction given to the trembling jailer who inquired what he should do to be saved, to be convinced of the groundless nature of this piece of criticism.

The speeches of Paul have been made the subject of a special, instructive discussion from the pen of Tholuck.[2] The principal part of his article is taken up with a comparison of the farewell address of the Apostle to the elders of Ephesus, at Miletus, with the writings of Paul—the purpose being to show the correspondence of that address with the Apostle's character and modes of thought. That the reader may be enabled to follow out this investigation for himself, we furnish here a very brief outline of most of the points in the comparison. The address is contained in the twentieth chapter of Acts. Paul's description of his pastoral fidelity (vs. 18–21), is shown to harmonize strikingly with allusions to the same topic in 1 Thess. ii. 10 and 2 Cor. vi. 3, 4. It is the habit of Paul frequently to appeal to his own life and conduct, partly in answer to calumnies, and partly to excite other Christians to follow his example, as in 2 Cor. i. 12; 1 Cor. xi. 1; Phil. iii. 15. The mention of his tears, in the address (ver. 31), brings out a characteristic of Paul which is also discovered from 2 Cor. ii. 4, where the Apostle says that he wrote to the Corinthians with "many tears." In each case

[1] Quoted in Lekeb., s. 235. [2] In the *Stud. u. Krit.*, 1839, II.

it is tears of love and of yearning over them for whose spiritual safety he is anxious. A little, yet striking mark of the authenticity of Luke's report is Paul's allusion (ver. 19) to what he had suffered at Ephesus from "the lying in wait of the Jews;" since in his narrative Luke had not mentioned any such persecution, but only the tumult raised by Demetrius. Had the address been invented by Luke, there would almost certainly be in the narrative an explanatory passage. In ver. 20, Paul reminds the elders of his preaching in private as well as in public; which falls in with 1 Thess. ii. 11, and with his exhortation to Timothy (2 Tim. iv. 2) to preach "in season and out of season." His boldness in preaching and his freedom from the fear of man (ver. 27), are the same qualities to which he adverts in 2 Cor. iv. 2 and 1 Thess. ii. 4, professing in the last passage that he did not speak "as pleasing men, but God which trieth our hearts." In ver. 22, he anticipates persecution in Jerusalem; in Rom. xv. 31, he expresses the same fear. How accordant is the Apostle's expression of the cheap estimate he puts upon life, if he might finish the ministry committed to him by the Lord Jesus (ver. 24, to be compared with xxi. 13), with the expression of self-sacrifice in Phil. ii. 17, and of triumph in 2 Tim. iv. 7! The presage of future dangers to the Church (vs 29, 30) may be compared with 1 Tim. iv. 1, and is shown by the Epistle to the Ephesians to have been verified. The same diligence and tenderness with which he had warned the Ephesians (ver. 31), we find him claiming to have exercised in regard to the Thessalonians, to whom he says (1 Thess. ii. 11), "ye know how we exhorted and comforted and charged every one of you, as a father does his children." The commending of the elders to God and the word of His grace, which was able "to build them up" (ver. 32), chimes with the benediction in Rom. xvi. 25, beginning: "Now unto Him that is able to establish you." In ver. 33, we hear the Apostle remind the elders how, coveting no man's silver, or gold, or apparel, he had sustained himself and his attendants by the labor of his own hands. His motives for pursuing this course are not explained here, but must be learned from the Epistles, in 1 Thess. ii. 9; 2 Thess. iii. 7–9; 1 Cor. iv. 12, ix. 12; 2 Cor. xi. 8. Especially worthy of note is the expression "these hands"—*αἱ χεῖρες αὗται* (ver. 34)—words requiring us to suppose a gesture to accompany them. Still more deserving of remark is the quotation of a saying of Christ not elsewhere recorded: "it is more blessed to give than to receive" (ver. 35). The saying itself is worthy to emanate from Christ, and is conformed to the spirit and style of his teaching. Coming in so simply and naturally, it seems to bear witness to the truth and fidelity of the entire report of the Apostle's discourse.

In the preceding observations we have employed for the purpose of refuting the Tübingen hypothesis—

except in the last remarks on the speeches of Paul—only the four Pauline Epistles accepted by Baur. But when we inquire for the grounds on which the genuineness of the remaining canonical Epistles ascribed to this apostle is denied, we find that the principal reason is the inconsistency of their representations with the theory which the four are supposed to authorize. On this ground, chiefly, even the Epistles to the Colossians and Philippians, which were never before doubted, and the marks of whose Pauline authorship are so irresistibly evident in their style and contents, are declared to be spurious! One would think that the inconsistency of these documents with Baur's theory would raise in his mind a strong presumption, not against them, but against that. But when we discover that his theory is overthrown by the testimony of the very documents on which he chooses to rely, and that his main objection to the genuineness of the other leading Epistles of Paul is thus taken away, we may resort to them for further illustration of the view which the Apostle took of the Jewish Christians. We find him, in the Epistle to the Ephesians, telling the Gentiles that they are no more "strangers and foreigners, but fellow-citizens with the saints, and of the household of God," and "built upon the foundation of the apostles and prophets" (Eph. ii. 19, 20). How fully does this harmonize with the spirit of the beautiful passage in the Romans, where Paul compares the Gentiles, in their relation to

Israel, to the wild olive-tree grafted upon the native olive and partaking of its "root and fatness" (Rom. xi. 17)! We find him in the 1st Epistle to the Thessalonians, saying: "for ye, brethren, became *followers of the churches of God which in Judea are in Christ Jesus*: for ye, also, have suffered like things of your own countrymen, even as they have of the Jews"—the Jews, who likewise "forbid us to speak to the Gentiles that they might be saved" (1 Thess. ii. 14 seq.). The Thessalonians, in the heroic spirit with which they had met persecution, had resembled their Christian brethren in Judea, whose firmness under such trial was well known. This one expression of honor to the faithful Christians of Judea, joined, as it is, with reprobation of the conduct of the unbelieving Jews, destroys the theory of Baur.[1]

[1] The attack of the Tübingen school upon the genuineness of most of the Pauline Epistles, resting as it does upon false assumptions, should not be allowed for a moment to affect the judgment which is founded on positive, abundant proofs. Take, for example, the 1st Epistle to the Thessalonians. Its Pauline authorship was never doubted until it was doubted by Baur. It is not only recognized by the great church teachers in the second half of the second century, but is found in the Syrian version, in the canon of Muratori, even in the canon of Marcion. Its language is Pauline. Its tone and spirit are Pauline. Its contents are adapted to a state of the Thessalonian church which may well be supposed to have existed. It has correspondences with the Acts, which are obviously uncontrived, yet exact. Compare 1 Thess. iii. 1, 2 with Acts xvii. 15, xviii. 5. And if the passage—iv. 15, 17—express a hope or an expectation of the παρουσία during the Apostle's lifetime, it demonstrates the Pauline authorship, since no writer of the second century would attribute such a disappointed expectation to

There are three other documents in the New Testament canon which throw important light upon the subject of this Essay. These are the 1st Epistle of Peter, the Epistle to the Hebrews, and the Apocalypse.

Paul. The objections of Baur to the Pauline origin of this Epistle are of no weight, and mainly rest upon misinterpretation.

There are thirteen canonical Epistles bearing the name of Paul. No criticism—save that of the Baur school—which by any stretch of charity can be called sober, pretends to deny the genuineness of the Epistles to the Philippians, to the Colossians, the two Epistles to the Thessalonians, and the Epistle to Philemon. The Pauline authorship of the Epistle to the Ephesians may be said to have been completely vindicated against the doubts suggested by De Wette and others. In fact, one of the main grounds of doubt—the absence of personal greetings—is an argument for the genuineness of the work; since, though we can only conjecture the cause of this peculiarity, it is one which a forger would last of all have permitted to exist. Of the Pastoral Epistles, the 2d of Timothy and the Epistle to Titus are fully proved to be Pauline, and recognized as such by unprejudiced critics, like Bleek and Meyer, who hold themselves at liberty to judge with perfect freedom of the claim of a book to a place in the canon. Of the 1st Epistle to Timothy, Neander says that he is not convinced of its genuineness with the "same assurance that he has in reference to the authorship of the other Pauline Epistles." *Pflanz. u. Leitung.* B. I. s. 538. N. Such misgivings, however, in respect to either of the Pastoral Epistles, are not shared by critics of equal candor and penetration; for example, by the late Dr. Arnold. As to the author of the Epistle to the Hebrews, a point about which the opinion of the ancient Church was divided, he is now generally conceded to have been, not Paul himself, but a disciple of Paul. This was the opinion, also, of Erasmus, Luther, and Calvin. It is the view of Neander, Bleek, Meyer, and, in fact, of all or nearly all the German critics. Its early date is, however, established; and if not written by Paul, it has the same relation to him as the writings of Luke have, and the same right in the canon as the second and third Gospels and the Acts.

The 1st Epistle of Peter is reckoned by Eusebius among the Homologoumena—the writings of undisputed genuineness. Among the witnesses to its authenticity are Papias and Polycarp.[1] It is addressed apparently to the first generation of converts from heathenism, and not to their children or grandchildren (e. g. 1 Peter i. 14). It purports to come from "a witness of the sufferings of Christ" (1 Peter v. 1); a fact introduced so briefly and naturally as to convince Schleiermacher that the expression was not put into the mouth of Peter, but was truly his own. It is addressed to "the strangers scattered throughout Asia Minor;" and yet the contents of the Epistle make it clear that Gentiles are meant; so that in this designation of them as *διασπορά*, the metropolitan character, so to speak, of Judaean Christianity is assumed in a manner natural to Peter. It was written from Babylon—the literal, as we think, and not the mystical, Babylon—where Jews were so numerous, and where Peter would naturally be drawn in the prosecution of his missionary labors. A suitable occasion for his writing was afforded by the journey of Silas (1 Peter v. 12), formerly a member of the Jerusalem church and afterwards concerned with Paul in founding and train-

[1] Eusebius, iii. 39, iv. 14. Those who deny the genuineness of the 2d Epistle of Peter, must yet place it not later than the beginning of the second century; and hence the testimony of this document (2 Peter iii. 1) to the 1st Epistle, as a work of Peter, is valuable. See on this and the other points of proof, Bleek's *Einl.*, s. 565 seq.

ing the very churches to which he now carried this letter. In these churches there were those who, as we learn from Paul in his later Epistles, had, through the influence of Judaizers, begun to fear that they had not received the true gospel. Now Peter reassures this class by simply saying at the close of his letter: "I have written briefly, exhorting and testifying *that this is the true grace of God wherein ye stand.*" It is an expression of confidence and fraternal sympathy from the Apostle "to the circumcision," written within a few years preceding the destruction of Jerusalem and shortly before his own death.

Another most interesting monument of the state of things at that critical time, is the Epistle to the Hebrews. It was written while the temple was yet standing, but not very long before the siege and capture of the city by Titus. It was addressed to Jewish Christians, and, as we believe, to the Palestinian Christians. It was written to keep them from apostasy—from lapsing into mere Judaism. This, every one must see, was the great danger so long as the Jewish Christians continued to cling to the ritual. It would seem that there were some of this class who had ceased to meet with their brethren (Hebrews x. 25). It is probable that with the rapid growth of the Gentile branch of the church, which was attended by a growing indifference to the ceremonial law still sacred to the native Jew, the disaffection of the Jewish Christians increased; and it is not improbable that in that class who are described as "forsaking the assembling of themselves together" is to be recognized the germ of heretical judaizing sects which become known to us at a later day. The great aim of the author of the Epistle is to persuade the Jewish Christian that in Christ the ritual is fulfilled; that in Him all that he had in the law is retained in a perfect and satisfying form.

Not less interesting as a memorial of the state of things which we are attempting to depict, is the Apocalypse. The Apocalypse was written—this fact, we take it, is now established, notwithstanding the continued dissent of a critic here or there—shortly after the Neronian persecution, and shortly before the destruction of Jerusalem. The Apostles Peter and Paul had been put to death. The bitter fanaticism of the Jews and all the signs of the times foretokened the judgments soon to fall upon the Jewish state. The condition of the churches in Asia Minor, coupled, we may well believe, with the persecuting animosity of his countrymen "according to the flesh" in Jerusalem, had drawn the Apostle John to Ephesus. The preponderance of proof, in our opinion, is in favor of the more common opinion that the Apostle is the author of the Apocalypse. But if not his work, it was certainly written by some one who belonged to his school and his neighborhood. Baur, who holds that the Apostle himself wrote it, has most unsuccessfully attempted to find in it a judaizing and anti-Pauline character. The distinction put upon the twelve apostles (Rev. xxi. 14) is one of his arguments. If this have any force, then Acts was written by a Judaizer (see Acts i. 21 seq.); and Luke's Gospel also (see Luke xxii. 30), which Baur considers especially Pauline in its spirit. Baur even discerns in the reference to false or pretended apostles (Rev. ii. 2) a side hit at Paul! Ewald, with just as little reason, considers them Judaizers. It is probable that they were leaders of the Nicolaitans, who seem to have been a sect of antinomian, gnostical libertines—abusing their freedom in the gospel by joining the heathen in licentious pleasures, and blending a sort of gnosis, which the writer designates a knowing of "the depths of Satan" (Rev. iii. 24); using, perhaps, the term *Satan*, as in the other phrase—the synagogue of Satan—where *they* would use *God*. A judaizing spirit is inferred by Baur from the distinct mention of the "hundred and forty and four thousand" from the tribes of Israel (Rev. vii. 4) who were among the redeemed. How ill-founded is this conclusion we see when we further read that those gathered from "all nations, and kindreds, and people, and tongues," instead of being a definite, symbolical to be sure, yet limited, number, were "a great multitude which no man could count" (ver. 9). But the Apocalypse affords a happy confirmation of the historical truth of the apostolic convention. Having alluded (Rev. ii. 20) as he had done before (ver. 14) to the obligation to abstain from fornication and from meat sacrificed to idols, the writer adds (vs. 24, 25), "I will put upon you *none other burden:* but that which ye have already"—namely, the true faith—"hold fast till I come." Here the context requires us to suppose that "burden" signifies injunction; and thus we are obliged to explain the passage by referring back to what he has said on the two points of duty above mentioned. In the requirement to abstain from fornication and from flesh offered to idols, he would add no other burden—*ἄλλο βάρος*—the very word used in the rescript of the apostolic convention (Acts xv. 21)![1] To our mind, this passage affords a striking corroboration of the narrative of Luke. A portion of the Asia Minor Christians had neglected the warnings of Paul, had abused their freedom, making it an obedience to lust, and had mingled with the heathen in their licentious feasts. Hence the need of imposing the old restraints, and the Apostle revives the rules suggested by that early conference in which he had himself taken part.

We may sum up in a few words the main points in the view we have taken. The apostles and most other Jewish Christians kept up the observance of the ceremonial law, and felt bound so to do until Christ should appear to abrogate that law, or in some other way should explicitly declare the old ritual abolished. Peter was divinely instructed in the affair of Cornelius,

[1] The interpretation we have given above is sanctioned by high critical authority, including that of Düsterdieck (in Meyer) and Alford.

that free intercourse with the Gentile convert was no sin. This lesson by him was not forgotten. At Antioch he ate with the Gentile believers, except when, under temptation, he was false to his convictions. The Jewish believers, seeing that the Gentiles had actually become Christians and received the Spirit without having been circumcised, cordially and thankfully acknowledged them as brethren, and refused to yield to the judaizing faction which required that they should be circumcised. At the same time there was a difficulty in overstepping the legal restrictions upon intercourse with them as long as the law continued to be observed. They could not cast aside all these restrictions without casting aside the law itself—a step for which they were not prepared. Hence the door was open for the efforts of the active party of Judaizers. These efforts, however, had not the sympathy or countenance of "the pillars" of the Jewish-Christian church. The fundamental error of Baur, as we believe, is the doctrine that *the Jerusalem apostles required the circumcision of the Gentile converts.* In supporting this error, he is obliged not only to attack the genuineness of the Acts and the moral character of the author, but also to do violence to the positive testimony of Paul himself in Gal. ii. The progress of the Gentile church led to the sharpening of the opposition from the side of the judaizing party, and probably to an augmentation of its strength. Only great providential events could clear the Christian Church of its connection with the

Old Testament system. These events at length came; first, the capture of Jerusalem by Titus, after the Jewish Christians had mostly fled to the neighborhood of the Dead Sea: then, after the insurrection by Barchochebas, the absolute prohibition by Hadrian (A. D. 135) of the temple-worship in the city, to which he gave the Roman name of Ælia Capitolina. This last event was the crisis that determined the fate of Jewish Christianity. Henceforward only a church on Gentile foundations could exist in Jerusalem. That portion of the former church which could not abandon the ritual became resolved into the heretical sect which lingered for centuries under the name of Ebionites, but consisting of two main subdivisions—one that of Ebionites proper, who refused to recognize the Gentiles as Christians; the other that of the Nazarenes, who clung with patriotic attachment to the ceremonies of the law, not denying, however, the Christianity of the Gentiles for not joining them in its observance. The headquarters of the Ebionite party was the region on the eastern border of Palestine, whither the Jewish Christians had originally taken refuge. The apostasy which to the author of the Epistle to the Hebrews was an imminent danger, actually occurred in the case of no small fraction of the Jerusalem church. And thus the saying of the Apostle John had a new and pathetic verification: "He came unto his own, and his own received him not."

ESSAY V.

BAUR ON EBIONITISM AND THE ORIGIN OF CATHOLIC CHRISTIANITY.

The rise of the ancient Catholic church, that church, which, with its unity in doctrine and creed, its type of theology too legal to be strictly Pauline, and its hierarchical order, emerges to view in the latter half of the second century, is one of the most interesting problems of history. If we take our stand at the time of Irenaeus, we find that genuine Christianity begins to be recognized as confined to one visible body, having for its great centres the churches supposed to be founded by the apostles, among which Rome, the see of Peter and of Paul, especially of Peter the head of the apostles, has the preëminence in dignity and respect—the *potiorem principalitatem*, to use the phrase by which Irenaeus affirms the distinguished reliability of its traditions.[1] Beyond the pale of this Catholic church there is no salvation. The outlying parties have no title to the blessings of the gospel. The church is comparatively pure in doctrine and free in government; yet the incipient and germinant Papal system is clearly discernible.

[1] Iren., Lib. iii. c. 3.

By what steps did simple, unorganized, apostolic Christianity attain to this new form? What agencies effected the transformation? Such is the problem to which we refer. It involves the whole question of the character of the Christianity of the apostolic age, as well as the nature of the changes it afterwards underwent. It has drawn to itself of late, in particular since the rise of the new Tübingen school of historical critics, the zealous attention of scholars.

One principal topic, the consideration of which involves the most important inquiries connected with the whole subject, is Ebionitism. Ebionitism is the general designation of that judaizing Christianity which existed during the first centuries, in several distinct parties, in separation from the Catholic church. The strict Ebionites—the vulgar Ebionites, as they are called in the classification of some German writers—not only observed the Mosaic ritual, but refused to fellowship any who failed to do likewise. The Nazarenes, another party, though observing the law themselves, willingly left the Gentiles to the enjoyment of their freedom. The former party was hostile to Paul and his doctrine; the latter was not. Both made use of Hebrew or Aramaic versions of the Gospel of Matthew, differing somewhat, however, from that Gospel, as they differed somewhat from each other. There was a third party, also, of theosophic or gnostical Ebionites, described by Epiphanius and represented in the Clementine Homilies, a spurious work of the latter part of the second century. It is an old and often-repeated assertion that primitive, apostolic Christianity—that Christianity which was established and fostered by the immediate followers of Christ—was Ebionite. This proposition was maintained by Socinian writers of a former day, who, considering the Ebionites to have been Unitarians, inferred that the early Christians held the humanitarian view of Christ's person. Hence the character and opinions of the Ebionite parties come up for discussion in the polemical writings of Bull, who combats the views of Zwicker, and in the spirited controversy, in the last century, of Horsley with Priestley. The subject was handled in a special dissertation by Mosheim, in an early essay of great merit by Gieseler, and has been further illustrated by Neander and the other masters in the department of church history. Of late the historical speculations of Baur have provoked new and fruitful investigations in the same field, and have called forth numerous publications, both from his followers and opponents.

In stating the theory of Baur upon this subject and upon early Christianity in general, we may remark at the outset that he agrees with the old Socinians in the statement that the Jewish Christianity of the apostolic age was Ebionite. But, unlike them, he holds that we find within the canon a great departure from, and advance upon, this humanitarian doctrine of Christ's person. He professes to discern in the

New Testament the consecutive stages of a progress, which, beginning with the Unitarian creed, terminates in the doctrine of Christ's proper divinity. To be sure, a considerable portion of these canonical writings, including all those which contain this last tenet, he pronounces post-apostolic and spurious. But he differs very widely from the Socinians in his exegesis of them, and approximates nearer, especially in regard to the sense of the writings of John, to the ordinary orthodox interpretations. Baur's general theory proceeds on the foundation of the hostility conceived to exist, in the apostolic age, between the Pauline and Petrine parties. In the study of the Epistles to the Corinthians, he supposed himself to have discovered that the long prevalent idea of the relation of Paul to the rest of the apostles, and of his doctrine to theirs, is mistaken; and for this new view he found support, as he thought, in the Epistle to the Galatians.[1] While the original apostles insisted that the Gentile converts should be circumcised and keep the law, Paul looked on circumcision as involving a forfeiture of the benefits of the gospel. Baur carries out his novel thesis with relentless consistency. He denies the Pauline authorship of all of the epistles usually ascribed to Paul, except four, and the genuineness of all the other books of the New Testament, except the Apocalypse. The

[1] For an interesting account of the growth of his critical theory in his own mind, see Baur's posthumous *Geschichte des 19tn. Jahrh.*, s. 395 seq.

Gospels, as to a part of their contents, are either monuments of this great division in the Church, or of the attempts to heal it. The Gospel of John is a fictitious product of the early part of the second century. The Acts is the work of a Pauline Christian of about the same date, who misrepresents the apostolic history for the sake of reconciling to each other the partisans of Peter and of Paul. At the close of the apostolic age, or at the death of these leaders, the Church had been left in this divided state. The Gentile or Pauline Christians, and the Jewish Christians, formed two opposing camps.[1]

We cannot enter into a detailed refutation of these fundamental positions of Baur, without repeating what we have said in another place. The assumption that the older apostles required that the heathen converts should be circumcised, and that Paul directly resisted the observance of the law by Jewish Christians as inconsistent with the Christian faith, is unproved and groundless. The mutual alienation of the Jerusalem apostles on the one hand, and of Paul on the other, is a figment of the imagination; as is shown by the direct testimony of Paul himself in documents which even Baur admits to be his.[2] The main objection to the credibility of the Acts is thus annulled. The positive proof of the genuineness of this book, as well

[1] For the full and final statement of Baur's positions, see his *Christenthum in d. drei ersten Jahrh.*, 2 A. 1860.

[2] Gal. ii. 9, 10; 1 Cor. xv. 9, xvi. 1, et al.

as of the rejected epistles of Paul, is abundant. The historical speculations of the Tübingen school, being built upon a false foundation, fall of themselves. There were, indeed, strong peculiarities belonging severally to the two branches of the Church in the lifetime of Paul; but with the exception of the judaizing party, there was no hostility between them. On the contrary, especially among the leaders, there was a cordial fellowship.

But at present we are concerned with the Tübingen theory so far as it relates to the Church of the sub-apostolic age. Baur pretends that after the death of Paul, there ensued the process of reconciliation between the two belligerent parties, to promote which, as we have explained above, most of the New Testament books were contrived. The Jewish Christians gave up circumcision, being satisfied with baptism, when regarded as necessary for salvation. Exactly how and when this remarkable step was taken, we are not informed. But most of the concessions were from the Pauline side. In fact, there occurred at the end, or before the end, of the apostolic age, a reaction of the Jewish Christianity, which with Baur is identical with the judaizing or Ebionite element, and this type of Christianity prevailed through the larger part of the second century. In the church of Asia Minor, little or no value was set upon the authority and the doctrine of Paul, which were supplanted by the Ebionite views of Christianity. The same was true of the Roman church, which Baur claims to have been, even at the beginning, chiefly composed of believing Jews. The diffusion and reception of the doctrine of the authority of tradition, of legal justification, of the saving efficacy of rites, of the superior merit of ascetic piety, of the clergy as a priestly class, of the primacy of Peter, and of other elements of Catholic theology, the Tübingen critics attribute to the great reaction and partial triumph of the Jewish-Christian, anti-Pauline party. So tenacious of life, we are told, was Judaism, that the powerful influence of the Apostle Paul was, to a large extent, neutralized and overcome by the revived power of the judaical element in the Church. Not that the Pauline element was ineffective. It was not without its representatives, and played a not unimportant part in the ferment from which Catholic theology resulted. Of course, these views of Baur affect his construction of the history of the doctrines concerning the Person of Christ and the Trinity. The first view of the Church respecting Christ was humanitarian. Then followed, according to Baur, the other form of Monarchianism, the Patripassian theory. The Logos doctrine was the intermediate, compromising theology, which was finally developed into the dogma of the Saviour's true and proper divinity, and the Nicene formulary.[1]

The topics which we propose to examine in the

[1] On this branch of Baur's theory, besides his "Christianity in the first Three Centuries," which has been referred to above, see his

remarks that follow, are, first, the alleged Ebionite character of the period immediately subsequent to the apostolic age, and then, in particular, Baur's representation of the early doctrine concerning Christ.

I. One marked vice of the Tübingen critics is the habit of attributing to a distinctly Jewish-Christian party or influence phenomena which more commonly originate in other causes. The tendency to regard Christianity as a system of laws, is not peculiar to the Jews and to Judaism alone. This tendency develops itself in other ages, even within the bounds of Protestant Christianity. Hence, when this spirit appears in an early Christian writer, to charge it forthwith to Ebionitism is an obvious fallacy. The same may be said of the overvaluing of external rites. A tendency to formalism may spring up independently of Jewish influences; in the nineteenth century as well as the third, in modern Oxford as well as ancient Rome. To say that religious phenomena, because they resemble each other, are historically connected, is a rash, and frequently unfounded, inference. This neglect to discriminate between what springs from a distinctively judaic party, and what merely bears some likeness to judaic principles, but only indicates an

extensive work on the History of the Doctrine of the Trinity, *Die Christl. Lehre v. d. Dreieinigkeit u. Menschwerdung Gottes in ihrer geschichtlichen Entwickl.* (1841), B. I.; and his *Dogmengeschichte*, 2 A. (1858), s. 104–112, 126–130.

analogous way of thinking, runs through much of the Tübingen criticism, as we shall hereafter illustrate.

But what are the proofs by which Baur would subvert the established views of early Christian history and verify his own hypothesis? In following the Tübingen critics through their classification of the ancient writers, we are constantly struck with the arbitrary character of the procedure. To make out that the Ebionite type of doctrine belongs to an early Father, they are under the necessity of ignoring expressions which are at war with such a view, and of magnifying the significance of artless phrases to which no emphasis is properly attached. One sign of the justice of our remark is the fact that these critics differ so widely among themselves in respect to the place to be assigned to the different writers—even to such a writer as Justin Martyr. Baur is constantly obliged to mediate between his two disciples, Schwegler and Ritschl, and to interpose the weight of his decision where these younger doctors disagree. Let us examine the proofs and witnesses which are adduced to establish the predominantly Ebionite character of the early Church. Even Clement of Rome, or the first epistle which bears his name, but which, wholly without reason, is denied by the Tübingen critics to be genuine, is made to stand on a neutral or half-way position between the Ebionite and Pauline doctrine—Clement, who speaks of justification as "not by ourselves, neither by our own wisdom, or knowledge, or piety, or the works which we have done in the holiness of our hearts; but by that faith by which God Almighty has justified all men from the beginning;"[1] who alludes to the epistle which "the blessed Paul the apostle had written to the Corinthians before;"[2] and whose view of Christ is so dissonant in spirit from that of the Ebionite! It is true that he associates Peter, as a martyr to be held in honor, with Paul.[3] And why should he not? It is true that Clement lays stress upon the practical duties of Christians, and often connects obedience with faith.[4] But the reason of this is found in the disturbed state of the Corinthian church, and the disaffection towards its officers.[5] Whoever will read the epistle from beginning to end will see that here is the motive for the enforcing of practical obligations, in conjunction with passages obviously derived, though not verbally cited, from the Epistle to the Hebrews.

Papias, in the fragments cited by Eusebius, is another of Baur's witnesses for the Ebionitism of the early Church. It is thought to be highly significant that in the scriptural books which are mentioned by Eusebius as having been cited by Papias, the Pauline epistles are not found; nor is it stated that Papias made mention of Paul. As if Eusebius professed to give all the canonical books to which Papias made reference, or Papias made reference to all the canonical

[1] C. 32. [2] C. 47. [3] C. 5.
[4] C. 10, 11, 12, et passim. [5] See C. 1, 48, etc.

books which he received! Of Polycarp, in like manner, Eusebius says that he made use, in his Epistle to the Philippians, of the 1st Epistle of Peter;[1] but we know, though Eusebius does not mention the fact, that he also made abundant use of the Epistles of Paul.[2] Eusebius had reasons of his own for specifying certain books in these allusions to the use of the Scriptures by earlier writers. We are not authorized to suppose that he intends to give an exhaustive list. The insinuation of a hostility to Paul on the part of Papias hardly merits a serious refutation. If he did not explicitly mention this apostle in his "Exposition of the Oracles of the Lord"—and whether he did or not we have no means of deciding—it would not be strange, since his aim was to gather up unrecorded reminiscences of the life and teachings of Jesus. His chiliasm, or millenarianism, is very far from proving him an Ebionite. He shared this doctrine not only with Justin Martyr and Irenaeus, but even with Barnabas, whom all the skeptical writers put on the Pauline side. Although chiliasm cannot be shown to have been the universal belief of the Church in the next age after the apostles, it was, without doubt, a very widely diffused opinion. It is not at all confined, however, to writers of a single school. In truth, as Dorner has clearly shown and we may stop here to observe, chiliasm, whatever may have been the first

[1] Euseb., Lib. iv. c. 14.

[2] See, for example, in *Polyc. ad Philip.*, c. v. (1 Cor. vi. 9, 10).

source of the belief, was widely diverse from the current Jewish expectation of a temporal reign of the Messiah.[1] The earthly reign of Christ after the second advent, even in the view of those inclined to conceive of the millennial period in too material a way, was a limited time, and was to be followed by a spiritual, heavenly life, to continue forever. But—to return to Papias—we need no other proof that he was not an Ebionite and had no inimical feeling towards Paul, than his friendship with Polycarp,[2] and the circumstance that Irenaeus, and Eusebius after him, with the writings of Papias before them, have no quarrel with him, except that Eusebius, as we should expect, objects to his chiliastic notions, and considers him, probably on account of them, a man of limited understanding.[3] Indeed, the circumstance which Eusebius mentions, that Papias made use of testimonies from the 1st Epistle of John and the 1st Epistle of Peter, is of itself conclusive against the Tübingen judgment concerning him.

Still more reliance is placed by Baur and his followers on the evidence drawn from the fragments of Hegesippus. This earliest historian of the Church came to Rome about the middle of the second century. He was an Ebionite, it is claimed; and as he had

[1] Dorner's *Entwickelungsgeschichte d. Lehre v. d. Person Christi*, B. I. s. 240 seq. See especially s. 240, N. 76.

[2] Irenaeus calls Papias a friend (ἑταῖρος) of Polycarp.

[3] Euseb., Lib. iii. c. 39.

travelled extensively for the purpose of visiting the churches, and had found them, according to his own statement, agreeing in doctrine, it is confidently asserted that the churches east and west, including the Roman church, which he especially commends, were also Ebionite. This deduction might be just, were the premise established. But what is the proof that Hegesippus was an Ebionite? In the first place, much is made of the description, quoted by Eusebius, of the character of James, the head of the church at Jerusalem, in which he is made out a punctilious observer of ceremonies.[1] That this fictitious portraiture accords with Ebionite taste, is granted. It is probable, however, that Hegesippus derived it from an Ebionite tradition. That he himself followed such a pattern of life, there is no more reason to think than there is to suppose the same of Gregory Nazianzen, who gives a similar description of Peter, and Clement of Alexandria, who gives a similar description of Matthew, both of which were also probably borrowed from Ebionite sources.[2] But Hegesippus reports that in every city "the doctrine prevails according to what is declared by the law, and the prophets, and the Lord;"[3] and this statement is seized upon as an undoubted sign of Ebionitism in the author! Hegesippus was zealous against the

[1] Euseb., Lib. ii. c. 23.

[2] See Schliemann, *Die Clementinen*, s. 429.

[3] Euseb., Lib. iv. c. 22.

Gnostics, and this mention of the Old Testament, which, however, would not be remarkable in any case, was very natural, it being a part of his testimony to the freedom of the churches from the taint of gnostical heresy.

But there is another passage from Hegesippus which was quoted by the Monophysite, Stephen Gobarus, and is found in Photius, in which he says that those who affirm that "eye hath not seen nor ear heard, nor hath it entered into the heart of man, the good things prepared for the just," maintain what is false and that this declaration is itself foolish. Here, we are assured by the Tübingen critics, is a direct condemnation of an expression of the Apostle Paul, and a condemnation of the apostle himself. Supposing Hegesippus to be quoted right, it is still not easy to judge of the real intent of a passage which is thus torn from its connection. There is little reason to doubt, however, that Hegesippus is attacking a gnostical interpretation or application of the passage, as was long ago conjectured. In the sense in which the Gnostics employed the expression, he might call it foolish. That he could not have designed to attack a statement of Paul, is demonstrated, first by the circumstance that Paul himself quotes the passage in question from Isaiah, and a censure of the apostle would involve a rebuke of the prophet; and, secondly, by the fact that in Clement's epistle to the Corinthians, which is approved by Hegesippus, this identical passage of Scripture is also found.[1] Hegesippus is, rather, a witness *against* Baur's theory. He says that the Church was united and unpolluted by heresy until the apostles and the generation taught by them had passed away.[2] How does this accord with the idea that the church of the apostolic age was rent in twain, and that Paul was considered then by the Jewish Christians to be a leader of heresy? "If there were any at all," adds Hegesippus, "that attempted to subvert the sound doctrine of the saving gospel, they were yet skulking in dark retreats." The surmise of Baur, that this expression relates to Paul, is so plainly a desperate effort to escape from a difficulty, that it requires no answer. How far from Ebionitism Hegesippus was, though probably a Hebrew Christian by birth, is evinced by his tracing even the gnostical heresies to a *Jewish* origin, by his approval of Clement's epistle to the Corinthians, and by his testimony that the church of Corinth, to which Clement wrote, had "continued in the true faith." The same thing is proved incontrovertibly to the sober student of history by the simple fact that Eusebius, himself hostile to Ebionitism, and surely not less able to detect its presence than any critic of the Tübingen school, and with the whole work of Hegesippus before him, speaks of this old writer with entire respect and approbation.

Against Hermas the charge of Ebionitism can be

[1] Clement, I. Cor. c. xxxiv.

[2] Euseb., Lib. iii. c. 32.

made with more plausibility; but even with reference to him it cannot be sustained. Although he does in terms make faith the parent of all Christian virtues, yet in his far-fetched and long-drawn allegories the gospel is generally presented in a legal aspect, as a system of commands, on obeying which salvation hinges. Moreover the idea of fasting as a meritorious act, and a general tendency to asceticism, correspond to certain features of Ebionitism. But we have here to reiterate the observation that was made before, that legalism and asceticism spring up in the Church from other causes than the influence of Judaism. Such is the fact in the case of Hermas and of the Church in the second century so far as it sympathized with his type of thinking. In Hermas there is no exaltation of the Jews as a nation, no recognition of their national pretensions, no ascription to them of a preëminence in privileges and hopes. Hence, however he may resemble the Ebionites in sundry points of doctrine, he is wholly distinct from them in historical position. A decisive proof that Hermas is not an Ebionite, is the doctrine he holds concerning Christ, to whom he attributes preëxistence and a part in the creation of the world. Another very striking proof of the same thing—a proof that his ritualism did not spring from an Ebionite root—is his notion that the Old Testament saints will have to be baptized by the apostles in the underworld, in order to be saved![1]

[1] *Pastor Hermae*, Liber III. Simil. ix. 16. "Hermas male intel-

We come now to the main prop of the Tübingen criticism, the Pseudo-Clementine Homilies. There existed from the beginning of the second century, in parts of Palestine and the neighborhood, a Jewish-Christian party called Elkesaits. They were composed of Ebionite sectaries, who had probably fallen under the influence of the Essenes, and whose creed was a compound of their old belief and their newly-gained ascetic tenets.[1] The Spirit of God had united itself, they held, with Adam, constituting thus the true prophet, and afterwards with a series of individuals—Enoch, Noah, Abraham, Isaac, Jacob, Moses, Jesus—who all taught in substance the same truth. Christianity was thus regarded as the restoration of the primeval religion, with which, also, primitive and pure Judaism was identical. The Elkesaits abjured the eating of flesh, and discarded sacrifices, which were

ligens verba Apostoli I Petr. 3. 19 haec scripsisse videtur," says Hefele in his note, p. 424.

[1] Gieseler attributes the theosophic ingredients of the Elkesait system to the influence of the Essenes. Schliemann, following Neander, would account for the same by the fusion of oriental elements with Judaism. But according to Neander, as Gieseler points out, Essenism itself is partly the product of this very fusion. See Gieseler's *K. G.*, B. I. § 32. n. 9.

The best edition of the Homilies is that of A. Dressel (1853). This edition contains the last two Homilies, which are not found in the edition of Cotelerius. A very thorough monogram on the whole subject of the Pseudo-Clementine writings is "Die Clementinen" of A. Schliemann (1844). Uhlhorn, the author of a later work on the same subject, gives a condensed statement of his views in Herzog's Real-Encyc., Art. *Clementinen*.

held to have come in through a corruption of the true religion. They advocated the obligation to renounce riches. The forgiveness of sins was procured by baptism, which, as it would appear, was often repeated. They rejected, among other scriptures, the Pauline Epistles.

The Pseudo-Clementine Homilies, which were written by some Roman towards the end of the second century, bring forward, with additions and modifications, the same tenets. The work falsely pretends to emanate from Clement, the first bishop of the Roman church after the apostles, who, being confounded, doubtless, with Flavius Clement, the relative of Domitian, is represented as a cultivated Roman of rank. Impelled by a thirst for truth, which he had sought in vain, he journeys to the east, and through the agency of Barnabas is introduced to Peter, whose instruction fully satisfies his mind, and who is made, in the room of Paul, the real apostle to the Gentiles, the founder and first bishop of the Roman church. Peter is portrayed as the antagonist of all sorts of errors, especially of the Gnostics in the person of Simon Magus. He combats, also, Chiliasm, the Hypostatic Trinity, and Montanism. Paul, though not mentioned by name, is made the adversary of Peter, and is regarded with hostility. Peter is made to teach the Elkesait doctrine of a primitive religion which was afterwards corrupted; of the identity of the true Mosaic system with Christianity; of the seven men, together with Jesus, in whom the true prophet was manifest; of opposition to sacrifices, abstinence from eating flesh, voluntary poverty, and frequent fasts and baptisms. In conjunction with these views, other notions are found. The earthly kingdom with Satan, its head, is set in antithesis to the heavenly kingdom, both forming together a pair; and a similar contrast or coupling is carried, in a series, through the whole history of the world and of man. Thus, Adam was endowed with all intellectual and moral gifts, but from him proceeded the woman, the source of sensuousness and weakness. So, along with the true prophet, false prophets are always found to pervert the truth. The hierarchical theory is decidedly supported, but chiliasm is opposed. Interwoven with the work is a not unattractive story, embracing the personal fortunes of Clement; and the whole is commended to credence by accompanying vouchers: a letter of Peter entrusting his discourses to James at Jerusalem, who is represented as the head-bishop of the whole Church; an attestation that the trust was faithfully discharged by James; and a letter of Clement to James, purporting to be written after the death of Peter, and transmitting the work which Clement had composed by his direction.

At a later period, it seems to have been thought that the Homilies were a work actually composed by Clement, but corrupted and interpolated by heretics. Accordingly, early in the third century, some one, probably an Alexandrian, undertook to clear them of supposed interpolations and restore them to the original form. The product was the so-called Recognitions of Clement. The Epitome is the result of a still later revision.[1]

Strange to say, the Clementine Homilies, a spurious production, the work of an unknown writer, and abounding in fantastic, anti-Christian ideas which could never have gained the assent of a sober-minded Christian, is made by Baur a sort of text-book for the illustration of the opinions of the Roman church, and of the churches generally, in the second century. Its authority is deemed sufficient, on many points, to outweigh the testimony of the approved writers who have heretofore been depended on by scholars of all theological affinities. Because this work is Ebionite and anti-Pauline, such must have been the prevailing Christianity of the time!

But the Clementine Homilies represented the opinions of an individual and not the sentiments of any important body of Christians. Not until after the Homilies were written did the party whose notions were, to a considerable extent, embodied in them, obtain adherents in Asia Minor, Cyprus, or Rome. Hence Origen, who was acquainted with the church at Rome, as well as with the churches elsewhere, speaks of this party as having "lately arisen."[2] The

[1] See Gieseler's *K. G.*, B. I. s. 285.

[2] Origen in Euseb., Lib. vi. c. 38.

most plausible and best supported hypothesis which we have met with, concerning the origin of this unique work, is that presented by Gieseler. The Roman church, as is well known, in the early centuries was far more practical than speculative. Instead of originating theological discussions, it gave a hearing to the more intellectual and versatile theologues of the East. In the second century in particular, Rome was the place to which theological sectaries resorted in order to gain, if possible, countenance from the influential church of the metropolis. In such a state of things it was natural that many should become unsettled in their faith and unable to satisfy themselves upon disputed questions. Among these was a young Roman, educated in philosophy, who determined to resort to Palestine, and seek for the truth among the remnants of the original, Judaean church. Falling in with the Elkesaits, he conceived himself to possess in their tenets a satisfactory system, and one on which divergent parties could be united. In opposing Gnostics and other parties with whom the Elkesaits had not come in contact, he was naturally led to amplify and modify the doctrine which he had learned, and to blend with it the results of his own speculation. This mode of accounting for the Homilie has the merit of being consistent with the known facts, and the bare statement of it will suggest how entirely exaggerated is the Tübingen estimate of the significance of the work.

The method which these critics adopt in dealing with the authorities from which the early history of the Church is to be deduced, we may illustrate by a modern parallel. Towards the close of the American Revolution, there appeared in London a history of Connecticut, from the pen of Rev. Samuel Peters, who had been a missionary in Hebron in that State, but had left the country in consequence of the unpopularity he had incurred by taking the side of the English Government. This work, though prefaced by protestations of fidelity and painstaking, is an odd mixture of fact and fiction. Among other fabulous stories, Peters promulgated the notion that unrecorded laws, which are styled "blue laws," of an ascetic and whimsical severity, were in force among the early Puritans of the colony. This singular, mendacious chronicle is thought worthy to be cited, though not without some expressions of distrust, by so recent an author as the learned Dr. Hessey in his Bampton Lectures upon the history of the observance of Sunday. Now what would be thought of an historical critic, who at some time in the remote future should take Peters for the governing authority in his investigation of the ancient history of Connecticut? Other documents, let it be supposed, are extant, which have been universally regarded as authentic. But these, together with historians like Bancroft and Palfrey, who lived much nearer the events and were in possession of a great amount of traditionary and documentary evidence which has since perished, he chooses to set aside. Such a course would match that taken by the critics who would convert the Clementine fiction into an authority sufficient to override the firmest historical testimonies.

That a judaizing party had sway in the Roman church in the next period after the apostolic age, is a declaration made in the face of convincing evidence to the contrary. Baur has contended that the church of Rome was made up, at the outset, chiefly of Jewish converts. But this proposition is refuted by the complexion of Paul's Epistle to the Romans. The fact of his writing an epistle to this church, which he had not personally planted and had never visited, is itself a strong presumption that the church was predominantly Gentile. The various expressions in the first chapter, relative to his calling to preach to the Gentiles and his willingness to fulfil it even at Rome (vs. 5, 6, 14, 15), would be out of place in an address to born Jews. And how unnatural is the hypothesis that the first eight chapters were written merely to serve as an introduction to the two chapters which follow! The observances of the Roman church were anti-Jewish. The custom grew up there of fasting on Saturday, or of continuing the fast of Friday through the following day, whilst Sunday was made a joyous festival. The Roman church, in the discussions of the second century concerning Easter, took ground against conforming to the Jewish calendar or continuing the

Jewish festivals. These are undeniable facts. They are met by the uncertified conjecture, that they indicate a Pauline reaction against the judaizing spirit which is assumed to have prevailed before! But this rejoinder is a subterfuge. If arbitrary conjectures of this kind are to pass for evidence, there might as well be an end of historical study.

The effort to trace the hierarchical theory and system to a distinctively Jewish-Christian and Petrine party, is not less unsuccessful. There was, without doubt, the transfer of the idea of the Jewish priesthood to the Christian clergy. The analogy of the Old Testament system was at once a model, and to some extent a motive, which determined the rank and functions of the Christian ecclesiastics. But the Jewish prejudice was peculiarly a *national* feeling. It was a feeling of pride in race and blood. This peculiar feeling, and the demands connected with it, hardly admit of being satisfied by the ascription of priestly prerogatives to Gentiles—by a seeming revival of the old religious system, attended, however, by the total loss of national preëminence. Jewish Christians, to be sure, might be liable to confound Old Testament with Christian ideas, and transform the preacher into the priest. This tendency, however, is to be distinguished from the technically judaizing spirit, which had its roots in a national jealousy. But even the Jewish-Christian feeling which was not judaizing, was far from being the controlling cause of that change in

Christian views which paved the way for the hierarchical system. Tendencies to such a system sprung up on heathen soil. Especially might this be the fact where the Old Testament, with its Levitical system, was in the hands of Christians, and when the question of the distinctive character of justification under the gospel no longer excited a living interest or continued to stir up controversy. The growth of the hierarchy, as a part of doctrinal belief and as a practical system, was imperceptible. It was rather due to the fact that the Church had become oblivious of the points of doctrine on which Paul insisted, or of the principles which underlie them, than to any distinct exertion or influence of an Ebionite party.

But how shall we explain the exalted rank which was given to Peter, and the position ascribed to him, of principal founder of the Roman church? These views, we reply, were not inspired by any anti-Pauline party. The whole tradition of Peter's visit to Rome and martyrdom there, as well as the later story of his episcopal supremacy in the Roman church, is attributed by the Tübingen critics to Ebionite partisanship. But as to the doctrine of Peter's headship among the apostles, it was not the offspring of an anti-Pauline theology. The idea of the hierarchy involved the need of an apostolic centre and head. And this place was naturally assigned to Peter. The reading of the Gospels and the Acts made the impression that Peter was the foremost of the apostles and was constituted their leader. Nor was this impression—however false the doctrine of an essential difference of rank between Peter and the rest may be—wholly unfounded. Even Paul in more than one place seems to regard Peter as the principal apostle, though a position hardly inferior seems to be held by James.[1] But the tradition of the visit of Peter to Rome and of his death there, antedates the hierarchical pretensions of the Roman church. Moreover, had the story been originated by a Petrine party in order to depress the consideration of Paul, as Baur pretends, it would have found instant contradiction from the Pauline party at Rome, instead of being attested, as it is, by the Presbyter Caius, himself a Christian zealous for the honor of Paul.[2] In truth, the idea that Peter helped to found the Roman church, and the association of his name with Paul in this work, is a sign that no partisanship respecting the merits and claims of these apostles existed. The notion that Peter was the first bishop of the Roman church, is something different from the tradition of his concern in founding it, and was probably set in circulation by the Pseudo-Clementine writings; first by the Homilies, but especially by the Recognitions, which passed for a genuine work. The inroads of Gnosticism and Montanism, and other agencies, contributed to combine orthodox Christianity into a more compact body. As the result of a variety of causes, the deepest of which lie in inherent tendencies of

[1] Gal. i. 18, ii. 7, 8.

[2] Euseb., Lib. II. c. 25.

human nature, an externalized conception of Christianity began more and more to prevail. The great, metropolitan church, in the city where Paul and Peter had died, the only church in the west claiming to be established and guided by an apostle, towered above all other western churches and even above all other apostolic sees. The idea of an apostolic primacy on the part of Peter insensibly connected itself with the story of an episcopal duty sustained by him in the Roman church. In these changes of doctrine and organization, we recognize, to be sure, the establishment of a system analogous to that of the Old Testament, and, in a great degree, with more or less consciousness, modelled after it; but we discern no evidence of the presence of a distinct, controlling Ebionite or judaizing party.

In the foregoing remarks we have not taken into view those important writings, the epistle of Barnabas, the epistle of Polycarp, and the Ignatian epistles,[1] the prevailing drift of which is confessed to be distinctly Pauline.[2] It has been possible, as we think, com-

[1] We may observe that the genuineness of the shorter Ignatian epistles—though they may have suffered interpolation—is not now impugned by judicious scholars. After the discovery of the Syrian version of three of these epistles, Bunsen came out with the hasty statement that only these, or so much of them as the Syrian version contained, are genuine. The Syrian translations, however, have been proved to be the product of an abridgment of the Ignatian originals, and to afford no evidence whatever against the genuineness of the remaining four.

[2] See Schwegler's *Nachapostolisches Zeitalter*, B. I.

pletely to refute the position of the Tübingen school by a plain analysis of their own evidence. Nor have we thought it necessary to answer the criticism which is quick-scented enough to detect in Justin Martyr a modicum of the judaizing leaven. Justin speaks mildly of the more liberal Ebionites who sought not to interfere with the freedom of the heathen converts;[1] and in the same spirit Paul would have spoken. Whoever will read with an impartial eye what Justin says of salvation by faith—that Abraham was justified "for the faith which he had being yet in uncircumcision"[2] (a statement doubtless borrowed from Paul), or peruse what he says of the sabbaths and fasts of the Jews,[3] or attend to his doctrine concerning the exalted dignity of Christ, will need no argument to convince him that Justin had no affinity with Ebionitism.

The Church in the era following the apostolic age was not swayed by Ebionitism. There was no party, save a party known and recognized as heretical, which was hostile to the Apostle Paul or called in question his right to be considered an apostle. However the Church may have gradually lapsed from his interpretation of the gospel, there was among orthodox Christians no conscious and wilful opposition to his doctrine. The whole theory of an anti-Pauline, Ebionite

[1] *Dial. c. Tryph.*, c. 47.

[2] *Dial. c. Tryph.*, c. 23.

[3] E. g. *Dial. c. Tryph.*, c. 19 seq.

Christianity in the second century, is not only unsupported by any solid evidence, but is positively proved to be false. Rather is it true that judaizing Christianity shrunk away and fell into a powerless sect, in the presence of the wide-spread establishment of the gospel among the heathen, and when Jerusalem, the sacred seat of the ancient worship, became a heap of ruins. Pauline Christianity achieved the victory; and then in Gentile churches themselves there sprung up conceptions of religion at variance with the spirit and tenor of the great apostle's teaching.

II. We proceed to the second topic which we proposed to consider—The Early Views concerning Christ, and the Doctrine of his Divinity.

In common with the older Socinians, Baur seeks to prove that the humanitarian view of the person of the Saviour was the original doctrine, or the doctrine of the Jewish Christians, partly on the ground that the Ebionites of the post-apostolic period, the remnant of the Judaean church, adhered to this conception, and were unitarians of the humanitarian type.

In order to test the validity of this argument, we shall have to state, as concisely as we can, what is known respecting the rise and character of the early Ebionite parties.[1]

[1] On this subject, there is nothing to supersede the lucid, masterly dissertation of Gieseler in *Stäudlin u. Tzschirner's Archiv für Kirchengeschichte*, iv. 2. Later investigations of Neander, Schliemann

There is no doubt, as we have said above, that there were in the apostolic age two branches of the Church. The Gentiles, or the churches composed of the disciples of Paul, and "they of the circumcision", were distinguished by the fact that the latter kept up the observance of the Old Testament ritual. It is a false position of Baur, as we affirm once more, that James, Peter, and the other Jerusalem apostles, together with the body of the Judaean church, were disposed to disfellowship Paul and his disciples. Yet there was a party of Jewish Christians—the Judaizers —imbued with a pharisaical spirit, and including many former members of the pharisaical sect, who were bent on making circumcision obligatory upon the heathen converts, and were inimical to the Apostle Paul. There is reason to believe that the judaizing party grew in numbers in proportion as the Gentile branch of the church gained in strength, and that their attachment to the ritual became more and more fanatical. At the destruction of Jerusalem, the Jewish Christians had taken refuge for the time in Pella and in the adjacent regions of eastern Palestine. But in consequence of repeated insurrections of the Jews, they were at length forbidden by Hadrian (A. D. 135) to enter the new city which he established on the site of Jerusalem; and the celebration of the Mosaic ritual,

(in the work already noticed), Dorner, and others, have rectified, however, the representations of Gieseler in certain particulars, and have brought forward some new information.

whether by Jews or Jewish Christians, was interdicted. Thenceforward the Christian church at Jerusalem ceased to observe the ceremonial law, and was externally, as well as in spirit, in full accord with the Gentile churches.

Not far from the time when this decree was issued, we find Justin Martyr[1] distinguishing between two classes of Jewish-Christian sectaries, with one of whom he can have no communion, while he looks upon the other with charity. The first class observe the ceremonial law and insist that Gentile Christians shall observe it; the second class, though observing the law themselves, which Justin counts a weakness, yet freely tolerate their Gentile brethren and make no attempt to put the yoke of circumcision and sabbaths upon them. It is plain that Justin has in mind the two parties which are known to later writers as Ebionites and Nazarenes; both however being frequently merged under the common name of Ebionite. Justin immediately proceeds to consider the opinion which was entertained by some Christians, that Christ did not preëxist, but is a man, not essentially distinguished from other men; and his language renders it clear that Jewish Christians are referred to. Irenaeus (who first uses the name *Ebionites*) and Tertullian treat Ebionitism as a heresy, and bring up the fact of the enmity of the sect to the Apostle Paul. This antagonism to Paul, however, belonged, as we

[1] *Dial. c. Tryph.*, 47, 48.

know, only to the strict Ebionites, and was not shared by the milder party of Nazarenes. Origen explicitly distinguishes these two divisions of the Ebionite class. The former, he says, deny and the latter accept the miraculous birth of Christ from the Virgin.[1] Eusebius describing both parties under the common designation of Ebionites, yet distinctly states that a portion of them did not deny "that the Lord was born of the Virgin by the Holy Ghost."[2] From Jerome and Epiphanius, in the latter part of the fourth century, we derive a more full explanation of the characteristic tenets of the different judaizing sects. Epiphanius describes a third class of Ebionites, who had mingled with their judaizing tenets theosophic or gnostical speculations and thus concocted a distinct and peculiar scheme of doctrine. One phase of this eclectic theology, as we have already explained, is presented in the Pseudo-Clementine Homilies.[3] The Homilies, it will be remembered, along with other elements which separate their system from the dogmas of either of the two parties which we have just described, are yet Ebionite in their hostility to the Apostle Paul, their rejection of the doctrine of Christ's divinity, and in various other points. Jerome, who lived in the neighborhood of the Jewish Christians and held intercourse with them, is our best authority, especially so far as the Nazarenes are concerned. Both these

[1] Origen, *c. Celsum*, v. 61, also c. 65.

[2] Euseb., Lib. III. c. 27.

[3] Epiph., *Haer.* xxx.

parties made use exclusively of the Gospel of the Hebrews, a gospel in the Aramaic dialect, which bore a near resemblance to the canonical Gospel of Matthew. The Ebionites proper, however, unlike the Nazarenes, rejected the first two chapters. Both observed the requirements of the ceremonial law. It is clear that the Ebionites proper considered Jesus to be a mere man, begotten by a human father; a prophet, receiving the messianic call at his baptism, and endued at that time with the Holy Spirit for the discharge of his office. Without circumcision, there was no salvation. Christ would come again to establish his throne at Jerusalem and bring all nations into subjection. Whether the Nazarenes held the chiliastic, or sensuous millennial, doctrine of the stricter Ebionites, we cannot determine.[1] But in many features the Nazarenes were broadly distinguished from this party of radical Judaizers. They rejected the pharisaical traditions and spirit. They believed that Jesus was conceived of the Holy Ghost and born of a virgin. They cherished a fraternal feeling towards the Gentile Christians. They honored the Apostle Paul. They waited, with longing, for the conversion of their Jewish countrymen to the faith in Christ.

Such, in brief, was the character of the Jewish-Christian sects, as it is gathered from the fragmentary information to be gleaned from the Fathers. We cannot fail to recognize in the Ebionites proper the

[1] See, on this topic, Schliemann, s. 457.

descendants of the party of Judaizers who, during the life of Paul, displayed a fanatical opposition to his principles and person. Nor do we err in regarding the Nazarenes as the successors of that milder party of Judaean Christians, who, under the lead of the apostles, observed, to be sure, the laws and customs of their people, but were in fraternal union with Paul and his Gentile churches. The territorial situation of these post-apostolic sects, in Palestine and the vicinity, together with all the rest of the knowledge we possess concerning them, corroborates this view. When and how did these parties separate from each other and form the rest of the church? We are not without the means of answering this question. Hegesippus, towards the end of the second century, states expressly that during the lifetime of the apostles, and down to the times of Trajan, there was no heresy or division in the Jerusalem church, and that the first movements of this sort occurred after the death of Simeon, the successor of James, or about the year 108. Up to this time the Church had remained a pure and unspotted virgin—a mode of expression signifying the absence of heretical parties.[1] It may be that little reliance is to be put upon the statement that an individual named Thebuthis was the first fomenter of schism, or that personal rivalry lay at the bottom of it; but as to the main chronological fact, there is no good reason for doubt. When the final decree expelling the Jews

[1] See Heinichen's note (8) to Euseb., Lib. III. 32.

and Jewish ritual from Jerusalem, was issued, a large number of Hebrew Christians abandoned the ceremonies of the law and identified themselves with the Gentile church.[1] But the Jewish Christians who were not prepared to take this step and were likewise unprepared to give up their Christian faith altogether, were thrown into the position of separate sects. The precise relations of the two divisions of the judaistic party to each other, it is not so easy to determine. But this we know, that the name of the Nazarenes had been applied from the beginning, by the Jews, to Christians generally;[2] and that the Nazarene party, in their principle relative to circumcision and their feeling towards Paul, harmonized with the liberal Jewish Christians of the apostolic age and were bitterly hated by the stricter Ebionites. It is natural, therefore, to suppose, with Gieseler, that the Ebionites proper—the strict Judaizers—broke off from the Nazarenes at the time when Hegesippus states that heresy and division began. When the Epistle to the Hebrews was written, or shortly before the destruction of Jerusalem by Titus, the judaizing party had shown signs of withdrawing itself from their more liberal

[1] Gieseler's Essay (in *Stäudlin u. Tzschirner*), s. 325. His references are to Epiph. de Pond. et Mens. § 15, and Sulpicius Severus, Hist. Sacr. II. 31. Where there is so great an inherent probability that the fact was as they state, these authorities may be considered sufficient.

[2] Paul was called by his Jewish accusers "a ringleader of the sect of the Nazarenes." Acts xxiv. 5.

countrymen and brethren. Here was the germ of the stricter Ebionite party. That the word Ebionite is derived from a person bearing the name of Ebion, a founder of the sect, is probably a fancy of Tertullian, since no mention is made of such an individual by Origen, Irenaeus, or any other previous writer. That the word signifies the narrow standpoint of the law, or the low views entertained concerning Christ, both of which interpretations are given by Origen, is equally improbable. It is more likely that it was one of the names of opprobrium early affixed by the Jews to believers in Jesus, on account of their actual poverty and social inferiority; though this poverty did not spring, as Baur would have it, from ascetic principles. This name continued to be applied to Jewish believers by their unbelieving countrymen, and was gradually appropriated, at least in Christian use, more specially to one branch of the Jewish separatists.

The unsoundness of the argument drawn from the opinions of the Ebionites, against the supposition that the divinity of Christ was a part of the faith of the apostolic church, is easily exposed. In the first place, it is not true that the Nazarenes—the only portion of the Ebionites whose opinion on the subject is pertinent in the discussion—professed the humanitarian doctrine. The Fathers unite in attributing to them a higher conception of Christ than was entertained by the more bigoted faction. They believed in his miraculous generation through the Spirit of God. We do not find, indeed, that the hypostatic preëxistence of Christ was an article of their creed; but the absence of this tenet from a theology not fully defined or developed, is very different from the distinct rejection of it. Dorner cogently defends the ground which was formerly taken by Horsley, that the Nazarenes are not to be counted among the disbelievers in the Saviour's divinity.[1] He shows that when Christ is styled, in a passage of their gospel, the Son of the Holy Spirit, it is not the Holy Spirit, the Sanctifier, but the spirit of God in the more general sense, or God himself, that is meant.[2] Dorner holds that their view, though undefined, had more resemblance to Patripassianism. But, in the second place, if the Nazarenes of the second and third centuries *were* humanitarians, it would be entirely unwarrantable to infer that the body of Jerusalem Christians in the apostolic age were of the same mind. The Ebionites did not represent the type of faith and feeling which belonged to Peter, James, John, and their disciples. We might as well infer that the faith of the Congregationalists of Boston at the end of the seventeenth century, must correspond to the faith of their descendants at the end of the eighteenth. Great changes of doctrine imperceptibly occur; and this is more easily the fact where doctrines are not scientifically defined. We have historical

[1] Dorner's *Entwickelungsgeschichte d. Lehre v. d. Person Christi*, B. I. s. 307 seq.

[2] Schliemann misinterprets these poetical expressions.

proof that such a change occurred in the case of the Jewish Christians. The Epistle to the Hebrews, written to Palestinian Christians a short time before the capture of Jerusalem by Titus, is a warning against these tendencies, of which actual apostasy on the part of some, and heretical Ebionitism on the part of others, were the proper fruit. Side by side with his arguments against keeping up the Mosaic ritual, the author of the Epistle lays stress upon the exalted nature of Christ. It appears altogether probable that the disposition to take a lower than the apostolic view of the person of Christ, as well as a tenacious clinging to the obsolete ritual, were manifest dangers which the writer of this epistle endeavors to meet and to avert. When the crisis occurred which compelled a choice, a portion of the Judaean Christians gave up the law and cast in their lot with the Gentile Christians. The Ebionites were *degenerate* Hebrew Christians. If there was an advance on the part of their brethren, on *their* part there was retrogression. Not only were they opposed to a logical and legitimate progress, they fell back from the tone and spirit of apostolic Christianity and a large portion of them settled down upon a lower view of Christ, according to which he was only a human prophet and lawgiver.

We are now prepared to judge of the truth of the oft-repeated statement that Christianity in its first stage was Ebionite. If this statement signify that the apostles and the church, as a body, at Jerusalem, required heathen converts to be circumcised, it is false. If it signify that they were humanitarians in the doctrine of Christ, it is likewise unfounded. If it mean that they were inimical to Paul, it is equally destitute of truth. If it mean that they made poverty a duty and were a band of ascetics, it is not less contradicted by the evidence. If it be intended simply that the Jewish Christians continued to worship in the temple and, for themselves, to observe the law, so much is true. In the proper and ordinary acceptation of the term, they were not Ebionites; and this appellation can be rightly applied only to schismatical parties of a later date.

When we follow Baur into the province of exegesis, we find his statements still more fallacious. We allow that Christ is not presented in just the same aspect in the various books of the New Testament, whether gospels or epistles. To say nothing of other grounds for a variety of representation, it is true of every great character in history, that the impression he makes on different persons varies with their varying individuality. One is taken up with a side which another partly overlooks. The Gospels do differ though they do not dissent, from each other. The Synoptics dwell more on the special proofs of messiahship and on the future disclosure of Christ's exalted rank in the exercise of his office of judge. In John, the glory of Christ to be exhibited at the end of the world retreats more into the background, whilst the fact of his preëxistence is distinct and prominent. But essentially the same conception of Christ is common both to the Synoptics and to John. The same underlying unity is also characteristic of the remaining portions of the New Testament.

1. Matthew, who is confidently claimed as a representative of the humanitarian view, really contains the same lofty conception of the person of Christ which is met with later in the New Testament. The Christ of Matthew is not merely a teacher and lawgiver, not simply a channel for conveying truth to men. He himself, as the head of the new kingdom, a central object of faith and love, stands in the foreground. The faith of the centurion in his supernatural power is applauded; the little faith in him, on the part of the disciples, when the lake is tossed by the tempest, is rebuked; the fervent faith confessed by Peter, or Peter as the representative and embodiment of this faith, is declared to be the rock on which the Church is built. Christ is to be loved more than father or mother. All men are to come to him to find rest. In his name the Gentiles are to trust. Into his name, or fellowship, they are to be baptized. He is greater than Jonas, greater than Solomon, Lord of the Sabbath-day. It is undeniable that the title of "Son of God," especially when associated, as it is, with the antithetical title of "Son of Man," is not only used

with a physical import, as referring to his miraculous birth, and an official import as an honorary title of the Messiah, but denotes, also, a metaphysical relation to God—a higher, divine nature. "*My* Father," is the usual and, as we think, the deeply significant mode in which Christ alludes to the relation of himself to God. Moreover, in the background of the eschatology in Matthew is the conception of Christ as divine. He is to come in the clouds of heaven, in the glory of his Father, attended by a retinue of angels, the most exalted of created intelligences. He is to summon together and to judge the entire race of mankind. How shall this be done without omniscience? To our mind, the impression which this whole representation is fitted to make, is wholly incongruous with the humanitarian doctrine. Very significant, as teaching that "Son of David" designates but one side of his being, and as likewise containing an implication of his preëxistence, is the question to the Pharisees: if David (in the 110th Psalm) call him Lord, how then is he his son? There are not wanting passages, even in Matthew, which closely resemble, even in language, the Johannean representation: "No man knoweth the Son but the Father, neither knoweth any man the Father save the Son and he to whomsoever the Son will reveal him;"[1] or, as it reads in Luke, "No man knoweth who the Son is but the Father, and who the Father is but the Son, and he to whom the Son will

[1] Matt. xi. 27.

reveal him."[1] How evident that "Son" is here not a mere official designation! Christ is the sole Revealer—in the language of John, the Logos or Word! He and the Father mutually know each other; and from the direct knowledge of either, all other beings are precluded! Here is presented a necessary incident, one of the constituent elements, we had almost said, of the Saviour's divinity. It is true that Christ is subordinate to the Father. The historical Christ, the Word made flesh, both in the New Testament and in the creed of the Church, is subordinate to the Father. A kind of subordination, not inconsistent with full and proper divinity, belongs even to the preëxistent Christ, as the Nicene formularies, in agreement with the New Testament, imply.

2. The Epistles of Paul which Baur chooses to consider genuine, teach the same doctrine concerning Christ as do the Epistles which he rejects. According to Baur, the principal peculiarity of Paul's doctrine is the ascription to Christ of a sort of celestial humanity, whereby he is distinguished from Adam. Dropping the interpolated *ὁ κύριος* from the text in 1 Cor. xv. 47, he holds that Paul sets the earthly, psychical nature of the first Adam, in which the germs of sin and death were inherent, in contrast with the second Adam, who, instead of springing from the ground, is constituted, so to speak, of a higher, heavenly stuff. Now Paul does, to be sure, in conformity with

[1] Luke x. 32.

Genesis, ascribe mortality to the unfallen Adam, the exemption from that lot having been the destined, but forfeited reward of obedience.[1] But his whole theology is utterly opposed to the conception of sin as originating in a physical imperfection and as forming a necessary stage in the development of humanity. Sin is man's act; it is *παράπτωμα*—transgression of a law, holy, just, and good. Sin with Paul is ethical, not physical. And as to the declaration respecting Christ, the second Adam, that he is from heaven (*ἐξ οὐρανοῦ*), it means either that thence he is to appear in his glorified body (comp. Phil. iii. 20)—such is the interpretation of Meyer; or, that he is a man supernaturally introduced into the race.[2] Baur's interpretation is not legitimately drawn from the passage, but read into it. In 1 Cor. viii. 6, the preexistence of Christ is distinctly and undeniably asserted, and with it the creation of the universe by him: "one Lord Jesus Christ, *by whom are all things.*" To refer this expression to the moral creation, or the redemptive work of Christ, as Baur does, though not without evident misgivings, is arbitrary and forbidden by the context—the "all things" in this clause being obviously identical with the "all things" of the clause

[1] Compare with these passages of Paul, Gen. iii. 19, 22, 24. The Scriptural doctrine respecting the connection of sin with death, together with the sense of 1 Cor. xv. 46 seq., is the subject of an able discussion in Julius Müller's *Lehre v. d. Sunde*, B. II. s. 400 seq.

[2] This last meaning Neander prefers, in his posthumous Commentary on the Epistles to the Corinthians.

preceding, where the creation is attributed, in opposition to polytheism, to one God. In 2 Cor. viii. 9, is another undeniable assertion of the preëxistence of Christ and of the incarnation: "Ye know the grace of our Lord Jesus Christ, that *though he was rich*, yet for your sakes *he became poor*, that ye through his poverty might be rich." The descent of Christ from a preëxistent glory to a state of humiliation is here definitely declared. The blessings of salvation come to us because Christ, from being rich, consented to become poor. It cannot mean, as Baur would have it, that in order to enrich us with grace, Christ, who was rich in grace, was in a condition of poverty; for if this were the sense, we must understand, if we would save the text from confusion of thought, that he became *poor in grace!* On the question whether Paul held to any real preëxistence of Christ, in any other way than as the typical man and as all types ideally preëxist, Baur is undecided but leans to the negative. The preëxistence of Christ in Paul, he says, "is vague and ambiguous."[1] On the contrary, we affirm that these passages, not to mention what other Epistles, falsely called spurious, furnish to the same effect, exhibit in different language the equivalent of John's doctrine of the Logos.

Baur finds in these other Epistles an advance upon the conception in the accepted four, but still a form of doctrine below that of John. He misinter-

[1] *Das Christenthum*, etc. s. 314.

prets, however, Phil. ii. 6—a text containing a view of Christ identical with that of the passage last commented on. "Who being in the form of God," says Paul, "thought it not robbery to be equal with God, but made himself of no reputation"—literally, emptied himself—"and took upon him the form of a servant." Here Baur confesses that preëxistence and a near relationship to God are predicated of Christ. But the equality with God—expressed in the *ἴσα Θεῷ*—was not possessed, Baur claims, until he had passed through the humiliation of an earthly life and the cross, and had been raised from it to that pitch of exaltation. But that the true and proper Divinity, expressed in the phrase just quoted, is predicated of the preëxistent Christ, is evident from the expression, "in the form of God," contrasted as it is with "the form of a servant" which he assumed. He was in the form of God; his mode of existence was divine; the attributes and glory of God pertained to him. In purposing to descend to save man, he chose not to appear in the glories of Divinity; he let go his condition of equality with God instead of being eager to keep hold upon it, or—as he is figured in the act of parting with it—to *lay hold of it*, and assumed humanity. Is there not here the precise equivalent of the Johannean doctrine of a relinquished divine glory, in which he is afterwards reinstated?[1]

The Epistle to the Hebrews and the Apocalypse

[1] John xvii. 5.

are ranked by Baur between the Epistles of Paul which he considers genuine, and the rest which bear his name.[1] They contain a doctrine, Baur says, between the humanitarian view and that highest view of Christ's person which he finds in the Gospel and the first Epistle attributed to John. But in the description of Christ, in the Epistle to the Hebrews, as the Brightness or Effulgence of God's glory, and the express image of his person, and as sitting down, after he had purged away our sins, at the right hand of the Majesty on High (Heb. i. 3), there is presented the same conception which we have found in Phil. ii. 6. And as to the Apocalypse, when Baur allows that in this book Christ "not only shares with God the same power and dominion and the same homage, but is also clothed with predicates which seem to leave room for no essential distinction between him and God,"[2] he virtually allows the validity of the orthodox interpretation, and his subsequent, halting attempts to qualify and invalidate this admission fail of their end.

In regard to the theological doctrine of the Person of Christ in the post-apostolic age, Baur is brought by his philosophy into an important disagreement with the older Socinians. Baur considers the Homoöusion of the Nicene creed to be the logical and legiti-

[1] We may observe that one of the Tübingen leaders, Hilgenfeld, has retracted his denial of the genuineness of the Epistle to the Colossians and the 1st Epistle to the Thessalonians. So mutable is "criticism."

[2] *Das Christenthum*, etc. s. 315.

mate development of the Christian idea. The forms in which the doctrine was stated—the Logos terminology, in particular—were taken from the Alexandrian Jewish philosophy. But the mature Christian doctrine, as to its contents, was not a conglomerate of beliefs before existing. It was not, as Socinians have charged, a theft from Platonism. Yet the reader would be deceived if he supposed that Baur regards Christ as the Nicene Fathers regarded him. The Homoöusion, in his theory, does not represent an exclusive and peculiar distinction of Christ. He, by the impression he made on men, only gave occasion to the process of speculation which terminated in the Nicene formula. This formula has value to Baur, only as a symbol expressive of the union of the finite and the infinite, the pantheistic oneness of man and God. With us the Homoöusion only defines what Christ was in reality—the rank that belonged to him in distinction from all other sons of men. The process of theology was the effort to state the impression produced by the person of Christ and by his declarations concerning himself. It did not add to the contents of the earliest faith; it simply evolved that faith in a scientific form. The Homoöusion was not the mere climax of a course of thought, of which the historical Person of Christ was the moving spring but which passed above and beyond the starting point. Christ *was* all that he was seen to be in the disciples' faith and declared to be in the mature form of the creed.

Connected with the false position of Baur that the earliest doctrine—the first step in the metaphysical process—was humanitarian, are historical statements either unfounded or exaggerated. The prevailing view of Christ which was taken in the Roman church through the greater part of the second century, Baur holds to have been Ebionite. This theory about the opinions of the Roman church has been thoroughly refuted. The intimate fellowship of Irenaeus with that church, as Neander has remarked, is sufficient to create the strongest presumption against Baur's hypothesis. But the Artemonites, Baur reminds us, affirmed that their doctrine, which was monarchianism in the humanitarian form, had been the doctrine of the church of Rome up to Zephyrinus. So they affirmed that their doctrine was that of the apostles, John included; for they received his Gospel. But Eusebius, to whom we are indebted for this information, adds that their declarations were denied and were met by appeals to the early writers and ancient hymns, in which the divinity of Christ was said to be attested.[1] Moreover, thanks to the newly discovered Hippolytus, it is not only ascertained that Zephyrinus was a Patripassianist, holding thus to an extreme formula of Christ's divinity, but it is now settled that

[1] Euseb., Lib. V. c. 28. In refutation of the statement that the humanitarian doctrine had prevailed up to Zephyrinus it was urged, as Eusebius states, that Victor his predecessor had expelled Theodotus the Currier from the church, for holding that opinion.

one, if not two, other bishops of the Roman church about that time, adopted the same doctrine. Patripassianism, of which the Sabellian theory is the offspring, could never have sprung from Jewish or judaizing influences. It is the antipode of the humanitarian doctrine. Yet the fact is, that while adherents of the latter doctrine gained no foothold at Rome, the Patripassianist leaders found great favor and even won over two, if not three, bishops to their opinion. It is thus demonstrated that the anterior opinions at Rome were in no sense Ebionite.[1] Indeed, we learn from Hippolytus—from whom it is ascertained that Zephyrinus embraced the Patripassianist doctrine—that the Trinity in the form of hypostatical subordinationism, in which, also, he is himself a believer, was the mode of view previously prevailing at Rome.

Baur would reverse the usual view of the course which history took. He claims that humanitarian, or Ebionite, monarchianism (for he confounds the two) was the first belief. This was followed by a Patripassian monarchianism. The Logos doctrine mediated between the two and culminated in the spurious gospel of John, while Artemonism or the humanitarian

[1] We should not forget to remind the reader that the humanitarian monarchianism differed from the ordinary Ebionite view in giving no such exaggerated importance to the baptism of Jesus and the endowments which he was thought to have then received. Neither unitarianism springing up within the Catholic church, nor ritualism there, is to be confounded, either historically or doctrinally, with Ebionitism.

party at the end of the second century, was a reaction in behalf of the original belief. But, apart from explicit proof of the early and widely diffused Logos terminology, how impossible that Patripassianism should have been the child of the humanitarian view lying at the opposite extreme! How impossible that Patripassianists should have been pacified and satisfied with the Logos doctrine! How singular that Patripassianists in seeking to support their own theory against it, should have appealed to this very gospel of John, a recent fiction of their adversaries! In truth, there is decisive proof that monarchianism sprung up by the side of the Logos theology, from the difficulty felt by certain minds in respect to the immanent Trinity; the humanitarian form among persons of a rationalistic turn; the Patripassian among those who were disposed to exalt Christ to the utmost.

In the study of ante-Nicene writers on the question of Christ's divinity, it is above all things important to understand the true principle of theological development. There is not an addition to the contents of Scripture nor to the truth embraced in faith; but theology is the scientific statement of the teaching of Scripture and of the objects of faith. The scientific statement may be, and at the outset is likely to be, defective. Some essential element is omitted. Some incongruous element is introduced. Subsequent investigation and the light shed by controversy, remedy the fault; and the doctrinal statement advances nearer to an exact interpretation of the Christian faith.[1] Controversialists on both sides have erred in overlooking this distinction. They have either hastily inferred that an ante-Nicene Father is Arian, because his phraseology is inexact and might indicate Arian opinions, if uttered two centuries later, when the line between the Arian and Athanasian doctrine had been sharply drawn; or they have attempted to strain these defective statements into coincidence with the Nicene watchwords. From this last error, in consequence of ignoring the true principle of doctrinal development, so great and deeply learned a writer as Bull is not free.

For ourselves, we are convinced that the ante-Nicene writers not only believed in the incarnation and the preëxistence of Christ, but also exalted him, in their faith, above the category of creatures. This is true when they are not consistent in their language, and fall into phraseology which clashes, not only with other statements of their own, but with the truth which they had at heart. "As concerns the church doctrine respecting the Son of God, the Church from the beginning has recognized in the person of Christ, as he had appeared on earth, a superhuman, yea, divine manifestation, nature, power, glory. This was even their peculiar doctrine—the object round which

[1] For good remarks on the distinction to be made between correctness of faith and correctness in the statement of it, see Dr. Shedd's *History of Doctrine*, Vol. I. p. 246 seq.

all their thoughts clustered. At first, just as was the case with the apostles, the foundation of this ideal apprehension of Christ rested more in feeling and in a living necessity of their nature, and the thought was grasped and held in a diversified, free form."[1] Such is the conclusion of one of the most impartial and thoroughly learned of the recent writers on the history of doctrine. He proceeds to add that the parties, in the first two centuries, who called in question this cardinal truth, were either, like the Ebionites, outside of the pale of the Church, or, like the Artemonites, alien from its spirit. As Neander has said, there was a consciousness that the Redeemer was he from whom the creation proceeded, through whom all things were made that *were* MADE. In the doctrine of the Son, or the Word, as the revealer of the invisible God, and of the necessity for such a mediator, the essential elements of the orthodox conception are really involved. "No man hath seen God at any time." As He is in himself, He is not directly visible, cognizable, to any creature. The Revealer must be, of course, another than God; and yet *not* another as a *creature* is another, because in this case he would, by the supposition, stand at a distance from the being whom he is to reveal, instead of really bringing that being to the knowledge and contact of created intelligences.

These remarks will be found to be verified by a candid examination of the early Fathers. Even

[1] Baumgarten-Crusius, *Dogmengeschichte*, B. II. s. 143.

Hermas, a Roman Christian, who is thought by some to be so infected with Ebionite tendencies, ascribes to Christ an existence prior to that of any creature, and a participation in the work of creation: "filius quidem Dei omni creatura antiquior est ita ut in consilio Patri suo adfuerit ad condendam creaturam."[1] How emphatically are the Saviour's preëxistence and divinity asserted in that gem of the early literature, the anonymous epistle to Diognetus![2] It is still doubted whether in Justin Martyr the preëxistent Word is hypostatic—personal—before God's purpose to create is about to be carried into effect; but Justin's idea of emanation takes the Word out of the category of creatures, even though, now and then, he may fall into expressions which are not logically coherent with this position. When he attributes all true knowledge of divine things, even among the heathen, to the enlightenment that proceeds from the Word,

[1] Hermas, Lib. III. simil. IX., XII. The use, in the early writers, of such terms as "Spirit" and "Holy Spirit," sometimes to designate the preëxistent Christ as an equivalent of Logos, and sometimes in a general sense for God, or the operative energy of God, has given rise to many mistakes. It has been erroneously concluded that the Holy Spirit, i. e. the Sanctifier, was not held to be an hypostasis distinct from the preëxistent Christ, and that the personality of the Holy Spirit, i. e. the Sanctifier, was not an article of belief. These mistakes are admirably exposed and explained by Baumgarten-Crusius, in a passage of his *Dogmengeschichte*, B. II. s. 178 seq.

[2] C. 7, 8. See also Clem. 1 Cor. cc. 36, 60, 16, 22; Barnabas, c. 6 (the comment on Gen. 1: 26); Ignatius, *ad Phil.* c. 9; *ad Magn.* c. 8; *ad Polyc.* c. 3; Polyc., *ad Phil.* c. 3, c. 7 (where is quoted John iv. 3).

and makes the preëxistent Christ the divine subject in the theophanies of the Old Testament, who speaks to the patriarchs and to Moses out of the fire, there naming himself the self-existent *I am*,[1] the character of Justin's theology is evident. The Nicene creed, be it remembered, though denying (against the Arians) that the Son had a beginning of existence, and predicating of him coequal divine perfections, did not reject all subordination. It denied that sort of subordination which would imply that the Son is not truly and properly divine, and would reduce him to the rank of a creature. In Irenaeus and Tertullian we discover the continued endeavor to grasp and combine the various elements that were involved in the Christian faith. A oneness of the Son with the Father, which is yet not an identity—an elevation of the Son above all creatures, above all things *made*—which yet shall not intrench upon a pure monotheism, are obviously aimed at in their doctrinal constructions. Origen contributes one important element, a clear statement of the timeless character of the generation of the Son. Finally the Nicene Fathers, having before them the opposite errors of Arius and Sabellius, hit upon a statement which excludes both.

There is no proof that the humanitarian doctrine of Christ—that type of monarchianism—ever prevailed extensively in the Church or at any time was the creed of more than a minor party, who were out of

[1] *Apol.*, I. 63.

sympathy with the general faith. Justin Martyr, in arguing with the Jew, mentions that some, whom the connection if not the proper reading of the text shows to have been converted Jews, considered Christ to be a mere human prophet. But the whole tone of the passage implies that they constitute a small party in dissent from the great current of belief. Tertullian, in the well-known passage in which he says that the unenlightened, who always compose the majority of Christians, are inclined to monarchianism, being perplexed by the economical or hypostatic trinity—a passage which even Hase wrongly applies to the humanitarian class—unquestionably has in mind the Patripassianists, against whom his treatise is directed. The same is true of certain passages in Origen, which have been sometimes quoted to prove the prevalence of a humanitarian theology.[1]

[1] Tertullian, *adv. Praxeam*, c. 3: "Simplices quique, ne dixerim imprudentes et idiotae, quae major semper credentium pars est, quoniam et ipsa regula fidei a pluribus diis saeculi ad unicum et verum Deum transfert, expavescunt ad οἰκονομιαν,"—the hypostatic trinity. "Monarchiam, inquiunt, tenemus." Neander justly understands this passage and corresponding statements of Origen, as referring to the Patripassian class of Monarchians. See his *Church History* (Am. transl.), vol. I. p. 578. The erroneous remark of Hase is in his *Kirchengeschichte*, s. 100.

The word *idiotae* has often been mistranslated. Even Horsley fell into the error of rendering it *idiots*—a slip which Priestley was not slow to remind him of, and which Horsley defended as well as he could. Bentley caught Collins in a similar error. See Bentley's *Phil. Lips.*, in his collected Works, Vol. III. p. 263. *Idiota* means originally a private person, in distinction from one in public station;

On the whole, we must conclude that the historical theory of Baur, although he has brought uncommon learning and ingenuity to the support of it, is an example, not of historical divination, but rather of arbitrary, artificial construction. It is one more illustration of the power of a preconceived theory to distort the perceptions of a strong understanding. Unquestionably, new light has been thrown upon the origin of the Church, but nothing has been brought forward which tends to alter essentially the received conception of early Christian history.

then an *unenlightened* person—a man of plebeian understanding. *Idiot* stands in Wicliffe's translation, in 1 Cor. xiv. 16, where *unlearned* is found in our version. People of this sort, Tertullian says, found it hard to see the difference between hypostatic trinity and tritheism. They preferred the Patripassian view because it was easier.

ESSAY VI.

THE MYTHICAL THEORY OF STRAUSS.[1]

THE peculiar form of unbelief which in our time has been brought forward to invalidate the testimony to the miracles of the Gospel, is the Mythical Theory; and the leading expounder and advocate of that theory is David Frederic Strauss. The Life of Christ, by Strauss, is an extensive and elaborate work. The author, if not a man of the profoundest learning, is nevertheless a trained and well-read theologian. Adopting a theory which, at least in the breadth of its application, is a novel one, he yet skilfully avails himself of everything which has been urged in the way of objection to the truth of the Gospel history from the side of ancient or modern skepticism. He knows how to weave into his indictment charges drawn from the most opposite quarters. He is quite ready to borrow aid from Woolston, the Wolfenbüttel Fragmentist, and other deistical writers, whose philosophy in general he repudiates. Thus, in his work, there are brought

[1] *Das Leben Jesu, kritisch bearbeitet, von Dr. David Friedrich Strauss.* 4 A. Tübingen: 1840.

Streitschriften zur Vertheidigung, &c., von Dr. David Friedrich Strauss. Tübingen: 1841.

together and braided together the difficulties in the New Testament history which all past study had brought to light, and the objections which the ingenuity of unbelievers, from Celsus to Paulus, had found it possible to suggest. It is the last and strongest word that skeptical criticism will be able to utter against the evangelical narratives. In the arrangement and presentation of his matter, the work of Strauss is distinguished by a rhetorical skill that is rarely surpassed. He knows what it will do to assert roundly, what is best conveyed by an insinuation, what is more effectively suggested in the form of an inquiry. He knows how to put in the foreground whatever seems to favor his position, and to pass lightly over considerations having a contrary tendency. The currency obtained by the work of Strauss, and its influence, are very much due, also, to the transparency of his style. In the exhibition of the most complex details, the remarkable clearness and fluency that belong to his ordinary composition are fully preserved. It will not be denied that Strauss has presented the most plausible theory which can be presented from the unbelieving side, and has made it as captivating as the nature of the case will admit. This theory we now proceed to examine.[1]

Although Strauss undertakes to construct a life of

[1] In connection with Strauss's principal work, the *Streitschriften*, or polemical tracts in reply to his reviewers, which he himself collected into a volume, will receive attention.

Christ, it is plain that the great question before his mind is the question of the truth or falsehood of the narratives in the New Testament which record miracles. Strange to say, he lays down at the beginning the critical canon that a miracle is never to be believed, and that the narrative in which it is found is, so far at least, unhistorical. That is to say, he begs the question which it is one prime object of his book to discuss. His entire work is thus a *petitio principii*. From a scientific point of view, therefore, it has, strictly speaking, no claim to consideration. When we call to mind the names on the roll of science which are counted among the believers in miracles, such as Pascal, Kepler, Sir Isaac Newton, not to speak of names proportionally eminent among scientific men at the present day; and when we think how much of the loftiest intellect the world has seen has likewise put faith in these New Testament narratives; when, moreover, we remember that mankind have generally believed, and do now believe, in miraculous events of some sort, we must pronounce the pretended axiom that miracles are impossible, to be, in every sense of the word, an assumption. We waive this point, however, and proceed to consider the positive theory of Strauss.

What is a myth? A myth is, in form, a narrative; resembling, in this respect, the fable, parable, and allegory. But unlike these, the idea or feeling from which the myth springs, and which, in a sense, it embodies, is not reflectively distinguished from the narrative, but rather is blended with it; the latter being, as it were, the native form which the idea or sentiment spontaneously assumes. Moreover, there is no consciousness on the part of those from whom the myth emanates, that this product of their fancy and feeling is fictitious. The fable is a fictitious story, contrived to inculcate a moral. So, the parable is a similitude framed for the express purpose of representing abstract truth to the imagination. Both fable and parable are the result of conscious invention. In both, the symbolical character of the narrative is distinctly recognized. From the myth, on the contrary, the element of deliberation is utterly absent. There is no questioning of its reality, no criticism or inquiry on the point, but the most simple, unreflecting faith. A like habit of feeling we find in children, who, delighting in narrative, improvise narrative. It is difficult for us to imagine that childlike condition of mind which belonged to the early age of nations, when the creations of personifying sentiment and fancy were endued, in the faith of those from whom they sprung, with this unquestioned reality. It is almost as difficult as to reproduce those states of mind in which the fundamental peculiarities of language germinate; peculiarities in respect to which the philological explorer can only say that so mankind in their infancy looked upon things and actions. But there is no doubt as to the fact that the mythologies had this character. They are the spontaneous growth of childlike imagination, originated and cherished in the full, because unthinking, belief in their reality. So the Greek mythology sprung into being.[1] The popular imagination, unhindered by any knowledge of laws and facts which science could not suggest, because science was not born, peopled the groves and mountains, the sea and air, with divinities, whose existence and whose deeds, forming the theme of song and story, were the object of universal faith. The ablest of the modern writers upon antiquity, such as Ottfried Müller and Mr. Grote, have made it clear that frequently there was no historical basis for these mythological stories, and that, in the absence of explicit evidence, we have no right to assume a nucleus of fact at their foundation. They may have been—fre-

[1] The reader will perhaps be reminded of the beautiful lines of Wordsworth:

"In that fair clime the lonely herdsman, stretch'd
On the soft grass, through half a summer's day
With music lull'd his indolent repose;
And, in some fit of weariness, if he,
When his own breath was silent, chanced to hear
A distant strain, far sweeter than the sounds
Which his poor skill could make, his fancy fetch'd
Even from the blazing chariot of the sun
A beardless youth, who touched a golden lute,
And fill'd the illumined groves of ravishment.
The nightly hunter, lifting up his eyes
Towards the crescent moon, with grateful heart
Call'd on the lovely wanderer, who bestow'd
That timely light to share his joyous sport:
And hence a blooming goddess and her nymphs."

quently, at least, they were—the pure creation of the mythopœic faculty ; the incarnated faith and feeling of a primitive age, when scientific reflection had not yet set bounds to fancy. Science brought reflection. The attempt of Euemerus to clear the mythical tales of improbabilities and incongruities, and to find at the bottom a residuum of veritable history, and the attempts of both physical and moral philosophers to elicit from them an allegorical sense, are, one and all, the fruit of that skepticism which culture brought with it, and proceed upon a totally false view of the manner in which the myths originate. When these theories came up, the spell of the old faith was already broken. They are the efforts of Rationalism to keep up some attachment to obsolete beliefs, or to save itself from conscious irreverence or popular displeasure. A state of mind had arisen, wholly different from that which prevailed in the credulous, unreflecting, child-like period, when a common fear or faith embodied itself spontaneously in a fiction which was taken for fact.[1]

[1] Upon the nature of the myth, see K. O. Müller's *Prolegomena zu einer wissenschaftlichen Mythologie* (1825). The recently published lectures of Schelling on the *Introduction to Mythology* (see Schelling's *Sämmtliche Werke*, II. Abth. I.), are a very able and elaborate discussion. Schelling examines at length the various theories which have been proposed to account for the origin of mythology, including those of Heyne, Hermann, Hume, Voss, Creuzer, and others. He disproves all the irreligious hypotheses and expounds in an interesting and profound way his own view, which is the same in spirit as that of Müller, although the latter, in the opin-

As we have implied, back of the authentic history of most nations lies a mythical era. And whenever the requisite conditions are present, the mythopœic instinct is active. The middle ages furnish a striking example. The fountain of sentiment and fancy in the uncultured nations of Europe divaricated, so to speak, into two channels, the religious myth and the myth of chivalry. When we have eliminated from the immense mass of legendary history which forms the lives of the Saints what is due to pious frauds (though these presuppose a ready faith), and what is historical, being due to morbid or otherwise extraordinary psychological states, and, if the reader so pleases, to miracle, there

ion of Schelling (p. 199), has not applied his theory to the first origination of the conceptions of the gods, but rather to their mythological doings—the mythological history. Schelling applauds the remarks of Coleridge on this subject, and says that he gives the latter a dispensation for the alleged free borrowing from his writings, in return for the single word which Coleridge has suggested as a proper description of myths. They are not *alle*gorical, says Coleridge, but *taute*gorical. Schelling also maintains that the primitive religion of mankind was "relative monotheism," that is, the worship of one God who is not known in his *absolute* character. Thence polytheism arose, so that this one God was only the first of a series.

We may also refer the reader to the sixteenth and seventeenth chapters of the first volume of Grote's *History of Greece*. Mr. Grote shows the spontaneity that characterizes the origin of myths. In some other important respects, his view is defective. No theory that does not explicitly take account of the truths expressed by Paul in Romans, i. 21, and Acts, xvii. 23 seq., can be considered satisfactory. A religious nature in man and a fall from the communion of the one living God, must be presupposed, if we would explain the mythologies.

still remain a multitude of narratives involving supernatural events, which last have no foundation whatever in fact, but were yet thoroughly believed by those from whose fancy, enlivened and swayed by religious sentiment, they emanated.

Strauss was not the first to suggest that portions of the biblical history are myths; but Strauss it is who has applied the mythical theory in detail and at length to the Gospel narratives, and with the aid of this theory has attempted to divest the life of Christ of all supernatural elements,—all these being pronounced mythological. Strauss opposes, on the one hand, believers in the miracles, and, on the other, the advocates of the so-called "natural exposition," of whom Paulus was the chief. Paulus was the German Euemerus, holding the New Testament narratives of miracles to be erroneous conceptions and amplifications of historical events which really fell within the sphere of natural law. Thus, the healing of the blind was accomplished by Christ through an efficacious powder applied to their eyes—a circumstance which was unnoticed or omitted by the lovers of the marvellous whose reports we have: the fact at the bottom of the record of the transmuting of water into wine, was the gift of a large amount of wine, which Christ, since he was to be attended by several disciples, brought with him to the wedding: instead of being expected to find a coin in the mouth of the fish, Peter was to obtain it by selling a fish in the market, and the Gospel narrative sprung from a mistaken view of the transaction: Christ did not walk on the water, as was supposed, but walked along the shore: the so-called transfiguration was the effect on the disciples of seeing Christ on a higher mountain-peak which was white with snow. Strange as it may seem, abundant learning and the utmost painstaking were expended in the support of this theory, which, however, had few adherents when Strauss gave it the final death-blow. Equal hostility is professed by Strauss to the form of infidelity which had charged the apostles and their Master with being wilful deceivers. He joins with the Christian believer in denouncing the coarseness and shallowness of that species of unbelief which found reception among pretended philosophers of the last century. He will propound a theory which involves no such condemnation of the founders of Christianity. He will propound a theory, moreover, which leaves untouched that inner substance of Christianity which is alone valuable to the philosopher. His construction will have the merit of sparing the sensibilities of the believer who is offended at hearing those whom he reveres, branded as impostors, and, at the same time, of relieving the men of the nineteenth century from giving credence to events which, it is quietly assumed, modern science pronounces to be impossible.

Omitting minor details, some of which we shall have occasion to bring forward in the progress of the discussion, the principal points in the doctrine of

Strauss may be briefly stated. There existed in Palestine, at the time when Jesus grew up to manhood, a wide-spread expectation of the coming of the Messiah. There was also a defined conception, the result of the teaching of the Old Testament and of later speculation, of the character of his work. Among other things, he was to work miracles, such as the opening of the eyes of the blind, the healing of the sick, the raising of the dead; and he was, generally, to outdo the supernatural works ascribed to Moses and Elijah and the other prophets of the former time. Jesus, who had been baptized by John, became at length persuaded that he was the promised Messiah. Endowed with lofty qualities of mind and character, he attached to himself disciples who shared in his belief concerning himself. He taught with power through the towns and villages of Palestine. But, encountering the bitter hatred of the ruling classes on account of his rebuke of their iniquities, he was seized upon and put to death under Pontius Pilate. Overwhelmed with grief and disappointment, his disciples, who had expected of him a political triumph, were finally comforted and inspirited by the mistaken belief that he had been raised from the dead. Hence the cause of Jesus was not crushed, but gradually gained strength. And out of the bosom of the young community, filled with enthusiastic attachment to their slain and (as they believed) risen Lord, there sprung the mythical tales which we find in the Gospels. Believing Jesus to be the Messiah, they attributed to him spontaneously the deeds which the prophecies had ascribed to that personage. In these mythical creations, the formative idea was the Old Testament description of the Messiah. This idea, coupled with the faith in Jesus, generated the Gospel history of Christ, so far as that is miraculous, and even exerted a very important influence in shaping and coloring circumstances in the narrative which are not supernatural. The Christ of the New Testament is thus the ideal Messiah. He is Jesus of Nazareth, glorified in the feeling and fancy of disciples by the ascription to him of supernatural power and supernatural deeds, such as lay in the traditional, cherished image of the Messiah.

It should be observed that Strauss does not reject the supposition of a conscious invention in the case of certain features in the New Testament reports of miracles, notwithstanding his general disavowal of an intent to impeach the moral character of their authors; but he claims a very mild judgment for a certain kind of artless, though not wholly unconscious, poetizing—the *arglose dichtung* of simple souls.[1] But how far Strauss and his school are able to adhere to their canon, which excludes wilful deception from a part in producing the miraculous narratives of the Gospel, will be considered on a subsequent page.

The denial of the genuineness of the four Gospels

[1] *Leben Jesu*, B. I. s. 95.

is an essential part of Strauss's theory. They cannot come, he maintains, from "eyewitnesses or well-informed contemporaries." The apostles could not be deceived to such an extent as we should be compelled to assume, if we granted that the Gospels exhibit their testimony. On the subject of the origin of the Gospels, Strauss is neither full nor clear; but this is affirmed, that they are the production of later, non-apostolic writers. This position he strives to establish by a critical analysis and comparison of these documents. The attempt is made to prove upon them such inconsistencies with each other, as well as violations of probability, as render it impossible to suppose that they came from the hand, or bear the sanction, of the immediate followers of Christ. The credibility of the Gospels is attacked, partly as a means of disproving their genuineness. And the method of the attack is to press the point of the improbability of the miracles, while, at the same time, the untrustworthy character of the narratives is elaborately argued on other grounds. The Gospels are dissected with the critical knife, their structure and contents are subjected to a minute examination, for the purpose of impressing the reader with the conviction that, independently of their record of miracles, these histories are too inaccurate and self-contradictory to be relied on. Their alleged imperfections are skilfully connected with the improbable nature of the events they record, so that the effect of both considerations may be to break down their historic value.

Having thus stated the main points in the theory of Strauss, we proceed to set forth the reasons why the mythical hypothesis is untenable.

I. The belief of the apostles and of Jesus himself that he was the Messiah, cannot be accounted for on the theory of Strauss, and could not have existed, were the assumptions of that theory sound.

Strauss puts his doctrine into a kind of syllogism. There was a fixed idea that the Messiah would work these various miracles; there was a fixed persuasion in the minds of the disciples that Jesus was the Messiah; hence the necessity that the mythopœic faculty should attribute these miracles to him.[1] These, we are told, were the conditions and forces by which the myths were generated. But if it was a fixed expectation that the Messiah would work these miracles, how could the disciples believe in Jesus *in the absence of these indispensable signs of Messiahship?* Recollect that this persuasion concerning the Messiah is represented to be so deep and universal as to move the imagination of the disciples of Jesus, after his death, to connect with him all these fictitious miracles. How, then, were they convinced of his claim to be the Messiah—so convinced that their faith survived the disappointment of some of their strongest and fondest anticipations relative to his kingdom, and survived even the shock of his judicial death? It must be manifest to every candid man that Strauss is thrown upon a dilemma. Either

[1] *Leben Jesu*, B. I. s. 94.

this previous ideal of the Messiah was not so firmly engraved upon the minds of the disciples, in which case the condition and motive for the creation of myths are wanting; or being thus firmly fixed, their faith in Jesus through his lifetime proves that miracles were really performed. A similar remark may be made of Jesus himself, since he is supposed to have shared, on this point at least, in the common expectation respecting the characteristic works of the Messiah. How could he maintain this unswerving faith in his messianic calling and office, in the absence of the one principal criterion, the exercise of supernatural power? To avoid one difficulty, the advocate of the mythical hypothesis creates another which no ingenuity can remove.

It is not to be supposed that Strauss ignores this difficulty. He endeavors to answer the objection. The impressiveness of the character and teaching of Christ supplied, in a measure, the place of miracles so long as he was bodily present. But this consideration is evidently felt to be quite inadequate, and hence Strauss makes prominent what he seems to consider a concession. Jesus, we are informed, did calm and relieve certain persons afflicted with nervous disease, which was thought to be the fruit of demoniacal possession. This effect was wrought, however, only by psychological influence—the natural influence of a strong and calm nature. Hence, it was only in cases where the type of the disease was mild and chiefly mental in its origin that such cures were effected. The cure of a case like that of the maniac of Gadara, or the child at the foot of the Mount of Transfiguration, would be a miracle, and is, of course, excluded.[1] Moreover, Strauss finds it convenient to maintain that the cure of so-called demoniacs was produced by others; that, in fact, it was not so uncommon. He appeals to the instance narrated by Josephus, of the cure effected in the presence of Vespasian,[2] and to the question of Christ: "by whom do your children cast them out?" So that, after all, this relief of less aggravated forms of nervousness is not a distinguishing act of Christ which could serve to attest his Messiahship. There is obviously no reason, beyond the necessities of a theory, why it should be allowed that Christ relieved this kind of infirmity, to the exclusion of all the other instances of healing, together with the raising of the dead to life, which are equally well attested. Nor are we assisted to understand how the disciples were so easily satisfied with the omission of all the other forms of miracle which they believed to be indissolubly connected with the Messiah's appearance. When they saw Jesus pass by the blind, the lame, the dumb, the leprous, even the severe forms of demoniacal frenzy, and do nothing greater than to quiet the less afflicted subjects of nervous hallucination, which others were in the habit of doing as well, how could they consider

[1] *Leben Jesu*, B. I. s. 106; B. II. s. 43, 45.

[2] Jos., *Antiq.* VIII. 2, 5.

him the Messiah? We cannot avoid perceiving that the same cause which is thought to have led irresistibly to the forming of imaginary miracles, would have effectually precluded a faith not sustained by miracles which were real.

II. The mythical theory is fully disproved by the fact of the absence of any body of disciples to whom the origination and dissemination of the myths can be attributed.

The advocates of this theory prefer to use vague terms and phrases in speaking of the source whence the so-called Christian mythology came. It sprung, says Strauss, from the enthusiasm of the infant church. But when he is called upon to explain his meaning more precisely, he admits that neither the apostles nor the community which was under their immediate guidance could have been the authors of these fictitious narratives. That the followers of Christ, who had attended him through his public life, could mistakenly suppose themselves to have been eyewitnesses of the series of miracles which the Gospels record, is too much for Strauss to believe. He claims that the apostles in their Epistles, or in such as he concedes to be genuine, do not bring forward the prior miracles, but dwell on the Resurrection of Christ. So far as they do not speak of the earlier miracles, the circumstance is readily explained, if we suppose them to have been familiar to the churches to whom the apostles wrote, and remember that, in the view of the apostles, the grand fact of the Saviour's Resurrection stood in the foreground, eclipsing, as it were, the displays of supernatural power which had preceded it. In the discourses of the apostles, recorded in Acts, these prior miracles *are* appealed to. But Strauss, be it observed, contends, and is obliged to contend, that the apostles were ignorant of any such miraculous events as these which the evangelists record. The myths did not originate within the circle of their oversight and influence. This would be evidently true, whoever were disposed to deny it; but Strauss concedes and claims that such is the fact. Where, then, did these myths grow up? Who were their authors? To this fundamental question the advocates of the mythical theory vouchsafe only the briefest response. Yet Strauss does say that they grew up among the dwellers in more secluded places in Galilee where Christ had tarried but a short time, and among those who had occasionally, or at seasons, companied with him.[1] There was, then, if we are to give credit to the mythical hypothesis, a community of Jewish-Christian disciples in Palestine, separate from the apostles and the Christian flocks over which they presided, and in that community, within thirty or forty years after the death of Christ, this extensive and coherent cycle of miraculous tales originated. We say a *community*, because a myth is not the conscious invention of an individual, or a conscious invention at all,

[1] *Leben Jesu*, B. I. s. 72. *Streitschr.*, s. 46.

but an offshoot of the collective faith and feeling of a body of people.[1] If, in certain cases, it proceeds from the fancy of an individual, it is presupposed that he stands in the midst of a sympathetic and responsive community who receive without scrutiny whatever falls in with the current of their feelings. We say "within thirty or forty years after the death of Christ," because in this period Strauss himself places the bulk of the so-called myths which are found in the New Testament.[2] Now, in reference to this extraordinary solution of the enigma as to the authorship of the myths, we offer several remarks.

In the first place, it must strike the reader as a singular fact that there is no evidence whatever of the existence of such a non-apostolic Christian community in the midst of Palestine. The assumption that a set of believers of this description existed in Galilee, removed from the knowledge and guidance of the apostles, is not supported by the slightest proof, and is in the highest degree improbable. The disciples of Christ, at the time of his death, were not very numerous. There was a sense of unity among them. They formed one body. Everything tended to draw them together. And the apostles were their recognized heads. It is certain, and will hardly be questioned by any one, that

[1] So Strauss. It is most essential to understand, he says, that at the foundation of the myth lies—"kein individuelles Bewusstsein, sondern ein höheres allgemeines Volksbewusstsein, (Bewusstsein einer religiösen Gemeinde.") *Leben Jesu*, B. I. s. 89.

[2] *Streitschr.*, s. 52.

the other disciples looked up to "the twelve" as their guides, and leaned on them for support and counsel.

But how could persons in the situation attributed to these obscure disciples, come to believe, or remain in the belief, that Jesus was the Messiah? We have shown the improbability that the apostles believed without miracles. But the difficulty of supposing these other hearers of Christ to have believed, in the absence of such evidence of his divine commission, is much greater. It is a part of the hypothesis that they knew comparatively little of Jesus, for to allow them an intimate knowledge of him would put them in the same category, as to the possibility of framing myths, with the apostles themselves. They had seen little of Jesus; they had seen none of the supernatural signs expected of the Messiah; he had wholly disappointed their idea that the Messiah was to be an earthly prince; and, finally, he had perished by the death of a culprit, which he endured without resistance, God not appearing to deliver him. Is it not inexplicable that casual hearers of Christ, who were thus placed, having seen, be it remembered, no miracle for their faith to rest upon, should continue to believe—believe, too, without a misgiving, with the childish simplicity and enthusiasm which are requisite for the creation of mythological tales?

Such hearers must have originally cherished the ordinary expectation concerning the Messiah, that he would sit, in the character of a temporal Prince, upon the throne of David and bring into subjection the heathen nations. The myths they would frame, if they framed any, would be in keeping with this expectation. A radical change in their conception of the Messiah would require us to suppose, at least, that they were well acquainted with the actual career of Jesus. But here, again, an acquaintance of this sort with the real facts of his history shuts out, by Strauss's own admission, the possibility of their connecting with his life a cycle of myths.[1]

But if we admit what is incredible, that a class of disciples of this character existed, and existed in such circumstances that they actually produced through the mythopœic faculty, and set in circulation, the narratives of which we have a record in the New Testament, we are not then clear of half of the difficulty. How can we suppose all this to be done with no knowledge or interference on the part of the apostles and other well-informed contemporaries to whom the facts of the life of Christ were well known? It will not be claimed that this mass of mythological narrative was shut up in the nooks and corners where it came into being. This pretended seclusion of the ill-informed believers in Christ, could hardly have been kept up for the whole generation during which the apostles traversed

[1] In this paragraph and in several remarks in the paragraphs which immediately follow under this head, we have been anticipated by Professor Norton, *Internal Evidences of the Genuineness of the Gospels*, ch. i. He is one of the few writers in English who have correctly apprehended Strauss.

Galilee and ministered to the church. The Jewish Christians continued to come up to Jerusalem to the great festivals; did these Galilean believers stay away from them? How happens it, we beg to know, that this type of belief, so foreign from that of the eyewitnesses and authorized apostles of Jesus, found no contradiction or exposure?

But an objection still more formidable remains to be stated. From whom did the Gentiles receive Christianity, and what type of Christianity did they receive? The new religion had been carried from Jerusalem to Rome before the death of Paul and Peter. Was it from the simple folk whose imagination is credited with the origin of the miracles—was it from them who knew so little of Christ as to indulge in these uncertified fancies, and too little of the apostles to have their self-delusion corrected—was it from these obscure disciples that Christianity went forth to the Gentile world? Did they have the energy to assume the missionary work confided to the apostles, while these and all the well-informed followers of the Messiah rested in idleness? And had they the ability to command a hearing and to crown the new religion with rapid and glorious success? It would be preposterous, in the face of probability and against all the evidence we possess, to assert this. The Christianity of the Gentile churches was apostolic Christianity. Their teachers were such as Peter and John, Paul and Barnabas, Silas and Timothy. Their conception of the history of Christ on earth was derived from the apostles and the Christian believers associated with them. Now, all of the canonical Gospels, except the first, are Gentile Gospels. The third was written by a Gentile, and this, together with the second and fourth, were written for Gentiles. Gentile Christianity did not flow from that quarter—that *terra incognita*—where the myths are said to have sprung up and been received. How then shall we account for the character of the Gentile Gospels, and, in particular, for the representation of the life of Christ which they contain! The conclusion is inevitable that this representation, including the narratives of miracles, was a part of that Christianity which the apostles believed and taught. But when this admission is made, the mythical theory breaks down; since, as we have before mentioned, Strauss admits that, in case these narratives are false, apostles and others who were well acquainted with Christ could neither have originated them nor have been persuaded to lend them credence.

III. The genuineness of the canonical Gospels, the proof of which it is found impossible to invalidate, is a decisive argument against the mythical theory.

Considering the importance of the subject, the observations of Strauss upon the authorship and date of the Gospels are very meagre. He denies, indeed, that we can prove a general circulation of Gospel histories during the lifetime of the apostles, or that our present Gospels were known to them.[1] At one time he was inclined to admit that John was the author of the fourth Gospel, but seeing, probably, the fatal consequences resulting to his theory from this concession, he withdrew it in a subsequent edition. But the proposition that John wrote the Gospel which bears his name, is supported by such an array of external and internal evidence as must convince an unprejudiced mind of its truth. In respect to this Gospel, Strauss and his friends are obliged to abandon the mythical hypothesis and to pronounce its contents the deliberate fabrications of a pretender who chose to subserve a doctrinal interest by assuming the character of John. The needless audacity which would lead a literary impostor in the second century to present a view of the course of Christ's life, which when compared with the previous established conception, is, in many respects, so original and peculiar, and his complete success in winning the confidence of the churches in all quarters of the Roman world, are mysteries not to be explained. The patristic testimonies to the genuineness of the Gospels of Luke and of Mark, as well as to the relation in which they severally stood to Paul and Peter, cannot be successfully impugned. Luke's preface to his Gospel harmonizes with the tradition of the church concerning him. His informants, he there states, were immediate disciples of Christ. He had acquired from the original sources "a perfect understanding" of the matters on

[1] *Leben Jesu*, B. I. s. 72.

which he wrote. Of Mark and his Gospel, we have an early account in the fragment of Papias, whose birth fell within the apostolic age, and who drew his information from the contemporaries and associates of the apostles.[1] When Papias states that Mark, having been the interpreter of Peter, and derived his knowledge of Christ from him, wrote down "the things spoken or done by our Lord," though not observing, as to the discourses at least, the historical order, he describes, without doubt, our second Gospel.[2] If there are critical questions pertaining to the authorship of the first Gospel, about which even believing scholars are not yet agreed, it is even more evident concerning this than any of the others that it emanates from the bosom of the apostolic Church. Of this, the evidence, external and internal, leaves no room for doubt.[3]

Renan, in his recent Life of Christ, has the

[1] Whether Papias was, or was not, acquainted with the Apostle John himself, is a disputed point. Irenaeus affirms it, but Eusebius is inclined to consider his statement an uncertain inference from the language of Papias. Euseb., Lib. III. c. 39.

[2] Whether the want of historical order is attributed by Papias to the record of the "things said" alone, or of "the things done" as well, depends on the sense of λόγια in the passage—a question which we have elsewhere considered.

[3] The critical questions to which we allude, are clearly stated by Meyer in the *Einl.* to his Com. on Matt., and Bleek in his *Einl. in d. N. T.* These questions do not affect the date of the Gospel, nor its origin in the apostolic Church. Meyer's view depends on his restriction of the sense of λόγια—in the τὰ λόγια συνετάξατο of Papias which is not made out. On the other hand, Bleek's hypothesis leave the early tradition concerning the authorship unexplained.

candor to acknowledge the early date of the evangelical histories, and, in general, though his views are here not free from inconsistency as well as error, their apostolical origin. He says that the composition of the Gospels was "one of the most important events to the future of Christianity which occurred *during the second half of the first century.*[1] As to Luke, "doubt is hardly possible."[2] "The author of this Gospel is certainly the same as the author of the Acts of the Apostles. Now the author of the Acts is a companion of St. Paul, a title perfectly suited to Luke." "One thing at least is beyond doubt, that the author of the third Gospel and of the Acts is a man of the second apostolic generation." "Chapter xxi., inseparable from the rest of the work, was certainly written after the siege of Jerusalem, but *soon after.*" "But if the Gospel of Luke is dated, those of Matthew and Mark are also; for it is certain that the third Gospel is posterior to the first two, and presents the character of a compilation *(rédaction)* much more advanced."[3]

[1] P. xiv. [2] P. xvi.

[3] Although we have more fully discussed these questions in other parts of this volume, we may observe here that whatever Papias meant by the λόγια of Matthew—whether the discourses alone, or the narratives also—Renan errs decidedly in saying that the Matthew which was known to Papias was simply the discourses (in Hebrew). When Papias says that the λόγια were written in Hebrew and ἡρμήνευσε δ' αὐτὰ ὡς ἠδύνατο ἕκαστος, he speaks of things in the past. It is certain that Papias had the first Gospel in its complete form, in the Greek. (See Meyer's *Einl. z. Matt.*, s. 11. N.) It is certain that the first Gospel had its present form before the date of the destruc-

Mark, we are told, "though not absolutely free from later additions, is essentially as he wrote it." "He is

tion of Jerusalem. (Meyer, *Einl. z. Matt.*, s. 21.) But Renan concedes that the second Gospel is "but a slightly modified reproduction" of "the collection of anecdotes and personal information which Mark wrote from Peter's reminiscences." P. 22. There is no proof whatever that Mark's work has undergone any "modification," if we except one or two passages which are thought by critics to be interpolated. The school of Baur have, to be sure, made Papias refer to an "Ur-Markus," a work supposed to be prior to, and the basis of, our second Gospel. But our Mark corresponds to the description given by Papias; so that the sole argument of the Baur school for their view is unfounded. The writers of the second century know nothing of any other work ascribed to Mark except our second Gospel. *It is an incontrovertible fact that this Gospel was composed by John Mark, an associate of the apostles.* The Baur school have made an attempt, which we are justified in terming *desperate*, to bring down the date of the writings of Luke to the early part of the second century. But apart from all the other evidences in the case, Baur's own method of argument requires him to suppose, and he does suppose, that the generation—γενεα—spoken of in Luke xxi. 32, still subsisted when the Gospel was written. But this term *will not bear* the loose sense which he gives it. We have set forth in another Essay the proof of the early date of the Acts. It is enough to state here, that the circumstance of the writer's making no use of the Epistles of Paul, in composing his work, is an insoluble fact on Baur's theory. *It is an incontrovertible fact that the third Gospel and the Acts were written by Luke, an associate of Paul.* The conjecture of Renan that the first two Gospels *gradually* borrowed anecdotes from each other, would be inconsistent with the agreement in the copies of each which were extant in the different parts of the world in the third century, and is, moreover, supported by no proof. But in holding that Luke was composed about the year 70, that Mark remains substantially as he wrote it, and that both Matthew and Mark are earlier than Luke, Renan admits all that we ask in the present discussion.

full of minute observations coming without doubt from an eyewitness. Nothing opposes the idea that this eyewitness, who evidently had followed Jesus, who had loved him and known him intimately, and who had preserved a lively image of him, was the Apostle Peter himself, as Papias says."[1] If the view presented by Renan concerning the origin of the fourth Gospel is less satisfactory, it is yet sufficient for the refutation of the leading propositions of Strauss. He holds that "in substance this Gospel issued, towards the end of the third century, from the great school of Asia Minor, which held to John—that it presents to us a version of the Master's life, worthy of high consideration and often of preference."[2] If the work was not by John, there is "a deception which the author confessed to himself"—a literary fact, says Renan, unexampled in the apostolic world. The Tübingen doctrine of its being "a theological thesis without historical value" is not borne out, but rather refuted, by an examination of the work.[3] In a "multitude of cases," it sheds needed light upon the Synoptics. "The last months of the life of Jesus, in particular, are explained only by John." The school of John was "better acquainted with the external circumstances of the life of the founder than the group whose memories made up the synoptic Gospels. It had, especially in regard to the sojourns of Jesus at Jerusalem, data which the others did not possess."[4] The conclusion appears to be that

[1] P. xxxviii. [2] P. xxv. [3] P. xxix. [4] P. xxxiii.

the narrative portions of the fourth Gospel are from the pen of John; and as to Renan's opinion of the origin of the discourses, we are left in doubt, for now he attributes them, and now denies them, to John. As to the last point, the record of the discourses is obviously from the same pen that wrote the rest of the Gospel and, also, the first Epistle which bears the name of John, the genuineness of which Renan will not deny. The statements of Renan in respect to the origin of the Gospels approximate to the truth. They are the admissions of a man of learning and a skeptic. They demolish the mythical theory as defined by Strauss. The evidence which proves the Gospels to be the productions of the apostles or their associates, at the same time subverts an essential part of that theory. In truth, every argument for the genuineness of the Gospels is just as strong an argument for their credibility.

IV. The mythical hypothesis falls to the ground from the lack of a sufficient interval between the death of Christ and the promulgation, in a written as well as oral form, of the narratives of miracles.

We were led, under the last head, in speaking of the genuineness of the Gospels, to allude to the subject of their date. There are grave difficulties connected with the twenty-fourth and twenty-fifth chapters of Matthew, but the apologist has, perhaps, a compensation in the demonstration afforded by them that the document of which they are a part was composed in its present form before the destruction of Jerusalem. The date of Luke, as before observed, is not far from that of Matthew. But we discover on inspection that a large portion of the matter contained in each of the first three Gospels appears, frequently in identical language, in the other two. Among the various hypotheses suggested to account for this peculiarity, it is held by some that Matthew was the earliest written of the three, and that a portion of Matthew was incorporated by Mark and Luke in their Gospels; while others maintain that Mark was the original Gospel and furnished the other two with the matter that is common to all. It has been, however, contended with much force of argument, that prior to the composition of either of the three, an original gospel, containing the matter to which we refer, must have existed, and existed in a written form. This earlier record of the teachings and miracles of Christ antedates, therefore, our present Gospels, and is a written monument standing still nearer the events. But whether this be, or be not, the true solution of the peculiarity in question, we have from Luke decisive proof of the early composition of written histories of Christ, in which the miracles had a place. "*Many*" such histories of what was "surely believed" in the apostolic church, Luke states, had already been composed. The Hebraized diction of various parts of his Gospel, differing from his own style, is a sufficient proof that he wrought into it portions of prior records.

This information, which comes from Luke, be it remembered, only a few years after the death of Paul, implies that there had been a desire among Christians for authentic lives of Christ, and that numerous narratives had been written to meet the want. It has been made probable, we may add, that the Apostle Paul made use of a written gospel, and although we cannot affirm that this document was more than a collection of the sayings and discourses of Christ,[1] yet the existence of it is an indication of the necessity that must have been felt for authentic records of the life of the Lord, and, also, of the ease with which, owing to the spread of Greek culture, this demand could be satisfied. For, as Neander observes, this was not the age of the rhapsodist, but an age of written composition.

We are thus, through the testimony of Luke, in our search for written narratives of the miracles of Christ, brought back into the heart of the apostolic age and to a point of time not far from the events themselves. We are obliged to allow that the New Testament miracles were not only believed by the generation of Christians contemporary with the apostles and under their guidance, but were, also, within twenty or thirty years, at the longest, after the death of Jesus recorded in written narratives. Now this interval is altogether too short for the growth of a Christian mythology. Unlike something made by the will, this

[1] See Neander's *Leben Jesu*, s. 10. *Pflanz. u. Leit. d. Kirche*, s. 173 seq.

must be the fruit of a long brooding over the incidents in the career of Christ and the prophecies relating to him. We cannot conceive this cloud of myths to arise, when the real circumstances in the life of Christ had just occurred and were fresh in the recollection of those who had known him. The sharp outlines of fact must first be effaced from memory before the humble career of Jesus could be invested by the imagination with a misty, unreal splendor. The sudden ascription to him of these numerous acts of miraculous power would be a psychological wonder. Strauss is not insensible to the force of this objection. His answer is that these narratives were, in a sense, prepared in the messianic expectations of the people, and it was only needful that they should be connected with Jesus. But there is a wide gulf between the general anticipation that the Messiah, when he should come, would heal the different forms of disease and outdo the works of the old prophets, and the concrete, circumstantial narratives which we find in the Gospels. Strauss fails, therefore, to evade the force of the objection, and it stands, an insurmountable obstacle in the way of his theory.

V. The mythical theory is incompatible with the character of the times in which Christ appeared.

It was an historical age; that is, an age in which history is studied, historical truth discriminated from error, evidence weighed; an age in which skepticism is found; in which, also, written records exist. It was the age of Tacitus and Josephus; the age when the influence of Greek culture and Roman law were felt to the remotest bounds of the empire. It was, moreover, an age when history had seemingly run its course and the process of decay had set in. How unlike the periods when a people, given up to the sway of sentiment and imagination, builds up its mythologic creations, never raising the question as to their truth or falsehood! Let us hear Mr. Grote upon the characteristics of a myth-producing age. "The myths," writes the historian, "were generally produced in an age which had no records, no philosophy, no criticism, no canon of belief, and scarcely any tincture of astronomy or geography; but which, on the other hand, was full of religious faith, distinguished for quick and susceptible imagination, seeing personal agents where we only look for objects and laws;—an age, moreover, eager for new narrative, accepting with the unconscious impressibility of children (the question of truth or falsehood being never formally raised), all which ran in harmony with its preëxisting feelings, and penetrable by inspired poets and prophets in the same proportion that it was indifferent to positive evidence."[1] It is true that the operation of the mythopœic faculty is not absolutely extinct in a more cultured time; yet its peculiar province is the childhood of a people. As Grote elsewhere says, "to

[1] Grote, Vol. I. p. 451.

understand properly the Grecian myths, we must try to identify ourselves with the state of mind of the original mythopœic age; a process not very easy, since it requires us to adopt a string of poetical fancies not simply as realities, but as the governing realities of the mental system; yet a process which would only reproduce something analogous to our own childhood." Of the point of view from which the myths were looked upon by the Greek, he adds: "Nor need we wonder that the same plausibility which captivated his imagination and his feelings was sufficient to engender spontaneous belief; or rather that no question as to the truth or falsehood of the narrative suggested itself to his mind. His faith is ready, literal, and uninquiring, apart from all thought of discriminating fact from fiction." If we turn to the age of Augustus, we find a condition of society at a world-wide remove from this primitive era of sentiment and fancy. Some are deceived by the supposed analogy of the middle ages, which, however, were wholly different, and more resembled the ancient nations in their period of immaturity. The Greek and Roman literature and science had passed away. Christianity, with its doctrines and miracles, had been received by the fresh, uncivilized peoples of Europe, and these, full of the new sentiments and beliefs which were awakened by Christianity, dwelling, so to speak, in an atmosphere of the supernatural, created the mass of mythical stories which fill up the voluminous lives of the saints. It was the work of unlettered, imaginative, uninquiring peoples, on the basis and under the stimulus of the miraculous history of the Gospels. "Such legends," says Mr. Grote, "were the natural growth of a religious faith, earnest, unexamining, and interwoven with the feelings at a time when the reason does not need to be cheated. The lives of the saints bring us even back to the simple and ever-operative theology of the Homeric age."[1] Totally different was the state of things among the old nations at the advent of Christianity. We must not forget that, so far as intellectual development is concerned, along with the downfall of ancient civilization the tides of history rolled back. New nations came upon the stage and a period of childhood ensued. Dr. Arnold, writing to Bunsen, points out the anachronism involved in Strauss's theory. "The idea," exclaims Arnold, "of men writing mythic histories between the time of Livy and Tacitus, and of St. Paul mistaking such for reali-

[1] Grote, Vol. I. p. 471. As to the loose habit of observation and great inaccuracy of mediaeval writers in describing ordinary objects, which justly excite incredulity in regard to their stories of miracles, see Dr. Arnold's *Lectures on History*, p. 128. He gives an instance of this carelessness from Bede, who was reputed the most learned man of his age. "I cannot think," says Arnold, "that the unbelieving spirit of the Roman world was equally favorable to the origination and admission of stories of miracles with the credulous tendencies of the middle ages." (P. 129.) No doubt bodily austerities, vigils, fastings, and the like, together with the spirit of unbounded credulity, might produce extraordinary phenomena, which could easily be mistaken for miracles.

ties!"[1] Strauss labors hard to create a different impression in respect to the character of the age of the apostles. He appeals to the occasional mention of prodigies by Tacitus and Josephus—as the supernatural sights and sounds attending the capture of Jerusalem. But if current reports of this sort of preternatural manifestation convict an age of an unhistorical spirit, there is no state of society that would not be liable to this charge. Even skeptics, like Hobbes, have not escaped the infection of superstitious fear. These passages in Josephus and Tacitus are chiefly remarkable as being exceptions to the ordinary style of their narratives. Strauss endeavors to make much of the two alleged miracles of Vespasian, at Alexandria, which are noticed by Tacitus and also by Suetonius. But whatever may have been the fact at the bottom, the circumstances in the narrative of Tacitus afford a striking exemplification of the historical spirit of the times, and, thus, of the falsehood of Strauss's general position. When the application was made to Vespasian by the individuals on whom the cures are said to have been wrought, he laughed at their request and "treated it with contempt."[2] The

[1] *Life and Correspondence of Arnold*, p. 293, N.

[2] Vespasian behaved like William of Orange, who sneered at the old practice of touching for the king's evil. This behavior of William gave great scandal to not a few. (See Macaulay's *Hist. of England*, Harper's ed., Vol. III. p. 432 seq.). Many invalids resorted to the king to be touched. Yet who will infer that the age of William was

applicants being importunate in their request, and pretending to make it by the direction of the god Serapis, Vespasian had a talk with the physicians, who stated the nature of the diseases and were quite non-committal on the question whether the Emperor could effect a cure in the manner desired. The entire passage in Tacitus shows at least a full consciousness that the event is wholly anomalous and not to be accepted without satisfactory proof. The truth is, that the creative period in the ancient nations when the mythological religions sprung up, had long ago passed by. Even the belief in them was fast crumbling away and yielding to skepticism. This engendered, to be sure, a superstition to fill up the void occasioned by the destruction of the old belief. Hence magic and sorcery were rife. The professors of the black art, to use a more modern phrase, drove a lucrative business, and found credulous followers, as the apostles discovered in their missionary journeys. But this despairing superstition was a phenomenon lying at the opposite pole from that action of the mythopœic tendency which belongs, as we have explained, to the freshness of youth. Pilate spoke

not an "historical" age, or suppose that a mythology could have arisen in England in the seventeenth century and established itself in the popular faith?

It is remarkable how often the cures by Vespasian have been made to figure in skeptical treatises. Hume dwells on them in his Essay on Miracles.

out the feelings of the cultivated Roman in the skeptical question, What is truth? Nor is Strauss more successful in the attempt to find among the Jews, in particular, a condition of society suitable for the origination of myths. Prophecy had long since died out. A stiff legalism, with its "traditions of the elders," had chilled the free movement of religious life. Nor is it true that among the Jews, in the time of Christ, a miracle had only to be stated to be believed. Miracles (unless exorcism be reckoned one) were not supposed to occur. They were considered to belong to an era of their history long past. A miracle was an astounding fact. "Since the world began," it was said (John ix. 32), "was it not heard that any man opened the eyes of one that was born blind."[1] The Gospels are full of parables, allegories, showing a state of mind, in teacher and hearer, inconsistent with the production of myths. In the parable, the idea is held in an abstract form, and a fiction is *contrived* to represent it. Otfried Müller, in answer to the question, how long the myth-building spirit continues, explains that the fusion or confounding of idea and fact, which constitutes the myth, could take place only so long as the habit did not exist of presenting the one apart from the other—either idea apart from narrative, or narrative apart from the mythopœic idea. But when ideas are apprehended as such, in an abstract form, or veracious history is

[1] See also Matt. ix. 33.

written, the mythical era is gone.[1] So far from there being a reign of credulity, there existed, in the Sadducees, an outspoken skeptical party who regarded with coldness and suspicion the supernatural elements in their own religion. How could myths arise among those who listened to debates like that which Matthew records between Christ and the Sadducees, "who say that there is no resurrection?"[2] So far from there being among the Jews in the time of Christ an irresistible tendency to glorify the object of reverence by attributing to him miraculous works, it is a fact, of which the advocates of the mythical theory can give no plausible explanation, that no miracles are ascribed to John the Baptist, though he was considered in the early Church to be inferior to no prophet who had preceded him. If there was this unreflecting and credulous habit which is imputed to the Jewish Christians, why is no instance of miraculous healing interwoven in the description which the Gospels give us of the career of the forerunner of Jesus? He was supernaturally enabled to designate the Messiah, but he himself, though he is characterized in terms of exalted praise, is not represented as endowed with supernatural power. It is, also, significant that the life of Jesus, up to the time of his entrance upon his public ministry, is left an almost unbroken blank. Had the disciples given

[1] *Prolegomena*, s. 170.

[2] Matt. xxii. 23 seq. Julius Müller refers to this passage in his cogent review of Strauss, in the *Studien u. Kritiken*, 1836, III.

the reins to their imagination, as the theory of Strauss supposes, they would almost infallibly have filled up the childhood of Christ with myths, after the manner of the spurious gospels of a later date.[1] But Mark and John pass over in silence the whole of the preparatory period of thirty years. Matthew passes immediately from his birth and infancy to his public ministry, while Luke interposes but a single anecdote of his childhood. Why this remarkable reticence, unless the reason be that the apostles chose to dwell upon that of which they had a direct, personal knowledge?

It may be objected to the foregoing remarks, that the original authors of the mythical narratives are supposed to be persons aloof from the great world and beyond the influence of its culture—Galileans of humble rank. The existence of a class of disciples, cut off from the guidance of the apostles, has before been disproved. But apart from this, the supposed authors of the myths were reflective enough to discriminate between the parable and the abstract relations represented under it. They were acquainted with the questions debated between the Sadducees and their opponents. Besides, it is undeniable that a spirit of opposition to Christ and his cause existed, and must have existed, wherever he had preached. The vindictive hostility of the Pharisees and rulers caused his death. In Galilee, as well as

[1] The Apocryphal Gospels were generally the offspring of pious fraud. They were composed, for the most part, to further the cause of some heretical doctrine or party.

Jerusalem, he had to encounter unbelief and enmity. Aside from the fact that the pharisaic influence ramified through the land, it appears that at Capernaum, Chorazin, Bethsaida, Nazareth, there were unbelievers and opposers.[1] There was a strong disposition among these to disprove the messianic claim of Jesus and to invalidate, in some way, the proofs on which it rested. There could be no disciples of Jesus—to say the least, no considerable number of disciples—who would not be instantly called upon to make good their cause in the encounter with objections and cavils. This necessity, if nothing else, would force them to reflection, and would thus break up the attitude of unquestioning fancy and blind credulity. They must give a reason for the faith that is in them. They must do this to the very persons among whom the incidents, on which their faith was grounded, were alleged to have recently occurred. The mythopœic faculty cannot work, it is clear, under a cross-examination. Fancy cannot go on with its creations in the midst of an atmosphere of doubt and unfriendly scrutiny. The state of the Church was the very opposite of that repose on which alone a mythology can have its birth. It holds true that the application of the mythical theory to the testimony of the early disciples, is a gross anachronism.

[1] It is one theory of the Tübingen school that the Pharisees followed Jesus into Galilee and that the hostility they felt to him was provoked there.

VI. The mythical theory is unable either to account for the faith of the apostles in the Resurrection of Christ, or to disprove the fact which was the object of this faith.

Strauss finds it impossible to deny that the apostles, one and all, *believed* that Jesus had risen from the dead and that they had held various interviews and conversations with him. This miracle, at least, it must be admitted that *they* received. Without this faith, their continued adherence to the cause of Jesus would hardly be explainable. And this fact was a main part of their preaching and testimony. It was immovably lodged in their convictions. Moreover, the Apostle Paul, in an Epistle whose genuineness is not disputed, is a witness to the existence of this belief and testimony on the part of the other apostles. He knew them; he had spent a fortnight with Peter in his own house. He had declared to the Corinthians, he says, that Christ died "and was buried, and that he rose again the third day, according to the Scriptures; and that he was seen of Cephas, then of the twelve: after that he was seen of above five hundred brethren at once, of whom the greater part remain to this present, but some are fallen asleep; after that he was seen of James; then of all the apostles." The whole manner of Paul indicates that he is giving the result of a careful inquiry. That the apostles *believed*, with a faith which no opposition could shake, that they had thus beheld the risen

Jesus, there is, therefore, no room for doubt. The main question is, how came they to this persuasion? The Gospel narratives furnish the explanation by describing his actual reappearance, and repeated conferences with them. Rejecting the miracle, Strauss is obliged to undertake the task, by no means a light one, of accounting for their unanimous belief in it; for the belief, also, of the assembly of more than five hundred disciples to whose testimony Paul refers.

The principal points in Strauss's attempted explanation are the following:[1] Christ had more and more impressed the disciples with the conviction that he was the Messiah. His death, so contrary to their previous conceptions of what the Messiah's career would be, for the time extinguished this conviction. But after the first shock was over, their previous impression concerning Christ revived. Hence the psychological necessity of incorporating into their notion of the Messiah the idea that he was to suffer and die. But as comprehending a thing, among the Jews of that time, only signified the deriving of it from the Holy Scriptures, the apostles resorted to these to see whether there might not be in them intimations that the Messiah was to suffer and die. This idea, Strauss affirms, was foreign to the Old Testament; nevertheless, the apostles would find the intimations, which they wished to find, in all the poetic and prophetic passages of the Old Testament, as Isaiah liii., Psalm xxii., in which

[1] *Leben Jesu*, s. 636 seq.

the men of God were represented as persecuted even to death. This obstacle surmounted, and having now a suffering, dying Messiah, it followed next that Christ was not lost, but still remained to them: through death, he had only entered into his messianic glory, in which he was invisibly with them, always, even to the end of the world. Having advanced so far, they would be moved to ask themselves how it was possible that he should refrain from personally communicating with them? And how could they, in the warmth of feeling kindled by this unveiling to them of the Scriptural doctrine of a suffering and dying Messiah, avoid regarding this new discovery as the effect of an influence exerted upon them by the glorified Christ, "an opening of their understandings" by Him—"*yea*," adds Strauss, "*as a discoursing with them?*" These feelings, in the case of individuals, especially women, rose into an actual (apparent) vision. In the case of others, even of whole assemblies, something objective, visible, or audible, perchance the sight of an unknown person, made the impression of a revelation or manifestation of Jesus. But another step in the psychological process was yet to be taken. If the crucified Messiah had really ascended to the highest state of blessed existence, then his body could not have been left in the grave; and since there were Old Testament expressions, like Psalm xvi. 10, "thou shalt not leave my soul in Hades, neither suffer thy Holy One to see corruption," and Isaiah liii. 10, in which the slain servant of Jehovah was promised a long life afterwards, the disciples could keep their previous notion that "Christ abideth forever" (John xii. 34), by means of the thought of an actual reawakening of the crucified; and, inasmuch as it was a messianic function to raise at a future day the bodies of the dead, the return of Jesus to life must be an actual anastasis—a resurrection of the body.

What shall be said of this chain of conjectures? We freely admit that all which Strauss asserts on this subject is *possible*. That the followers of Christ came to believe in his resurrection in the way above described, without the objective fact to excite this belief, is not absolutely beyond the bounds of possibility. It is not pretended that the fact of the miracle is susceptible of strict demonstration. Nay, we concede that if a man holds a miracle, under the circumstances, in connection with the establishment of Christianity in this world, to be more improbable than any method, which is not literally irrational, of explaining it away, he may accept the above solution of Strauss But even he cannot shut his eyes to the tremendous difficulties which attend that solution. In order to set forth some of these difficulties, we must restate the hypothesis of Strauss, adding other particulars in his view, some of which have not been mentioned. A young man—such is the theory of Strauss—comes to the baptism of John with the same motive which led others to the prophet, and takes his place among his disciples. After John is thrown into prison, he begins himself to teach. He draws about him a band of disciples. Gradually he comes to believe himself not merely a prophet, but even the expected Messiah. But at first, though inculcating spiritual truth, he shares in the political theory of the Messiah's kingdom until the unfavorable reception accorded to him and his doctrine modified the view he took of the character and prospects of that kingdom. He may, not unlikely, have anticipated that the opposition excited against him would, at no very distant day, result in his death. But when seized by the Jewish rulers, he was not looking for an immediate death. This is a point which Strauss is obliged to maintain in order to avoid conceding to Christ supernatural knowledge. On a sudden he is seized in the midst of his followers, and executed as a culprit. All their expectations had been disappointed. They had expected the Messiah to work miracles; but they had witnessed none. They had looked for a political Prince, and been encouraged in their view, for a time, by Jesus himself; but behold their imaginary Prince nailed to the cross! He is solemnly adjudged to death by the rulers of the nation, by those who sat in Moses' seat! And the civil power of the Romans carries out the sentence He dies, receiving no succor from God, apparently incapable of offering resistance! Add to this that they, as was natural, dispersed in terror. Can we, adopting Strauss's interpretation of the previous history of Jesus, think that the souls of the disciples were enthralled to that degree that they still clung to their faith in him? If Strauss were willing to admit that Jesus had before exhibited supernatural powers and had performed the miracles recorded of him in the Gospels, it would be less difficult to account for a mistaken belief of his disciples in his resurrection; but in that case, the motive for discrediting the reality of the miracle would no longer exist. But the theory of Strauss respecting the previous life of Christ disables him from explaining how a myth of this portentous character could spring up and obtain universal credence among his disciples. There was nothing in the Master's career to prepare their minds to believe, much less anything to predispose their minds to originate, such a report. And then the idea of all of them, with none to dissent, reviving from their terror and despondency; changing essentially their notion of the Messiah to suit the circumstances; attributing their new interpretations of the Old Testament to an inspiration from Christ; conceiving themselves, on this account, to be holding personal intercourse with him, then proceeding to the further inference that his body had been awakened to life! Add to this that on the strength of this faith, the offspring of a series of the veriest delusions, they went forth proclaiming the resurrection of Jesus, and this with a courage they had never before manifested or felt—went forth—these illiterate visionaries—to the spiritual conquest of the world! Notwithstanding the inventions of Strauss to account for it, the revolution in the feelings of the apostles so soon after they had "mourned and wept," having thought that the kingdom would be restored to Israel, and hid themselves out of "fear of the Jews," remains, unless we suppose a great objective transaction to produce the change, an unexplained marvel. For in their deep dejection of mind, there was nothing that could awaken a vision such as Strauss imagines. Misery does not beget enthusiasm.

But if we admit for the moment that his conjectures on this point are well founded, he is immediately confronted by another difficulty, to surmount which he is obliged to set at defiance the testimony in the case. The most of the interviews with the risen Christ, which Strauss calls visions, took place in Jerusalem. There they met him—first, individuals, and then the eleven together, on the day but one after he had been laid in the tomb. They had the means of testing whether his body was, or was not, still in the embrace of death. They would certainly have made inquiry. They would certainly have gone to the tomb. Sensible of this difficulty, Strauss takes it upon him to transfer the scene of these interviews to Galilee. In Matthew, where the account bears all the marks of being an abbreviated summary, Jesus appears to "Mary Magdalene and the other Mary" on the first Sunday, and the disciples are directed to go into Galilee to meet him there. There Strauss places the scene of the supposed visions.[1] But in taking this view he is obliged to contradict the more full narratives of the other evangelists, including John. They are confirmed, in this particular, by the unquestioned testimony of Paul. For he states that the reappearance of Christ was on the third day after his burial. The commemoration of Sunday in the apostolic age, of which the New Testament affords convincing evidence, proves the same thing. There is no plausible explanation of the constant affirmation of the disciples that the resurrection occurred on the third day, unless we suppose that Jerusalem was the place of his reappearance to them. The next declaration of Paul, that "He was seen of Cephas," falls in with the statement incidentally made by Luke (Luke xxiv. 34), of the appearance of Christ "to Simon" on the Sunday of the resurrection; and it is natural to identify the interview with the twelve, which Paul mentions immediately after in the same verse, with the interview mentioned by Luke as taking place in the latter part of the same day (ver. 36). So that the denial by Strauss that these interviews, whether real or imaginary, took place in Jerusalem and soon after the burial of Christ, is in the teeth of unimpeachable testimony.[2]

[1] Strauss throws aside, however, Matthew's account of the interview of Jesus with the two Marys. It is one of a multitude of instances in which Strauss follows an evangelist just so far as, and no farther than, it suits his convenience.

[2] Baur, the Prince of the Tübingen critics, appears to give up the Straussian notion that the disciples forsook Jerusalem. "It proves,"

But to remove the theatre of the so-called visions to Galilee does not suffice. It will not do to allow that the apostles began *so soon* to believe and to preach their dream as a reality for which they were ready to lay down their lives. For this inward change, time was required. There must be, in their Galilean seclusion, a silent preparation—a *stille Vorbereitung.* To secure this advantage for his theory, Strauss does not hesitate to contradict the statement of Luke, in the Acts, that within a few weeks from the Master's death, on the day of Pentecost, they preached with great power and proclaimed his Resurrection.[1] Observe that the author of the Acts is not credited with a myth, but is charged with conscious deception.

But all this violent criticism is really insufficient, because, apart from the testimony of the evangelists, the testimony of Paul makes it evident that it was not visions, but interviews and conferences, which the apostles had with the risen Christ. Strauss, indeed, tries to show that Paul's own sight of Jesus was only

he says, "the great strength of their faith and a greatly strengthened confidence in the cause of Christ, that the disciples immediately after his death *neither scattered outside of Jerusalem, nor assembled in a remoter place*, but in Jerusalem itself had their permanent centre." See *Das Christenthum*, etc. s. 41. He gives up the attempt "to penetrate by psychological analysis into the inward spiritual forces," by which the unbelief of the apostles at the death of Christ was supplanted by the faith in his resurrection: s. 40. In this particular, then, Baur seems to repudiate the long-drawn hypothesis of Strauss.

[1] *Leben Jesu*, B. II. s. 639.

a vision, or a seeming vision, and then leaps to the inference that the other interviews of the disciples with Christ, after his death, were of a like nature. But Paul evidently regarded the appearance of Christ to him at his conversion, to which he here refers, as an objective, visible, actual manifestation. This late manifestation of the ascended Christ, he connects with the appearances of Christ to the other apostles *before* his ascension. There is no warrant, therefore, either for the assertion that Paul, in his own case, was referring to a vision, or, even if he were, that the manifestations of Christ to the other disciples were of this kind. If it were admitted that Paul's sight of Jesus was an illusive impression, a seeming vision, as Strauss pretends, yet that implies psychologically a state of feeling on his part, whether it were incredulity or incipient faith, which nothing but the proclamation of the resurrection of Jesus by the apostles could have produced. And *their* supposed visions, at least, no prior fact of this kind can help explain. But this theory of visions is excluded by the fact that he was seen, as Paul declares, more than once by the whole company of the apostles simultaneously, and still more by the fact of his appearance to an assembly of more than five hundred disciples at once. The simultaneous imaginary vision of Christ by so large a number would be unaccountable. The nature of those meetings of the disciples with Christ, which Paul records with so profound a sense of the vital importance of them, feeling that "if Christ be not risen, our faith is vain," is set forth in the more circumstantial narratives of the evangelists. It was fact, not fancy, on which the preaching and the unconquerable faith of the apostles were founded.

VII. The mythical theory is inconsistent with the book of Acts.

We have just alluded to one point in this testimony. The book of Acts is the continuation of the third Gospel by the same author. It was written for the benefit of the same Theophilus to whom the Gospel was addressed (Acts i. 1). It is a work of a person who was the beloved companion of the Apostle Paul during a part of his missionary journeying.[1] The testimony of the Acts is of the highest value and importance. We here see the apostles, a few weeks after the death of Christ, proclaiming in Jerusalem his resurrection. We find them referring in their discourses to "the miracles, and wonders, and signs," which Christ had performed "in the midst" of the people to whom they spoke (Acts ii. 22). We find that the apostles themselves were endowed with power to work miracles.[2] The Acts prove, thus, that the earlier miracles of Christ were believed and preached by the apostles. They furnish the most decisive proof of the supernatural events connected with the founding of Christianity.

[1] Col. iv. 14; Acts. xvi. 10–17, xx. 5–15, xxi. 1–18, xxxii. 1 seq.

[2] Besides passages in the Acts, see on this point Rom. xv. 19; 2 Cor. xii. 12; Hebrews ii. 4.

Strauss, in his Life of Christ, prudently abstained from considering at any length the testimony of the Acts. Other adherents of the Tübingen school, especially Baur and Zeller, have endeavored to supply this deficiency. But the mythical theory proves insufficient. It is found necessary to charge the author of the Acts with intentional fraud and falsehood. In defiance of the explicit, as well as incidental, evidence afforded by the Gospel, both works are remanded to the early part of the second century, while the passages in the Acts in which the "we" occurs, are declared to have been thus left for the purpose of deceiving readers into the belief that the date of its composition was earlier. So the old infidelity is brought back again. Candid men will sooner put faith in the direct statements, made by the author of the third Gospel and of the Acts respecting himself, fully corroborated as they are by internal evidence of an incidental nature which could not have been manufactured, and confirmed, too, by the authority of the early Church, than accept the theory that we owe these precious histories of Christ and the apostles to a cheat.

VIII. The mythical theory is proved untenable by the fact that the supernatural elements in the life of Christ, are inseparably connected with circumstances and sayings which are plainly historical.

The advocates of the mythical theory undertake to

dissect the Gospel histories, and to cast out everything supernatural. Out of the residuum they will construct the veritable life of Christ. Now if it be true that the natural and the supernatural, the historical and the (so-called) fabulous, are incapable of this divorce, but that both are parts of each other, so that if one be destroyed the other vanishes also, then the miracles must be allowed to stand. And such is the fact. These narratives will not suffer the decomposition that is attempted upon them. The two elements, the natural and the miraculous, will not admit of being thus torn apart. We have space for only a few proofs and illustrations of our proposition; but these, it is hoped, are sufficient to show its truth. The first illustration we have to offer is the message of John the Baptist from his prison, to inquire of Jesus, "Art thou he that should come, or do we look for another?"[1] The two disciples of John witnessed the various miracles of healing performed by Christ. Jesus then said to them: "Go and shew John again these things which ye do hear and see: the blind receive their sight, and the lame walk, the lepers are cleansed, and the deaf hear, the dead are raised up, and the poor have the gospel preached to them: and blessed is he whosoever shall not be offended in me." The messengers departed; and Jesus proceeds to speak, with earnest emotion, to the people who are present, of the sacred character and the position of John. Now it is obvious

[1] Matt. xi. 2 seq.; Luke vii. 18 seq.

that if one part of this narrative is given up, the rest falls with it. There is no way of escaping the miraculous, as the procedure of Strauss evinces, except by denying the whole—denying that John sent the message. But how irrational to suppose that the disciples of Christ would have falsely attributed to John the doubt as to the Messiahship of Jesus, which occasioned the message.[1] Had Strauss no theory to maintain, he would be the last to assume a thing so improbable. We have, then, an example in which the miracles are an indissoluble part of a transaction undeniably historical.

We proceed to another illustration. The evangelists record four instances of the miraculous healing of aggravated diseases on the Sabbath, each of which led to a conversation, inseparable from the incident that provoked it, and yet manifestly historical.[2] Let us briefly notice one of these instances—that of the man healed of the dropsy. On this occasion, in reference to the lawfulness of healing on the Sabbath-day, Christ put to the lawyers and Pharisees the question: "Which of you shall have an ass or an ox fallen into

[1] That such was the motive of the message seems clear. See Meyer on Matthew, s. 244. The momentary uncertainty of John may have been owing to the circumstance that Jesus remained in retiracy and gave no signs of inaugurating any political change, from the expectation of which John was, perhaps, not wholly free.

[2] 1. The case of the man with a withered hand, Matt. xii. 9 seq. (Luke vi. 6 seq.; Mark iii. 1 seq.). 2. The man afflicted with dropsy, Luke xiv. 5 seq. 3. The woman bowed down with a chronic infirmity, Luke xiii. 10 seq. 4. The lame man at the pool of Bethesda, John v. 2 seq.

a pit, and will not straightway pull him out on the Sabbath-day?" Strauss cannot bring himself to deny that Jesus proposed this question. The expression, both in doctrine and in form, is too characteristic of his method of teaching. Nor can he avoid admitting that it was spoken in connection with some act of Jesus in ministering to the diseased. He even concedes that the inquiry would be inappropriate unless the case were that of a person rescued from a great peril. After making various suggestions which fail to satisfy himself, Strauss is at length inclined to fall back upon the (so-called) natural exposition, which he is wont to handle, in general, so unmercifully.[1] If Jesus ministered among his disciples to bodily as well as spiritual infirmities, and had been giving remedies on the Sabbath, the question may have been put by way of self-defence. After following Strauss in the perpetual attack he makes, with logic and satire, upon the interpretations of Paulus, which, to be sure, are equally destitute of reason and taste, one cannot help being struck with surprise to find him resorting, in order to avoid the miracle, to one of that critic's favorite notions. Nothing could more clearly indicate the stress of the difficulty which is created by the evident verity of the New Testament report.

The evangelists state that on numerous occasions, after working a miracle, Jesus directed that the fact should not be noised abroad. Not only would he be

[1] *Leben Jesu*, B. II. s. 118, 119.

concerned to avoid a premature conflict with the Jewish rulers, which might cut him off before his work was finished, but the prohibition was with reference to the eagerness of the people for a political Messiah, and in order that the number of his disciples might not be swelled by a multitude on whom no deep spiritual impression had been made; who would, therefore, abandon their faith as soon as their carnal expectation should be balked. In some instances, the evangelists inform us, the injunction of Christ on this point was not complied with. That Christ should utter these prohibitions, was in itself a remarkable circumstance. It must fix itself, and *did* fix itself, in the recollection of his disciples. But if the miracles are dropped, what becomes of the prohibition to report them? Strauss's talent for conjecture is here put to a severe test. He concludes that Christ, after he began his public ministry, at first regarding himself as only a forerunner like John, and only by degrees indulging the idea that he is himself the Messiah, was, so to speak, struck with fear at hearing that distinctly suggested from without which he hardly, in his own bosom, dared to conjecture, or had only shortly before come to believe! That is, in homelier phrase, Christ wished nothing to be said on the subject till he had made up his own mind! We need offer no comment on this theory, save to remind the reader that it does not touch the proof that this injunction most frequently had reference to miracles.

Still another example of the truth that the natural and the supernatural are bound up together in the Gospel history, is afforded by the narrative of the Saviour's agony in Gethsemane. This disclosure of the sinking of his heart in the near prospect of death, and of the struggle through which he passed, is *felt* by the reader to be historical. Least of all would Strauss be expected to impeach the verity of it. His axiom is that the disciples were swayed by a desire to glorify their master. He strangely attributes the circumstance that the disciples are said to have fallen asleep, even here in the garden, and on the Mount of Transfiguration, while Christ was awake, to a secret desire to ascribe to him a certain superiority. How, then, could they have been prompted to falsely represent him in a state of feeling, which, in the judgment of the world, however superficial that judgment may be, is less noble and worthy than the placid manner of a Socrates? And yet Strauss, after long criticisms of the several Gospel narratives, pronounces the whole story of the agony of Jesus in the garden unhistorical![1] He has, moreover, a reason for this judgment. This agitation, whatever causes produced it, was conditioned by the knowledge that death was at hand. Now, as the plot was a secret one, to admit that Jesus was possessed of this knowledge would be tantamount

[1] ——"jener ganze Seelenkampf, weil auf unerweislichen Voraussetsungen ruhend, aufgegeben werden muss." *Leben Jesu*, B. II. s. 454.

to the acknowledgment of his supernatural foresight. Strauss makes a laborious endeavor to show that none of the words of Jesus in the record of the institution of the Supper, imply an expectation of an immediate death. Thus, to avoid the supernatural, he strikes out of the history of Christ a passage which bears the most unmistakable stamp of being historical, and which his own fundamental postulate forbids him to reject!

Other proofs of a more than human knowledge on the part of Christ, are left upon the Gospel page. Christ predicted the destruction of Jerusalem, the overthrow of the Jewish state, and the forfeiture of its rank and privilege, as the seat of the worship of Jehovah. When the city stood in all its strength and splendor, he set the date of its downfall within the lifetime of the generation then on the stage. He foretold, what is even more impressive to a thoughtful mind, the progress of the Christian cause to a universal triumph. In the parables of the mustard-seed and the leaven, he depicted the small beginnings and the future extent and power of the Christian religion. What a gaze was that which thus looked far down the stream of time! The unaided faculties of no man, in the situation of Jesus, could have thus forecast the drama of history.

IX. The arbitrary and sophistical character of the criticism applied to the contents of the Gospels in order to prove them untrustworthy, is conclusive against the mythical theory.

The method of Strauss, as we have indicated before, is to overthrow the credibility of the Gospels, to the end that he may disprove their genuineness. He wishes, by an analysis of the testimony, to show that it cannot emanate from eyewitnesses or qualified contemporaries. Hence, the greater part of his book is taken up with the detailed examination of the Gospels, his aim being to show them to be destitute of historical authority. Strauss has forgotten the admonition of his countryman, Lessing: "if Livy, and Dionysius, and Polybius, and Tacitus, are so candidly and liberally treated that we do not stretch them upon the rack for a syllable, why should not Matthew, and Mark, and Luke, and John be treated as well?" We characterize his criticism as generally unfair and sophistical. His manner is precisely that of a sharp advocate who sets himself to pick to pieces the testimony of a company of artless, but honest and competent witnesses. Variations are magnified and harped upon; whatever is stated by one and omitted by another is laid to some occult motive either in the one or the other, or in both; meanings are read into the record which never occurred to those who gave it; and by other arts familiar to the advocate the impression is sought to be produced that the testimony is entitled to no credit. To fan suspicion is the prime object of Strauss. His method would destroy the credibility of all history. A parody, where the subject is an established, notorious historical fact, is the most effective method of refuting this criticism which rests on suspicion. If Whately's Life of Napoleon is not a valid refutation of Hume, inasmuch as no natural fact, however unexampled, can be put in the same category with a supernatural fact, this little work, nevertheless, well illustrates with what facility doubt may be cast upon sound and credible testimony. A clever parody upon Strauss was written in Germany, in the form of a Life of Luther.[1] The fact of "two birthplaces," for example, Bethlehem and Nazareth, which, at the outset, calls out the skepticism of Strauss, is put by the side of circumstances equally surprising in the case of Luther, whose parents, before he was born, had come from Möhra to Eisleben, and shortly after that event moved to Mansfeld. An able writer[2] has finely parodied the reasoning of Strauss through which he aims to impeach the credit of the evangelists, by trying the same method upon the ancient testimonies describing the assassination of Julius Caesar. And he proves that Caesar was never killed, by the same species of argument which Strauss employs to disprove the healing of the Centurion's son, or the transfigura-

[1] The title is as follows: "The Life of Luther, critically treated by Dr. Casuar Mexico, 2836." (Tübingen: 1839. The work was written by Wurm). A learned doctor, a thousand years hence, takes up the documents pertaining to the life of the Reformer, and, following strictly the method of Strauss, proves their untrustworthiness.

[2] Professor Norton, in his *Internal Evidences of the Genuineness of the Gospels*.

tion. The one effort is just as successful as the other. The advocates of the mythical theory are very zealous in their repugnance to forced harmonizing, but forced *dis*harmonizing is surely not less unworthy. What is the issue raised by Strauss? It is not the question whether the Gospels are free from discrepances; nor is it the question whether these narratives are inspired, or what kind and degree of inspiration belongs to them; nor is it, in general, the question how far they may, or may not, partake of imperfections, from which competent and credible witnesses are not expected to be wholly exempt. But the essential truth of these narratives is the proposition which he impugns, and which, as we affirm, he utterly fails to overthrow.

A great many causes besides error, either innocent or wilful, may introduce modifications into the form of a narrative. Of this all are aware who have pursued historical investigations, or are conversant with courts of law, or even observant of ordinary conversation Where brevity is aimed at, not only an omission, but some modification, of features of a narrative is often required. A peculiar interest in one element of a transaction may have the same effect, or may lead a reporter to change the order of circumstances. For the sake of making a transaction intelligible to a particular person or class, some addition or subtraction may be necessary. At one time, an event may be stated in the dryest form; at another, the same event may be pictured to the imagination. Two reports of the same transaction will often seem irreconcilable, but a new fact, coming to light, removes the contradiction. These are universally acknowledged principles. To hold living witnesses, or documents, to a mathematical accuracy of statement, or to an absolute completeness, on the penalty of being cast out of court, is disreputable sophistry.

These are grave charges against the critical method of Strauss, and we proceed to substantiate them by examples. On account of the demand made by the Pharisees that Jesus should give them "a sign," or "a sign from heaven"[1] (Mark viii. 11, 12; Matt. xii. 38 seq., xvi. 1 seq.; Luke xi. 29 seq.), and the refusal of Jesus, Strauss affirms that Christ is here said to disclaim the working of miracles! That is, the evangelist, in each case, so stultifies himself as to put on the same page with the record of miracles such a disavowal by Christ! The simple truth is, that the "sign" was a peculiar manifestation in the sky, expected to attend the advent of the Messiah, and which the Pharisees demanded *in addition* to all the other miracles.[2] Strauss says that Jesus, in forgiving the sins of the paralytic (Matt. ix. 2), recognized the Jewish doctrine of the allotment of evil in this life in exact proportion to the sin of the individual.[3] Yet

[1] *Leben Jesu*, B. II. s. 4.

[2] See Neander on John vi. 30 (*Leben Jesu*); Meyer on Matt. xvi. 1.

[3] *Leben Jesu*, B. II. s. 75 seq.

this doctrine is plainly inconsistent with what Christ said on hearing of the Galileans "whose blood Pilate had mingled with their sacrifices;" with the declarations in the Sermon on the Mount; with the parable of the Rich Man and Lazarus, and with the statement in respect to the man born blind (John ix. 3). That an opposite doctrine is expressly taught in several of these passages, Strauss allows. It is only needful to suppose that in the particular case of the paralytic, his disease was directly occasioned by some sin,[1] or that Jesus saw that his conscience was troubled.[2] On how slender a foundation is a gross inconsistency charged upon the Great Teacher, or upon the historians who report him!

A specimen of numerous minor perversions of the sense of Scripture, is the remark of Strauss upon Matt. xxi. 7, where it is said that the disciples "brought the ass and the colt, and put on them their clothes, and they set him thereon." The last word, the translation of *ἐπάνω αὐτῶν*, Strauss refers to the animals, and strives to make the evangelist utter nonsense;[3] whereas the pronoun refers to the clothes:[4] and even if the construction of Strauss were correct, he could only in fairness convict the evangelist of using a loose, colloquial expression. A similar instance of quibbling is the effort to foist upon John the error of

[1] So Meyer, ad loc.

[2] So Bleek, *Synopt. Erkl* s. 75.

[4] So Neander and Meyer.

[3] *Leben Jesu*, B. II. s. 274.

supposing that the High Priesthood was an annual office, because he alludes to an individual as "High Priest that year."[1] In the narrative of John, Peter is made to go first into the sepulchre, according to Strauss, out of respect to the vulgar notion concerning Peter; and John must be made out to be the first to believe in the Resurrection.[2] But why not rather give to Peter the last distinction, or to John the first? Is it possible for criticism to be more arbitrary and groundless? The relation, we are told, in which John is placed to Peter, in the fourth Gospel, is "suspicious"[3]—*verdächtig* is a favorite word with Strauss—but the position of John among the disciples is attested not only in the Acts but also by Paul, who styles him, Peter, and James, the pillars of the church at Jerusalem.[4] Peter's confession of faith (Matt. xvi. 16) is construed into a proof that even the disciples had not before taken Jesus for the Messiah. But the fervor and depth of Peter's faith, the peculiar source of it, and perhaps, the glimpse of the higher nature of Jesus involved in it, together with the fact that it was uttered at the moment when others were deserting him, constitute its peculiarity and explain the marked commendation by Christ. To what reader of the passage did the notion of Strauss ever occur? Who ever felt any difficulty of the sort? Noteworthy is the timidly-asserted imputation of an admixture of

[1] *Leben Jesu*, B. II. s. 361. [2] *Leben Jesu*, B. II. s. 582.
[3] *Leben Jesu*, B. I. s. 582. [4] *Leben Jesu*, B. I. s. 497.

political elements in the plan of Jesus.[1] The abstaining from every effort to organize a political party, the explicit abjuring of a design to found a kingdom of this world, the acknowledgment of earthly magistrates, the essentially spiritual character of all the doctrines and precepts of Christ, are not denied. One would think that this were enough to acquit him of the slightest participation in the current Jewish notion of a political Messiah. All that Strauss brings to support his charge from the words of Jesus, is the promise that the disciples should sit on twelve thrones, judging the twelve tribes of Israel. But this was to be at the *παλιγγενεσία*—in the future spiritual kingdom of the new heavens and the new earth. If this proves a temporal idea of the messianic kingdom, then the declaration of Paul that the saints shall judge the world, would prove that he held the same. The promise of Christ presents, in a tropical form, the reward of an ultimate participation in his own heavenly glory. The insinuation of Strauss that the entrance of Christ into Jerusalem, riding on an ass, was a claim for political recognition, does not merit a reply.

Under this head may be mentioned the neglect of Strauss to adhere to his own theory, in the frequent implication of a wilful deception on the part of the evangelists. This peculiarity of his criticism is worthy of marked attention. He is perpetually crossing the

[1] *Leben Jesu*, B. I. s. 518 seq.

line that separates the mythical from the mendacious. He thus proceeds frequently upon a theory which he professes to reject. A consciousness on the part of an historian that his statements are not conformed to the truth, makes him guilty of intentional falsehood. Then we have not myth, but lie. When Strauss says that the cases of the healing of the blind are much more numerous than the instances of the healing of lepers, because the former admit of a greater variety of circumstances;[1] when he states that the healing of the impotent man (John v. 1 seq.) was framed on the basis of narratives in the other Gospels, and made to take place on the Sabbath, because the words "take up thy bed and walk," would furnish the most suitable text for the dispute, that follows, about the observance of the Sabbath;[2] when he says that the prediction by Christ of the mode of his death was attributed to him from a desire to relieve the feeling which was excited by the shameful character of the cross; when he affirms that the foreknowledge of the treason of Judas was falsely ascribed to Jesus from a like motive;[3] when he says that the reference in John (John xviii. 26) to a kinsman of Malchus is artificial and unhistorical, being put in simply to fix Malchus immovably in the narrative;[4] when he charges that the account of Pilate's washing of his hands, sprung from a desire of Christians to make the innocence of Christ seem

[1] *Leben Jesu*, B. II. s. 64.
[2] *Leben Jesu*, B. II. s. 122.
[3] *Leben Jesu*, B. II. s. 371.
[4] *Leben Jesu*, B. II. s. 475.

clear and certain;[1] and in numerous other places, some of which have been touched upon under former topics, Strauss virtually accuses the sacred writers and early disciples of conscious falsehood. He thus falls back upon a scheme of infidelity which the advocates of the mythical theory are fond of decrying as obsolete and as supplanted by their own more refined and charitable view.

Of the unwarrantable attempt to fix a contradiction which shall impair their credit, upon the Gospel writers, where no contradiction really exists, there is a multitude of examples in Strauss. Thus, in comparing the healing of the paralytic in the record of Matthew (Matt. ix. 1 seq.,) with the narrative of the same event in Mark and Luke (Mark ii. 3 seq.; Luke v. 18 seq.), he intimates that the two latter, in saying that a multitude came to Christ, start with an exaggeration of the simpler story of Matthew; although Matthew *closes* the account of the miracle with the words, "*and when the multitude saw it,* they marvelled."[2] It would seem no great inaccuracy in Luke and Mark to mention at the beginning what Matthew mentions at the end of the narrative. If one evangelist is more circumstantial than another, the additional matter is at once pronounced a later, fictitious addition. In the healing of the Centurion's son, because Matthew abbreviates the incident, omitting to mention the messages sent by the

[1] *Leben Jesu*, B. II. s. 37.

[2] *Leben Jesu*, B. II. s. 503.

Centurion, these are at once set down as exaggerations of the original story.[1] As if a writer were bound, in all cases, to give details! The main points—the faith of the Centurion and the healing from a distance—are clearly presented in Matthew; and these are the essential points in the incident. On similar grounds the charge of exaggeration is brought against Mark and Luke (Mark v. 22 seq.; Luke viii. 41 seq.), on account of the narrative of the cure of the daughter of Jairus, which Matthew (Matt. ix. 18 seq.) also gives in an abbreviated form. Such criticism upon secular history would be scouted. Strauss labors hard to make out a contradiction between certain statements in John concerning Judas (John xiii. 27–30), and the statement of the synoptical writers, that he had previously bargained with the priests; but John says nothing inconsistent with this. So Strauss would set the other evangelists in opposition to John, in reference to the statement of the latter, that Judas went out from the Supper, although the fact is that they say nothing about it one way or the other. A baseless charge of contradiction is founded on the statement of John that Christ bore his cross, and the statement of the other evangelists that, on the way to the place of crucifixion, it was laid upon a man named Simon.[2] It is a poor cause which requires such perverse interpretation to prop it up.

[1] *Leben Jesu*, B. II. s. 94 seq.

[2] *Leben Jesu*, B. II. s. 509.

Besides the artificial interpretation in the work of Strauss, his criticism is marked by a pervading fallacy. He reasons in a circle, using now the authority of the Synoptics to disprove a statement in John, and now the authority of John to disprove a statement of the Synoptics. He is ever calling back this or that witness whom he has himself driven out of court, and seeking to make out a point by the use of his testimony.

Another fallacy runs through Strauss's work and vitiates much of his reasoning. He is continually ascribing features in the Gospel narratives to the desire or tendency of the disciples "to glorify their master." This tendency or desire is *assumed* without proof. Being thus arbitrarily assumed, it is freely used to throw discredit on the narratives, while it is only on the foundation of the assumed falsehood of the narratives that the existence of such a desire or tendency is supposed!

X. The connecting of the various portions of the Gospel history with predictions and incidents which, it is alleged, served as a spur and model for the mythopœic faculty, is generally far-fetched and forced.

If Strauss fails in his negative work of proving the falsity of the New Testament history, his failure to account for the construction of it is not less signal

If Christ was to heal the sick, some degree of resemblance between his miracles and those wrought by the Old Testament prophets was to be expected. Yet Strauss seldom finds a resemblance near enough to render the assertion plausible that one event could have stimulated the fancy to the production of the other. In various cases, where there is a palpable difficulty in applying his theory, he takes refuge in the arbitrary, unsupported affirmation that features originally belonging to the Gospel narrative have been effaced and other features substituted for them. In regard to other miraculous occurrences described in the Gospels, he is unable to fasten decidedly on anything which could have put the imagination of the disciples upon framing them. But, of course, one test of his theory must be its applicability to the details of the New Testament history.

The justice of the preceding remarks may be evinced by illustrations. Strauss makes the healing of the Centurion's son a myth, founded on the healing of Naaman by the prophet Elisha (2 Kings v. 8 seq.).[1] But only in the one circumstance, that the prophet did not go out personally to meet Naaman, do the two miracles resemble each other; and even here there is the marked difference, that in the case of Naaman a message promising a cure was sent to the diseased person himself. Moreover, the Centurion's son was a paralytic, while Naaman was cured of the more terrible

[1] *Leben Jesu*, B. II. s. 3.

disease of leprosy; but a leading canon of Strauss is that the messianic miracle will be an exaggerated copy of the Old Testament original. The healing of the withered hand (Matt. xii. 10 paral.) is said to be a fancy-copy of the healing of Jeroboam's hand (1 Kings xiii. 6). But the prominent point, which would not have been forgotten, in the latter narrative, is the character of the king thus healed. He stretched out his hand unrighteously, and could not draw it back. For the miracle of calming the sea, Strauss vainly searches for some Old Testament parallel. He is obliged to fall back on passages (Ps. cvi. 9; Nahum i. 4; Ex. xiv. 16, 21), all of which relate to the *drying up of the sea.*[1] Whence the extraordinary deviation in the Gospel narrative? Strauss can think of no other solution than the fact that, being in a ship, Christ could not be well conceived of as making bare the bed of the sea! But if there was this difficulty, could not the myth-makers have taken care to place him in a more convenient position? The account of the miraculous draught of fishes in John (c. xxi.), is pronounced a mythical combination of Luke v. 4 seq. and Matt. xiv. 22 seq. But Strauss is embarrassed by falling into conflict with two of his own axioms, one of which is that the later account has most of miracle, and that in John, especially, the miraculous is carried to the highest point: whereas, in the case before us, John represents Peter as *swimming* to the shore, while, in

[1] *Leben Jesu*, B. II. s. 166.

the earlier narratives, he walked on the sea. The miracle of the transfiguration occasions Strauss great trouble. There is, indeed, the account of the shining of the face of Moses, although this was after his descent from the mountain, and of the voice out of a cloud; but it happens that the chronology of this miracle of the transfiguration is so definitely fixed, the event is so connected with things before and after, that the historical character of the narrative cannot well be doubted.[1] For the miracle of the stater in the mouth of the fish, no antecedent prophecy or incident can be found. The same is true of the miracle of the healing of the ten lepers; and Strauss resorts to the supposition that a parable has here been mistaken for a fact. It is only by searching the Old Testament and the Rabbies, and combining one scrap here with another there, as the necessities of each case demand, that Strauss is able to make any practical application of his theory. The most that he shows, when he is most fortunate, is that a given narrative might *possibly* have grown out of this or that story or prediction. But, *possibly* not; *possibly* the narrative is the record of a fact. A *probability* is what Strauss fails to make out.

We leave here the special criticism contained in Strauss's work. But there remain to be presented several considerations of a more general character.

[1] See Bleek's *Synopt. Erkl.*, B. II. s. 56–67.

XI. The mythical theory is inconsistent with a fair view of the temper and character of those immediately concerned in the founding of Christianity.

Christ chose twelve disciples to be constantly with him, in order that an authentic impression of his own character and an authentic representation of his deeds and teaching, might go forth to the world. We find them, even in Paul, designated as "the Twelve," and a marked distinction is accorded to them in the early written Apocalypse.[1] The nature of their office, even if, contrary to all reason, the testimony of the Gospels were rejected, is made abundantly clear by those writings of Paul which are acknowledged by the skeptical school to be genuine. Their function was *to testify* of Christ. Understanding their office, it was natural that, as Luke relates, they should feel called upon, after the defection of Judas, to fill up their original number by selecting a person who had "companied" with them through the public life of Christ, to be, as they said, "a witness with us of his resurrection."[2] A doubt of this last fact, in Paul's estimation, was equivalent to charging the apostles with being *false witnesses.*[3]

[1] 1 Cor. xv. 5; Rev. xxi. 14. The Revelation, it is allowed by the Tübingen school, was written about A. D. 70.

[2] Acts i. 21, 22. Passages adverting to this office of the apostles are, as we should expect, numerous in the history, given in the Acts, of their preaching. Among passages elsewhere to the same effect are Luke i. 2, xxiv. 48; John xv. 27; 1 Peter v. 1; 1 Cor. xv. 15.

[3] 1 Cor. xv. 15.

The disciples wêre not enthusiasts, but sober-minded witnesses, distinctly aware that they held this position.

But the principal remark we have to make under this head strikes deeper. There is one quality which pervades the teaching and the religion of Christ, and that is holiness. This attribute is, also, a marked element of the Old Testament religion, in distinction from the religions of the Gentile world. The Sermon on the Mount touches the deepest chords of moral feeling. It speaks to the conscience. They who were drawn to Christ strongly enough to persist in following him, were brought face to face with moral obligations and with the infinite consequences depending on moral tempers. But holiness must affect the intellectual operations. It introduces the principle of truthfulness into the soul. It puts an end to the vagaries of fancy. It opens the eye to realities. Holiness becomes, in this way, the safeguard against self-delusion. Now, in the case of the Master himself, it is irrational to think that he whose holiness was free from the alloy of sin, could cherish a miserable, self-exalting illusion concerning himself. Could that holiness which rebuked the least admixture of sin in the motives and spirit of his dearest followers, be so mixed with the wildest enthusiasm? His disciples, not the twelve alone, but all who were willing to incur the peril and the odium of permanently attaching themselves to his cause, must have partaken of his spirit. The distinction of good and evil, of truth and falsehood, was everything in their eyes. The comparison of the beauty-loving Greek with the truth-loving Hebrew, even when we are treating of an earlier age, involves an evident fallacy. Much more is the comparison of the Hebrew on whose ear not only the decalogue but the holy doctrines and precepts of Christ had fallen, with the Greek of a primitive age, fitted only to mislead. In the New Testament writings we breathe an atmosphere of truth and holiness. We are in contact with men who feel the solemnity of existence. We are continually impressed with the tremendous issues depending on the right use of the powers and faculties of the mind. We are among those who are solicitous, above all things, to be found faithful. Is it an error to expect from the holy a clearer discernment of truth? Is it an error to suppose that holiness clarifies the vision? that holiness will save men from confounding the dreams of fancy with fact? If this be an error, then the nature of man was made to be an instrument of deception and delusion. Then we must deny that "if the eye be single, the whole body shall be full of light."

Whoever looks into the Gospels will see that the pardon of sin is the great blessing promised and sought. It was they who craved this blessing who came to Christ, and remained believers, when those who had followed from a lower motive forsook him. But the sense of unworthiness, and enthusiasm, do not coexist.

The feeling of guilt may engender unfounded fears, and run into superstition; but nothing is more foreign from that play of the imagination which is implied in the theory we are opposing. That conviction of personal unworthiness, growing out of self-judgment and moral thoughtfulness, which led men to Christ, is wholly averse from enthusiasm. The desire to see miracles was not the deepest feeling in those who adhered to Christ. Rather was it the desire of forgiveness and salvation. The miracles were a welcome proof that Christ "had power on earth to forgive sins;" but the moral and spiritual benefit was uppermost in their esteem. They stood on a plane altogether above that occupied by a people in their intellectual childhood when the higher faculties are in abeyance, and the understanding is under the absolute sway of fancy and the craving for the marvellous.

XII. Christ and Christianity receive no adequate explanation from the skeptical theory.

This theory makes the character of Christ, as depicted in the New Testament, to be largely the product of the imagination of his disciples. The conception of that character, so excelling everything known before or since, combining all perfections in an original and unique, yet self-consistent, whole, the unapproached model of excellence for the ages that were to follow, must be accounted for. The features which the skeptical theory must tear from the portraiture are essential.

Take them away, and there is left only a blurred, mutilated image of one in whom good and evil, truth and pitiful error, were strangely mixed. If the Christ of the Gospels, says Julius Müller, be the creation of the disciples, if from their souls emanated this glorious and perfect conception, we must, then, revere *them* as the redeemers of the world!

But Christianity—this mighty and enduring movement in the world's history—how is that explained by the Straussian theory? The New Testament writings bear witness on every page to the depth and power of the movement. It was a moral and spiritual revolution, reaching down to the principles of thought and action, and leading thus, of necessity, to a transformation of the entire life of men. It was literally *a new creation in Christ Jesus.* In the case of the Apostle Paul, for example, we see that there was not merely a belief in the messianic office of Jesus. But Paul has become a new man, in the sentiments, purposes, motives, hopes, which constitute his inward being. A community sprung up, in which old things had passed away and all things had become new. And how shall we explain the effect of this movement upon history for so many centuries? It will not do to say that the Amazon, rolling its broad stream for thousands of miles, and spreading fertility along its banks, is all owing to a shower of rain one spring morning. The mind demands a cause bearing some just proportion to the effect. There are movements which affect only the surface of society. There are movements which produce a wide commotion at the outset, but are soon heard of no more. But Christianity is no superficial, no temporary, no short-lived, movement. On the contrary, its beginning is humble and noiseless. Even the most impressive natural phenomena, which are yet transitory, are no adequate symbol of the deep and permanent operation of Christianity. It is not like the tempest which, after a day or a week, is found to have spent its power. It is rather to be likened to the great, silent force of gravitation, exerting, age after age, its unexhausted energy. Now this movement, beyond what is true of almost every other in history, emanates from a single person. Whatever the previous preparation, whatever the attendant circumstances were, Christianity proceeds from Christ. The force that must lie back of this prodigious movement, inheres in him. He introduced and set in motion the energies that have wrought the whole effect. Let the reader try to form an estimate of this effect, in its length and breadth, as far as history has yet revealed it, and then turn to the solution of it offered by the skeptical theory. It was all produced, we are told, by a weak young man—an untaught Galilean Rabbi, who brought under his influence for one, or two, or three years, a few unlearned Jewish laborers! We say "a weak young man," for only great weakness or great depravity can explain the monstrous delusion that is imputed to him. Now, is this an adequate solution?

In view of the power which has been exerted by Christianity to subvert rival and long established systems of belief, to command the homage of the highest intellect, to reform and mould society; in view also of the adaptation of Christianity to the human mind and heart, of its harmony with natural religion while providing for great wants which reason discovers but cannot supply, an eloquent writer has justly said: "it seems no more possible that the system of Christianity should have been originated or sustained by man, than it does that the ocean should have been made by him."[1]

XIII. The Straussian theory is connected with a false and demoralizing scheme of philosophy.

At the conclusion of his work, Strauss describes the apparently ruthless and destructive character of his own criticism. He confesses that in appearance he is robbing humanity of its chief treasure. But all this he pretends to be able to restore in another form. Christianity is the popular expression of philosophical truth. This last he has no intention of sacrificing, but he will return to the believer all that he has wrested from him, though he will return it in a different form. Proceeding to inquire wherein lie the substance and power of Christianity, Strauss examines the various definitions given by the older Rationalism, and discards

[1] *Evidences of Christianity*, by President Hopkins, Section VII.

them. It is not as a collection of ethical precepts, it is not as a legal system, he holds, that Christianity has its characteristic quality and power over mankind. This distinguishing quality and power inhere in Christianity as a religious system, and proceed from the great central doctrine of a union of God and man in Jesus Christ. This branch of his discussion is carried forward with a penetrating analysis. How, then, does he propose to modify Christianity? What is the philosophical truth underlying this popular conception of the unity of divinity and humanity in Jesus Christ? The real truth, answers Strauss, is, not that God and man are one, or God becomes man, in a single individual, but rather in mankind collectively taken. That is to say, God is in each individual, in each the infinite becomes the finite, yet not fully or exclusively in any one; but for the indwelling and full expression of the infinite, all the members of the race are required. In plainer language, there is no Divine Person, with a self-consciousness separate from the consciousness of men. There is no being higher than man, who can hear prayer. If a man prays, he prays to himself. God is man, and man is God. Jesus Christ is divine, so far and in the same sense as every other individual of the race is God. Men are the transitory products of the evolution of impersonal being. Freedom, sin, accountability, personal immortality, are merged and lost in an all-engulfing necessity. Such is the apotheosis of man and denial of God which constitute the philosophy of Pantheism, and which we are invited to accept as an equivalent for the living personal God and the incarnate Redeemer! The demoralizing tendency of this necessitarian and atheistic philosophy is obvious to every serious mind. Strauss gives a specimen of the fruits of his philosophy by no means fitted to recommend it, when he elaborately justifies the continued preaching of the facts of Christianity, including the resurrection of Christ, by those who have espoused his interpretation of them, and, therefore, disbelieve in their historical truth. We can scarcely suppose that Strauss is in earnest in pronouncing his speculative dogmas the sum and substance of Christian doctrine. He is rather paying a decorous outward respect to history, in which Christianity has performed so mighty a part, and to the Church whose faith he has assailed. But let it be observed that his work is an attack upon the truths of Natural as well as of Revealed Religion. That God is a Person, that man is free and accountable, that sin is the voluntary and guilty perversion of human nature, are denied not less than the miracles attending the establishment of Christianity. The postulates, on which the need of revelation is founded, being thus put aside, it is natural that Christianity itself, and the miracles which attest it, should receive no credence. A clear perception of the primary truths which God has written upon the heart, might have induced in Strauss an appreciation of the Christian system and its founder, such as led Thomas Arnold to feel that miracles are but the natural accompaniments of Christian revelation; accompaniments, the absence of which would have been far more wonderful than their presence.[1]

[1] Arnold's *Lectures on History*, Lecture II.

ESSAY VII.

STRAUSS'S RESTATEMENT OF HIS THEORY.[1]

STRAUSS has well-nigh outlived his own theory. His restatement is to a large extent a retraction. He still holds, indeed, that myths are found in considerable number in the Gospel histories. But as an exclusive, or even predominant, mode of explanation, he gives up his old hypothesis and adopts another which in form and spirit is wholly diverse from it. Yet, anxious to retain the name of *myth*, he contrives a new definition of the term. Thus he partially disguises his "change of base," and gives his new position a verbal identity with his old.

This change is due to the influence of Baur. Baur has been ready to sanction the negative and destructive portion of the labors of Strauss. He gives Strauss the credit of showing that the several Gospel narratives are incapable of being reconciled with one another or depended upon as authentic histories. But for the positive construction of Strauss, Baur manifested less respect. He pointed out the logical impossibility of convicting the Synoptics of error by appealing to the

[1] *Das Leben Jesu für das deutsche Volk*, &c. 1864.

authority of John, and, at the same time, John of error by appealing to the authority of the Synoptics. Strauss was in truth continually seeking to prove his points by witnesses whom he was himself continually impeaching. Baur said rightly that the relative authority of the several documents must first be determined, and some firm standing-place be found, before anything could be proved or disproved by means of them. Then he also denied the general applicability of the mythical hypothesis to the contents of the Gospels. How could the fourth Gospel, which emanated from a single author who professes to be an eyewitness, be composed of myths, when myths are explained to be the involuntary creation of the enthusiastic fancy of the young Christian community? Baur supplanted the mythical theory by the so-called *tendency-theory*. A great portion of the narratives of miraculous events were declared to be the product of invention, and conscious invention in the interest of one or another of the theological parties which, as it was held, divided the early Church. In this way, the whole Gospel of John, no small part of the Gospel of Luke and the Acts (which were both declared to be moulded and colored to subserve a theological motive), and a less but not inconsiderable part of the Gospels of Mark and Matthew, were declared to have originated. Matthew was pronounced by Baur to have more of the character of a faithful record than either of the other Gospels, and was taken. therefore, for a starting-point and the chief authority in the criticism of the evangelical history. Now Strauss has adopted these doctrines of Baur, and to this extent has relinquished his own theory. At first, he apparently welcomed these new discoveries of the Tübingen master, or at any rate cheerfully adopted them. But in the present work, he chafes under the censures of Baur which have appeared in the posthumous writings of the latter, and gives vent to his dissatisfaction. Yet he does not withhold his assent from the conclusions of his more learned and sturdy compeer, and refashions his theory in accordance with them.

How can wilfully invented narratives be styled myths? Strauss meets the exigency by proposing that this term be used with more latitude. He will change the sense of it so as to include under the denomination of *myths* all narratives which spring out of a theological idea, even though they are the deliberate fabrications of an individual. He argues that theologians need not abide by the meaning which classical scholars now give to the word. The motive of this innovation, and wide departure from his own previous definition, is obvious. Strauss will still be the father of "the mythical theory," even if he must baptize a new child, a very different sort of child, with the old name.

But names are comparatively of little consequence. It is more interesting to remark that Strauss has abandoned, as far as much of the Gospel history is concerned, his fundamental conception, and espoused a conception which he had formerly repudiated. Of intentional falsification he professed to acquit the Gospel authorities. The originators of the narratives which they contain, were artless, enthusiastic devotees, carried away by a common enthusiasm and unwittingly mistaking fiction for fact, the products of their own imagination for veritable occurrences. Now they are made to be skilful theologians, bent upon pushing forward certain tenets or allaying some doctrinal strife, and not scrupling to resort to pious fraud to accomplish their end. This is a change of ground which no alteration of the significance of words will avail to cover up. The old infidelity is exhumed, with the difference that the mendacity imputed to the Gospel writers is attributed to another motive, and the attempt is made to disprove the genuineness of the canonical histories for the sake of disconnecting them from the apostles and thus avoiding the necessity of directly impugning their testimony, which would be an inconvenient, as well as ungracious, task.

For this reason, that part of the new *Life of Jesus for the German People* which is most entitled to examination, is the part relating to the origin of the New Testament historical documents. Most of what Strauss has to say on this topic has been directly or indirectly answered on preceding pages of this volume. He has set himself to supply the defect of his previous work, where, strange to say, the discussion of the sources of knowledge concerning the life of Jesus is extremely brief and meagre. His present treatment of this important subject is in the spirit of a partisan, and not in that of a conscientious scholar. When he says that "in those times everything passed for genuine that was edifying," and that dogmatical grounds with the Fathers, among whom he expressly mentions Eusebius, determined everything, he makes a statement which every well-informed student knows to be false. Every scholar knows that Eusebius, Origen, and the earlier writers, as Clement of Alexandria, Tertullian, and Irenaeus, did not govern themselves by any such canon as that which Strauss imputes to them. Every scholar knows that each of these Fathers depended on historical evidence and intelligently submitted to this test the writings which claimed to be apostolic, some of which they accepted and others they rejected. Strauss takes particular notice of the testimony of Papias, who says of Matthew that he "wrote the oracles (τὰ λόγια) in the Hebrew tongue, and every one interpreted (or translated) them as he could." This passage is construed into an implication that every one altered or recomposed the Hebrew Matthew to suit his own taste, and then the inference is proclaimed that on the basis of an original Hebrew Gospel, containing we know not what, our Greek Matthew, the apocryphal Gospel of the Hebrews, and various other works, were composed. There is not a syllable in Papias which remotely implies that any such liberty was taken with the work which he describes as the original of Matthew. If one, writing among Englishmen and giving an account of Strauss's former Life of Jesus, says that it was written in German and every one translated it as he was able, who would understand him to imply that various persons had altered and essentially recomposed that work? Whether Papias be right or wrong in supposing that the Greek Gospel of Matthew which he and his contemporaries had in their hands was the translation of a Hebrew original, the meaning of his language is clear. He means that at first Greek readers had to use the Hebrew Gospel, as all men now have to use an untranslated book in a foreign tongue. They have to render it into their vernacular as well as they can. That Papias was not acquainted with our Mark is deduced from his statement that Mark did not set down his matter "in order" (ἐν τάξει); a conclusion in itself most precarious, and entirely precluded when it is remembered that no mention of any other Gospel of Mark than that of the canon is to be found in any ancient writer. Strauss has the boldness to tell his readers that Luke does not pretend to have received his information from apostles, although in the proem of his Gospel he explicitly includes himself among those to whom the eyewitnesses had delivered their knowledge of the Master's life, and in the Acts impliedly places himself among the attendants of Paul. In reference to the passages in the Acts, from which we derive this fact, Strauss takes refuge in the untenable theory that they are a quotation. Justin is admitted to have made use of the first three Gospels. Respecting the Gospel of John, Strauss is more than usually sophistical. In the first edition of his former work, he had expressed doubts of its genuineness. Afterwards, in deference to the arguments of Ullmann and Neander, he retracted these doubts and declared his belief that John was the author. Still later, perceiving the fatal effect of this concession on his whole theory, he recalled it and went back to his old opinion. Among other observations in the present book, Strauss brings forward the alleged silence of Papias concerning a Gospel by John as a proof that such a work was not known to him. In the first place, we know not that Papias was thus silent; it is an uncertain inference from the circumstance that Eusebius does not speak of any reference by him to this Gospel. In the second place, he may not have had occasion to refer to or quote the Gospel of John, even though he used it. But, in the third place, he did, according to Eusebius, make use of the 1st Epistle of John, and the attempts of Strauss both to cast suspicion upon the correctness of Eusebius in this particular and to call in question the evident community of the Gospel and Epistle as to authorship, are alike futile. Strauss is desirous of showing that the Pseudo-Clementine Homilies in common with Justin derived quotations, which are not found in the first three Gospels, from the Gospel of the Hebrews. In one place (p. 60), he expressly enumerates these four as the probable sources whence the writer of the Homilies drew his citations. Now Strauss knew that this writer had the Gospel of John in his hands and quoted from it; for on a subsequent page (p. 69) Strauss expressly acknowledges the fact. Why not make this acknowledgment earlier? Was it because the author of the Homilies is thus proved to have drawn the passage upon the necessity of being born again, from the Gospel of John, and not from any apocryphal Gospel, so that the pretence that the similar passage in Justin did not come from John is deprived of its frail support? Other points in the remarks of Strauss on John hardly require to be noticed. He reiterates the objection that had Marcion been acquainted with the Gospel of John he would not have rejected it, although Tertullian explains that Marcion was misled by a false understanding of Gal. ii., and rejected the other apostles from their supposed hostility to Paul. Strauss also does not scruple to deny the correctness of Tertullian when he says that Valentine made use of the Gospel of John; he parades the opposition of the insignificant Alogi, who also rejected the Apocalypse which Strauss himself considers genuine: and he borrows from Baur the far-fetched hypothesis that the author of the fourth Gospel shaped his narrative even to the extent of misdating the crucifixion of Christ, for the sake of suggesting that He is the true paschal lamb. The fourth Gospel saw the light, according to Strauss, ten or fifteen years after the controversy of Polycarp with Anicetus, or some time between A. D. 160 and 175! He makes the Clementine Homilies one or two decades later than the principal works of Justin, or in the neighborhood of A. D. 160; so that, if we are to believe Strauss, the first certain reference to the Gospel is found in the Homilies. It is demonstrable that very shortly after this date the Gospel of John is found in use throughout the Christian Church, in every quarter of the Roman world, among the orthodox and among heretics, as a revered and authoritative document, the undoubted work of the Apostle, and handed down from the generation contemporaneous with him. Irenaeus, Clement, Tertullian, are among the witnesses to these unquestionable facts. Moreover, Irenaeus was in the vigor of life at the time when Strauss pretends that the Gospel first appeared. And Polycarp, to whom Irenaeus in his early youth had listened and from whom he had heard personal recollections of John himself, lived until A. D. 169 or until Irenaeus was not far from thirty years old. We say nothing of the satisfactory testimony of Justin and other earlier writers. The proposition of Strauss respecting the date of this Gospel must be maintained, if maintained at all, in reckless disregard of the evidence.

Having turned his back on the only authentic sources of knowledge, how is Strauss to compose a Life of Christ? Where is he to obtain the facts? It is obvious that no resource remains to him but to draw on his imagination. In truth, his work might better be entitled *Conjectures concerning the Life of one Jesus by a Disbeliever in the Authenticity of the Gospels and the Existence of God.* The aim is to frame a self-consistent account which shall exclude the supernatural. An evangelist is followed or discredited according to the exigencies of the moment. He is believed on one point and disbelieved on another point, when he could not be acquainted with one without knowing the other. A scrap torn from its connection in one Gospel is connected with a scrap torn in like manner from another, and the two, perhaps, are cemented by a wholly unproved conjecture. Strauss never hesitates to accept on the authority of the Gospels any fact that suits his need. There is nothing to satisfy a conscientious inquirer in this arbitrary proceeding. There is no firm footing anywhere. We are only provided with a mosaic of guess-work. There is no need of following Strauss into the details of his criticism. This has been sufficiently done in the examination of his earlier work.

In tone and spirit the second Life of Jesus, when compared with the first, gives evidence of a mournful degeneracy. In that earlier production there was an almost total lack of reverential, religious feeling. But in addition to this defect, the present work is marked by a bitter and scornful treatment of the fundamental verities of religion. In the dedication to a brother who, having been long an invalid, died before its publication, he expresses his pride and satisfaction that the sufferer had endured his pains without resort to any supernatural source of help and comfort, and that in moments when the hope of the continuance of life was extinguished, he had kept up his courage and composure, "never yielding to the temptation to deceive himself by resting on a world beyond." Stoicism is then the practical philosophy on which Strauss falls back in lieu of Christianity. The cold and barren spirit of endurance, where no design and no use are attributed to the sufferings which befall us, is the substitute for the faith and humility of the Christian. There is little danger that this blind and hard philosophy will acquire a lasting popularity. Christianity once overcame it and supplanted it; Strauss may well apprehend that the same result may follow again.

A rancorous tone, especially towards the Christian clergy, is an unpleasant feature of the present work. The author sees that Christianity remains in undiminished vigor, notwithstanding his supposed demolition of it nearly a generation ago. He is obviously soured by the disappointment, and he pours his resentment and chagrin upon the heads of the ministers, in a tone which, as he seems himself to anticipate, sounds demagogical. He despairs of overthrowing their influence until faith in miracles shall be extirpated from the minds of the people. To this class he now addresses himself, in the hope to have better success with them than he had with the scholars and teachers. No very deep reflection might suggest to Strauss that this hold of the ministers upon the hearts of the people, which he thinks to be so deplorable, would be impossible, were there not in the human soul an ineradicable sense of religion and faith in the supernatural, and he might thus be saved from cherishing too high expectations of the effect to be looked for from the influence of his books.

ESSAY VIII.

THE LEGENDARY THEORY OF RENAN.[1]

M. Renan, in the opening of his learned work on the *History of the Semitic Languages*, remarks upon the characteristic traits of the Semitic branch of the human family. He reckons among these traits an inbred attachment to monotheism. This observation illustrates at once the author's habit of incorrect, rash generalization, and the effect of his bias towards naturalism in warping his historical judgments. With the exception of the Mohammedan movement among a single people, and the religion of the Jews, all the members of the Semitic race were involved in polytheistic idolatry, and that commonly of a gross kind. Among the Arabian descendants of Abraham, the monotheistic faith of their progenitor had probably never been utterly extinguished; and as to the Jews, we know from their own records that for ages they were continually lapsing into the corrupt worship of their neighbors. Take out these people who trace their descent immediately to Abraham, and where is the monotheism of the Semitic race? Not among the Assyrians, the worshippers of Baal and Astarte and

[1] *Vie de Jésus* par Ernest Renan, membre de l'Institut. 1863.

other divinities, nor among the Babylonians, the devotees of a like idolatry, in whose foul ritual prostitution was a religious duty. Not among Syrians nor among Phoenicians or their colonists, the Carthaginians, by whom there was added to the lascivious cultus of the more eastern peoples the service of Moloch, the "horrid king," who was propitiated in the best days of Tyre and Carthage by casting children alive into the flames. In truth, the nation which, if we except the descendants of Abraham, has made the closest approach to a monotheistic religion, namely, the Persian, belongs not to the Semitic, but to our own Indo-European stock. How, then, can it be contended that the Semitic nations are naturally, by a law of race, monotheistic? The motive is obvious. The design is to suggest the inference that the pure conception of God which the Hebrew Scriptures present, was not supernaturally taught, but spontaneously generated. Evidences of a Pantheistic mode of thought are not unfrequently met with in the writings of Renan. "Two elements," he remarks in one place, "explain the universe; time and the tendency to progress."[1]

Renan's *Life of Jesus* clearly betrays the influence exerted by this naturalistic philosophy in determining

[1] See Renan's article in the *Revue des Deux Mondes* (Oct. 1863) bearing the title: Les Sciences de la Nature et les Sciences Historiques. See, also, Frothingham's Translations from Renan, entitled *Religious History and Criticism* (New York, 1864), p. xxx. seq.

the author's theory of the origin of Christianity. The comments we have to offer upon this production, which, partly in consequence of its attractive style, has had a wide circulation, will relate to four principal topics: the author's estimate of the documents which constitute the chief sources of knowledge; his treatment of the narratives of miracles in the Gospels; his methods of interpretation; and his conception of the character of the personage whom he undertakes to describe.

1. In respect to the date and authorship of the four Gospels, Renan is, on the whole, much more reasonable than most of the German unbelievers. He says of the Gospels: "all, in my judgment, date back to the first century, and they are substantially (*à peu près*) by the authors to whom they are attributed."[1] This concession is important, but the value of it is lessened by other remarks which stand in connection with it. The precise opinions of the author, it is not always easy to ascertain; for, on this topic, he frequently advances an assertion only to retract or essentially modify it in the next sentence. He confidently affirms that the title, the Gospel *according to Matthew*, and the corresponding titles of the other Gospels, originally denoted, not authorship, but rather the source whence the traditions found in the several Gospels were drawn.[2] The Manichaean Faustus is said by Augustine to have broached the same idea,

[1] *Vie de Jésus*, p. xxxvii.

[2] *Vie de Jésus*, p. xvi.

and, as far as we know, he was the first to do so. The phraseology of the titles admits of this hypothesis, but the early Fathers without exception interpret them as designating the authors, and such, in all probability, was their primitive significance.[1] Upon the authorship of the Gospel of Luke, Renan is fully satisfactory This Gospel, he says, is certainly written by the same person who wrote the Acts of the Apostles. It is "a regular composition, founded on authentic documents," and having "the most perfect unity." The author was a companion of St. Paul, was thus a man of the second apostolic generation, and wrote the Gospel "after the siege of Jerusalem, and soon after."[2] In regard to the fourth Gospel, the position of Renan is somewhat vacillating. Yet he admits that without the light derived from this Gospel, important portions of the Life of Jesus could not be understood. His conclusion, after suggesting various conflicting hypotheses, seems to be that the narrative parts of the Gospel are the work of John, and that the discourses emanate from his disciples, who modified and amplified what they had heard.[3] Renan deserves credit for his emphatic contradiction of the Tübingen theory respecting the fourth Gospel, and for his decided affirmation, which is well supported by proofs, that the Gospel had the early date which is commonly

[1] Bleek, *Einl. in das N. T.*, p. 87; De Wette, *Einl. in das N. T.* (5 A.) p. 130.

[2] *Vie de Jésus*, pp. xvi., xvii.

[3] *Vie de Jésus*, p. xxiv. seq.

assigned to it. It is plain that his misgivings in regard to the discourses in John are wholly subjective, and are incompatible with the external evidence for the genuineness of the Gospel, which he himself adduces. A great part of the discourses in John are linked inseparably with incidents in the narrative. If the discourses are given up, the narrative must share their fate. In his comments on Matthew and Mark, Renan has committed the gravest errors. He assumes that the discourses recorded in the first Gospel formed the basis of the work, to which the narrative matter was afterwards added; and, likewise, that the Gospel of Mark has been enlarged since its first composition. The collection of Discourses, he thinks, took up narrative matter from the primitive Gospel of Mark, and this Gospel in turn took up sayings of Christ from the *Discourses*. The theory is built on the foundation of the testimony of Papias, and this is done after Renan has expressly admitted that the descriptions of this Father "correspond very well to the general physiognomy" of the first two Gospels in their present form.[1] This admission is just, as we have shown in a previous Essay. If Papias *did* refer to an original collection of discourses, the basis of the first Gospel, which is very improbable, yet it has also been shown that he describes a state of things which lay in the past, and that he himself had in his hands the same Greek Matthew that is found in our Bibles. Renan has allowed himself to be misled in this par-

[1] *Vie de Jésus*, p. xix.

ticular, in consequence of overlooking the aoristic form in which the statement of Papias appears. The only other ground on which Renan would infer this mutual indebtedness of the two Gospels to one another, is the well known frequent similarity in the phraseology employed. This proves, indeed, either that one of the two was partly founded on the other, or that both drew from a common source of information, either oral or written. But either of these hypotheses is more probable than the theory proposed by Renan. At the same time, had he confined himself to the statements cited above, he would leave untouched the substantial authenticity of the first two Gospels. He only finds a part of Matthew in Mark and a part of Mark in Matthew. But he finally gives to this borrowing system a far greater latitude. Founding his statement on the remark of a single individual, Papias, concerning himself, and exaggerating the purport of that remark, he affirms that in the early Church "little importance was attached" to the written Gospels. He proceeds to say that for a hundred and fifty years the evangelical texts possessed little authority; that there was no scruple about inserting additions, combining them diversely, or completing some by others;" that the early Christians "lent these little rolls to one another: each transcribed on the margin of his copy the sayings and the parables which he found elsewhere and which touched him."[1] Now these extraordinary propositions are not only without proof, but

[1] *Vie de Jésus*, p. xxxii.

can be demonstrated to be false. The habit of citing passages inexactly and *ad sensum*, which belongs to Justin and other writers of his time, proves nothing to the purpose; for this is not peculiar to them, but belongs equally to Fathers of the next age, and Justin's quotations from the Old Testament are marked by the same kind of inaccuracy. Does Renan mean his readers to believe that down to "the latter half of the second century," Christians individually altered their copies of the Gospels *ad libitum* by interpolations of the character described? This appears to be his design. Yet conjectures of this nature have been proved to be not merely uncertified, but inconsistent with known facts.[1] The number of copies of the received Gospels in the early part of the second century must have been great. These copies were early multiplied and widely scattered over the Roman Empire, wherever Christians were found. Any essential variations in the text of either of the Gospels would inevitably have perpetuated themselves, and would appear in the later transcriptions. The essential agreement of all the manuscripts of the Gospels which are now extant, demonstrates that no changes of the character supposed by Renan could have taken place. Besides, he admits that Luke's Gospel is from a single pen, and was composed about the time of the capture of Jerusalem.[2] Why did not Luke's Gospel undergo

[1] See the argument of Norton, *Genuineness of the Gospels*, Vol. I.

[2] *Vie de Jésus*, p. xvii.

similar transformations? What protected that from the lot which befell its companions? But Renan involves himself in a labyrinth of inconsistencies on this subject, for Luke is declared to be later than Matthew and Mark, and "a compilation much more advanced."[1] And the resemblance in phraseology between the third Gospel and each of the first two presents the same problem as does the resemblance between the first and second.

Such is Renan's treatment of the question of the origin of the Gospels. Compared with the theories of the German skeptical critics, it deserves commendation. The most serious defects of it are the view taken of the discourses in John, and the notion that the Gospels, at least the first two, were long subject to arbitrary changes in their contents; a notion, however, which is incongruous with Renan's own previous concessions.

2. As concerns the history recorded in the Gospels, and especially the accounts of miraculous events, Renan adopts what may be styled the *legendary*, in distinction from the mythical, theory. These accounts were rather the transfiguration of fact, than a pure creation of pious enthusiasm. Renan is decided in affirming that at least a great part of these accounts emanate from the apostles themselves, and that acts which passed for miraculous figured largely in the life of Jesus. On this point he cannot acquit the Master

[1] *Vie de Jésus*, p. xviii.

at the cost of the disciples. He himself permitted the belief that he miraculously healed the sick and raised the dead. Renan is driven to this conclusion by his more sober view of the evangelical documents. What explanation of the testimony of the Gospels and of the extraordinary phenomena in the life of Christ, can be given? Renan replies that the Gospels are legendary narratives, like the lives of some of the mediaeval saints; and that the events in the life of Jesus which seemed miraculous, wore this character partly through the blind enthusiasm of the apostles, and partly through pious fraud in which they had an active, and their Master a consenting, agency. In defending his thesis, Renan declares that Jesus had no idea of a natural order governed by laws, and was not conscious of the distinction between the natural and the supernatural, the normal and the miraculous. The attentive reader of the Gospels will not need to be assured that this proposition is devoid of truth.[1] When Jesus says that God makes the sun to rise and the rain to fall, did he mean or does he imagine that the shining of the sun, or a shower of rain, is a miracle? Did he not know full well that the growth of the grass in the field is a totally different sort of event from the multiplying of the loaves, albeit the power of God is requisite for both? Did he not understand that his miraculous works belong in a different category from the ordinary labors of the physician? After the cure

[1] See, on this point, J. Müller's *Essay on Miracles*, p. 33. N.

of a dumb demoniac, Matthew records that "the multitudes marvelled, saying, 'It was never so seen in Israel.'" The miracles of Christ excited among the witnesses the same kind of amazement which events of a like character would occasion now.[1] Equally unfortunate is Renan's comparison of the company of Christ with St. Francis and his followers. We have already, in the review of Strauss, pointed out the mistake of transferring to the apostolic church the characteristics of the mediaeval age. The disciples of St. Francis were full of the spirit of their master; and enthusiasm that falls below absolute madness, can rise no higher than in the example of this monk. His asceticism stopped short of no austerities which the body could endure. His inward life, like his outward career, was a continual romance. His mystic fervor betrayed itself in his ordinary speech—in his apostrophes to birds and beasts and even to inanimate things. "His life," says Milman, "might seem a religious trance. Incessantly active as was his life, it was a kind of paroxysmal activity, constantly collapsing into what might seem a kind of suspended animation of the corporeal functions." As to the witnesses to the "wounds" of Christ on his person, one of them testifies to seeing the *soul* of St. Francis, after his death, in its flight through the air to heaven! And we are to believe that the author of the Sermon on the Mount and the Gospel Parables, together with

[1] See, for example, John ix. 32; Mark iv. 41.

the chosen disciples who sat at his feet, were the victims of the same sort of hallucination! But hallucination, as Renan feels and frankly allows, will not serve to explain these events in the Gospels. They were either miraculous, or there was fraud. He faces the dilemma and does not scruple to call in the aid of the *fraus pia* to account for them. The resurrection of Lazarus was a pretended resurrection, which the disciples contrived for popular effect, and in which Jesus reluctantly, but knowingly and wilfully, played his part! It is a hateful supposition; Renan himself, notwithstanding the sentimental apologies which he offers for the conduct of the parties to whom he attributes a proceeding so low and deceitful, finds his own theory ungrateful.[1] Yet he adopts it because, unable to believe in a miracle, he is fairly cornered by the evidence, and knows no other escape. There is a condition of mind in which devotional sentiment has broken from its natural alliance with conscience, and the moral sense is lost in the haze of an artificial morality, when a man may think he can serve heaven by cheating his fellow-men even in the things of religion. Pious frauds are the spawn of this terrible delusion, that one may "lie for God." But who that is not blind to the marks of simple, faithful, uncompromising rectitude, can entertain for a moment the suspicion that Jesus and his apostles were untruthful? that they sought to forward their cause by means of

[1] *Vie de Jésus*, pp. 265, 266.

disgusting frauds? The supposition is too irrational, and will find few, if any, to embrace it.

Renan's work, regarded from a scientific point of view, has the effect of an argument for the Christian faith and for the verity of the Christian miracles. For the alternative to which we are brought by his discussion is that of believing in the miracles or charging Christ and his apostles with fraud. We have either truth or gross cheating. Such is the real alternative, and Renan has unintentionally done a service to the Christian Church by impaling unbelief upon this dilemma.

3. The special criticism in Renan's work, if not sophistical like much of the criticism of Strauss, may be justly termed lawless. Starting with his unproved assumption that the canonical Gospels are legendary narratives, he seems to be governed in his beliefs and disbeliefs, in his acceptance and his rejection of their statements, by no fixed rules. This part of the narrative is accepted, and that thrown out, when frequently there is no assignable reason beyond the critic's arbitrary will. But in styling Renan's critical procedure lawless, we had chiefly in mind his exegesis of the New Testament, and in particular his interpretations of the teaching of Christ. It is often true that while these interpretations are in some degree plausible, they are unsound and false. The effect of them, not unfrequently, is to foist upon Christianity and its author doctrines which he never taught. The reader must

permit us to vindicate this judgment by some illustrations. Witness the mode in which Renan seeks to support the false assertion that the Saviour enjoined poverty and celibacy. We may first observe, however, that the most which the Roman Catholic interpreters have pretended to find in the Gospels, is a *recommendation* of these monastic virtues. They are placed by the Roman Catholic theology among the *Evangelica consilia*,—as not being commanded, not essential to salvation, but as qualities of the higher type of Christian excellence. The charge that the renunciation of property is required, as a condition of salvation, finds no support in the invitations of Christ addressed to the poor, in common with all who were in suffering, nor in the implication, which was the actual fact, that a spiritual susceptibility, not usually found in the more favored classes, belonged to them. Confronted by a fact like the discipleship of the wealthy Zaccheus, of whom no surrender of his property was required, Renan says that Christ made an exception in favor of rich men who were odious to the ruling classes! As if Jesus could think that the sin of possessing wealth was washed out when the rich man happened to be unpopular! Renan's perverse interpretation of the Saviour's rebukes of covetousness and an ungenerous temper towards the poor, he supports by appealing to the parable of the Rich Man and Lazarus. "Afterwards," he says, "this was called the parable of the 'wicked rich man.' But it is purely and simply the parable of the 'rich man.'"[1] As if the rich man were sent to a place of torment for being rich! His desire, we must infer, to return to the earth "to testify" to his five brethren, was a wish to warn them not to possess property! But what of the response of Abraham: "If they hear not Moses and the Prophets, neither will they be persuaded, though one rose from the dead!" Even Renan will not contend that the *Old* Testament considers the possession of property a sin. He would be much more apt to dilate on the earthly character of the rewards promised there to the pious. Renan derives from Matt. xix. 10–13, a law of celibacy, instead of the lawfulness of celibacy when spontaneously practised, as in the case of Paul, for the sake of greater freedom in promoting the progress of the kingdom of God,—which is the real sense of the text. He is even disposed to follow Origen in the revolting absurdity of literally construing the phraseology (Matt. xix. 12) by which the Saviour describes the condition of celibacy. In the context of this very passage, the Saviour implicitly puts honor upon marriage. It was at a wedding that he first manifested forth his glory. The married state and the family are held sacred in the gospel. Yet Renan does not hesitate to found upon the injunction to for sake father and mother, in obedience to the higher law of Christ, the charge that he required, as an indispensable condition of discipleship, the rupture of all

[1] *Vie de Jésus*, p. 175.

the ties of kindred! These preposterous interpretations are refuted by numerous places in the Gospels themselves and by the whole history of the primitive church. But these inconvenient passages it is easy for Renan to ignore or summarily cast out. Other examples of arbitrary and unfounded assertion in Renan's work are the statement that the Eucharist originated long before the Last Supper; that Judas was led to betray Christ out of jealousy of the other disciples; that John exhibits in his Gospel a feeling of rivalship towards Peter,—though Renan must have observed that Peter and John are frequently brought into conjunction in the Acts as well as in John's Gospel; that Christ had not the least idea of a soul as separate from the body,—as if he did not speak of "*both* soul *and* body," and imply the same distinction in a hundred passages besides; that Jesus, for the moment, thought of using force to prevent his arrest,—an interpretation which, if it came from anybody but a professed orientalist, would be held to indicate a singular incapacity to understand the tropical method of instruction, which was habitual with Christ, and, in this case, was employed to impress on the disciples the change in their situation, involving dangers to which they had not before been exposed. These examples of baseless criticism might be indefinitely multiplied.

4. The impossibility of forming a consistent conception of Christ, when the supernatural is rejected, is strikingly shown by the abortive essay of Renan. The

most incongruous assertions are made concerning Christ. Now he is credited with sublime attributes of intellect and heart, declared to be the greatest of the sons of men, a character of colossal proportions, and now he is charged with a vanity that is flattered with the adulation of the simple people who followed him; is accused of weakly yielding to the enthusiasm of his disciples, who were anxious that he should be reputed a miracle-worker, and is said to have given way to a gloomy resentment and to a morbid, half-insane relish for persecution and martyrdom. He is thought—this highest exemplar of mental and moral excellence, of wisdom and goodness, that has ever appeared or ever will appear on earth—to have not only cherished the wildest delusion concerning himself, his rank in the universe, and his power to revolutionize the Jewish nation, but he is also said to have declared against civil government and the family ties, and thus to have attempted a movement, most impracticable and mischievous, for the virtual disorganization and overthrow of society! Renan describes under the name of Jesus an impossible being. Although incompatible actions and traits are imputed to him without necessity, even upon the naturalistic theory, yet the prime, the insurmountable obstacle in the way of the task which Renan has undertaken, lies in the impossibility, so long as the supernatural elements of the narrative are rejected, of attributing to Jesus the excellence which undeniably belongs to him.

ESSAY IX.

THE CRITICAL AND THEOLOGICAL OPINIONS OF THEODORE PARKER.

THEODORE PARKER will be known, not as the inventor, but as a bold expositor and propagator, of new opinions. His Theology was a not very well digested compound of doctrines drawn from various and conflicting schools of Naturalism. Notwithstanding his robust intellect and his wide knowledge of books, his discriminating admirers will hardly claim that he was either an accurate scholar, or a consistent thinker.

In a review of the second edition of the Life of Jesus by Strauss, which Parker published in April, 1840,[1] he takes a tone of opposition to that writer, implies his own belief in the resurrection of Christ and in other miracles, and welcomes the partial admission of the genuineness of John which Strauss then made, but afterwards recalled. In May of the next following year, Parker delivered the noted Sermon, in which he avowed his disbelief in the Gospel miracles. Afterwards, in his *Discourse of Religion* and elsewhere, he adopts the Tübingen theories

[1] *Christian Examiner*, Volume XXVIII.

concerning the Gospels and the canon—but scarcely undertakes to support them by regular argument. His critical remarks, unconnected as they are, and resting on no independent researches, are possessed of little scientific value. Of the canonical Gospels, he says, "we must reject the fourth as of scarcely any historical value. It appears to be written more than a hundred years after the birth of Jesus, by an unknown author, who had a controversial and dogmatic purpose in view, not writing to report facts as they were; so he invents actions and doctrines to suit his aim, and ascribes them to Jesus with no authority for so doing."[1] "The Gospel ascribed to John is of small historical value, if of any at all."[2] Of Matthew, he says that "the fragmentary character of this old Gospel" is clear;[3] and of the Synoptics generally, that we know not "when they were written, by whom, or with what documentary materials of history."[4] These are the familiar propositions of Baur and his followers, and have been sufficiently examined on preceding pages of this volume. From his premises Parker deduces the proper inference that the Gospels are untrustworthy and full of errors.[5]

If this be so, what are we to believe respecting Jesus? The answers to this question are indecisive and self-contradictory. Now we are told that the

[1] *Discourse of Religion*, p. 236.
[2] *Ibid.*, p. 258.
[3] *Ibid.*, p. 237.
[4] *Ibid.*, p. 236.
[5] *Ibid.*, (e. g.) pp. 231, 339.

Gospel writers "would describe the main features of his life, and set down the great principles of his doctrine, and his most memorable sayings, such as were poured out in the highest moments of inspiration." In the same breath it is affirmed that no stress can be laid on particular events recorded in the narratives; that they are a mass of truth and error, collected about a few central facts.[1] In his practical use of the documents, Parker is not less arbitrary than his Tübingen compeers. He believes where it suits him to believe, and elsewhere the authority of the evangelists goes for nothing. For example, though he holds that the Gospel writers have egregiously erred in reporting the sayings of Jesus, and, among other things, in the application of general predictions, wishes, or hopes to specific times or events,[2] he still confidently appeals to some of these predictions, to prove the fallibility of Jesus.

There is one entire class of events which form no small part of the Gospel histories, which Parker pronounces wholly fictitious. It need not be said that we allude to the miracles. He agrees with Strauss in styling the narratives of supernatural events "mythical stories;"[3] and like Strauss he deviates from the mythical theory to make room for the diverse hypothesis of Baur. But why should Parker deny the truth of this portion of the Gospels? Unlike Baur

[1] *Discourse of Religion*, p. 233, and Note.

[2] *Ibid.*, p. 233.

[3] *Ibid.*, p. 234.

and Strauss, he professes to be a Theist, and to believe that miracles are possible. Why should he not believe them actual? Absence of competent testimony cannot be the reason, for it is plain that disbelief in the miracles is the real cause, and not the consequence, of his impeachment of the testimony. To render a satisfactory answer to this question, attention must be directed to Parker's theological principles. It will appear that the denial of miracles is part and parcel of the denial of Revelation, and that the latter springs from a failure to perceive the ground of the need of Revelation.

The fundamental point of Parker's theology is his doctrine of the absolute religion. With his eloquent paragraphs on the universality of the religious sentiment, and on the indestructible power which religion exerts over mankind, we cordially sympathize. They constitute a fine refutation of the Positivist assumption that religion is an excrescence to be lopped off in the progress of the race from childhood to maturity. But our concern now is with the doctrine about the absolute religion. Absolute religion, or religion in its pure, complete form, is sometimes described by Parker, in accordance with the Kantian definition, as obedience to the moral law regarded as the will of God,[1] and sometimes as love to man from love to God, or simply as love to God and man. Probably he would modify Kant's definition by introducing the element

[1] *Discourse of Religion*, p. 43.

of love. Religion, then, is declared to be expressed in the law enjoining love to God and love to man. The wonder is that Parker should seem to suppose that this definition is in any sense original or peculiar. There is hardly a symbol, catechism, or systematic treatise on theology, from any branch of the church, whether Latin, Lutheran, Reformed, Socinian, or Quaker, which does not set forth the same truth. The greater wonder is that Parker should suppose that Christianity, as generally understood, is superseded by this idea of religion. Christianity is a method of redemption from evil, and evil is the control acquired in the hearts of men by the principle antagonistic to this law. That is to say, Christianity is the means of salvation. To hold up the idea of the absolute religion in the midst of a world under the sway of ungodliness and selfishness, can only be compared to the conduct of one who, when the plague is raging, runs about with an excellent definition of health. Parker is naturally gratified at seeing the law in its simple form; but Paul's reply is: "the law *worketh wrath;*" "*we know* that the law is spiritual," we subscribe to all your laudation of it, "but *I* am carnal, sold under sin," "for what I would, that do I not, but what I hate, that I do;" "*who shall deliver me?*"

Thus, Parker's rejection of revealed religion (which is only the disclosure of the divine redemptive system) is logically and practically connected with his rejection of the Christian doctrine of sin. If the Bible doctrine respecting the present moral condition of mankind is false, the falsity of the Gospel is the proper corollary. But Parker's shallow apprehension of the great fact of the bondage of mankind to evil, which heathen religions as well as Christianity acknowledge, and to which not Paul alone, but earnest and discerning men in every age, have borne painful witness, is the fatal defect in his theology. He could see the outbreakings of sin in oppressive institutions and the selfish conduct of individuals, and these particular expressions of sin he denounced without stint. But he attained to no deep and large apprehension of the principle of sin, which pertains exclusively to no individual and no class of men.

The consequences of this fatal ignorance are easily traced. The attribute of holiness was almost stricken from the conception of the divine character. Justice was hardly distinguished from the personal passions of hate and revenge. Hence, the Bible representation of the character of God excited the strongest feeling of repugnance. This narrow view prevented Parker from attaining to any just appreciation of the Old Testament. He stuck in the phraseology, and was never weary of scoffing at the idea of a "jealous" or an "angry" God. But the New Testament, in its doctrine of the desert and penalty of sin, was scarcely less offensive. How Jesus, whom he professed to consider the highest embodiment of love and excellence, could be all this at the same time that he cherished these obnoxious ideas and feelings, is a problem which is left unsolved.

Though he was professedly a Theist, and though a volume of his prayers has appeared in print, Parker's theology is strongly tinctured with Pantheistic modes of thought. In the first place, his expressions in regard to the nature and origin of sin are more Pantheistic than Pauline. He speaks of sin as the tripping of a child who is learning to walk; that is, a necessary, and, if his illustration holds, an inculpable, stage in human progress. The idea that sin is a phase in the development of the soul and of the race, and is eliminated by the operation of a physical law, is only consonant with a feeble impression of the guilt of sin, and properly belongs in a system of Pantheism. The confounding of natural law with ethical law, and constitutional imperfection with moral transgression, is a mode of thought which Christianity regards with intense antipathy. Iniquity and innocent infirmity belong in totally different categories. The Pantheistic doctrine virtually calls evil good, and good evil, puts darkness for light and light for darkness, puts bitter for sweet and sweet for bitter. The free and responsible nature of man is really denied, and admitted only in words. If sin is not a voluntary apostasy from obedience to a law which commands but constrains not, the foundation of the Christian system is gone, and the superstructure must of course suffer a like fate. In the second place, Parker discusses the question of the history of religions in a Pantheistic spirit He adopts the Positivist speculation, tracing Monotheism to Polytheism, and Polytheism back to Fetichism.[1] That is, the most degraded type of religion was first. This doctrine is against history, which gives no instance of a nation spontaneously exchanging Polytheism for Monotheism. Polytheism may generate skepticism, as in Greece, but does not lift itself to a better faith. Heathenism generally brutifies and degrades humanity. But the hypothesis of such an upward progress is consistent with the general theory that the mutations of religion obey a natural law of progress, and that religion is one effect of civilization, so that in the infancy of mankind heathenism, and the lower forms of it, necessarily prevailed. In the third place, when Parker comes to define his conception of God, he differs little from Spinoza. There is no definite ascription to God, of the distinctive elements of personality, self-consciousness and self-determination. "We talk of a personal God. If thereby we deny that He has the limitations of unconscious matter, no wrong is done." "God must contain in Himself, potentially, the ground of consciousness, of personality—yes, of unconsciousness and impersonality." "All mental processes like those of men are separated from the idea of Him."[2] His language implies not creation, but emanation—a development

[1] *Discourse of Religion*, Chapter V.

[2] *Ibid.*, pp. 152, 153, 158.

of the world out of a prior potential existence. Parker's doctrine appears to come to this, that God is the infinite essence of which matter and spirit are the divine manifestations. He does not express himself with philosophical precision or strict consistency. But this appears to be the prevailing representation at the bottom of his remarks. It is the proposition of Spinoza. In fact, from Spinoza and Schleiermacher the principal ideas of Parker on this subject appear to have been learned.

It is true that in other places in the writings of Parker, expressions hardly consistent with that representation, and decidedly theistic in their purport, may be met with. But this is just the characteristic of his position—an uneasy equilibrium between the two systems. Had Parker been thorough in his theism, he would have attained to profounder views on the subject of sin, and might have advanced to the proper corollary, the need of supernatural redemption. Had he been thoroughly logical in his Pantheism, other elements in his system, especially his practical dealing with the evils of the day, would have been sensibly modified. As it was, he walked in neither path with firmness and consistency; and therefore, though his popular influence was large, he will leave no durable mark on scientific theology.

It would not be difficult to show that generous ideas of philanthropy have no stable foundation except in the Christian doctrine respecting man and human sin. Theories of the origin of heathenism and of the origin of evil, such as are broached by Parker, have a close affinity with the philosophy which treats portions of our race as semi-human, or at least hopelessly degraded. Slavery and other sorts of barbarity seek in this philosophy their theoretical support. But let the doctrine of Paul that paganism is the fruit of a fall and degeneracy be held; let his solemn arraignment of the human family in the opening of the Epistle to the Romans be heartily subscribed, and the connected principle that "God has made of one blood all men" will not be given up. Only in the pure atmosphere of Christian theism, can the law of human brotherhood take root and flourish.

ESSAY X.

IN EXAMINATION OF BAUR AND STRAUSS ON THE CONVERSION OF THE APOSTLE PAUL.[1]

When we speak of the conversion of the Apostle Paul, we mean not only the adoption by him of new religious tenets which he had before denied, but likewise the moral revolution in his tempers of feeling and principles of action. We refer to that great transformation which rendered him "a new creature." He was convinced that the crucified Jesus of Nazareth was in truth the Messiah; but his conversion also induced and included a new moral spirit and an all-absorbing consecration to the cause which he had previously hated. This entire change Naturalism attributes exclusively to the operation of physical and psychological laws.

The theory propounded by Baur in his *Life of the Apostle Paul* is reiterated with some variations in the last *Life of Jesus* by Strauss.[2] A zealot for the Phar-

[1] Lord Lyttelton's little work on the *Conversion of St. Paul* is a sound argument. It is largely taken up, however, with proving that Paul was no impostor; and the remarks to show that he was not an enthusiast, though judicious, are not adapted to meet the more recent skeptical theories.

[2] *Leben Jesu für d. deutsche Volk*, p. 33.

isaic type of religion, Paul was irritated and alarmed at the progress of a sect which held the ceremonies of the law to be of subordinate consequence, and pretended that their crucified Master was the promised King of Israel. His vehement spirit impelled him to active measures of persecution. Yet the nobler feelings of his nature could not fail to be touched by the demeanor of the dying Stephen; nor could he wholly suppress the misgivings which the unfaltering testimony of the disciples to the resurrection of Jesus stirred up in his breast. To him, a Pharisee, it was no impossible event; and if it were true, the difficulty occasioned by the ignominious death of Christ was removed or alleviated. In this divided state of feeling, when the will was maintaining a half-conscious struggle with the better impulses which rose against his present determination and his life-long convictions, and his soul was agitated with contending forces, he seemed to himself to behold in a vision Jesus rebuking him for the conduct for which he had begun to rebuke himself. Perhaps he was struck by lightning while on an errand of persecution; and this circumstance, together with the physical effects that followed, may have been the immediate occasion of the imaginary vision. Strauss argues that an infirmity of the nervous system probably belonged to Paul and partly accounts for remarkable experiences which he attributed to a supernatural cause. Baur, especially in his earlier discussion of the subject, dilates upon the tendency of the mind to pass from one extreme to the opposite. The more ardently and thoroughly a man enters into an erroneous system, the more likely he is, we are told, to be awakened to the falsehood of his position. In proportion to the intensity of his zeal is the force of the self-induced reaction.

To the credit of Baur it must be added that afterwards he appears to have become dissatisfied with his own solution. In the last edition which he prepared, of his *History of Christianity in the First Three Centuries,* he says that "neither psychological nor dialectical analysis can explore the mystery of the act in which God revealed to him his Son." He even says that in the conversion of Paul, "in his sudden transformation from the most vehement adversary into the most resolute herald of Christianity, we can see nothing short of a miracle (wunder)."[1] And the same word he soon after applies again to the same event. If we are not at liberty to suppose that Baur admits in this case a strictly supernatural agency—an admission which would fundamentally alter his whole theological system—yet it is something to find him willing to use the obnoxious word, and to acknowledge the impossibility of accounting for the conversion of Paul. Baur explains that, however mysterious the transaction was, the turning-point in the great change which took place in the mind of Paul was a new view of the death of Jesus. He came to understand that his death

[1] Baur, *das Christenthum*, etc. (2 A.) p. 45.

might be the transition to a more exalted life. With this new view, his prejudice against a *crucified* Messiah vanished, but with it his Jewish *particularism* disappeared also; since the Christ in the heavens was raised above the narrow Jewish conception of the Messiah, and their exclusive, carnal theory of his office and relation to men fell to the ground. What portion of truth is contained in these interesting suggestions we shall inquire in the course of the remarks which follow.

1. It is important to notice the testimony of the authorities and to compare the statements of Strauss and Baur with that. The conversion of Paul is three times circumstantially related in the book of Acts, once by Luke himself (c. ix.), and twice by the Apostle—the first time, in his address to his countrymen at Jerusalem (c. xxii.), and again in his speech before Agrippa (c. xxvi.) The variations in these three narratives relate to slight matters of detail, and are unimportant. Yet Strauss, as might be expected, expends upon them his trivial criticism. Paul was journeying towards Damascus for the purpose of seizing Christian men or women whom he might find there, and dragging them to Jerusalem. Suddenly a bright and dazzling light shone down upon him and his attendants. The whole company were filled with consternation. But the "trembling and astonished" Paul distinctly heard the words that were addressed to him. Then followed his blindness and his conjunction with Ananias at

Damascus, each having been supernaturally guided to the other. The skeptical critics do not scruple to avail themselves of any circumstances from Luke which fit into their scheme. Thus, the presence of Paul at the murder of Stephen is a fact of which Luke is the only witness. Strauss even supposes an effect on Paul from disputations with Christians, while the only evidence he offers that such disputation took place is Acts ix. 29, where Paul's disputing with the Jews after his conversion is alone mentioned. In the Acts we have the testimony of one who had been for a time associated with Paul, and who had resorted for his information (see Luke i. 5) to the authentic sources. But we cannot here enter into the question of the credibility of Luke, which, as we believe, has been fully vindicated in a previous Essay. Happily we have the testimony of the Apostle himself, in his undoubted Epistles, to several of the main facts, if not to the special circumstances, of his conversion. He tells us that prior to that event he had "beyond measure persecuted the church of God and wasted it" (Gal. i. 13). He says that he deserves not to be called an apostle, because he had "persecuted the church of God" (1 Cor. xv. 9). He had made himself famous among the churches of Judea as a persecutor (Gal. i. 22, 23). He had outrun the Jews about him in his fanatical zeal (Gal. i. 14.) He was unquestionably a furious enemy of the disciples and their cause. A Pharisee, he had entered with all his heart into the measures of his party for exterminating the infant Church. Moreover, it is undeniable from his own statements in the Epistles that his conversion was sudden. It was the result, as he declares, of a revelation of Jesus Christ to him. And when he connects with his claim to be an apostle the declaration that he too had seen Christ (1 Cor. ix. 1), it is rendered in a high degree probable that his conversion was one of the occasions when this occurred. The most of what has just been said, the skeptical critics allow. They generally concede that Paul's conversion resulted from a vision in which he supposed himself to behold Christ. They would only resolve this vision into a mere subjective impression, the product of intense mental excitement.

2. The skeptical theory assumes without evidence and against the evidence, that the mind of Paul before his conversion was deeply exercised with misgivings as to the rectitude of his course. The naturalistic solution requires the supposition that an inward tumult and conflict of this sort prevailed in his soul. This hypothesis not only lacks support, but is positively excluded by the proofs. It is founded on the words of Christ, in Acts xxvi. 14—the same passage in Acts ix. 5 is interpolated—"it is hard for thee to kick against the pricks." The "pricks" are the goad with which the ploughman from behind urged forward the oxen. The phrase was a proverbial one, and is thus correctly explained by Dr. Hackett: "the meaning is, that his opposition to the cause and will of Christ must be un-

availing; the continuance of it would only bring injury and ruin on himself."[1] The illustrative passages from Wetstein establish this interpretation. There is no implication that the Apostle was struggling against conscientious impulses: the opposite rather is indicated. He was engaged in a resolute, pertinacious, but ineffectual endeavor to stop the progress of the Christian cause. When we turn to Paul's own words we find satisfactory evidence that he was disturbed by no misgivings, but was wholly absorbed in the work of persecution. He had been, he says, a blasphemer and persecutor, but found mercy because he "did it ignorantly, in unbelief."[2] He says again: "*I verily thought with myself* that I ought to do many things contrary to the name of Jesus of Nazareth."[3] He was sincere and perfectly confident that he was striking at a heresy. When he "made havoc of the church," entering into private houses and hurrying to prison women as well as men, and when he left Jerusalem to hunt down the fugitive disciples in other cities, he had no doubt that he was performing an acceptable service to God. The idea that he rushed into extreme measures of cruelty to drown the rebuke of conscience is pure fancy. Everything shows that it was the depth and ardor of his conviction that stimulated him to outdo his Pharisaic brethren in his exertions to crush

[1] Hackett, *Commentary on the Acts*, p. 402. See, also, Meyer and De Wette, on Acts xxvi. 14.

[2] 1 Tim. i. 13. Acts xxvi. 9.

the new heresy. The foundation of the skeptical solution of the problem of his conversion is therefore taken away.

3. Baur's conjectural explanation of the change in the religious ideas of Paul is essentially defective. The earlier notion that great zeal in a bad cause naturally leads the subject of it to reverse his course, will obtain little applause. We do not find that Torquemada was converted to Protestantism and to gentleness by the excess of his own cruelty in managing the Spanish inquisition. Nor will it avail to answer that Paul was of a milder and more generous nature. . As Neander has remarked, there were among those who beheld the burning of Huss many good men who saw in the spectacle nothing but the just punishment of a contumacious and mischievous heretic. There is no ground for supposing that the death of Stephen made a different impression on Paul.

Baur is right in holding that the conversion of Paul from narrow Pharisaism to the broadest Christianity, however that conversion may have begun, involved a process. It was a rational change of principles and views. He attained to a new conception of the nature of religion, as not consisting in the punctilious observance of ceremonies, nor ultimately in any works of legal obedience, but in faith which worketh by love. Unquestionably he saw, as Baur affirms, a meaning and use in the death of the Messiah, which rendered that event no longer repugnant but grateful to his feelings. The proximate cause of this change, however, was the awakening of a sense of sin and a conviction of the utter inadequacy, from a legal point of view, of that obedience which he had been able to render. His feeling respecting the death of Christ was the correlate of his consciousness of sin and of the helpless condition into which sin had brought him. But all this peculiar experience, as far as we are able to ascertain, was posterior to that revelation of Jesus as the Messiah, which first broke up his feeling of self-satisfaction. Reflection upon the death of Jesus, as long as Paul was imprisoned in his Pharisaic conception of the Messiah, could only serve to confirm him in his opposition to the Christian cause. That Jesus had suffered death was of itself sufficient proof that his pretensions were false and his followers heretics and apostates. Not until Paul was convinced of the reality of the resurrection of Jesus, could he put faith in his claims and become reconciled to the fact of his death. This is allowed by Strauss; and now the question is, how Paul became convinced that Jesus had really risen from the grave. Strauss conjectures that Paul was overcome by the testimony of the disciples, the event to which they bore witness being one which he, as a Pharisee, must admit to be possible. But Strauss ignores the essential circumstance that the whole career of Jesus, terminating as it did in the crucifixion, constituted in the judgment of Paul an overwhelming presumption against the probability of his resurrection and against the credibility of his disciples' testimony. Moreover, it is clear from the Apostle's own language that it was not the weight of human testimony, in the first instance, that caused him to believe, but a supernatural revelation, or something which he supposed to be this. There is not a shadow of proof that he had begun to consider with himself whether the testimony of the disciples might not be true. On the contrary, he thoroughly disbelieved it, and, inspired with the fanatical hatred of an inquisitor, he was eager to exterminate the new sect. The naturalistic criticism in vain casts about for some explanation of this sudden, total revolution of opinion which was attended by a revolution equally signal in character and conduct.

4. There is no proof that the revelation of Christ, which caused the conversion of Paul, was a vision; and if it were, there is no explanation of it save on the supposition of its reality.

In a vision, through a powerful impression made on the mind there is a real or supposed direct perception of objects not presented to the senses. Were the event which changed the career of Paul shown to be a vision, not a step would be taken towards proving it an illusion. For the skeptical criticism will not be permitted to assume that the human mind cannot be supernaturally acted upon, and that the visions recorded in the Bible are the product of an excitement having its origin exclusively in the mind itself. It has been shown already that this criticism has wholly failed to point out any psychological preparation in Paul for such a deceitful exercise of imagination. A vision, even though it be unreal, cannot spring from nothing. Little is gained, therefore, were we to concede that Paul's first conviction of the resurrection of Jesus was through a vision.

But even this concession there is no warrant for making. It is true that Paul at various times in his life, after his conversion, had visions, as he himself relates. But it is also true that he makes no mention of his conversion as one of these, since the vision to which he refers in 2 Cor. xii. 1–4 occurred fourteen years prior to the time of his writing, whereas his conversion was at least twenty years before the date of the Epistle. Nor is there reason to think that Paul could not distinguish between the phenomena of a vision and an affection of the outward senses.[1] We find this distinction explicitly made by Luke in Acts xii. 9, where it is represented that Peter who had followed the angel out of the prison was in such perturbation of mind that he "wist not that it was true which was done by the angel, but thought he saw a vision (ὅραμα)." That which was "true" (ἀληθές), or actual, is expressly discriminated from the vision, or subjective impression. Peter knew not for the instant whether his liberation had been supernaturally represented to his mind with the vividness of reality, or

[1] For valuable remarks on this topic, see Beyschlag's Article, *Die Bekehrung des Apostels Paulus*, Studien u. Kritiken, 1864. 2.

whether he had been actually set free. There is no warrant for supposing that the strong understanding of Paul did not make the same distinction between vision and external fact. And when he says that he, as well as the other apostles, had seen Jesus, and connects his apostleship with this circumstance (1 Cor. ix.), we properly conclude that he refers to something besides a purely spiritual, inward perception, or such a perception as a vision could vouchsafe. Peter had seen Jesus in his bodily presence, and Paul puts himself in this regard on a level with Peter.[1] And the objective reality of this transaction on the road to Damascus can be disproved only by discrediting the thrice-repeated narrative in the Acts.

[1] Beyschlag shows that the argument of Paul for the resurrection of believers (1 Cor. xv.), which is founded on the resurrection of Jesus, implies a perception of Christ in his bodily presence. A sense of the presence of Christ, however vivid it might be, which did not exhibit him *in the body*, could not constitute a basis for this argument.

ESSAY XI.

THE NATURE AND FUNCTION OF THE CHRISTIAN MIRACLES.

THERE are those who find it hard to believe in a miracle, because the word is associated in their minds with the notion of a capricious act, or of a makeshift to meet an unexpected exigency. They conceive of a miracle not as an event planned and fitting into an established order, but as done in obedience to a sudden prompting, as a kind of desperate expedient to prevent the consequences of a previous neglect or want of forecast. Such an act, they properly feel, cannot be attributed to God. Anxious to remove the prejudice just described, another class of writers set up definitions of a miracle which destroy the distinction between a miracle and an event occurring in the course of Nature. In flying from one error, they plunge into another lying opposite. The mistake in the conception which they would correct can be exposed without confounding a miracle with a natural event, or stripping the former of the distinguishing attributes that constitute its value as a proof of divine revelation. A miracle belongs in a wholly different category from natural events; yet it forms no element of discord, is due to no mistake in the structure of the world, which requires to be remedied, and it conspires with natural events to produce harmony in the whole system.

In this Essay we shall make the attempt to define the nature, and determine the appropriate and appointed use, of miracles. Objections and errors of recent origin call for a fresh discussion of this important subject. And if the path of our inquiry leads in part through a field not unfamiliar; yet more precise conceptions of accepted truth are sometimes of hardly less value than new discoveries. For the sake of greater clearness, the remarks that follow will be arranged under a series of special topics.

WHAT IS THE IDEA OF A MIRACLE?

In answering this question we reject at the outset what the Germans call *the relative nature* of the miracle, or the notion that the miraculous quality of such an event is merely relative to human feeling and apprehension. This definition does not go beyond the etymology of the term. But an event which excites wonder in an extraordinary degree is not thereby constituted a miracle. The authority of Augustine has often been pleaded in favor of this faulty definition. He says that a miracle is not contrary to Nature, but only to that Nature which is known to us. The ordinary operations of Nature, he says, were they unfamiliar, would excite not less amazement, and are in reality not less wonderful, than miracles. But in

Augustine's view, which results from his anti-manichæan philosophy, *all* the operations of Nature are immediate exertions of the Divine will. In this respect, therefore, he can place miracles in the same category with the every-day operations of Nature, while he holds, at the same time, that the miracle, when regarded from another point of view, is an altogether exceptional event.[1] Spinoza, identifying God with Nature, is consistent in denying that any distinctive characteristic of an objective kind belongs to a miracle. This term, he says, has respect only to the opinions entertained by men, and signifies no more than this, that we, or at all events they who narrate the occurrence in question, are unable to explain it by the analogy of any other event familiar to experience. On Spinoza's scheme, a miracle in the proper sense is a complete absurdity.[2] Schleiermacher, never wholly able to es-

[1] Augustine, *De Civ. Dei*, xxi. 8, 2. Omnia quippe portenta contra Naturam dicimus esse : sed non sunt. Quomodo est enim contra Naturam, quod Dei fit voluntate, cum voluntas tanti utique Conditoris conditæ rei cujusque natura est? The will of God—the *voluntas* of the Creator—*is* Nature.

[2] Spinoza devotes c. vi. of the Tract. Theolog-Polit. to the subject of miracles; and further considers the subject in his Letters—Epist. xxi. and xxiii. He says (in the chapter above referred to): "Ex his —sequitur, nomen miraculi non nisi respective ad hominum opiniones posse intelligi, et nihil aliud significare, quam opus, cujus causam naturalem exemplo alterius rei solitæ explicare non possumus, vel saltem ipse non potest, qui miraculum scribit aut narrat." With Spinoza *leges naturales* are one and the same with *Dei natura*. See the context of the passage.

cape from the atmosphere of Pantheism, comes no nearer the true idea, when he says that any event, even the most natural, may be styled a miracle, provided the religious view of its origin is spontaneously awakened in the mind, with a forgetfulness of the proximate natural causes.[1] The relative notion of the

[1] Wunder ist nur der religiöse Name fur Begebenheit: jede, auch die allernatürlichste, sobald sie sich dazu eignet, dass die religiöse Ansicht von ihr die herrschende sein kann, ist ein Wunder. Mir ist alles Wunder, &c. Reden (6 A.) s. 106. See, also, N. 16, s. 145. Schleiermacher's views are more fully set forth in his System of Theology—the *Glaubenslehre*—§ 14 Zusatz, § 34, 2, 3, and § 47. Though not rejecting the New Testament miracles, as historical occurrences, he still professes his agreement with those who hold "dass Gott die Wunder auf eine uns unbegreifliche Art in der Natur selbst vorbereitet gehabt." B. I. s. 240. But his reasoning to prove that a divine act must be performed through the system of Nature and be provided for in that system, is unsound and of a Pantheistic tendency.

Schleiermacher has again discussed the subject of miracles in his Lectures upon the Life of Jesus, published lately for the first time. He has taken, however, no new positions. In his endeavor to refer the miracles of Jesus to energies belonging to Nature, he is perplexed by the control which Christ exercised over inanimate existence, as in stilling the tempest, multiplying the loaves of bread, and raising the dead. (See p. 223.) Such events, he perceives, can be attributed to no mysterious natural energy, which is supposed to have enabled him to produce extraordinary effects—for example, in healing—in contact with living men. Yet the miracles of the class mentioned above are *historically* as well attested as any of the rest. This fact Schleiermacher is constrained to allow, and hence finds it impossible to extricate himself from the difficulty into which he is thrown, and which is due to the false assumption as to the *relative* nature of the miracle, with which he sets out.

A view homogeneous with that of Schleiermacher has been at-

miracle fails to separate it objectively and really from a natural event—an event occurring by natural law. Neither the degree of astonishment with which events are regarded, nor the question whether they can be referred to a previously ascertained law, nor, again, the question whether they are attributed spontaneously to the power of God, forms the defining characteristic of a miraculous occurrence. An attentive observation of the *common* phenomena of Nature, as Augustine and after him Luther and many others have forcibly pointed out, may well kindle wonder, and in a reli-

tributed to Stanley on the foundation of passages in his work on the Old Testament History, and is styled the *providential* theory. (See Frances Power Cobbe, *Broken Lights*, p. 31). Events recorded in Scripture are said to be neither strictly natural nor strictly supernatural, but specially providential. They are such as to suggest impressively the agency of God, and are related to each other as parts of a great, consistent plan. This theory seems not to differ essentially from that of Schleiermacher. Whether it be justly ascribed to Stanley's interpretation of the Old Testament History, we do not assume to determine.

That the miracles of Christ could not have been performed by any power embosomed in Nature—as, for example, by an energy belonging naturally to preëminent human virtue—would seem to be an obvious truth. Yet a recent writer (Furness, *Veil partly Lifted*, p. 216) takes this position, even respecting the resurrection of Jesus. Aside from the tremendous difficulty of supposing such anomalous events, as the miracles recorded in the Bible, to be due to any power latent in human nature, we are cut off from that supposition by the testimony of Christ himself, and are obliged to refer them to a supernatural author. It is true respecting some, though not respecting the writer last referred to, that this theory springs from a reluctance to admit the agency of a living, personal God.

gious mind will carry up the thoughts to God. But such phenomena are not, on this account, to be deemed miraculous.[1]

In defining a miracle we pledge ourselves to no particular theory concerning the constitution of Nature. If the new doctrine of the persistency of force—the correlation of forces, Mr. Grove calls it—should be established; if all the phenomena of matter should be found to be due to varieties of motion—to be varied manifestations of one essence; our present discussion would not be sensibly affected. If occasionalism be adopted as the true philosophy; if it be maintained that the operations of Nature proceed immediately from the volitions of God, the efficiency of second causes being denied, or even that the phenomena of Nature are indistinguishable from these volitions, what we have to say, would, with some verbal modifications, hold good. For occasionalism does not question the reality of the *facts* of Nature; nor does it scruple to admit the sequences of Nature, the system in which these facts conjoin. We proceed, however, upon the position which is commonly taken by theists, that secondary causes are real—that matter is an entity manifesting forces, though requiring the direct sustenance and co-working of the power of God. The

[1] For good remarks on the relative notion of a miracle, see the valuable Essay of Julius Müller on the subject of Miracles, to which we shall again refer, c. iv. Relativa quam vocant miraculi notio examinatur.

forces resident in Nature subsist and act, but they subsist and act, not without the Divine preservation—the *concursus Dei*.

A miracle is an event which the forces of Nature, or secondary causes, operating thus under the ordinary Divine preservation, are incompetent to produce.[1] Secondary causes may be concerned in the production of a miracle. For a miracle (except in the case of creation *de nihilo*) is wrought in Nature, or in the realm of second causes; but these are insufficient to explain it. It is an event which only the intervention of the First Cause is adequate to produce. Beyond the constant upholding of Nature in the normal exercise of its powers, there has been an interposition of God to effect that which otherwise could not have taken place. Pascal has exactly hit the true nature of a miracle, when he terms it a result exceeding the natural force of the means employed. If the axe floats on the water, some power is exerted above the powers of Nature. They, if left to themselves, would necessarily carry it to the bottom.

[1] In this definition we use the term *Nature* as a synonym for the sum of second causes, or the creation in distinction from God. If the term be taken less comprehensively, as embracing only man and the material universe, or that portion of the material universe of which he has any knowledge, then in order to differentiate a miracle from *other* supernatural events—events, for example, which it may be thought possible for superhuman, created intelligences to bring to pass—we must add another element to the definition and *explicitly* connect the miracle with a volition of God.

IS A MIRACLE TO BE CONSIDERED A SUSPENSION OR VIOLATION OF NATURAL LAW?

More commonly this question has been answered in the affirmative. Yet the point is one on which theologians are not yet agreed. For example, Dr. N. W. Taylor, whose discussion of the general subject is marked by his wonted acuteness, styles a miracle a "deviation" from some law of Nature, and appears, also, to sanction the statement that miracles may involve a violation of natural law.[1] On the contrary, Dr. Julius Müller considers the statement improper and unfounded.[2]

The difference is really due to the different mode in which the phrase, "law of Nature," is defined by the parties respectively. Dr. Taylor means by a law of Nature "that established course, or order, of things or events, which depends solely on the constitution, properties, or nature of any created thing, and which admits of no deviation by any created power." The stated connection between a given event and a certain set of physical antecedents, which that event is observed invariably to follow, is taken as the idea of a law of Nature. Under this conception, a miracle is properly said to involve a counteraction, or suspension, or violation of natural law; for in the case of the miracle the presence of a given set of physical antecedents is not followed by the usual event. When a

[1] See Dr. Taylor's *Moral Government*, Vol. II. pp. 388, 390.

[2] Müller's *Essay on Miracles*, Caput III.

leper is healed, as the effect of a word uttered by a human voice, the connection usually observed to subsist between physical antecedent and consequent, is dissolved. If the law of Nature be this stated connection, then of course the natural law is suspended or violated.

But there is another and more exact meaning to be given to natural law, which does not involve this consequence. What is natural law but the method in which a force or energy is observed to operate? The laws of Nature are the method of the operation of the forces which inhere in Nature. Such laws are not a norm for an energy that is outside of Nature, or is imported from without. We need not affirm—we are not authorized to affirm—that a miracle involves a change in the constitution of matter or mind, or in the law under which they act. And if it *did* involve such change—so that matter, for example, were transformed into something different from matter—even then the miraculous event would be no violation of the laws of *matter*, since matter, by the supposition, has ceased to exist, and has been displaced by a substance endowed with diverse properties. Suppose the axe to float miraculously upon the water. There is here no violation of the laws of Nature. For the extraordinary event is not due to the abnormal action of the energies that belong either to the water or to the iron; but is owing rather to the introduction of a new and extrinsic cause which operates according to a law of its own.

There is no more violation of natural law than if the axe were upheld upon the water by the human hand. The effect which a given antecedent, or sum of antecedents, would otherwise produee, may be counteracted by the presence of other forces which are also natural. This is done whenever a stone is thrown into the air, or water raised by a pump, or lightning diverted from a building by an iron rod. In these cases there is not, as we conceive, any violation of natural laws. For the law of gravitation is *not properly stated* when it is made to involve the bringing to the earth of a stone in those circumstances under which we observe the stone to rise; and the same is true of the other examples of a supposed infringement of natural law. So the resurrection to life of a man who has once died is an effect which the natural causes connected with the event could not have produced, but, acting by themselves, must have excluded. But this change of event is not to be ascribed to an alteration of the norm under which they act, but wholly to the introduction in connection with them of a new and supernatural cause. The effcct which the physical antecedents, if *left to themselves,* would have produced, is set aside—in consequence, however, of an added antecedent, the Divine power supernaturally exerted.

We conclude, therefore, that a miracle, strictly speaking, is neither a suspension nor a violation of natural laws, but rather an event which *would be* this, were it not for the fact that with the physical antecedents there has been associated a supernatural agency.

The English writer who deserves credit for clearly refuting the idea that a miracle suspends or violates the laws of Nature, is the Scottish philosopher, Brown.[1] However he may err in unwarrantably extending the sense of the term *Nature* (a point on which Dr. Taylor animadverts), and however defective may be his general theory of causation, his observations on the particular topic before us appear to be conclusive.

IS A MIRACLE CONTRARY TO EXPERIENCE?

Here, likewise, attention is required to the meaning of terms. If experience be a synonym for the course of things as deduced from observation, then a miracle *is* contrary to experience. If we are told that a leper is cured by a word from human lips, we are told of an event which is contrary to experience—that is, inconsistent with what has heretofore been observed to follow upon the same natural antecedents. If we submit the case to experiment and reiterate the trial, using the utmost scientific caution in applying the test, no such event is observed to follow.

But if the opposition to experience that is predicated of a miracle be understood to involve the idea that in asserting a miracle we ascribe to the same set of causes an event different from that which they have

[1] Brown's *Inquiry into the Relations of Cause and Effect.* Appendix, Note E.

always been observed to produce, then a miracle is *not* contrary to experience. For a miracle, we repeat, implies no contradiction to the maxim that the same effect is to be expected to follow the same causes. A miracle is, by the supposition, an event resulting from the association of a new cause with a given set of physical antecedents. It is true that (save in the cases, the reality of which is under discussion) we have no experience of this association of the supernatural agency with the physical antecedents. But this last fact is better expressed by the statement that a miracle is *above* or *beyond* experience—transcends experience—than by the statement that it clashes with experience. That a miracle should occur when the power of God is specially exerted in connection with physical agencies, does not clash with experience.

THE POSSIBILITY OF MIRACLES.

The possibility of a miracle is the next topic to be considered. Is it necessary to argue this point before a believer in God? Is *omnipotence* incompetent to produce events that outreach the capacity of created Nature? Has He who gave existence to second causes, exhausted His resources of power in the act of producing and sustaining them? Was not the production of these causes itself a stupendous miracle?

There is nothing in our knowledge of the constitution of matter, and of the internal processes of Nature, of which only the phenomena are presented to our observation, to afford the shadow of a support to the presumptuous proposition that events like the recorded miracles of the Bible are inherently impossible to be effected. How in the regular course of nature the handful of grain multiplies itself in the harvest which springs from it, is an insoluble problem. It is an inexplicable fact which, after the closest observation of the successive phenomena attending the change, we still find to be a mystery. That the five loaves should be multiplied by an agency both different from that of Nature and superior, so as to furnish food for five thousand, is another mystery, but a fact which none but the atheist can consistently declare impossible. A man who would otherwise sink in death is restored to health by a medicinal agent administered by a physician's hand. We can only point out the visible antecedents of the effect. How they do their work in the hidden laboratory of Nature, we cannot go far in explaining. We cannot pierce through the veil that hides the interior process from our eyes. In this respect, we believe where we cannot see or explain. But if it be asserted that the invalid can be restored in a briefer time and by the exertion of a power different from any remedial agent in the natural world—say, by the direct volition of God—who is bold enough to affirm, who has the slightest ground for affirming, that the thing is impossible?

That a miracle is possible is a proposition commended to credence by the survey of the actual phenomena of Nature in its various kingdoms. We see that higher forces so far control the action of lower that the latter cease to produce the effects which would result from their exclusive activity. Mechanical forces are subordinated to chemical attraction. Inorganic nature is subjected to the operation of vital forces. Vegetable and animal existences are endued with powers which are, so to speak, superior to the forces of unorganized matter. The force of gravitation, for example, gives way, or is apparently overborne, by a heterogeneous and superior agency. If we could suppose ourselves divested of all knowledge of organic Nature, we should then have the same right, no less and no more, to deny, on account of the force of gravitation, the possibility of the upward growth of a tree, as the skeptic has now to deny the possibility of a miracle. The former event would be not less foreign to experience, not less unprovided for in the existences which we had beheld, and in the causes whose operation we had observed, than is the instantaneous cure of blindness by a volition, or the raising of a dead man to life. Nature is the spectacle of realm above realm, where the subordinate order is taken up and embraced within the superior. Ascending from one grade to another, we meet with new and diverse phenomena, and with a seeming reversal of the laws which operate on the plane below. This change is due, however, to the incoming and modifying agency of a new and heterogeneous class of causes.

Still more suggestive is the relation of the intelligent will of man to the forces of the unintelligent creation. Here, within the domain of Nature, effects are produced analogous to the miracle. The will in relation to the matter with which it is connected and over which it has power, is a heterogeneous and supernatural cause. The changes in matter which it produces take place, to be sure, in agreement with the laws of matter, yet they are changes and effects which originated not in the sphere of matter, but in a motor outside and above material forces. A gesture of the hand is the result of a train of causes—as the action of the brain, the nerve, the muscle—a train, however, which begins in a volition. It is true, there is no analogy, as far as we can judge, between the influence of the will upon existences exterior to it, and the exertion of *creative* power. The will, in its action on matter, can modify that which already existed, but cannot call into being what is not. Here the limits of human power are reached. A miracle that involves creative power has no parallel, as far as we can judge, with any possible exertion of man's voluntary agency. But with this exception, the control of the human will over matter bears a striking resemblance to the more potent operation of the Divine will, and exhibits impressively the possibility of such a miraculous operation.

THE PROBABILITY OF MIRACLES: THE PRESUMPTION ADVERSE TO THE OCCURRENCE OF MIRACLES.

That a miraculous event, looked at by itself, is improbable, needs no proof. The incredulity which the report of such an event awakens in an educated mind, implies an anterior presumption opposed to its occurrence. There are some defenders of Christianity who are inclined to put a miracle, in regard to the proof required to establish it, on the same footing with an ordinary event. They take, as we conceive, an untenable position, and one that is likely to harm more than it helps their cause. It is freely admitted that a presumption lies against the occurrence of a miracle. But before we can measure the strength of this presumptive disbelief, we must inquire into the sources of it.

This presumption is founded in our belief in the uniformity of Nature. But what is the nature and ground of this belief?

It is not, as some philosophers have held, an instinctive faith that things will continue to be as they are—that the future will reproduce the present.[1] For our belief in the uniformity of Nature points backward, as well as forward. It relates to what has occurred in the past, not less than to what is expected to occur hereafter. Moreover, the supposed axiom is

[1] Just objections to this form of statement are presented by J. S. Mill, in his *Logic*.

inexact in leaving room for the assumption of a *kind* of sameness in the recurrence of physical phenomena, which experience disproves. For example, the climate of our latitude has not always been what it is now; nor is it now what it will be hereafter. The globe and the whole physical universe, by the mere operation of physical causes, have undergone vast and various changes. New and before unobserved phenomena have sprung into being. The saying, that things will be what they are or have been, describes no original belief of the mind, or is, at best, a vague and inaccurate statement of any such belief.

The presumptive disbelief of the educated mind in miracles is founded in our conviction that there is *a system of Nature.* Scientific investigation has inspired a belief in the sway of general laws, as opposed to preternatural intervention. The progress of science, from Thales downward, has largely consisted in the elimination of supposed divine interferences and in the disclosure of an established order. One department of Nature after another has been brought within the circle of ascertained law. Phenomena, seemingly capricious, have been found to recur with a regularity not less unvarying than the succession of day and night. Events that were once thought to be wholly owing to a preternatural cause can be predicted in advance by a process of mathematics. Not two centuries ago, leading ministers of New England considered a comet to be a special messenger from God to forewarn men of punitive calamities which were impending over them.[1]

The conviction which is excited by the results of scientific investigation, relative to the unvarying control of natural law, is not without support from another quarter. Such an arrangement, generally speaking, best harmonizes with our ideas of the wisdom and majesty of God. We should expect that He would stamp regularity upon the operations of Nature. Moreover, the uniformity of Nature—the exemption, in general, of Nature from supernatural intervention—is a most benevolent arrangement. The fixed course of Nature is a vast and indispensable blessing to man. It is essential that we should be able to count upon the future; to anticipate the rising of the sun at a given hour; to foresee that the bread which we take for the nourishment of life will not turn out to be poisonous; to be certain that when vitality is gone there is no hope of revoking the principle of life. Were it not for the order of Nature, all human calculations would be baffled, human judgments left without

[1] See, for example, Dr. Increase Mather's "Κομητογραφια, or a Discourse concerning Comets, wherein the Nature of Blazing Stars is enquired into," &c., &c., with "two Sermons occasioned by the late Blazing Stars." Boston: 1683. We have quoted but a small fraction of the title. In the Discourses are stated "the horrible massacres, fires, plagues, tempests, hurricanes, wars, and other judgments" which have followed the appearance of Comets in all ages. It is an amusing instance of the fallacious confounding of the *propter hoc* with the *post hoc*.

a foundation to rest upon, and infinite disorder and confusion everywhere prevail. The ends of a wise benevolence are best met by marking out the course of Nature and leaving it to move on the appointed track.

Such is the force of these considerations that we unhesitatingly reject the testimony by which most alleged miracles are supported. In reading early historians, like Herodotus, or mediaeval chroniclers, like Gregory of Tours, or in listening to the modern necromancers, whenever we perceive, and in proportion as we perceive, that an event which they report involves a miracle, we instantaneously disbelieve the narrative. Such disbelief is felt to be the dictate of reason.

And this aversion of the mind to give credence to a miracle is augmented by the necessity under which the historical student is placed, of rejecting so vast an amount of miraculous narrative. It may be said, to be sure, that the evidence from testimony is defective; for such is the truth in numberless instances of pretended miracle. Yet, in some cases, were the events which are too much for our faith, unmiraculous, we should deem the testimony on which they rest to be sufficient. In these cases we deny credence simply and solely on the ground of a rational reluctance to believe in miracles. For example, we credit Herodotus in a thousand places, where the proofs—apart from the character of the events reported—are no greater than those which he brings forward in relating the miraculous.

We fully concede, then, that there is an antecedent, rational presumption against the truth of a narrative involving miracle, a presumption resting proximately upon the experience of the uniformity of Nature, and ultimately upon our conviction of the wisdom and desirableness of such an arrangement; and acquiring additional force from the knowledge, which history and observation afford, of the credulity of mankind and the prevalence of superstition.

HOW MAY THE PRESUMPTION ADVERSE TO MIRACLES BE REMOVED?

The uniformity of Nature, in the sense of excluding supernatural intervention, is not an intuitive truth—a truth of reason. That like causes will produce like effects is indeed—as far as the physical world is concerned, for we leave out of consideration the will—an axiom of reason. But the uniformity of Nature involves another proposition, namely, that the sum of forces operating in Nature remains the same—with no introduction of supernatural power. And our belief in the uniformity of Nature has no greater strength than belongs to the presumption that supernatural interposition will not occur.

But every theist knows that supernatural interposition has occurred in the past; that all things which he beholds owe their existence to such an exertion of the Divine will. For he traces them all to an act of creation.

Moreover, science affords a kind of historical proof that acts of creation have occurred. The origination of all the types or species of living beings found on the earth, requires the supposition of a creative act, since Geology points back to a time when no germs of animated being existed on the globe. If the old doctrine of the original distinctness of existing species be still held, which no facts have thus far disproved, we are led to the necessary assumption of a series of creative acts. The uniformity of Nature is thus seen to be no absolute truth.

But for what end does material Nature exist? Surely not for its own sake. The end for which Nature exists must be sought outside of Nature itself. Nature is only a part of a more comprehensive system. Nature is an instrument, not an end. The moral administration of God is superior and all-comprehensive. The fixed order of Nature is appointed to promote the ends of wisdom and goodness. The same motive which dictated the establishment of this order may prescribe a deviation from it; or rather may have originally determined that the natural order should at certain points give way to supernatural manifestation.

That is to say, if the object to be secured is sufficiently commanding, or, in other words, if the benefit to result outweighs all the evils which may be supposed to attend a Divine intervention, the antecedent presumption against the miracle is set aside and overborne.

Supposing an end worthy of the intervention of God, a miracle is perfectly consistent with the immutable character of the Divine administration. This lies in the unity of the end. The same end is pursued, but the means of attaining it are varied. Now He makes use of natural law, and now of special intervention. There is no disturbance of the grand harmony that pervades the Divine administration. The acts of Divine Providence, both natural and miraculous, form together one consistent whole. A commander, who commonly issues his orders through subordinates, does not interfere with the ends he has in view, if he chooses, now and then, to ride over the field and personally convey his commands. He is guilty of no fickleness, if he alter the disposition of his forces to suit a new set of circumstances. This alteration may even have been embraced in his foresight. Nor is the Ruler of the country inconsistent with himself, when he augments, or diminishes, or wholly disbands, the military force which he has himself organized. For this force does not exist for its own sake. It was created for a special end outside of itself, and is moulded with sole reference to the benefit sought. A miracle is not a prodigy, a mere wonder (τέρας), fulfilling no moral end, a disturbance of the natural order, carrying with it no advantage. But a miracle is also a sign (σημεῖον), signifying something, fulfilling an idea, and serving an end.[1]

Hence, a miracle implies no afterthought on the part of God—as if he resorted to a measure which He had not originally purposed. In the plan of this world, miracles not less than natural events had their appointed place. The Divine Being as truly determined to exert supernatural power at the points where miracles occur, as to act elsewhere through general laws. In short, miracles are fully accordant with the laws of the Universe, or of the universal system which includes God. A departure, in one sense of the terms, from the law of Nature, they are yet harmonious with, and required by, the laws of the Universe. The higher law prescribes their occurrence.[2]

[1] Of the three terms used in the New Testament to designate a miracle, τέρας corresponds to *miraculum* and denotes the subjective effect on the mind; σημεῖον denotes the significance of the event; and δυνάμεις the supernatural energies to which it must be due.

[2] It is a relief to turn from the vagueness of many modern writers to the greater precision of the Schoolmen. Thomas Aquinas (*Summa*, P. I. Quæst. 105, Art. 6) handles the question whether God can do anything *praeter ordinem rebus indutum.* He explains that every order is dependent upon a cause, and that one order may be subject to another that is higher and more comprehensive: as the family which is dependent on the father is embraced in the city, which, in turn, is included in the kingdom. A miracle is no violation of the order of things, *as dependent upon the First Cause.*

In another passage (P. I. Quæst. 110, Art. 4), Thomas discusses the question *utrum angeli possint facere miracula.* He admits that superhuman creatures can bring to pass events which are miracles *quoad nos;* that is, events which surpass the power of any created causes with which we are acquainted. But he responds to the ques-

It will be objected that we are unqualified to say when a moral emergency that calls for a miracle is constituted. To a certain extent, this may be granted. We cannot take into view the entire Divine system. We may be disposed to set up a claim for the intervention of God in cases where a wiser being would be of another mind. This, however, may fairly be demanded of every theist, that as he believes in an intervention of God at the successive epochs of creation, so he shall be prepared to expect a similar intervention at epochs equally momentous in the new spiritual creation, or the redemption of mankind from their bondage to evil. The antecedent presumption against the occurrence of miracles may exist in different degrees of strength. It may, in a given set of circumstances, be greatly weakened without wholly disappearing. But a crisis can be conceived to exist, an exigency can be conceived to arise, where this presumption wholly vanishes and even yields to an expectation of the opposite character. The need of Revelation, and of miracles to verify and give effect to Revelation, constitutes an occasion justifying the Divine intervention.

THE FALLACY OF HUME'S ARGUMENT.

The preceding remarks suggest the proper answer to the reasoning of Hume against the possibility of

tion negatively, because a miracle, properly speaking, is *praeter ordinem totius naturae creatae*—something, therefore, which only God can do proving a miracle. He ignores the fact of a supernatural moral government over the world of Nature and of men. Our belief both in the constancy of Nature and in human testimony, says Hume, is founded on experience. In regard to the former point, this experience is uniform (since the cases of supposed miracle, being under discussion, are not to be assumed as exceptions). In respect to the credibility of testimony, however, if we suppose apparently credible testimony to be piled never so high, nothing more is required for believing it to be falsely given than to suppose a violation of natural law; that is, of the laws connected with the giving of credible testimony. But if we accept the testimony, and believe the fact it alleges, we are obliged to assume the same thing; namely, the violation of natural law. In other words, we are required by the reporters of a miraculous event to accept one miracle in order to avoid another! We have stated the gist of Hume's argument. The fallacy does not consist in the postulate that a miracle is contrary to experience; for there is a logical propriety in this provisional assumption. But the fallacy lies in the assumption that a miracle is *just as likely to occur in the one place as in the other;* that we may as rationally expect a miracle to be wrought in the matter of testimony, whereby the laws of evidence are miraculously converted into a vehicle for deceiving and misleading mankind, as to suppose a miracle in the physical world, like the healing of the blind. Hume's argument is valid only on the hypothesis that God is as ready to exert supernatural power to make truthful men falsify, as to perform the miracles of the Gospel. Introduce the fact of a personal God, a moral Government, and a wise and benevolent end to be subserved through miraculous interposition, and Hume's reasoning is emptied of all its force.[1]

THE SPECIAL FUNCTION OR USE OF MIRACLES.

This is a topic deserving of more full examination. Why is Revelation attended with miracles? What particular end is subserved by supernatural manifesta-

[1] Most of the opponents of Hume have failed to overthrow his reasoning. Assuming that the uniformity of Nature is ascertained from testimony, they have claimed that testimony does not prove this uniformity to be unvarying, and that Hume, in taking the opposite position, begs the question in dispute. If they are correct, there is no greater *a priori* improbability of a miracle than of a natural event; and the same amount of proof which satisfies us that a man has sunk in the water, suffices to prove that he has walked on the water or subdued the billows with a word. If they are correct, an event inexplicable by natural laws is as credible as the every-day phenomena of Nature. They forget that the uniformity of Nature is *a legitimate generalization* from experience. It is not a bare record of facts and observations, but an authorized (though not absolute) generalization on the basis of them. It is true that J. S. Mill and philosophers of the Positivist type, who exclude an *a priori* element from induction, have no good warrant for any generalization—any dictum more comprehensive than the cases actually observed. Hume, to be sure, is logically involved by his philosophical theories in the same embarrassment. But on a *sound* philosophy, we are obliged to admit a presumption against miracles, which requires to be removed.

tion in connection with Christianity? These are the questions to be considered.

It has been sometimes thought that the miracles of Christ were to prove His Divinity. But this, in our judgment, is an error. The miracles of Christ do not differ in kind from those which are attributed to the prophets of the Old Testament. By the prophets the sick were healed and the dead revived. Nothing in the quality of the works wrought by Christ, therefore, can authorize us to put this interpretation upon them. If we look at the teaching of the New Testament, we discover that neither Christ nor the apostles attach this peculiar significance to His miraculous works. On the contrary, they are explicitly said to be performed by the Father, or by the Father through Him. They are said to be effected by a power which, though it permanently abide in Him, was yet given Him of God. They are sometimes preceded by the offering of prayer to the Father. They are declared to be a manifestation of the power and majesty of the Father. And in keeping with these representations is the circumstance that no miraculous works proceeded from Jesus prior to the epoch of His baptism and entrance on His public ministry. The Divinity of Jesus is a truth which rests upon His testimony and that of the apostles, and not upon the fact that He performed works exceeding human power.[1]

[1] The scriptural proof that the miracles of Christ were not to prove his Divinity, is presented more in detail in the Essay of Müller.

The old view that miracles are to authenticate the divine mission of a religious teacher, is the correct view. They are a proof which God condescends to afford, that the person by whom they are wrought is clothed with an authority to speak in His name. This being their special office, Christ never performed miracles for the promotion of His own personal comfort. That miracles are in this way a testimony of God, is declared by the Saviour. "The works which the Father hath given me to finish, the same works that I do, bear witness of me, *that the Father hath sent me*."[1] "'If thou be the Christ, tell us plainly.' Jesus answered them, 'I told you and ye believed not; the works that I do in my Father's name, they bear witness of me.'"[2] We need not cite the numerous passages in which the miracles are set forth as the proper signs of Messiahship. An emphatic example is the response of Jesus to the messengers who came from John the Baptist with the question whether He was indeed the Christ. The miracles of Christ, then,

See Mark vii. 34; John xi. 41, 42, v. 36, ix. 25, 33, xiv. 10, xi. 40; cf. Luke ix. 43. See also Acts ii. 22, cf. Acts x. 38. There is only one passage (John ii. 11) which could be thought to suggest a different view. But the δόξα which Christ manifested forth by the miracle at Cana was the *messianic* glory, implying, indeed, in the view of John, divinity (see John i. 14); yet not identically the δόξα for which Christ prays in John xvii. 5. Hence John ii. 11 cannot be considered as inconsistent with the general tenor of the New Testament representations on this subject, which is seen in the passages above cited, many of which are from John.

[1] John v. 36. [2] John x. 24, 25.

are the testimony of God to His supernatural, divine mission; and the miracles of the apostles have a similar design and import.[1]

Is this end unimportant? Surely, if the Christian religion is important, it is essential that its authoritative character should be established. Whether the doctrine is of God, or Christ speaks of himself; whether the Gospel is only one more experiment in

[1] Müller has attempted, successfully, as we think, to show that the miracles of Christ were also intended to be *symbolical* of His spiritual agency, and of relations in His spiritual kingdom. The miracles of healing symbolized, and commended to faith, His ability to cure the soul of its disorders. The feeding of the multitude set forth the possibility, through Him, of accomplishing great things in His cause by apparently insignificant means. His resurrection from the dead is a standing symbol, in the writings of Paul, for the spiritual awakening from the death of sin.

That the miracles of Christ, besides the principal end of authenticating his mission, had other collateral motives and ends, is not questioned. They undoubtedly serve to impress the mind with the fact of the *personality* of God. They are thus an antidote to Pantheistic sentiment, as well as to the Deism which puts God far off. They are, also, a natural expression of the compassionate feelings of Christ towards all in distress. Says Chastel, in his excellent *Études Historiques*, upon the Influence of Charity in the early Church, p. 30, "*C'est parce que Jésus aimait que*, tout en publiant la nouvelle du royaume des Cieux, il guérissait, dit l'historien, les maladies et les langueurs du peuple (Matt. iv. 23, 24). Cette même compassion qui le saisissait à la vue de la foule errante et sans guide (Matt. ix. 36), l'attendrissait aussi sur d'autres souffrances; il allait de lieu en lieu faisant du bien et laissant partout des marques de son inépuisable sympathie." This is true; yet there was another, which was, also, the principal motive—the attestation of His messianic mission and office.

speculation, one more effort of erring reason to solve the problems of life, is surely a question of capital importance. Every sober and practical mind desires, first of all, to know if the Gospel can be *depended upon.* The *authority* and *certainty* of the Christian system are of inestimable value; and these are guaranteed by miracles.

Just at this point we encounter one of the most popular objections to the attestation of a Revelation by miracles. A miracle, it is urged, is an exertion of power. But how can a display of power operate to convince the reason or quicken the sense of obligation? The binding force of a moral precept lies in its intrinsic character. Obedience on any other ground is worthless. Now can a miracle add to the obligation to follow that which is right? or create a sense of obligation which the law itself fails to excite? Is not a miracle in such a case something heterogeneous, impertinent? The objection is equivalent to the discarding of the principle of authority in religion altogether. We answer, that as far as Christianity is preceptive, the force of authority is a distinct motive superadded to the perceived rectitude of the law, and is both a legitimate and effective motive—as truly as parental authority, including the whole influence of a parent's will and a parent's love, is a proper influence in the heart of a child. As far as Christianity is a testimony to truth which the human mind cannot discern or cannot to its own full satisfaction prove, everything depends on having this testimony fully established. And, in general, there is a fallacy in the supposition that religious truth must be either discerned intuitively and with perfect clearness, or be cast aside as of no use. Reason may be educated up to the understanding and appreciation of what was once comparatively dark and unmeaning. The outward reception of that which is commended by authority may be followed by insight. This is that elevation of reason to the level of revealed truth which Lord Bacon declares that we are bound to accomplish. We recognize the principle of authority whenever we devote ourselves to the study of a scientific treatise which we know to be true, but have not yet mastered. Every boy who engages in the study of Euclid, does this with the prior conviction that his text-book contains truth, but truth which he can appropriate to himself not without strenuous exertion. The Gospel system, when attested by miracles, makes an analogous claim upon the soul. It calls for obedience, consecration; it rewards these with apprehension, insight. The credentials which attest it put the mind in the right attitude for inwardly receiving its lofty and inspiring lessons.

While it is the office of the Christian miracles to verify the supernatural, divine mission of Christ, we are far from considering that they are the exclusive, or even the foremost, proof of this great truth; or even that, by themselves, they are adequate to the production of an inward faith. But of their relation to the other sources of Christian evidence, we shall speak more fully under another head.

A recollection of the end for which miracles are wrought, will expose the fallacy of the current skeptical objection that miracles would imply a flaw in the constitution of material Nature, which needs to be repaired through a special intervention. The need of miracles is not founded on the existence of any defect in Nature. The system of Nature is good and is worthy of God. It is fitted, in itself considered, to disclose the attributes of the Creator and to call forth feelings of adoration in the human mind. The defect is not in Nature. But the mind of man is darkened so that this primal revelation is obscurely discerned; his character, moreover, is corrupted beyond the power of self-recovery, in consequence of his apostasy from God. Now, if God shall mercifully approach with new light and new help, why shall He not verify to man the fact of His presence, by supernatural manifestations of His power and goodness? In this case, Nature is used as an instrument for an ulterior moral end. The miracle is not to remedy an imperfection in Nature, but is, like the Revelation which it serves to attest, a product of the condescension of God. He *condescends* to address evidence to the senses, or to the understanding through the senses, in order to open a way for the conveyance of the highest spiritual blessing to mankind. Material Nature, be it remembered, does not include the end of its existence in itself. It is a subordinate member of a vaster system, and has only an instrumental value.

Of a piece with the objection just noticed, is the vague representation that something sacred is violated by a miracle. Hume styled a miracle a *transgression* of natural law—skilfully availing himself of a word which usually denotes the infringement of a moral law, and so carries with it an association of guilt.[1] Several recent writers have more directly propounded a like notion. Such views may be pertinent under a scheme of sentimental Pantheism where Nature is deified. Only he who holds, with Spinoza, that Nature is God, can deem a miracle repugnant to the attributes of God. When the attempt is made to connect such notions with any higher theory of the universe, they deserve no respect, but rather contempt. As if it were derogatory to the Divine Being to save a human life by any other than physical agencies, even when the principal end to be attained is the verification of a heaven-given remedy for the soul and for the disorders which sin has brought into it!

THE RELATION OF MIRACLES TO THE MORAL PROOFS OF CHRISTIANITY.

The question has often been discussed whether the strongest proof of the divine origin of Christianity is found in its doctrine or its miracles. Some have gone

[1] Hume's *Essays*, Vol. II. Appendix, K.

so far as to say that the doctrine proves the miracles, not the miracles the doctrine. The truth on the subject has been more properly set forth in the aphorism of Pascal: "Doctrines must be judged by miracles; miracles must be judged by doctrines."

It is plain that a doctrine which the unperverted conscience pronounces immoral or inconsistent with the perfections of God, cannot be received on the ground of alleged or supposed miracles attending it. This principle is declared in the Bible itself, in a memorable injunction given to the Israelites.[1] We must conclude, to be sure, that all wonders which the teacher of such doctrine performs, are "lying wonders;" that they are either the product of jugglery or are wrought by supernatural evil beings whose force surpasses that of men, and who are, therefore, able to counterfeit the works of Divine power.

In accordance with the tendency of this principle, is the reply of Jesus to the charge that his miracles were wrought by the power of Satan. He does not deny that works, surpassing the power of men, may be done through the aid of devils; but he responds to the charge by a moral consideration. An evil being would not work against himself and exert power against his own minions.

So much is clear, then, that a doctrine must be negatively unobjectionable on the score of morality or of moral tendency, in order to challenge our faith,

[1] Deuteronomy xiii. 1–4.

whatever wonderful works may attend the annunciation of it.

But a still more positive and important place belongs to doctrine in the evidence for the divine origin of Christianity. The foregoing discussion has evinced that in order to prove miracles, the anterior presumption adverse to their occurrence must be set aside. The necessity of Revelation and of a method of salvation which man is unable to originate, partially prepares the mind to expect miracles. But the contents of the professed Revelation are of not less moment in their bearing on this anterior expectation. The more excellent the doctrine, the more it seems to surpass the capacity of the unaided human faculties, the more it appears adapted to the necessities of our nature, in fine, the more worthy it is to have God for its author, so much the more credibility is given to the miracles which, it is claimed, have accompanied it. The doctrine and the miracles are two mutually supporting species of evidence. The more the mind is struck with the divine excellence of the doctrine, the more likely does it seem that this doctrine should be attended with miracles. If the doctrine is noble and worthy and sufficient, we naturally look for miracles, and only require that they shall be recommended to belief by faithful testimony.

In these remarks we have compared *the doctrine* with the miracles, as sources of proof. The moral proofs of Christianity, however, comprehend much more than what is understood by Christian doctrine. As affecting the presumption relative to the occurrence of miracles, we must take into view the character of Jesus, the entire spirit and plan of his life, all the circumstances connected with the planting of Christianity in the world. It is unwarranted and unwise to isolate one element of Christianity, as the miracles, or the doctrine, from the other elements which are connected with it, and form, as it were, one vital whole. Christ and Christianity, as they are presented in the New Testament Scriptures, stand out as one complex phenomenon, which we are called upon to explain. Nothing can be appreciated by itself, but everything must be looked at in its organic relation. The moral evidence of the supernatural origin of Christianity includes the teaching of Christ and the Christian system of doctrine, but it embraces much more—much that is inseparably associated with the doctrine.

Farther still, we are required to consider Christianity in the light of a mighty historic movement, beginning in the remote past, extending in a continuous progress through many ages, culminating in the advent and life of Christ, and in the establishment of his Church, but flowing onward in its effects, through an ever-widening channel, down to the present day. We have to contemplate the striking peculiarity of this great historic movement, which embraces the unfolding, through successive stages, or epochs, of a religion distinct in its spirit as well as in its renovating power from all other religions known among men. And we have to connect with this view a survey of its subsequent diffusion and leavening influence in human society. Comparing this religion with the native characteristics of the people among whom it appeared, and from whose hands the priceless treasure was at length delivered to mankind, we are to ask ourselves if this religion, so pure and salutary, so enduring and influential, so strong as to survive temporary eclipse and withstand through a long succession of ages, before the full light appeared, an adversary as powerful as human barbarism and corruption, can be the product of man's invention. And whatever reason there is for rejecting this supposition as irrational, is so much argument for the Christian miracles.

It deserves remark that miracles appear especially at the signal epochs in the progress of the gradually developing system of religion. This circumstance has been pointed out by Christian apologists.[1] In connection with Moses, who marks an era in the communication of the true religion; then, after a long interval, in connection with the prophets, who introduce an era not less peculiar and momentous, and then, after a long suspension of miraculous manifestation, in conjunction with the final and crowning epoch of Revelation, with the ministry of Christ and the founding of the Church, the supernatural is seen to break into the course of history. There is an impressive analogy be-

[1] See Dr. A. P. Peabody's *Christianity, the Religion of Nature.*

tween the spiritual creation or renewal of humanity, and the physical creation, where successive eras are inaugurated by the exertion of supernatural agency in the introduction of new species, and after each epoch history is remanded, as it were, to its natural course in pursuance of an established order. Miracle would seem to be the natural expression and verification of an opening era in the spiritual enlightenment of mankind, when new forces are introduced by the great Author of light and life, and a new development sets in.

In this place may be noticed a criticism which is frequently heard, in these days, from the side of disbelief. Miracles, it is said, are put forward as the evidences of Revelation, but miracles are the very thing which require to be proved. "Miracles," it is triumphantly asserted, "instead of affording satisfactory proof of anything, are now usually found in the dock instead of the witness-box of the court of criticism."[1] To this we reply, that when the testimony of a witness is such as to conclude the case, and that witness is impeached, of course the main effort is turned in the direction of establishing his credibility. When a messenger brings a communication of a momentous nature, the character of his credentials becomes a question of vast consequence and draws to itself a proportionate degree of attention. Are these credentials genuine, the contents of his message will command respect.

[1] Mackay, *The Tübingen School*, &c., p. 56.

Are the credentials fabricated, his message is devoid of authority. To scrutinize the credentials and, in case they are worthy of credit, to remove the doubts of the skeptical, is thus a matter of prime importance. But the fallacy of the objection implied in the quotation above, does not rest on this consideration alone. If miracles attest the Christian Revelation, they are also a part—one side—of that Revelation itself. They are *constitutive* of Revelation, so that in proving them we are establishing not so much a collateral circumstance as a part of the main fact. They are one element in the immediate manifestation of God. The doctrine is divine, but the works also are divine.

The presumption in favor of the miracles, that is created by the excellence and credibility of the doctrine, does not supersede the need of miracles, nor does it supersede the need of faithful testimony to their occurrence. He has a poor understanding of logic who does not know that two sources of evidence may lend to each other a mutual support. The excellence of the doctrine sustains the testimony to the miracles; the proof of the miracles establishes the divinity of the doctrine.

It is sometimes urged that if miracles are necessary in the original communication of Christianity, they are not less to be expected in the propagation of it. And the question is asked why we refuse to give credit to reports of more modern miracles, or why such miracles are not wrought now in conjunction with missionary labor? We do not consider the supposition that miracles have been wrought since the apostolic age to be so absurd as many seem to regard it. So thorough a historical critic as Neander hesitates to disbelieve the testimony to the miracles said to be performed by that devout and holy preacher, St. Bernard, and so great a man as Edmund Burke takes the same ground in respect to the miracles attributed to early Saxon missionaries in Britain. But there is generally a defect in the character of the testimony, in the habits of careful observation, or of trustworthy reporting, which, apart from other considerations, prevents us from giving credit to the Catholic miracles. It is remarkable that some of the most eminent mediaeval missionaries disclaimed the power of performing miracles. This is true of Ansgar, the famous apostle of the North of Europe, and of Boniface, the still more celebrated apostle of Germany. They were ready to give credence to the pretensions of others, but for themselves professed to be endued with no supernatural powers. Besides this, however, there is another consideration of almost decisive weight. The origination of Christianity, a method of salvation, is beyond human power; not so the propagation of the religion which is once communicated. We agree that the general method of the Divine government is that of leaving men to discover for themselves what the unaided human faculties are competent to find out. The laws of astronomy, the physical structure and history of the globe, with all the sciences and arts which belong to civilization, it is left for human investigation, in the slow toil of centuries, to develop. But the true knowledge of God was practically inaccessible; salvation was something which fallen man could not achieve of himself. It accords, therefore, with the method of God to leave the *diffusion* of the blessings of Christianity, when they are once communicated, to the agency of men, withholding miraculous (though not supernatural) assistance to their endeavors.[1] It is plain that in the Divine administration there is what has been called an economy, or sparing use, of miracle. The Saviour's whole manner of speaking on the subject, as well as the course which he pursued, appears to indicate that miracles are an accommodation to human weakness, and are granted in response to an unwonted exigency. Comparing ourselves, or any heathen nation, with the age contemporary with Christ, we find ourselves in possession of other proofs derived from the operation of Christianity in the world, which may well stand in the room of any ocular demonstration of its heavenly origin.

[1] That supernatural agency of God which is not *manifestly* supernatural, but which is so connected with the operation of natural causes that its presence is not palpable, we do not style miraculous. To this supernatural, but not miraculous, agency, belongs the Regeneration and Sanctification of the soul. Providential answers to prayer may fall under the same head—to prayer, for instance, for the restoration of the sick.

The foregoing remarks will prepare the reader for the observation that miracles are an inferior species of proof, compared with the moral evidence of the divine origin of Christianity, and, independently of the impression made by this last kind of evidence, must fail to convince. Such is undeniably the rank assigned to miracles by the Saviour himself. Apart from miracles, there was proof of his divine mission, as he considered, which ought to satisfy the mind. But if this proof left the mind still skeptical, he pointed to the miracles. "Believe me that I am in the Father, and the Father in me; *or else* believe me for the very works' sake."[1] A weak faith, an inchoate faith, miracles might confirm. Where there was a receptive temper, some degree of spiritual susceptibility, miracles were a provocative and aid of faith. But where there was an entire insensibility to the moral side of the gospel, or an absence of any such craving for the truth as gave it a degree of self-evidencing power, the Saviour refused to work miracles. Miracles have for such minds no convincing efficacy. They would be referred either to occult natural causes or to diabolical agency. Miracles could develop and reinforce the faith which moral evidence had partially awakened. They could not create that faith outright. They could not serve as a substitute for the proofs which touch directly the reason and conscience. They could not kindle spiritual life under the ribs of death. They were an appeal to

[1] John xiv. 11.

the senses, symbolizing the spiritual operation of the gospel, and subordinately aiding the confidence of the darkened soul in the divine reality of the gospel. All the teaching of Christ concerning the place and use of his miracles, and concerning the comparative value and dignity of the proof from miracles and from the moral evidence of his divine mission, corroborates the doctrine we have laid down, that the former are subsidiary and secondary, and are due to the condescension of God, who affords an extraordinary prop, and one we have properly no right to demand, to that hesitating, incomplete faith which has been excited by the superior appeals flowing directly from the Christian system itself and the character of its Author.

It was the tendency of the school of Paley to give the greatest prominence in the Evidences of Revelation, to the miracles. The internal argument in their hands often received less than justice. Belief was sought to be produced by the constraining influence of authority through the medium of supernatural interposition. In that reaction against this school, of which Coleridge more than any other individual was the efficient promoter, the position of the two sources of proof was reversed. It became common to speak of the evidence from miracles in disparaging terms, as if it was deserving of no respect. This tendency of course found support from such as rejected the supernatural altogether from any concern in the origin of Christianity. In some quite recent writers, the pendulum oscillates again to the former place. The sound view, in our judgment, lies between the two extremes, and this view has the sanction of the Saviour himself.

ESSAY XII.

THE CREDIBILITY OF THE TESTIMONY OF JESUS CONCERNING HIMSELF.

PHARISEES on a certain occasion taunted Jesus with pretending to be a witness to his own claims. A record which he bore of himself, they said, deserved no credit, on the accepted principle that a man cannot be witness in his own case. He replied that his testimony, although it related to himself and his own pretensions, was nevertheless true and credible. To be sure, there was, besides, an objective proof answering to the subjective witness of his own consciousness, and verifying that witness to others, if not to himself. There was, namely, the testimony which God gave through the works which Jesus wrought; works which man without God could not have done. Yet his own testimony, the testimony of his own consciousness, his inward conviction or intuition relative to his mission, and to the office that belonged to him among men, he justly held to be of itself, under the circumstances, a valid proof.[1]

[1] John viii. 14: "Though I bear record of myself, yet my record is true." Only in verbal opposition to this affirmation is John v. 31. "The seeming contradiction between the present declaration and the former concession of Jesus is explained, if we suppose that he there

To develop and support this proposition is the purpose of the present Essay.

In respect to the contents, or proper interpretation, of the testimony of Jesus regarding himself, there is, of course, some difference of opinion. But the points, to which we now draw attention, certainly formed a part of it, as all sober criticism must allow. In the first place, Jesus claimed to act in virtue of a special divine commission. He had been sent into the world in a sense altogether peculiar, and for the discharge of a mission which was of strictly supernatural origin. This was the primary, the generic, the often-repeated, claim of Jesus, which it were idle to attempt to fritter away or to resolve into a figure. He was preëminently, and by supernatural appointment, the Messenger of God in this world. In the second place, he affirmed of himself a lofty and peculiar relationship to God. We need not here say all that we believe upon this point. It is sufficient for our present argument to notice his claim to a knowledge of that invisible Being,

thought proper to follow the common human rule, and to adduce the testimony of others in his behalf; whilst here, on the contrary, he proceeds in conformity with the higher principle that the Divine can only be testified to and proved by itself. Besides, there is in the thing itself no contradiction. His self-testimony, resting upon the consciousness of his divine mission, corresponds in a sense to the testimony of his works (John v. 36), inasmuch as these always presuppose such a consciousness." (De Wette on John viii. 14). See, also, Meyer (on John v. 31), where Euthymius is quoted to the effect that in this passage Jesus is merely anticipating the objection of the Jews—not uttering his own sentiment.

which in kind and degree surpasses that possessed by all other men, and to a spiritual union with Him as intimate as language is capable of expressing. He professes to stand in this exalted, mysterious fellowship with God; to be a partaker of divine prerogatives; and, after departing from the world, to sit on the throne of universal dominion. In the third place, he assumes towards men an office the most elevated which imagination can conceive. He claims to be the moral Guide and Deliverer of mankind. He does not hesitate to style himself, in this relation, the Light, or the Illuminator of the world; taking the same place in the kingdom of souls that belongs to the Sun in the material system. In the exertion of the office committed to him, he forgives sin. This awful prerogative, which it were impious for a mortal to take upon himself, he does not hesitate to exercise. He invites the world of men, in their conscious infirmity and guilt, to rest upon him. He undertakes to procure for them reconciliation with God. He bids them pray with confidence, in his name. He promises, even, to work within them moral purification through potent agencies of which he is the prime mover. In short, he assumes to be the Deliverer of the souls of men from their bondage to sin and exposure to retribution. How exalted, how unparalleled the claim! And to crown all, judgment over the race is lodged in his hands. He is the arbiter of destinies. "Before him shall be gathered all nations."

In this sketch of the extraordinary claims of Jesus, we have exaggerated nothing, but rather have purposely stopped short of their full magnitude. They are all included within his consciousness. That is to say, his conscious relation to God involved all this. "I *know*," he said, "whence I come, and whither I go." Back of all these claims was a full, inward persuasion or intuition of their reality.

Now the question is, Was this consciousness of Christ veracious or deceptive? Did it represent the reality, or was it the fabric of enthusiasm? Plainly such is the alternative to which we are brought. It is understood that we leave out of sight for the present, the miracles—the objective verification of the consciousness and the claims of Christ. Is this consciousness—for so we may be allowed to style the intuitive conviction to which we refer—of itself, in the case before us, trustworthy? Or, have we in these claims an instance of unexampled self-delusion?

We proceed to offer reasons why this last hypothesis cannot rationally be entertained.

One very remarkable feature of the Gospel history, which has an important bearing on the present inquiry, we must notice at the outset. The peculiar claim of Jesus was most deliberately made, and was made persistently in the face of all the opposition and scrutiny which it underwent. Moreover, the utmost stress was laid upon it by Jesus himself. It cannot be said that he was not distinctly aware of the momentous import of the claim which he put forth. This he understood in all its length and breadth. It is plain that he had a calm, yet full and vivid, appreciation of its nature. Had he needed any spur to reflection, this would have been furnished by the unbelieving and inimical attitude of almost all around him. Never were pretensions more constantly and ingeniously challenged. Think how assured his own spirit must have been, to pass through this life-long ordeal without sharing, in the faintest degree, the misgivings and distrust of the surrounding world! Among the rulers and leaders of the nation, among his own kindred, on every side, there was pitying or scornful disbelief. Yet he did not doubt himself! Moreover—and this is a point of especial significance—he made this belief in him the cardinal requirement, the turning-point, and test. His extraordinary claims and assertions respecting himself and his mission are not left in the background. On the contrary, they stand out in bold relief. Confidence in them is the one great demand, the first and fundamental duty which, in the preaching of his religion, men are called upon to perform. How much do we read about belief and unbelief on the pages of the New Testament! The same question was agitated then, even in the very presence of Christ, that is discussed now. Was he, or was he not, worthy of belief? Was he, indeed, sent from God, or did he speak of himself?

Now it is adapted, we cannot but feel, to make a strong impression on every thoughtful mind, to reflect that this question of believing or disbelieving in him was clothed, in the estimation of Christ himself, with all the importance that justly attaches to it. However vast his claim, he knew and felt how vast it was. Not only did he stake his all, and sacrifice all, in the maintenance of it, but he concentrated, so to speak, his whole system in it, by making the full assent to this claim the one foremost and essential requirement. "This is the work of God, that ye believe on him whom He hath sent." He examined his disciples as to the view which they took of his person and office. Who think ye that I am? was his question to them. He was acquainted with the various theories concerning him that were entertained by his contemporaries. When there was everything to excite self-questioning, the consciousness of his divine mission was not in the least disturbed. Through all denial of him, under the frown of men in power as well as the fierce outcries of the fanatical mob, in view of his apparently unsuccessful career, even amidst the terrors of death, the consciousness of his divine mission remains a deep, immovable conviction. It was a conviction which reflection — self-knowledge — had no tendency to weaken.

Self-deception, in a matter like this, is incompatible with the transcendent holiness and goodness of Christ.

It would argue such a degree of self-ignorance and self-exaggeration as could spring only from a deep moral perversion.

We shall not enter into an elaborate argument to prove the spotless character of Christ. It is enough to convince us of his sinless purity, that while his moral discernment was so penetrating and sure, and his ideal of character absolutely faultless, and his dealing with others marked by a moral fidelity so searching, he had yet no consciousness of sin. When the tempter came he found nothing in him—no province in his heart, no strip of territory, which he could call his own. The teaching of Christ presents the purest description of rectitude and holiness. Every man finds in it practical rebukes of sin—of his own sin—which are more pointed and awful than he can find elsewhere. His precepts are the embodiment and expression of a pure conscience. Yet the feeling of self-reproach never entered the heart of Jesus. It is impossible to account for this, except on the supposition that he was absolutely free from sin. Without dwelling on the excellence of Christ, on that blending of piety and philanthropy, that union of the active virtues with the passive graces of character, that exquisite combination and harmony of virtues, we may still advert to one or two special features in which his perfection shines out. Men who rise far above the common level of character are still frequently open to temptation from two sources, ambition and friendship.

In each of these particulars, Jesus affords an example of stainless virtue. The love of power and worldly advancement was kept far away from his heart. He was proof against self-seeking in this enticing form of personal aspiration. Even more difficult is it to resist subtle temptations to yield something of truth or duty for the sake of friendship. But Jesus, though patient and tender towards all the erring, is unsparingly faithful in dealing with his most intimate disciples. There is no exception, no tacit indulgence, no accommodation of the moral standard, out of favor to them. The foremost of them, when he would suggest to Jesus a departure from the hard path of self-sacrifice, is sternly rebuked under the name of Adversary and Tempter.[1] Even their resentment at injuries offered to him brings upon them his disapprobation.[2] He tolerates in the best loved, and in the seclusion of private intercourse, no temper of feeling which is repugnant to the principle of goodness.[3]

Now we aver that the holy character of Christ precludes the possibility of a monstrous self-delusion such

[1] Matt. xvi. 23. [2] Luke ix. 55.

[3] Among the delineations of the character of Jesus, the pregnant aphorisms of Pascal in the *Pensées* have, perhaps, never been surpassed. Ullmann's little work on *The Sinlessness of Christ* (much enlarged and improved in the later editions) is convincing and impressive. *The Christ of History*, by John Young, a Scottish writer, is a forcible argument on the same general subject. As an extended portraiture of the excellence of Christ, the chapters in Horace Bushnell's *Nature and the Supernatural*, on "the Character of Jesus," besides their eloquence, are full of instructive suggestion.

as must be attributed to him in case his claims are discredited. The soul is not so made as to fall a victim to this enormous self-deception, whilst the moral part is sound and pure. The principle that if the eye be single the whole body is full of light, is applicable here. There is a shield for the judgment in thorough moral uprightness. God has not made the intelligence of man to mislead him so fearfully, provided he abides in his integrity. The mind is a witness to the truth, and was made for that end. To assume that the inmost consciousness of a holy, unfallen soul, in the full communion of God, is no criterion of truth, would be almost equivalent to supposing that the world is made and governed by an evil being. We found the credibility of the consciousness of Christ on his perfect goodness.

This conclusion is fortified when we consider, in particular, the humility of Jesus. Notwithstanding the extraordinary dignity to which he lays claim, humility marks his whole demeanor. He is careful to keep within the bounds of his calling; for himself, regarded apart from the relationship he sustains to God and from his office, he exacts nothing; from every symptom of an elated mind, from every feeling of self-glorification, he is utterly exempt; while, in his intercourse with his fellow-men of every rank, there appears a winning lowliness of heart. This mixture of humility with so lofty claims—elements seemingly incongruous, yet in the evangelical portraiture of Jesus so naturally uniting—makes his character altogether unique. Asserting for himself a station so exalted, he is yet the impersonation of self-renouncing regard for others. The singular humility of Christ, emanating, as it does, from the very core of his character, renders it well-nigh inconceivable that he could have been bewildered and blinded by a self-exalting delusion respecting his rank in the universe and his authority among men. Such an impression, if it be false, must have its roots in an immoderate self-estimation. Nothing short of a most inordinate self-love could breed a persuasion of this nature, if there was in truth no foundation for it. But if this occult misleading principle had been operative, other and offensive manifestations of it would have appeared. On the contrary, a rare humility before God and men is one of the striking characteristics of Jesus. It would seem as if he were desirous of requiring for himself the least that he could require in consistency with truth. And even this he requires, not from any personal love of honor or power, but rather in the interest of truth, and as compelled in the faithful performance of the work which it was given him to do. Had he been a lover of power, conspicuity, authority, rule, we might possibly account for the rise in his soul of a delusive sense of personal importance. But in one who was actuated by motives wholly antagonistic, in whose eyes the doing of the humblest act of love was nobler than to wear a coronet, in him who was "meek and of a lowly heart," the existence of a self-magnifying illusion of this nature is psychologically insoluble.

No case analogous to that of the founder of Christianity can be cited from the abundant records of religious enthusiasm. It is true that multiplied examples of such enthusiasm exist in the past. There have been professed prophets and founders of religions, who have believed in their own pretensions, which were yet the offspring of a morbid imagination. But none of these, in respect to character and to surrounding circumstances, resembles Christ, or helps us to explain his consciousness. There is this radical difference, that none of these have been exempt from the corrupting operation of sin. The effect of that deranging, disturbing force, has been experienced not only in the character, its immediate seat, but also in the intelligence. Because they who are groping in the dark lose their path, it follows not that such will be the lot of him who walks in the day. Point us to the prophet or saint who can claim the unclouded vision which is the attribute of the unfallen soul, and we admit the parallel. But let us glance at some of these leaders whose names are sometimes flippantly coupled with the name of Jesus.

Confucius cannot be placed in the category of religious teachers pretending to a divine mission. He was simply a teacher of moral and political axioms; entitled to credit, indeed, for certain commendable features in his ethical doctrine, but disclaiming any special knowledge of the invisible world. He laid claim to no higher character than that of a sage, drawing from no other fountain than human wisdom. Buddha was likewise a moral reformer, a true philanthropist, the propounder of humane ethical precepts. Though subsequently invested by his followers with a halo of supernatural glory, it is not ascertained that this monk and mystic himself claimed to be the organ of a divine revelation. His work, as far as it was religious, was chiefly negative, consisting in the deliverance of his followers from the slavish superstition of the brahminical system, by denying the reality of the objects of their previous worship. The speculative part of his system was his own discovery, and was atheistic. Of Zoroaster too little is known to enable us to judge intelligently of his mental characteristics. If he claimed to have received communications from heaven, we know too little of his history to determine the shape and extent of this pretension. How far he was really infected with a mystic enthusiasm, and how far the supernatural elements in the traditional accounts of his career have sprung from the fancy of later generations, we are not in a situation to decide.[1] Skeptics have sometimes endeavored to draw a parallel between

[1] A tolerably full, and doubtless in the main authentic, account of Zoroaster and Buddha, and of the wide-spread religious systems called respectively by their names, may be found in Duncker's *Geschichte des Alterthums* (Vol. I.), a work which offers a consecutive and readable, as well as learned, exhibition of the results of modern

Apollonius of Tyana and the author of the Gospel. But the earliest life of Apollonius, the work of Philostratus, was not written until a hundred years after he lived, and the resemblance of his pretended miracles to the miracles of the Gospel is probably, for the most part, a designed parody of the Saviour's history. Of Apollonius we know little more than that he was one of the more famous of the roving magicians and dealers in the preternatural, who, in that epoch of spiritual distraction, found a ready hearing in the Roman world.

The appeal to Mohammed, as a notable example of sincere but unfounded confidence in one's own divine mission, has been urged with more frequency and persistency. Happily the investigations which have been made into the history of the Arabian prophet, have furnished the explanation of his remarkable self-delusion. This solution is found in a great degree in his peculiarly morbid physical constitution. Subject from his youth to a form of epilepsy, and combining with this nervous infirmity a mystic fervor of religious aspiration, he conceived the impression that the extraordinary states of body and soul into which he occasionally fell, were due to the action of celestial beings, and at length came to consider himself the organ of a divine revelation. His zeal for a rigorous monotheism inflamed the fanaticism of his fiery temperament, and finally impelled him to missions of conquest; though

investigation in the department of oriental history. It is understood that the more recent researches into the Zoroastrian system yield important fruit.

it seems to be admitted that after his establishment at Medina, and with his advancing success, he lost much of the comparative sincerity and singleness of his motives. A large alloy of base ambition became mingled up with the enthusiasm of the zealot. In the case of Mohammed, there were present all the materials which are needful for the composition of an enthusiast. His hot blood, his morbid temperament, his inward yearnings and conflicts, the seasons of hallucination through which he passed, his solitary vigils and self-mortification, are sufficient to explain the origin of the delusion which gained possession of his mind.[1]

[1] The best biography of Mohammed is the late work of Dr. Sprenger, who has had the command of wider materials than were before accessible. He describes with much fulness the maladies to which Mohammed was subject. In the portions of this copious work which we have read, the author makes the impression of great knowledge on the subject, but of small literary skill, with a tendency to prolixness. The English biography of Mohammed, in best repute, is the recent work of Mr. Muir. In one of his articles in the *Calcutta Review* (which are incorporated into his subsequent work), Muir discusses "the Belief of Mohammed in his own Inspiration." He traces with plausibility the psychological origin of this belief. "How far," says Muir, "the two ideas of a Resolution subjectively formed, and involving a spontaneous course of action, and of a Divine Inspiration objectively imparted and independent of his own will, were at first simultaneously present, and in what respective degrees, it is difficult to conjecture. But it is certain that the conception of a divine commission soon took entire and undivided possession of his soul; and, colored though it often was by the motions and inducements of the day, or mingled with apparently incongruous desires, retained a paramount influence until the hour of his death." (P. 320.) Of Mohammed at Medina, Muir says (p. 330): "Ambition,

But there were men, we are sometimes told, in the ancient world, of another make and of a different order of mind from this, who were yet believed by themselves to be charged with a divine mission. Pythagoras was one. Unfortunately, the earliest extant biographers of Pythagoras, Porphyry and his pupil, Jamblichus, did not write until seven or eight hundred years after the philosopher whom they commemorate, flourished; and the best of the biographers whom they cite date no further back than about two centuries after their master's death. In the absence of contemporary witnesses, the knowledge we possess both of the mental and moral character, and the pretensions, of Pythagoras, is scanty and, to a considerable extent, inferential. It would be nothing strange if a man like him, at that time, imagined that natural gifts of knowledge were imparted to him by a special inspiration of the divinity. It is difficult to see how anything can be gathered unfavorable to the claims of Christ, from the example of a heathen mystic so indistinctly known, and standing, withal, at the dawning period of scientific thought.

There is, however, one man of antiquity, who, in some other respects, has not unfrequently been set in comparison with Jesus, and the conjunction of whose name with that of Christ may give a less shock to reverential feeling. Yet, in the points in which the

rapine, assassination, lust, are undenied features of his later life, openly sanctioned by an assumed permission, or even command, from the Most High!"

position of Socrates is more usually compared with that of Christ, Socrates is better likened to the forerunner of Christ; as, indeed, he was styled by the Platonist of Florence, Marsilius Ficinus, the John the Baptist of the ancient world. The Socratic philosophy prepared many noble minds for the reception of the gospel, by its congenial tone, and by the cravings which it awakened but failed to satisfy.

But Socrates believed himself to have been entrusted with a divine mission, and believed that he enjoyed an inward supernatural guidance. We are quite willing to consider this persuasion on the part of the greatest man of the ancient heathen world, for the reason that a careful consideration of the character of this belief of Socrates and of the nature of his pretensions generally, will serve to corroborate strongly the argument which has been presented on the foregoing pages.

Socrates, like all the Greeks of the time, save individuals here and there who may have disbelieved in anything divine, thought that the gods made known their counsels through the medium of dreams and oracles. This will be called a superstition. So, he thought that the study of physical science, when carried beyond the small stock of knowledge indispensable for the practical pursuits of life, was an impiety —a meddling with what belonged to the gods. This, too, was a superstition. Such views simply indicate that we are not to look, even in Socrates, for a miraculous degree of enlightenment. But we are concerned here with the view which he took of himself and his mission. And here it is to be observed that in reference to the opportunity of being taught by dream and oracle, and the like, he claimed nothing more for himself than what he attributed to others. In this matter all stood on the same footing. The gods heard prayer, he held, and gave answer in these ways. In respect to the work to which he devoted himself, the verdict of the Delphian oracle in favor of his preeminent wisdom doubtless had an important influence in leading him to the career which he embraced of a public interrogator and exposer of pretended knowledge, and teacher of such as cared to learn of him. And this work he considered a calling, in the literal sense, which he was not at liberty to forsake. He supposed, also, that an inward monitor, whose restraining impulse he experienced on various occasions, was given him to hold him back from a mistaken or injurious course of action. For the office of the demon, according to what must be considered the statement of Socrates himself, in the Apology, was negative—never suggesting what to do, but simply, on occasions, interposing resistance to stay him from unwise action.[1] Now, it

[1] Apologia, c. xix. Socrates says of the inward voice: ἀεὶ ἀποτρέπει με τούτου, ὃ ἂν μέλλω πράττειν, προτρέπει δὲ οὔποτε. Compare, also, c. xxxi., where Socrates says that through all the legal proceedings in his case, the voice in his soul had interposed no check to the course he was taking, and where he defines the function of the supernatural Monitor in the same way. The representations of Xenophon in the Memorabilia (I. 1, 4, *et al.*), as is well known, are

may be held, that this supposed demon was the intuitive moral impulse of Socrates himself, which, in the promptitude of its action, struck him as the voice of another in his soul; or, in common with some of the Christian Fathers, and with others whom it were harsh to tax with credulity, we may even suppose that supernatural enlightenment was not withheld from this man by the Being before whom those in every nation who fear Him—even though their knowledge of Him be imperfect—and work righteousness, are accepted.

But when we look at the claims of Socrates respecting himself, we find that he is far from assuming preëminence or authority. It is true that he considered his work an important one, and himself not a harmful but a needed and useful citizen. But this was the limit of his pretensions. He distinguished himself from other men, not through any superiority of knowledge which he thought himself to possess, but through that consciousness of ignorance which belonged to him and which they lacked. He, like them, knew nothing, but, unlike them, *he knew* that he knew nothing. He asserted for himself no greater knowledge, and no more certainty of knowledge respecting the future life, than other men had. He claimed to exercise no authority over the opinions or the conduct of others. If

less accurate; and those contained in the Theages (like the work itself) come not from Plato. Yet in this Dialogue it is stated, in conformity with the Apology, that the demon only forbids, never instigates.

the demon negatively guided him, he received thereby no authority or wisdom for the control of other men. He was simply a man among men; a humble searcher for truth; pretending to the exertion of no authority save that which was willingly accorded to the force of his reasonings. In fact, a principal charm of Socrates is his humble sense of the narrow boundaries of human knowledge, and his waiting for more light.

Let us now change the picture which history presents of this remarkable man. Let us suppose that Socrates had claimed to be invested with all power in heaven and on earth, had required the acceptance of his doctrines on his mere authority, had demanded of all men an implicit obedience to his will, had styled himself the lord and master of his disciples, had assumed to pardon impiety and transgression, had professed an ability to allot to men their everlasting destinies, besides delivering them from the bonds of death, and had declared himself to be the constituted judge in the future world of the entire race of man. The question we put is, whether assumptions of this character, notwithstanding acknowledged virtues of Socrates, would not evince either a demented understanding or an ingrained, monstrous self-love and self-exaggeration, only to be explained on the supposition of a deep moral perversion? Should we not be driven to conclude that claims so extravagant and presumptuous in a sane mind imply that character is off its true foundations? How else could self-deception and self-exaltation reach this height? And would not complacency for certain traits and actions of Socrates be lost in the repugnance we should feel for this arrogancy of pretension? An enthusiast is ordinarily looked upon with compassion by sober minds. But when enthusiasm leaps so high, and leads to the usurping of a rank far beyond the allowance of truth and the moral law, it inspires a feeling of moral aversion.

Had Jesus stood forth simply in the character of a promulgator of some high, and, perhaps, forgotten truth in theology or morals, with which his whole being was penetrated, we might look upon the mistaken belief in a supernatural mission with a less unfavorable judgment. It is conceivable that the light which flashes on the intelligence should be wrongly attributed to a supernatural source, that the intuition should be taken for miraculous revelation, and that a glowing, absorbing conviction should be held to come from above in a supernatural way. Such, we should be willing to grant, was the principal source of Mohammed's original faith in his own inspiration. The feebly recognized truth of the sovereign control in this world of one almighty will came home to his soul with a vividness which nothing, in his view, but preternatural influence could account for. In this, or some similar way, a man comes to recognize himself as the chosen repository of a great, vital truth, and the chosen instrument for propagating it. And such a conviction is even consistent with humility, so long as the truth is kept uppermost and the function of the prophet is felt by himself to be merely subordinate and ministerial. Nay, the very contrast between the sublimity of the truth of which he has been made the recipient, and his own poor merits, may intensify the feeling of personal unworthiness. The prophet or saint feels abashed at being made the channel for conveying the divine communication. It is true that pride ever stands near, and self-flattery and arrogance gain easy admission. The humility is apt to be retained only in semblance, while it is really supplanted by a principle wholly antagonistic. Still more important is it to remember that even this sort of self-deception belongs to men who, whatever may be thought of their earnestness and relative excellence, partake of the sinfulness of humanity. If they fall into the error of supposing that they are specially chosen agents of heaven when they are not, this is among the delusions which are due to the darkening influence of the sin that is common to mankind. Apart from this consideration, there was, in fact, no one idea of religion to which the mind of Jesus was surrendered, and in which he was swallowed up. The fertility, the variety, the consistency, and symmetry of his teaching, not less than its whole tone and temper, forbid this hypothesis respecting him. But the decisive answer to the suggestion that he was an enthusiast of this description is gathered from what was said in the beginning of the extent of his claims. These claims are far from being satisfied when he is looked upon as the simple repository and organ of a divine communication. His exalted claims, then, in case they are not allowed, must be credited to the self-seeking which corrupts the simplicity of the enthusiast, and moves him to put himself before his truth. Pride and ambition, however hidden and subtle in their working, are at the root of this gross, unwarranted self-elevation.

We are brought back to the dilemma which was proposed in the earlier part of this discussion. The unbelief of the time professes to reject all claims of a supernatural sort which were put forward by Jesus, at the same time that it loudly professes admiration for his personal excellence. It is true that Renan throws out the suggestion that he was guilty of a tacit concurrence in pious frauds; but, as far as we know, Renan stands alone in a view which is repugnant to the common sense of every sober-minded student, whether infidel or believing, of the evangelical history. And even Renan allows that Jesus had full faith in his own Messiahship. Infidelity must take the ground, and, at the present day, almost universally does take the ground, that Jesus was a religious enthusiast. His ethical system and, perhaps, a part of his religious teaching, are praised, but his distinctive claim to be the Messiah of God is rejected as decidedly as it was by the Jewish elders who crucified him. As if to make up for this dishonor put upon his pretensions, abundant laudation is bestowed, as we have said, upon the character of Jesus. Skeptical writers of the present day have much to say of the fine balance and equipoise of his faculties. Even Strauss, in his latest work, pays homage to the harmony of his nature. But these writers frequently go farther; they describe him as the embodiment of whatever is pure and good, the highest exemplar of moral excellence.

We deny the consistency of their position. We deny the justice of this judgment concerning Jesus, if, indeed, as they tell us, his extraordinary claims were founded in illusion. We are obliged with all solemnity to affirm, that the indulgence of the thought that these awful claims were the fruit of self-deception, carries along with it, as a necessary consequence, a feeling towards Jesus quite opposed to the reverence and abundant admiration which they are still disposed to lavish upon him. In other words, the cherishing of a delusion of this character is incompatible with that moral soundness, that clear and thorough truth of character, the lack of which debars one from being the legitimate object of such reverence and admiration. In short, the skeptical view of the claims of Christ strikes indirectly, but with equal effect, at his character. It is impossible to stop with attributing to him the weakness of an enthusiast. Such a delusion, though it be unconscious, can have no other ultimate source than moral infirmity. That profound truth of character, which ensures self-knowledge, clarifies the intellect, and keeps a moral being in his own place, can no longer be supposed. A sentiment of mislike—of aversion—must take the place of moral reverence. In ordinary life, any one who dreams himself entitled to more of honor and deference than belongs to him, and more of control than he has a right to exert, excites a natural disesteem. Men divine that false pretensions, even when they are unconsciously false, spring from some occult fault of character. And when claims are mistakenly put forth which would lift the subject of them to a higher than earthly pinnacle of dignity and power, the same verdict, with proportionally augmented emphasis, must follow.

The supernatural claims of Jesus are thus identified with the excellence of his character. Both stand or fall together. Trust in him has a warrant in his transcendent goodness. He could not be self-deceived, and therefore his testimony respecting himself is credible. He who lived and died for the truth was not himself enslaved by a stupendous falsehood. But respecting himself, not less than in respect to the other great themes of his teaching, he saw and uttered the truth. "To this end," he said, "was I born, and for this cause came I into the world, that I should bear witness unto the truth. He that is of the truth heareth my voice."

ESSAY XIII.

THE PERSONALITY OF GOD: IN REPLY TO THE POSITIVIST AND THE PANTHEIST.

THE truth of the Personality of God is impugned, in these days, by two diverse and mutually repugnant systems, Positivism and Pantheism. Agreeing in this negation, they stand at a world-wide remove from one another, as to the grounds on which it is based. Positivism is hardly to be called a Philosophy unless we abandon the ancient and proper sense of this much abused term.[1] It rather disdains philosophy, in the usual acceptation of the word, as a fictitious and now obsolete phenomenon in the progress of thought. It cannot be denied that M. Comte has displayed considerable ingenuity in framing his classification of the Sciences, though in this task he is far from being without rivals to dispute with him the palm of merit, if not of originality; and so far as his classification of the objects of science ascends above unintelligent nature and draws in men and society, it is open to the essential objections which lie against his system in general. Man, as an individual, is placed under the

[1] See Hamilton's *Metaphysics* (Am. Ed.) p. 45. It will be understood that we refer, in these remarks, exclusively to the philosophy of Comte. J. S. Mill and Herbert Spencer, whose systems pass under the general designation of Positivism, oppose Comte's depreciation of Psychology.

head of Physiology; and if the social man is honored with a separate rubric, no better reason is assigned than that every animal develops a distinct set of qualities in intercourse with his kind. Mental philosophy, in its recognized ends and methods of obtaining them, Comte not only casts out of his scheme, but treats with scorn as a pretender to the name of science. The old and often refuted pretension, by which the impossibility of Psychology is sought to be demonstrated, that the introspective act of consciousness puts a stop to the mental operation which consciousness would observe, Comte parades anew with the air of a discoverer. He acknowledges, in his principal work, that he has not read Kant, Hegel, and other great modern writers in the field of Metaphysics.[1] The great business of the human intellect, according to Positivism, is to observe facts and to register them by the rules of chronological sequence and of similarity. That false imaginations are not to be suffered to cloud the mind of the inquirer, so as to hinder him from a full and unprejudiced investigation of the phenomena presented to experience, is in truth a legitimate lesson of the Baconian system, and of high practical importance, especially in the physical sciences. Nor is Positivism to be denied the merit of having brought prominently forward this valuable truth. The mischief is that this truth is presented in both an exaggerated and one-sided form. For even in physical studies the inquirer

[1] *Cours de Philosophie Positive*, T. I. p. xxxvi.

is piloted by that scientific imagination which awakens hypotheses in respect to the producing and final causes of phenomena; and it was in the light of theories which were conjectural until observation had established them, that some of the finest discoveries, in Astronomy and Chemistry, for example, were made. Hypothesis, in the sense just defined, like a torch, has lighted the explorer on his path. Of this fact, ignored by the Positivist school, Whewell has given some noteworthy illustrations. But the Positivist is generally one-sided in the application of his favorite maxim. There are phenomena in the moral, religious, and aesthetic experience of man which are undeniable, and which are, as they have always been, most potent in their influence, which yet are tacitly ruled out of the realm of truth acknowledged by the votaries of this school. If we are to be confined to the observation of facts, let not that observation be narrowed down to that single class of phenomena of which the senses take cognizance. Otherwise Positivism is nothing better than materialism under a less odious name.

But the fatal defect in Comte's handling of the axiom to which we have adverted, and the vice, at the same time, of his whole system, is his denial of efficient and final causes.[1] The universe is the sequence of

[1] *Phil. Positiv.*, T. I. p. 14, and *passim*. J. S. Mill states (Westminster Review, April, 1865), that Comte does not deny the existence of causes beyond phenomenal antecedents, but that he simply

phenomena which are connected, as far as we know, by no causative agency, and related to no intelligible ends. The felicity of him who explores into the causes of things, which has heretofore been deemed his strongest incentive and best reward, is no more to be

affirms that they are inaccessible to us. Comte's language is that the Positive Philosophy considers, "comme absolument inaccessible et vide de sens pour nous la recherche de ce qu'on appelle les causes, soit premières, soit finales." But the question is whether there be causation—causative *agency*—dependence of one thing on another, such as invariable sequence, or, to adopt Mill's improved formula, "unconditional invariable sequence," does not express. On this point, all the language of both Comte and Mill seems to imply a negative answer. The inquiry into causes Comte abandons "à l'imagination des théologiens, ou aux subtilités des metaphysiciens." *Philosophy* knows of nothing but sequences of phenomena. Mill, in his Logic, notwithstanding his general disclaimer, constantly implies that the belief in *causation* (beyond stated sequence) is without scientific warrant. "Nothing," he says, "can better show the absence of any scientific ground for the distinction between the cause of a phenomenon and its conditions than," etc., (Mill's *Logic*, B. II. c. v.). "Force" and "attraction" (the former, as well as the latter) applied to the earth, he pronounces logical fictions. He declares that the relations of succession and similarity among phenomena are the only subject of rational investigation. He protests (c. xxi) against taking necessity of thinking as a criterion of reality. Events, he thinks, may be conceived of as occurring at random. The law of causation is a generalization by simple enumeration. In distant parts of the stellar system, he says, the law of causation (uniformity) may not prevail. If we remember right, he derides the notion of "a mysterious tie" between the cause (antecedent) and consequent.

The essential question is whether there be such a thing as *efficiency*, and whether this is the peculiar property of a *cause* in the strict sense of the term. And on this question, Mill's position is sufficiently clear. His theory has little advantage over that of Hume.

looked for. He may find out what is, but must abjure the thought of seeing a rationality in what is.[1] Now as far as the first point in the Positivist skepticism is concerned, the denial of the validity of the principle of causation is the rejection of one of the necessary deliverances of the human mind. We are under the necessity of thinking that every change is mediated by the exertion of power, is connected with a force or agency existing in its antecedents. If the necessity of thought is not to be accepted here as the criterion of truth, then Comte has nothing on which to rest his faith in the reality of the external world. The alternative, in fact, is universal skepticism. Now, that our belief in efficient causation *is* necessary, can be made plain. Let any one suppose an absolute void, where nothing exists. He, in this case, not only cannot think of anything beginning to be, but he knows that no existence could come into being. He affirms this —every man in the right use of reason affirms it—with the same necessity with which he affirms the impossibility that a thing should be, and not be, contemporaneously. The opposite, in both cases, is not only untrue, but inconceivable—contradictory to reason.

[1] Comte admits that besides the practical and economic use of positive science, there is a higher advantage from it. We are under the necessity of having *some* arrangement of facts—for example, to escape the painful feeling of *astonishment* which a disconnected phenomenon produces, and to keep off metaphysics and theology! This verily reduces the ideal interest of scientific study to a minimum. See *Phil. Positiv.*, T. I. pp. 63, 64.

Such is the foundation of the principle, *ex nihilo nihil fit.* But if a phenomenon is wholly disconnected from its antecedents, if there be no shadow of a causal nexus between it and them, we may think them away, and then we have left to us a perfectly isolated event, with nothing before it. In other words, it is just as impossible to think of a phenomenon which stands in no causal connection with anything before it, as it is to think of an event, or even of a universe, in the act of springing into being out of nothing. Futile is the attempt to empty the mind of the principle of efficient causation; and were it successful, its triumph would involve the overthrow of all assured knowledge, because it would be secured at the cost of discrediting our native and necessary convictions.

Not less ill-founded is the Positivist opposition to the doctrine of Final Causes. One may cavil at particular forms of statement in which this doctrine has been embodied; but that, in the various kingdoms of Nature, there is a selection of means with reference to ends, is a truth which is irresistibly suggested to the simplest as well as the wisest; as the reception of it by mankind, in all nations and ages, sufficiently attests. Speculation cannot dislodge this conviction from the human mind, for it will return again with every fresh view of the objects of nature. It has been the clue, as is well known, to important discoveries, for instance in Animal Physiology. The use of a given organ, its fitness to an end, its designed office in a system, has enabled the naturalist to anticipate observation and complete the fragmentary animal structure. Witness the remarkable discoveries of Cuvier. Of the place of the doctrine of Final Causes in the argument for Theism we shall speak hereafter. Here we simply affirm that the fact of a singular adaptedness of means to ends, such as cannot be fortuitous, but must be the fruit of selection, is established by universal observation, and is not shaken by any arguments from the Positivist side. What inference we are authorized to make as to the being of God, is a question reserved for a subsequent part of this Essay.

Comte's well-known description of the stages of human progress, of which the first is the Mythological, the next the Metaphysical, and the last the Positivist,[1] though at the first sight it strikes one as ingenious, will not bear the historical test, and is moreover vitiated by an underlying fallacy. There is no proof that the principal nations of the Indo-germanic and the Semitic stocks ever practised fetish-worship, in the lower sense of this term, or that they ascended from the meanest types of mythological religion to something higher. All the proof is the other way. There is no proof that mankind were originally on the lowest stage of religious knowledge and feeling. Apart from revelation even, the hypothesis of a fall and degradation from a primitive state which was morally more elevated, is equally rational, and, in our judgment, far better sus-

1 *Phil. Positiv.*, T. I. p. 3 seq. and Tome v.

tained, than the supposition of a gradual ascent from a moral and spiritual life little superior to that of the brutes. The phenomena of conscience, which the philosopher has no right to overlook, sustain the Christian hypothesis and are incompatible with its opposite, while the existence of a law of progress, such as the anti-Christian theory assumes, cannot be inductively established, but is rather disproved by the facts of history and observation. Comte's imaginary law of succession is inconsistent also with facts in one other particular. The three eras, to use his own phraseology, the Mythological in which personal deities are believed in, the Philosophical in which notions, such as essence, cause, and the like, are substituted for them, and the Positivist or the era of facts, are not found to succeed each other in this fixed order. Comte allows, to be sure, that one may overlap the other; but this concession falls far short of the truth. Who will venture to affirm that a metaphysician like Hegel belongs in an earlier era of intellectual progress than his contemporary, Comte? In the case of the former, there is not only the supposed advantage of living in the same advanced period with the latter, but of being immensely superior in mental power and in the range of his acquisitions. Who will affirm that Kepler and Newton believed in God, either for the reason that Positivism had not been announced, or because they were too unphilosophical to receive it? Skepticism and disbelief in the supernatural are not peculiar to modern times. They have appeared and re-appeared in the world's history ever since men began to speculate. This generalization of Comte is, therefore, hasty and incorrect.

But a most glaring error connected with this theory of Comte is the assumption that the mythologies sprung from the scientific or intellectual motive. The mythological epoch is pronounced the earliest effort of the human mind to explain the changes occurring in nature. The religious motive, the instinct of worship, the yearning for the supernatural and divine, is for the most part, or wholly, left out of the account. How strangely superficial this view of the religions of the world is, no thoughtful scholar needs to be told. As if religion, with all its tremendous power in human feeling and human affairs, were simply a form of knowledge, the crude offspring of curiosity! Were the Positivist to look deeper into human nature and history, he would see that religion, even in the perverse and corrupt forms of it, rests on other foundations; and this perception would uncover the groundlessness of his whole hypothesis. For if the religions of the heathen have their root in the constitution of the soul, and spring from ineradicable principles in our nature, it follows that, although they may pass away, religion will not cease, but will survive this wild outgrowth, in a life undying as the soul itself. The advancement of science has no more tendency to extirpate religion than it has to extirpate morality. A better understanding of nature may enlighten religion and tend to purify it from certain errors, but to destroy it—never. One might as well contend that the progress of Art tends to annihilate the sense of beauty, or that clearer and truer conceptions of the family relation tend to eradicate the domestic affections.

Positivism is Atheism. It would bind human knowledge down to a bare registry of facts, and chiefly to facts which the senses observe and arithmetic calculates. Other facts, the most real, the most precious, and the most influential upon human happiness and human destiny, it scornfully throws aside. Instead of offering an answer to the great problems which we cannot banish from thought without a conscious abasement of our nature and a choice of indifference and torpor instead of a noble disquiet, this system bids us cast them away as unpractical and fictitious. If Paganism be, as Positivism asserts, the lower plane of knowledge, one may still be pardoned for preferring to stand upon it, and for exclaiming, in view of a system so unsatisfying as this

—"I'd rather be
A Pagan, suckled in a creed outworn,
So might I, standing on this pleasant lea,
Have glimpses that would make me less forlorn;
Have sight of Proteus rising from the sea,
Or hear old Triton blow his wreathed horn."

More fascinating to a mind of a speculative cast, because more rich in contents and more coherent and self-consistent in form, are the later systems of Pantheism. Pantheism, negatively defined in its relation to religion, is the denial of the Personality of God. Pantheism is the doctrine that God is synonymous with the totality of things, and attains to self-consciousness only in the finite consciousness of men. It is the doctrine that all things are the forms, or manifestations, or developments of one being or essence. That being is termed God. Monism, or the identifying of the world as to its substance with God, is the defining characteristic of Pantheism.

Philosophy early started in quest of a common ground or essence of all existence. Ancient systems, one after another, suggested their crude solutions of the problem. The Pythagoreans, for instance, were disposed to find the groundwork of all being, or the one originant and pervading principle, in numbers. These early theories which are so fully handled in the great work of Cudworth, as well as by later historians of philosophy, we have no call at present to examine. The founder of modern Pantheism was Spinoza. Assuming the monistic doctrine, he laid down the proposition that the one and simple substance is known to us through the two Attributes of infinite thought and infinite extension. Neither of these Attributes implies personality, the essential elements of which are denied to the Substance.[1] The latter is

[1] In the interpretation of Spinoza's system, the difficult point is the relation of the Attributes to the Substance. Does he mean that

self-operative, according to an inward necessity, without choice or reference to ends. All finite existences, whether material or mental, are merely phenomenal. Spinoza also laid down the famous axiom: *omnis determinatio est negatio;* or all predication is limitation. To attach predicates or qualities is to reduce to finitude. In this notion, whether consciously or not, Spinoza was following in the track of Christian theology itself, which, as represented by Augustin and other Platonic theologians, had claimed that Deity is exalted above the distinction of essence and attribute. Some had even maintained that God is hyperousian, or that the term *essence* or *substance* is inappropriately applied to the Being who is truly Ineffable. It need not be said that, with the exception of that anomalous product of the ninth century and marvel in the history of philosophy, John Scotus, theology had never organized itself into Pantheism, from which

these Attributes belong objectively to the Substance, or are they only relative to the intellect of the individual beholding it? The last is the more usual interpretation of Spinoza. So says Erdmann, *Geschichte der Neuern Phil.*, I. (2) 59 seq.; Ritter, *Geschichte der Christ. Phil.*, vii. 224; Ulrici, *Geschichte der Neuern Phil.*, I. 44 seq.; Schwegler, *Geschichte der Phil.*, s. 107, and other critics. The opposite interpretation is upheld by another class of writers. Passages favoring the former opinion may be quoted from Epistles of Spinoza, especially Ep. xxvii. It also harmonizes better with the maxim, *omnis determinatio*, etc. The second interpretation, however, better accords with the mathematical character which Spinoza endeavors to give to his system, in the Ethics. In whatever way this question may be decided, it is plain to all that the "infinite thought" which is attributed to the Substance excludes self-consciousness and choice.

all the great teachers of the Church would have shrunk with horror. Their object in these statements was to elevate God to the greatest imaginable height by affirming His incomprehensible nature. The system of Spinoza is built up, with an attempt at mathematical demonstration, on the primary assumption respecting the one and simple substance—the *una et unica substantia.* Of course, the personality of God, a supernatural Providence, miracles in the proper sense, and Revelation, are given up. Of the effect of the Spinozistic system upon the conception of moral liberty and responsibility, we shall speak hereafter.

Although Spinoza borrowed his definition of substance from Des Cartes, he is original in the main features of his scheme. He is the forerunner of the later German systems, as some of their leading representatives, including Hegel, have allowed. Yet these systems would not have arisen, but for the impulse communicated from an intervening thinker, himself a firm believer in the principles of theism, the foremost philosopher of modern times, Immanuel Kant. In undertaking to criticise the knowing power, and to determine how far knowledge is a product of the subjective factor, a resultant from the operation of the mind itself, Kant took hold of a great problem of philosophy. He set out to dissect knowledge, and to separate its constituent elements according to their origin whether subjective or objective. This involved an inquiry into the nature of things—the nature of being—the object as well as the subject of knowledge. The question to be determined was, what is given to the knowing organ and exists independently of it, and what does this organ itself contribute. The conclusion of the theoretical philosophy was that we are assured of nothing save the bare existence of the object which sets in motion the mechanism of thought. All else that constitutes knowledge is of subjective origin. Space and time are *a priori* forms of sensuous intuition —the frame in which objects are set by the perceiving subject. The so-called categories—substance and accident, cause and effect, and the rest—are the *a priori* forms of the judging faculty, a description of the nature of the understanding, not of the nature of things. The ideas of Reason, the ultimate conceptions presupposed in the three forms of logical judgment, or the three phases of the unconditioned—namely, the Soul as a thinking substance, the World as a whole, and God, the highest condition of the possibility of all things—are only the rubrics under which the categories are reduced to unity. Not having an empirical, but an *a priori*, origin, they do not admit of an application to external objects, nor can they be assumed to represent realities; and if this be done, the antinomies, or logical contradictions, that inevitably result, warn us that Reason is out of its province, and that the undertaking is illegitimate. The objective factor was thus reduced to a minimum. In this department of his philosophy Kant stopped only one step short of universal skepticism. For of what avail that *a-priori* truth is supported, against Hume, by the criteria of universality and necessity, if this truth is after all endued with no objective validity? Of what value is a subjective certainty which simply reveals a law of thought, but contains no assurance of a corresponding law of things? The practical philosophy of Kant rescued his system from the consequences so fatal to religion. But the theoretical philosophy was the starting-point of the subsequent systems.

Fichte took the short step which Kant steadfastly refused to take. He drew the object itself, whose bare existence was all that is known concerning it, within the subjective sphere. If the object is assumed merely as a cause to account for states of consciousness, while the principle of causation is itself purely subjective, merely a law or mould of thought, then Idealism seemed to be logically inferred.

The Idealism of Fichte evolves the external world (so called) from the thinking subject. All things which constitute the objects of thought are modifications of consciousness which are wholly due to the self-activity of the subject. The impression of externality results from the check put upon this self-activity by its own inward law. It is not, however, from the particular, individual ego, that all existence thus issues forth, but rather from the absolute, impersonal Ego, which evolves at the same time the individual subject, and the object which is inseparably related to it. The relativity of consciousness, in which the ego and the object of thought stand in correlation, belongs to the finite subject, and not to the Absolute Being; yet the Absolute is viewed as a subject and denominated the Ego.[1]

Schelling modified Fichte's conception of the Absolute. The Absolute, the root of all particular existences, is no more to be called subject than object. It belongs equally to the thinker and the thing. In truth, it lies equidistant from both poles of consciousness, the subjective and the objective. It is the indifference-point between them. That is to say, both the external world and the percipient subject are identical in essence and in origin. They flow from the same fountain, which is the absolute, impersonal being. Connected with this view, was Schelling's dynamical conception of Nature. Nature is made up of forces. Nature is pervaded through and through with rationality. For this reason, it is possible for Nature to be an object of knowledge. The mind and Nature are bound to each other by the closest affinities. The knowledge of Nature is Nature itself attaining to self-consciousness. For knowing is a form of being—of the identical being of which Nature is a lower expression. But how to cognize the hypothetical Absolute? Relation and dependence cleave inseparably to conscious thought, and the thinking sub-

[1] The different phases or modifications of Fichte's system we do not here attempt to describe.

ject can escape from itself—get behind itself—only by abolishing thought. But this does not secure the end, for the cessation of thought is not the cognition of the Absolute. Hence Schelling supposed a peculiar organ of Intellectual Intuition, by which the soul, freeing itself from the ordinary bonds of consciousness, gains a direct vision of the Absolute. He took refuge in a mystical theory, which reminds us of Plotinus.

It is no wonder that the rigorous intellect of Hegel was dissatisfied with this mode of bridging the gulf between finite and infinite being. Accepting the general notion of the Absolute, as defined by Schelling, Hegel professed to set forth the process in which the entire universe is necessarily evolved. Thought and being are identical: hence the universe, including God, nature, self, is resolved into a thought-process, or a chain of concepts self-evolved through an inward necessity, and comprising and exhausting in themselves all reality. Indeterminate being, the notion first in order, necessary and self-supported, implies, or, according to the Hegelian language, changes into, another notion, and the two in turn are merged in a third which is more specific than either; and so the process goes forward until all concrete existences take their places in the series of concepts. To the philosophic eye all reality is summed up in this realm of concepts. But the philosophic view is the last stage in the development of consciousness. It is interesting to inquire what account Hegel gives of sense-perceptions as they are found in the common consciousness of men. Schelling was not a Berkleian. Notwithstanding his dynamical, idealistic theory of Nature, and his monism, the object had not less reality, in his system, than the subject. The external world was real, as well as the mind that perceives it. The same is affirmed by Hegel. Yet he constantly speaks of a transmutation of consciousness from the state of perception to that of conception, and of the transmutation of the *thing* also, which is the object of perception, into the mental concept. It is plain that with Hegel both subject and object, thinker and thing, are engulfed in the logical thought-process, and that both coalesce and are identified in the Absolute. The object has nothing more than a transient reality. The ordinary sense-perception is only the first stage in a movement which soon liberates consciousness from this impression of a distinct externality in the object, and in the consummation of which both object and subject resolve themselves into the one, identical, absolute being. Then all reality is fathomed, and thence, as from a new starting-point, the universe is reconstructed by the philosopher, or rather rises of itself, by its own inherent and necessary movement, in his consciousness This process as it takes place in the consciousness of the philosopher, is the self-unfolding of the innermost nature of things. In it and through it Deity attains to self-consciousness.[1]

[1] Among the multitude of German dissertations which have a

The Hegelian school pretended to find an equivalent for the objects of Christian faith and the propositions of Christian theology in the dogmas of their system. The latter were said to be the pure and final rendering of that which Christianity presents in a popular form. The substantial contents of both were averred to be identical. The Trinity, the Atonement, and the other doctrines of the orthodox creed had now —so it was claimed—received a philosophical vindication; and the vulgar Rationalism which had flippantly impugned these high mysteries, was at length laid low. These sounding pretensions could only mislead the undiscerning. A philosophy which denies the distinct personality of God, and consequently must regard prayer as an absurdity, can by no legerdemain be identified with Christian doctrine. The appearance of the *Life of Christ* by Strauss, and the subsequent productions of Baur and his school, through the applications which they made of the Hegelian tenets to the New Testament history and the teaching of the apostles, placed this conclusion beyond a doubt.

Having thus noticed the leading forms of Pantheism, we offer some remarks which may serve to evince the untenable character of this philosophy.

1. The fundamental assumption of Pantheism that

bearing on the origin and character of the new philosophy, we may refer here to one, the beautiful Essay of Schelling *über die Quelle der Ewigen Wahrheiten*, which was read in the Berlin Academy in 1850. See Schelling's Works (II. Abth. I.), p. 575.

all things are of one substance, whether taken in the Spinozistic sense, or in that of the later German philosophers—is not supported by evidence, but is contrary to the truth.

The doctrine of one Substance, this grand postulate of Pantheism, is an uncertified dogma for which no proof is vouchsafed. Yet it forms the foundation on which the Pantheistic systems rest.

There is the best reason for concluding that the objects of perception are essentially distinct from the percipient mind. These objects are seen face to face, and known as external. In their manifestations they are totally diverse from the characteristics of mind, which are revealed in consciousness. It is a just inference that materialism and idealism, the two forms of the monistic theory, are alike false.

As concerns the Hegelian scheme, Schelling, in his new system, has suggested a sufficient refutation. If the logical development in Hegel were allowed to be throughout coherent and demonstrative, we have only a string of abstractions. We have only a theory, or ideal framework, of the universe, but no reality, no real being. If there are no realities corresponding to the idea and known through experience, the universe is still a void. It were as rational to confound the plan of a castle with the actual edifice, as to identify a concept with a real being, or the aggregate of concepts with a universe of realities. Therefore, Hegel's logic at best describes only the possibility of things.

It is a merely negative philosophy. If this philosophy were all, and if real being were not brought to our knowledge through experience, the result would be Nihilism. Thought and being are distinct, and with the admission of the truth of this proposition, Pantheism falls to the ground.

2. The Pantheistic dogma, even though it were admitted, does not solve the problem which it pretends to explain. Knowledge is not accounted for by being wholly resolved into self-knowledge; for self-knowledge is a phenomenon not a whit less mysterious and inexplicable than the knowledge of not-self. The Pantheist takes it for granted that the knowledge of anything distinct in substance from the knower, is out of the question: as if the knowledge which the knower has of himself were a thing more easy to understand.

3. The Pantheistic conception of the Absolute is self-contradictory and false.

We believe in an Absolute Being, that is, in a being for whose existence no other being is necessary, or who stands related to no other being, as a condition of existence. But the Pantheistic Absolute includes in itself and develops out of itself the relative. Here is the contradiction. The Absolute is placed in a necessary relation to finite, relative existences. They emanate *de necessitate naturae* from the bosom of the Absolute. The conception of the latter is thus directly violated; and this inconsistency cannot be removed from the Pantheistic scheme.

4. The deduction of finite existence from infinite being the Pantheist fails to make conceivable.

How cogitative and incogitative existences are developed out of the characterless substance, Spinoza wholly fails to render intelligible. How is the world and all things in it to issue forth from unlimited, uncharacterized being? What is the moving force, and what the *modus operandi?* Hegel, in his system, is obliged at the outset to proceed on the supposition that motion or activity belongs inherently to the primitive notion, and thus introduces a quality with which we become acquainted through experience; but even then the transition from being without attributes to being specially characterized, from nothing to something, is effected by sleight of hand.

5. The Pantheist's conception of God does not satisfy his own description of the infinite and absolute being.

The God of the Pantheist is dependent on a process of development for the realization of his own being. It is only in the last stage of this progress that self-consciousness is reached; and then in no individual, but only in the human race collectively, through the course of its history. But what kind of God is that which must emerge by slow gradations from a merely potential existence to the manifestation and comprehension of his own being?

6. At the same time, the objections of the Pantheist to the theistic conception are groundless.

(1) The Pantheist objects that self-consciousness cannot belong to God in Himself considered, because for the awakening and development of consciousness an external object is required. But this statement is an unauthorized inference from what is true of personality in man. We are connected with a material organism, and placed in a relation of dependence upon it for the unfolding of our spiritual natures. But we have no right to conclude that this peculiarity attaches, as a necessary condition, to *all* personality. The uncreated, eternal spirit is subject to no such condition.

(2) Nor does personality clash with infinitude of perfections. God is infinite, because all conceivable perfections belong to Him, and belong to Him without limit in their measure. Infinity is a negative predicate. As applied to a given quality in God, it means that this quality is not partially possessed, but possessed in the fullest conceivable measure. As applied to the sum of excellencies, it denotes that this sum admits of no addition.

(3) Nor is the existence of the world as distinct in its essence from God, inconsistent with His being the Absolute. If the world were a necessary existence, if God would not be God without the world, if He were constrained to give being to the world, then indeed the assertion of the Pantheist might be true. But the limitation which God puts upon himself in creation is voluntary. It is a *self-limitation.*

Creation is no wise essential to the realization of His attributes, but is a most free act, performed in the exercise of benevolence.

We have touched upon the weakness of Pantheism when regarded from a speculative point of view. There is another objection of a different kind, but of decisive weight, against all the Pantheistic systems.

7. Pantheism runs counter to our moral intuitions.

This is a practical objection, an objection to the consequences of the Pantheistic philosophy, but not the less pertinent and valid on that account; for a system which involves among its legitimate consequences the denial of known truth, is thereby effectually disproved.

Every Pantheistic scheme is, and must be, thoroughly necessitarian. The world is not a creation, but a necessary development. All events take place by the same rigid necessity. A holy or a sinful act must be when and where it is, just as a star must revolve or a plant grow. Moral liberty, as apprehended by the common understanding of men, is illusive. The distinction between physical and ethical experiences of the soul is extinguished. Even personality itself is only phenomenal. Evil is not evil, save to finite apprehension; seen from a loftier plane it is a form of good. The one is equally essential and desirable with the other. Crime, remorse, the self-approval of virtue, are robbed of their essential significance. Moral responsibility, in the deep and true sense in which conscience affirms it, has no place.

These consequences, though sometimes disguised under an obscure or sounding terminology, inevitably attend Pantheism in all its forms. The ablest advocates of this philosophy, including both Spinoza and Hegel, have involuntarily betrayed the embarrassment which these conclusions are well fitted to awaken. Against them the moral sense of every unperverted mind will forever lift an indignant denial. But the irresistible protest of conscience tells with equal effect against the whole system with which they are inseparably connected.

The Pantheistic systems of philosophy which have appeared in Germany since Kant, regarded as exertions of intellectual power, have hardly been surpassed since the best days of the Greek philosophy. But they are built upon a false foundation, and hence, though they contain materials of high and lasting value, they are structures which cannot stand. Their splendor is like the deceptive lustre of that "fabric huge" which was reared by the fallen spirits, where

> "from the arched roof,
> Pendent by subtle magic, many a row
> Of starry lamps and blazing cressets, fed
> By naphtha and asphaltus, yielded light
> *As from a sky*."

There are two generic opinions among Christian theologians respecting the origin of our belief in God

By some it is considered to be implanted in the mind and spontaneously developed; by others it is thought to be imported into the mind, or to be the result of a process of reasoning. Perhaps the difference might be resolved into a verbal one; since the first class generally allow that this native belief is educed by training and the view of the works of God, and the second confess that an original tendency to believe in God belongs to the human soul. And such an original tendency is hardly distinguishable from a *nisus*—a germinant belief. This disagreement in regard to the genesis of our faith in God is generally connected with differences in Psychology, or in the mode of stating the functions and the early operations of the mind. It must be conceded that those who hold that the knowledge of God is intuitive, have often failed to state their doctrine with clearness, or to set it in connection with acknowledged principles of mental philosophy.

Our own position is that the belief in God does not originate in external, traditionary teaching, like a fact in history or science, which is handed down from one generation to another; it does not originate, properly speaking, from the view of the objective manifestations of God, for instance in the works of Nature, or the course of history; nor does it flow from any empirical source. But this belief is potentially inherent in the mind, and is obscurely present in the earliest operations of intelligence. Dependent for its full explication upon instruction, and upon the various proofs which corroborate at the same time that they explicate and develope it; subject, also, in common with the moral sense, with which it is vitally connected, to the darkening and perverting influence of evil, faith in God is yet seminally native to the soul, and is seldom, if ever, so extinguished that it may not, in favoring circumstances, again revive, and even assert itself against every attempt of the will to eradicate it.

The tremendous hold which religion has had upon mankind in all nations and ages forbids the supposition that it owes its origin to tradition merely, to processes of argument, or even solely to a perception of the marks of design in Nature. A phenomenon so deep and universal must be due to a profounder cause, and a cause more directly operative. The shallow theory which ascribed religion to the craft of priests and lawgivers was long ago exploded. The theory, which is only a little less superficial, that religion took its rise from the alarm excited by startling occurrences in Nature, is also well-nigh obsolete. Impressions from this source are fleeting, and impressions of terror are quickly effaced by those of a different character, which are awakened by opposite aspects of Nature. Faith, moreover, is too deeply imbedded in the moral feelings to be accounted for by this external and accidental cause. If it be said that religion is due to the personifying imagination of uncultured men, we have the same answer. This may account to some extent for the form which heathen religions take; but without a prior belief in the supernatural and yearning for it, without the principle of worship, and the sense of accountability to a higher Being, the religions of Paganism could never subsist. Nor is the argument from design, important as this argument is in its place, to be considered either the primary source, or the principal ground, of the belief in God.

It may be objected that the belief in a supernatural Power is not universal, and that religion in some peoples is feebly manifested. The Chinese are said to be such a people. But if the religious feelings are susceptible of decay, the same is true of the moral feelings, the sense of ethical justice and ethical truth. If the feebleness and corruption of conscience does not militate against the doctrine of a native and universal principle of rectitude, the same is true of a similar low state of religious convictions. In both cases, the seeming exception establishes the rule.

The two essential characteristics of the human mind are self-consciousness and self-determination. The one is indispensable to the other; for if the determination of the will is a cônscious act, it is not less true that if the voluntary power were absolutely inactive or wanting, that distinct separation of self from the world without, which is involved in self-consciousness, is not supposable. Now, for the realizing of self-consciousness, the mind is thus dependent upon the existence of the world without us, and in our mental states are always found elements derived from this outer world to which we are so closely united. In this dependence, we have decisive proof that the soul—the spiritual part—is not self-originated. At the same time we know equally well that it is not derived from material nature, for it is *toto genere* distinct from the world of matter, and in the sphere of Nature the law holds that like produces like. In this twofold conviction lies the first suggestion of an infinite personality, the living creator and God, from whom our finite soul derives its being. Intimately connected with this presage or incipient faith, is the conscious subjection of the will to an authoritative law which yet the will does not impose upon itself, but which is identified with the will of the Being from whom the soul springs, while at the same time through this law, his holy character, if not clearly discerned, is indistinctly divined. Thus in the background of our moral and spiritual natures, God is immediately revealed, the ground of our being, at once our Creator and Lord. Thus we can understand how, with every fresh awakening of conscience, God is vividly present to the consciousness; and the natural voice of guilt, as well as of dependence, is prayer.[1]

[1] The doctrine of the preceding paragraph is presented, in substance, by Julius Müller, *Lehre von der Sünde*, I. 101 seq. Compare the argument of Hugo of St. Victor from the existence of the soul, and the similar argument of Locke (*Essay on the Understanding*, B. iv. c. 10). The main proposition of Locke is that cogitable existence cannot be produced out of incogitable, the minor premise being that the human mind is a cogitable existence.

It should be observed that we have not been framing an argument to prove the existence of God. What we have said is rather an analysis of consciousness for the purpose of unfolding the elements that enter into it, and of showing that the consciousness of self involves as a condition, not only an immediate knowledge of the external world, but equally a faith in God. The world, self, and God, are the three factors, which are the elements of our personal consciousness.[1]

It is the prevailing habit of German writers to describe our immediate faith as *the consciousness of God* [Gottes-bewusstsein]. We are said to be conscious of that which is the object of immediate knowledge. That we are conscious of the outward world, or the objects of sense-perception, is phraseology sanctioned in the philosophy of Sir William Hamilton. That we are conscious of self, or phraseology equivalent to this, is current in speech. The external object so directly manifests itself to us that we know that it exists. Thus, also, self or the conscious ego, is so manifested in consciousness that we know that we exist. The analogous fact respecting the Divine being is denoted by the term God-consciousness, or consciousness of God.

The phenomena of our religious consciousness would be imperfectly described, if we pointed out sim-

[1] That faith in the unconditioned being is "an original factor of our thinking," not derived from the law of causality, but implied in it, is well shown by Ulrici, *Gott und die Natur*, p. 606.

ply the belief in God which is awakened in the manner delineated above. Vitally associated with this awakening faith, is the attraction towards communion with God, or the inward gravitation of the soul towards the Being in whom it lives, which forms an essential foundation of prayer and worship.

Attention is also required to the fact that faith in God is primarily a matter of feeling. They who are wont to consider the mind a congeries of faculties, in which thought, feeling, and will are coördinate, find it hard to comprehend this.[1] But when we look to the genesis of our ideas, to the process in which intelligence is developed, we discover that feeling is antecedent. In regard to the knowledge we have of the outer world, sensation, in which the mind is acted upon, precedes perception. Now the feeling of God, or, to use a more expressive term, the sense of God, precedes the distinct idea. The recognition of God, though including an activity of the intelligence, is grounded in, and pervaded by, feeling. The error of Schleiermacher did not consist in his founding piety in feeling, as a psychological fact, but it lay in his confining piety to the incipient stage of faith. He would shut up the mind, as far as the exercise of piety is concerned, to the consciousness of its own state, with no reference

[1] "Eine Psychologie, die aus Erkennen, Begehren und Fühlen drei *coordinirte* Formen des Bewusstseins macht, hebt alle Möglichkeit auf, in dieser Sache etwas zu erklären." Nitzsch, *System d. Christ. Lehre*, p. 23. Compare the note on p. 27, in reply to Schwartz.

of that state to a distinct personal object. It is just as if we were to stop with simple sensation, instead of through sensation advancing to the perception of the world without us. We are supposed to be conscious of a certain mental state, the feeling of dependence, as we are sensible of an ache in a limb, and there, as far as piety is concerned, the matter ends. Schleiermacher was also wrong in resolving piety wholly into the feeling of dependence; since the yearning for communion with God, not to speak of the feeling of obligation, is an equally essential element; but this is comparatively a venial error. The mystic, who makes feeling directly percipient, is still more at fault. As we humbly conceive, the truth is that the mind is affected in certain ways, in the department of feeling, by the great Being in whom we live and move, just as self and the outward world make themselves felt in consciousness; and the states of consciousness thus originating from God involve and beget an immediate faith in His existence—a faith, however, in which feeling, as it is the root, is likewise the predominant element. For example, remorse of conscience includes a sense of accountability, and this implies a sense of God. The feeling itself is God's work in the soul, and is felt to be so. God is believed in, through this feeling, not by a process of argument, but immediately. He is, literally speaking, manifesting Himself to the soul. It is true that men may discredit the manifestations of God in the soul, and disbelieve in him. So they may speculate themselves out of the belief in the reality of the external world, or even of their own existence. They may deny, and have denied, the reality of a moral law binding on the conscience, and quench this light that is in them. The belief in God is, also, largely dependent on the state of the will; in this respect, that the alienation of the will and heart from that Being may weaken and well-nigh deaden this faith. Nor should we overlook the truth that it is also dependent upon the will of God, who may withdraw or intensify those manifestations of Himself in which it originates. Unquestionably, the effect of sin is to reduce this implanted faith, so that in most men it appears as an obscure yearning after an object distant and dimly conceived. This state of the sinful mind is described in Scripture as a feeling after God. Men grope, as in the dark, for Him "who is not far from every one of us," but whom we "did not choose to retain in our knowledge."[1]

It is remarkable that in Germany almost all the writers of note, of all schools in philosophy, unite in regarding belief in God as an immediate act of the soul, and as rooted in feeling. This is conceded even by the Hegelians. They allow that such is the character of this faith in the primitive stage, and only contend, in accordance with their system, that such faith

[1] Clear psychological explanations relative to our primitive religious faith or feeling may be found in the excellent work of Ulrici, *Gott und die Natur*, pp. 610, 620. The entire chapter is valuable.

is only a rudimentary condition of consciousness, to be supplanted by its maturer development. Theologians who, though influenced by Schleiermacher, have constructed their systems in an independent spirit, such as Nitzsch and Twesten, Julius Müller and Rothe, in common with Trendelenburg, Ritter, Ulrici, and other philosophers of various schools, substantially agree in the doctrine that religion originates in an immediate faith, and emanates from no empirical source. Such, in fact, is the old doctrine of theology. An obscure knowledge of God—a *notitia dei*—was held to be implanted in the soul, and to be the immediate witness to God's existence. Such is the doctrine of Calvin and Melancthon, to say nothing of their forerunners and followers.[1]

What now is the purport and the force of the several arguments for the existence of God? We reply that these proofs are the different modes in which faith expresses itself, and seeks confirmation.

[1] Calvin pronounces it an incontrovertible truth that "the human mind, even by natural instinct, has some sense of Deity"—divinitatis sensum. He affirms that "men universally know that there is a God;" that "some sense of the Divinity is inscribed on every heart." "Unde colligimus," he adds, "non esse doctrinam quae in scholis discenda sit, sed *cujus sibi quisque ab utero magister est*." There is a natural "propensity to religion" in men, says Calvin, and an ineradicable knowledge of God, which manifests itself in the worst men in spite of their will. See the *Institutes*, B. I., cc. ii. and iii. Melancthon says: "vult enim deus agnosci et celebrari; et fulsisset illustris et firma notitia Dei in mentibus hominum, si natura hominum mansisset integra." *Loci Communes*, I. De Deo.

In them, faith, or the object of faith, is more exactly conceived and defined; and in them is found a corroboration, not arbitrary but substantial and valuable, of that faith which springs from the soul itself. Such proofs, therefore, are neither, on the one hand, of themselves sufficient to create and sustain faith, nor are they, on the other hand, to be set aside as of no weight.

The arguments for the being of God are capable of being classified in various ways. We shall consider them here under the three heads of the ontological, the cosmological, and the teleological arguments—the moral argument being embraced under the teleological, where it properly belongs.

1. The Ontological proof proceeds from the idea of God, attempting to deduce therefrom the truth of His existence. The germ of this proof is in Augustin. It appears in its riper form in the celebrated argument of Anselm. The objection that the idea of the most perfect being imaginable is after all only an imagination, Anselm endeavored to parry by the statement that this idea is far from being an arbitrary notion, like the image which fancy forms of the lost island (the illustration of Gaunilo), but is strictly a necessary idea, in the sense that the mind cannot escape from entertaining it. The argument of Anselm stands in vital connection with his Realistic philosophy.[1] But he

[1] A being in the mind and a being *in re*, require the supposition of a genus—hence a being, according to Realism—embracing both. The true sense of Anselm's argument is best appreciated by Ritter.

fails to show that existence *in re* is an attribute entering into a concept, and falls into the error of inferring the existence of a thing from the definition of a word. Des Cartes assumed the existence of God to account for the presence in the human mind of the idea of the infinite and perfect being. As much reality, he thought, must belong to the cause as is found in the effect; and this holds good where the effect is an idea. The idea of the infinite and perfect God cannot be produced in the mind by the things that surround us in the world. It implies, therefore, for its cause the Being himself. This reasoning does not carry full conviction; and if the additional fact of a yearning to break through the bonds of our finite being and to commune with a higher Power, be introduced, we are brought back to the original faith which precedes logical argument.

Yet the ontological argument, even though it be fallacious, is not without an indirect value. It presents a true conception of God, regarded as a possible being. The being than whom no higher can be conceived, in case He exists, exists necessarily.

Geschichte d. Christ. Phil., III. 337. The validity of Anselm's argument is maintained by the Cambridge Platonist, Henry More, in the early part of his *Antidote to Atheism*. It should be observed that Anselm's argument is to be found in the *Proslogium*, and in the Reply to Gaunilo. The earlier form of the argument in the *Monologium* resembles more nearly the argument of Augustin. Yet it is important as showing the Realistic foundation on which the later argument rests.

2. The Cosmological argument starts from the contingent character of all things presented to observation. Their changeful and dependent character implies the existence of an unchangeable and independent Being. The principle of causation unquestionably involves a belief in a First Cause, or a Cause which is not at the same time an effect: otherwise existences are traceable to no cause, and the principle of causation is made void. An eternal series is an absurd hypothesis, since it would be a series of effects without a cause. Eliminate the element of time (which is not a cause), and the series becomes like a single momentary event, which would be an event without a cause. We are, therefore, compelled to believe in something which is eternal and independent. The defect of the argument is that it contains no strict proof of the personality of this eternal Being. It does not carry us necessarily beyond the Absolute of Pantheism.

This is the defect of Dr. Samuel Clarke's attempted demonstration of the being of God from the attributes of necessary existence. When he would prove the intelligence of the necessary being, he falls back upon the *a-posteriori* proof from marks of design in the world.

Thus the cosmological argument establishes the existence of an eternal being, the cause or ground of all things, but does not fully satisfy the mind that He is intelligent and free.

3. The Teleological argument is the proof from

final causes. We discern, for example in the structure of our own bodies, and in the material existences around us, features which, as we involuntarily feel, presuppose the agency of a free and intelligent cause. Through the action of our minds and the works of man, we are made familiar with the operation of intelligence; and when we are confronted by phenomena strikingly analogous to the known expressions of our intelligence, we are authorized to attribute them to a like cause.

The theory of a plastic force, or blindly working agency in Nature, similar to the supposed working of instinct in an animal or of the principle of growth in the plant, is sometimes brought forward in opposition to the doctrine of final causes. The objection is fallacious; since the admitted "blindness" of that which is conceded to operate with the wisdom and precision of intelligence, is the very circumstance which carries us beyond the secondary cause and inspires the belief in a free and intelligent Power.

Sir William Hamilton affirms that the argument from final causes is not valid, unless it be presupposed that the human mind is a free intelligence.[1] It is true that if the human mind itself be the product of an unintelligent force, as materialistic theories imply, the external world might not irrationally be thought to emanate from the same source. Both man and nature might be thought to be due to a common cause. It

[1] Hamilton's *Metaphysics* (Am. Ed.), p. 22.

should be added, however, that the impression made by external Nature is a sign of our inbred conviction that we do indeed originate our actions, in the exercise of intelligence and freedom; and under this supposition, the argument from final causes in Nature retains its force. To set before it ends and choose means for attaining them is the distinctive act of mind.

The physico-theological proof, or the proof from design in the works of Nature, is one of the oldest, most universally impressive, and justly convincing of the various arguments for a personal God. It has been set forth by a series of writers from Socrates and Cicero to Paley, and acquires fresh illustration with every new discovery in physical science. It is brought forward in the Scriptures, as being sufficient to render ungodliness a sin. The devotional parts of the Bible abound in appeals to the testimony to the existence of God which his works present.[1]

The validity of this argument is not destroyed by the Darwinian theory that all living species are descended from a common parentage; unless indeed this theory is allowed to run into materialism by bringing the human soul into the same category with animal and vegetable life. Were the Darwinian speculation established as a truth of science, the physico-theological proof would still be good. For if all species are re-

[1] One of the most impressive discussions of the subject of Final Causes is the chapter on the *Zweck*, in Trendelenburg's *Logische Untersuchungen* (revised ed.).

duced to one, the same marks of design still remain in that one comprehensive species; and however far back we go in tracing the genesis of living things, the signs of the agency of a superior intelligence are indelibly stamped upon the whole system.

Yet it must be confessed that the physico-theological argument, considered in the light of a strict proof, lacks completeness. In the first place, it rather suggests the idea of a builder or moulder of matter, than of an original Creator. To be sure, the Being who constructed Nature must have a profound knowledge of the properties of matter; but then there have been philosophers, ancient and modern, who have held that matter itself is eternal.[1] In the second place, Nature is at best a finite product, and we are not authorized, in strict logic, to infer an infinite wisdom and power in its Maker. To identify omnipotence with exceedingly great power as Paley does, is to reason loosely and to abandon the proper conception of God. We will not dwell on seeming infelicities which meet us in the constitution of Nature, and which occasion perplexity. Finally, it is possible, without any violation of logic, to consider Nature to be the product of unintelligent forces operating in pursuance of an inherent law. The Pantheistic hypothesis is logically admissible.

[1] Yet, this objection of Kant proceeds on the notion of a possible separation of matter and force, which science does not favor. See Ulrici, *Gott und die Natur*, p. 401.

The office of the physico-theological argument, therefore, is, first, to educe and, secondly, to corroborate the faith in God which, as we have before explained, is an original possession of the human soul. It is a probable argument, deriving its probability from the anticipating faith which is defined and fortified through these outward manifestations of God in Nature.

There is a teleology in History, as well as in Nature. Events conspire, through long periods of time, for the accomplishment of certain ends. All things are seen to work together for the securing of these ends. The thoughtful student of History is not less impressed with the proofs of forecast and far-reaching providential control, than the thoughtful student of Nature is struck with the traces of creative wisdom and will in the material world.

The moral argument is put by Kant in the following form: we are made for two ends, morality or holiness, and happiness. These two ends, in the present state of existence, frequently fail to coincide; the former is chosen at the expense of the latter. Hence we are obliged by the practical reason to suppose a future state, and a God by whom the system is adjusted or completed, and righteousness connected with happiness.

Far more impressive is the proof which lies in the more direct evidences of a moral administration over this world. The distribution of natural good and evil, even though the system of moral government is unfinished in this life, is sufficient both to prove the existence of a divine Governor, and to evince, as Butler has cogently argued, that He approves of virtue and condemns vice. History is the record of judgments exercised over beings endued with a free and responsible nature. Rewards and punishments are allotted to individuals and nations, and the spectacle is one which is adapted to convince reflecting minds that God reigns.

Yet this argument is not one that compels acquiescence. It is possible for the mind to rest in the theory of a self-executing moral system or moral order, to the exclusion of the agency of a personal being. Nor are there wanting adherents of such a theory. True, it seems untenable save on a necessitarian philosophy in which moral liberty is sacrificed. Yet the theory is one from which its adherents can be driven by no compulsion of logic. As in the case of the previous arguments, we have to fall back on the immediate feeling of the mind. Faith is elicited and confirmed, but not begotten, by the traces of a righteous moral administration, which are observed in the course of this world's history.

INDEX.